STRANGERS AT THE GATES

Strangers at the Gates

New Immigrants in Urban America

Edited by
ROGER WALDINGER

UNIVERSITY OF CALIFORNIA PRESS
Berkeley   Los Angeles   London

University of California Press
Berkeley and Los Angeles, California

University of California Press, Ltd.
London, England

© 2001 by
The Regents of the University of California

Library of Congress Cataloging-in-Publication Data

Strangers at the gates : new immigrants in urban
America / edited by Roger Waldinger.
        p.   cm.
    Includes bibliographical references and index.
    ISBN 0-520-23092-2 (cloth : alk. paper) —
ISBN 0-520-23093-0 (pbk. : alk. paper)
    1. Immigrants—United States—Social
conditions.   2. Immigrants—United States—
Economic conditions.   3. Alien labor—United
States.   4. Cities and towns—United States—
I. Waldinger, Roger David.

JV6475 .S77 2001
305.9'0691—dc21
                                    2001027085

Printed in the United States of America
08   07   06   05   04   03   02   01
10   9   8   7   6   5   4   3   2   1

The paper used in this publication is both acid-free
and totally chlorine-free (TCF). It meets the minimum requirements of ANSI/NISO Z39.48-1984
(R 1997) (*Permanence of Paper*).

כְּאֶזְרָח מִכֶּם יִהְיֶה לָכֶם הַגֵּר ׀ הַגָּר אִתְּכֶם וְאָהַבְתָּ לוֹ כָּמוֹךָ כִּי־גֵרִים הֱיִיתֶם בְּאֶרֶץ מִצְרָיִם

"The stranger who lives with you shall be to you as one of your citizens; you shall love him as yourself, for you were strangers in the land of Egypt."

Lev. 19:34

To the memory of my grandparents,
Lola and Maximillian Kessler and Beatrice and Ernst Waldinger

CONTENTS

FIGURES AND TABLES

Figures

Tables

ACKNOWLEDGMENTS

This book owes its origins to Demetrios Papademetriou, long one of the most thoughtful and knowledgeable figures on the immigration scene. Demetri sought to engage me in a project that was then only a glimmer in his imagination: an international effort to bring together researchers, advocates, and policy makers to increase understanding of immigrants' transformation of the urban regions on which they were converging throughout the world. As anyone who knows Demetri would have predicted, the idea soon became reality; the Metropolis Project, as it is now known, has repeatedly demonstrated the value of the endeavor Demetri initiated. This volume, funded by a generous grant from the Ford Foundation, represents part of the U.S. research contribution to the Metropolis Project. It is a pleasure to express my gratitude to Demetri, for involving me in Metropolis, and to Mary McClymont, vice president of the Ford Foundation, and Taryn Higashi, program officer, for seeing value in this study of new immigrants in urban America.

I am no less grateful to UCLA, my home university, both for its institutional support and for the lively intellectual environment it has provided. This project was initiated when I was director of the Lewis Center for Regional Policy Studies, a unit of UCLA's School for Public Policy and Social Research. I wish to thank Founding Dean Archie Kleingartner and his successor, Dean Barbara Nelson, for their support of me and of the center. Many thanks also to Margaret Johnson, the center's assistant director, and Belinda Vigil, then the center's administrative analyst, for their dedication and for their assistance on behalf of this project and the many others I carried out while director.

The best part of this project was the intellectual company it entailed. The colleagues I enlisted in writing this book saw value in an effort to coordinate our voices, which meant that we spent considerable time together discussing matters of substance and methodology. I am grateful to them for what they taught me and for their interest and good humor in bringing this project to fruition.

A special word of thanks is needed for my two closest collaborators: Claudia Der-Martirosian and Nelson Lim. In addition to her contribution to this volume, Claudia supervised the overall project, doing so with her customary meticulousness and care, for which I remain most appreciative. Nelson's enthusiasm and expertise never failed to move the project ahead. Thanks also to Vincent Fu, Youxin Huang, and Eric Kostello for their invaluable research assistance.

Naomi Schneider, my editor at the University of California Press, was always encouraging and did much to see this book through to publication. Naomi's authors universally ring her praises, and I now know why.

Without a sabbatical, I would never have found the time for the writing and editing required to finish this book. A year of uninterrupted writing and reflection was an extraordinary privilege, putting me in debt to the taxpayers of California, who ultimately made it possible. I hope the Californians among the readers of this volume will conclude that it indeed merited their support.

Many thanks also to my wife, Hilary, and to my children, Max, Mimi, and Joey, who cheerfully put up with my book-writing preoccupations but correctly reminded me that immigration was not the be-all and end-all of life. I am also grateful to Silvia Reyes, whose assistance contributed immeasurably to keeping our household afloat.

This book is dedicated to the memory of my grandparents, who arrived in the United States as refugees at the very eve of World War II. They were always proud to have become Americans. But they would have been happier if others had been equally fortunate—for they never forgot the disaster that befell those who could not escape.

Chapter 1

STRANGERS AT THE GATES

Roger Waldinger

As America enters the twenty-first century, it is clear that the twentieth was the century of immigration. True, the doors closed in the mid-1920s—and for many, especially during the dark days of World War II, they remained fatally shut until it was too late. But even during the heyday of immigration restriction, the back door remained open, which means the Mexican presence also then grew. A temporary migrant farm labor program in 1943—known as the Bracero program—augured the shape of things to come: immigration began growing in the late 1940s, and the path since then has been ever upward, indeed at an ever-steepening slope. By the end of the century, the numbers of newcomers equaled the flow seen at the century's dawn.

Immigration is again transforming the United States—and does so in a particular way, since the newcomers head for urban America. Today's newcomers are far more likely than their native-born counterparts to live in the nation's largest urban regions, making immigration, now as in the past, a quintessentially urban phenomenon.

Thus, the immigrant masses are once again huddling. They are also congregating, as before, in a handful of places. Nonetheless, the new map of immigrant America looks very different from the old. New York still ranks as a premier immigrant destination; likewise, Chicago retains a significant attraction for the foreign-born. But immigration's center of gravity has decisively shifted south and westward. San Francisco, earlier an immigrant town, remains a magnet for the foreign-born, its pull intensified by the region's vastly greater population. But the capital of today's immigrant America is unquestionably Los Angeles, that ill-defined blob sprawling over five southern California counties. And at the other end of the country, Miami, though a much smaller metropolis than the rest, holds the nation's densest concentration of immigrants; it was the very first to receive the new immigrant tide and is still an entry point of extraordinary magnitude.

The newcomers' tendency to gravitate toward this particular cluster of places affects immigration's impact; it also influences the prospects for immigrant America. The urban centers at the heart of immigrant America have very limited attraction for the native-born, which is why much of the United States has been slow to be touched by the reemergence of mass immigration, the expanded foreign-born population notwithstanding. By the same token, the impact of immigration is magnified in those few places on which the newcomers converge— precisely why established residents of regions such as Miami, Los Angeles, or even New York have been so prone to immigration anxiety. There may well be an irrational side to these allergic responses to immigration, but one should not underestimate the rapidity of the ethnic shifts engendered by immigration and the unsettling effects of these changes. Moreover, one can find plenty of good reasons to think that immigration's effects may not be completely benign. After all, these very largest places earlier welcomed other migrants, most notably African Americans and Puerto Ricans, who started out at the bottom and then lingered there, as did a disheartening number of the migrants' offspring. The advent of a large group of newcomers may spell bad news for those urban residents still at the margins, struggling to move ahead at a time when the changing shape of urban economies puts all less-skilled workers at risk.

Life in the big city scares off the native-born, who, voting with their feet, have been departing the immigrant metropolis for other places, where, as it happens, the foreign-born are not so frequently found.[1] But the metropolis offers something essential to the foreign-born: their friends, kin, and compatriots, whose presence provides most, if not all, of the resources needed to get started. Immigration is a network-driven phenomenon, with newcomers naturally attracted to the places where they have contacts and the buildup of contacts facilitating later moves to the key immigrant centers. The importance of networks explains why immigration is so geographically channelized: the decisions of *prior* migrants exercise a long-term effect on the options available to those who follow them.[2]

But if immigrants find virtues in congregating together, it is not quite so clear that they have selected the best places. Much of urban America has gone through the wringer over the past half century. Many cities have actually lost population, and manufacturing, long the key to the urban economic base, has been severely hemorrhaging jobs. Still, immigrants have generally stayed away from the least robust urban centers. Los Angeles, Miami, and San Francisco have all been gaining jobs and people during recent decades, despite their ups and downs, most notably the deep slump into which Los Angeles fell during the first half of the 1990s. As for New York and Chicago, although their periods of greatest dynamism belong to history, the economies of these number one and number three urban centers have shown remarkable buoyancy throughout the past several decades.

Each of the top immigrant destinations represents a going enterprise—and how could it be otherwise, since immigrants always move in search of jobs. The potential problem with the continuing attraction of urban centers for the foreign-born lies in the job structure. The economy of today's immigrant metropolis has been completely overhauled. Large urban economies still contain plenty of jobs for people who arrive with few skills and must start at the very bottom. But, relatively speaking, there are far fewer such positions than in the past and the number is continually dwindling. While the same generalization holds for the U.S. economy in general, it applies with particular force to these capitals of immigrant America, whose persistent role in the economic landscape rests on a particularly deep transformation in the ways of making a living. The leading immigrant destinations have shifted heavily to jobs requiring higher skills and education. Although this change does not stop newcomers from finding an entry berth, it may well make it harder for them—or their children—to hew to the path of upward progress followed by earlier immigrants and their descendants. And immigrant concentration is unlikely to make matters any easier, with job and wage competition among immigrants an inevitable side effect of the newcomers' tendency to cluster.

Of course, all of these processes are likely to work themselves out in distinctive ways: the leading immigrant destinations are far from uniform in structure or history; more important, they have come to harbor immigrant populations of very different types. The axes of variation are multiple, involving national-origin composition, the degree of ethnic heterogeneity, and skill makeup, to name just the most important. And it is not simply a matter of East versus West Coast, or older metropolis versus new. Each immigrant destination is in important ways distinct from any other, reflecting both the ways in which geographic and historical particularities shape immigrant flows and the impact of the region's place in the urban hierarchy on the options available to arrivals from abroad.

Thus, this book is an attempt to reckon with the new immigrant America in those places where its presence is most pronounced: the urban regions of Los Angeles, New York, San Francisco, Miami, and Chicago, listed in order of the size of their respective immigrant populations. Though the book touches on aspects related to the impact of immigrants on these regions, its main concern is the issue at the heart of the contemporary immigration debate: can today's newcomers make it?

Many researchers have already weighed in on that question, but no one has yet taken full account of immigration's fundamentally urban aspect. That so many new arrivals come with relatively low skills is a central aspect of today's reality, but other considerations are also key. Of equal importance, immigrants flock to those places where the low-skilled worker—regardless of ethnic background—is in particular trouble. It is for that reason that immigration's urban convergence calls out for special attention.

This book builds on the research of the many scholars who have concerned themselves with the urban dimensions of immigration. Even so, gaping holes in our knowledge base reflect the striking degree to which scholarly attention has been skewed toward some urban regions and away from others. Consider, for example, the contrast between New York and Chicago. The Chicago School of Sociology emerged in the 1920s as an attempt, in part, to understand the ways in which the immigration of the early twentieth century worked itself out in its urban context. Though the intellectual influence of the Chicago School persists, research on the new immigrant Chicago is virtually nonexistent. By contrast, New York, home to many "New York schools," but none of sociology, has proved fertile ground for immigration researchers, whose thread of important, insightful publications spans from the early 1970s to today. Until recently, Los Angeles received relatively little serious scholarly attention, perhaps because few researchers had met the prerequisite for serious study of the region: overcoming their prejudices against LA's particular form of urbanism and urban living. But researchers appear to have moved beyond their bias; the past few years have seen an outpouring of books and other publications on Los Angeles, many of them zeroing in on immigration and the region's ethnic transformation. Immigration scholars have also been hard at work studying Miami, a city that shares many traits beyond its sun belt location with Los Angeles. Immigration studies in Miami, however, have tended to give short shrift to the demographic side, and the great majority of work focuses on the dominant group, the Cubans. By contrast, San Francisco, a region with almost as many immigrants as Miami, though of entirely different origins, has been almost completely—and unaccountably—neglected, an occasional monograph excepted.

This book therefore seeks to consolidate our understanding of these leading immigration centers, adding to the established scholarship where it exists and extending the information for those more neglected immigrant urban regions. But we are also attempting something different: to go beyond the single case study to compare the immigrant experience across this tier of leading immigrant destinations. While we certainly expect to find some similarities, the unique characteristics of each of the places and the differences in their respective immigrant flows highlight the ways in which the urban context matters.

Like many other studies of immigration, this book relies on the decennial censuses of population—long the workhorses of immigration research. For all their utility, however, the censuses suffer from one crucial flaw: they rapidly become dated. The 1990 census painted a portrait of America as it looked in the spring of that year, a picture of diminishing utility in the early twenty-first century. At a time when the relevant results from the 2000 census are not yet available, however, we do possess an alternative instrument for apprehending immigration's contemporary reality: the Current Population Survey (CPS), the Census Bureau's monthly vehicle for tracking population during the intercensus years. In years past, the Census Bureau periodically added a question about place of birth and parents' place of birth, but these items appeared only every few years. Starting in 1994, however, the bureau made questions about place of birth and parents' place of birth a permanent feature of each month's survey, enabling us to capture the changing reality of immigration through the late 1990s.

Although the CPS universe is far smaller than that of the census, one can combine surveys from subsequent years to build up a sample of very respectable size—indeed, one sufficiently large to study particular places, such as our five urban regions, or subgroups, such as immigrants and their descendants. This book makes particular use of a combined

TABLE I.I.   SAMPLE SIZE, WEIGHTED:
CURRENT POPULATION SURVEY,
1994–1998, MERGED DATABASE

Total Population			
	Native-born	Foreign-born	Total
Los Angeles	17,135	7,569	24,704
New York	23,762	6,695	30,457
San Francisco	7,952	2,214	10,166
Chicago	10,858	1,622	12,481
Miami	3,604	2,193	5,797
All other	310,204	18,712	328,915
Total U.S.	373,514	39,006	412,520

Ages 25–64			
	Native-born	Foreign-born	Total
Los Angeles	7,386	5,109	12,495
New York	11,349	4,532	15,881
San Francisco	4,049	1,601	5,650
Chicago	5,344	1,122	6,466
Miami	1,517	1,435	2,951
All other	155,396	12,159	167,554
Total U.S.	185,041	25,957	210,998

Note: Totals fail to sum to 100 due to rounding errors.

sample concatenating observations from the 1994 through 1998 Current Population Surveys.[3]

Admittedly, we pay a price for our effort to bring the story up to date. Although the total combined sample is quite large ($N = 412,520$), sample sizes diminish as we move to units of smaller geographic scale and, within them, break down the population by ethnicity or nativity. Consequently, we have focused on the larger urban region rather than the key city that lies at its center or even the somewhat larger metropolitan area attached to the urban core. Thus when we write of New York, Chicago, or any other of the urban places to which we refer, we mean the urban region, or "consolidated metropolitan statistical area," to use the official Census Bureau designation, and not the city. (See table 1.1 for weighted frequencies for the total population and for persons ages 25 to 64 years old in Los Angeles, New York, San

Francisco, Chicago, Miami, and all other areas combined, cross tabulated by nativity.)

Although the regional focus necessarily eclipses the differences between urban and suburban areas that have so long lain at the heart of much urban analysis, it is in many respects a more useful unit than any of the smaller alternatives. The distinction between urban and suburban lacks meaningful reality in newer urban regions such as Los Angeles, Miami, and most of San Francisco, with the exception of the rather small cities of San Francisco, Berkeley, and Oakland. From the beginning, the sun belt cities had little urban concentration and rates of density far lower than those in the East; their sprawl made for a multinucleated metropolis, where any given center possessed limited economic function. Moreover, the self-proclaimed cities of the sun belt are best thought of as cities in only a nominal sense. While the City of Los Angeles contains the most extraordinary combination of urban and suburban within a single municipal jurisdiction, much of the urban core, as defined in terms of urban functions, lies entirely outside the boundaries of the city of Los Angeles. Chicago and New York, of course, remain much more in the nineteenth-century mold, their downtowns ever dense and still packed with employment within a range of higher-order economic functions. Nonetheless, growth is increasingly on the periphery; these areas have absorbed many of the central city functions and, as in the sun belt, spread out over a wide space. In other words, the city, such as it is, has been steadily embedded within a regional economy, in which the broad suburban expanse is increasingly urbanized and finds itself attracting a population of ever greater diversity—of which the immigrants are one important component.

Urban Fates and Immigrant Destinies

This book looks at the nexus between urban fates and immigrant destinies. Each chapter responds to the question posed earlier—Can today's newcomers make it?—tackling the issue from different perspectives. Drawing on data from the five gateway regions, the chapters provide fruitful regional, interethnic, and native-born comparisons, focusing on wage trends, rates of employment and adequate employment, displacement, ethnic niches, poverty, and the new second-generation immigrants. Although the raw material is quantitative, all of the authors have sought to make the discussion accessible even to readers with little or no background in statistics. Throughout the book, our emphasis is on graphic display of quantitative findings, which makes the numbers easier to apprehend. Many of the chapters use more complex statistical procedures, but the details are always relegated to the footnotes, and we have tried to present results in ways that lend themselves to intuitive interpretation. The remainder of this chapter, however, places our work in its appropriate intellectual context, outlining the key debates that we have sought to address.

Immigration and the Urban Condition

"The problem of the 20th century," announced W. E. B. DuBois almost 100 years ago, "is the problem of the color line."[4] At the time, the acuity of the insight may not have been crystal clear, and few were then ready to pay much attention to the arguments of a DuBois. At the turn of the twentieth century, the United States was in the throes of a mass migration, the arrival of so many apparently swarthy migrants from southern and eastern Europe the main source of ethnic disturbance for American elites of the day. In relatively short order, the foreign-born became the unwanted, as restrictionist legislation passed first in 1921, and then modified in 1924, fundamentally closed the gates. Without replenishments from abroad, the teeming immigrant masses Americanized; although still viewed with derision until well past midcentury, the degree of hostility and apprehension lessened.[5]

The fading of immigration from Europe more or less coincided with the advent of the Great Migration; as African Americans headed for northern cities in search of opportunity, they provided a convenient target on whom Euro-Americans, new and old, could project their anxieties and fears, a process that also allowed the racially dubious new immigrants to eventually become "white."[6] For African Americans, however, the urban promise soon turned to disillusion. Like their immigrant predecessors, African Americans initially found a place at the very bottom of urban social structures, but the task of moving up from and consolidating those initial gains proved deeply problematic.[7]

Accounting for this difference in experience became one of the central social science preoccupations of the past several decades, and researchers put forth various explanations. The most deeply influential view, enunciated with greatest force by the Kerner Commission more than three decades ago and reiterated and strengthened by a number of commentators, most notably the Harvard sociologist William Julius Wilson, emphasized the role of timing.[8] From this perspective, African

Americans had the great misfortune of entering the large urban areas just when their economies began to shift in ways that decreased opportunities for the less skilled. The basic bottom-level, entry positions began to disappear. Opportunities somewhat farther up in the job hierarchy became increasingly hard to obtain. White workers, after all, were never all that willing to help African Americans get good-paying factory jobs, and as the most desirable blue-collar jobs became less available, resistance to integration stiffened. Geographic shifts in production and residence made matters still worse: jobs went to the suburbs, but the force of residential segregation made it hard for black workers to follow; over time, even the suburban factory base eroded, as jobs leaked out to low-cost areas, first in the United States and then abroad. In some urban centers—Buffalo, Detroit, St. Louis, and Youngstown, to name just a few—deindustrialization delivered a knockout punch. Elsewhere, most notably in the very largest urban agglomerations with which this book is concerned, a different type of urban economy, organized around the processing and transmission of information, emerged. But this new economy did little for less-skilled African American workers, who once may have managed to hold a job in the factory sector but lacked the proficiencies required by employers in the service sector. Those too young to have known the blue-collar city in its heyday grew up with other problems. In the well-known views of William Julius Wilson, the unhappy coincidence of events—the disappearance of the factory sector, the out-migration of the black middle class, and the resulting social isolation of the poor—gave rise to an "urban underclass." Lacking the regulative structure of work, as well as the institutions, informal connections, and role models provided by the more complete ghetto community of old, African American ghetto dwellers altered behavioral patterns and attitudes, responding to the changes around them in self-defeating and self-reproducing ways.[9]

Just as Wilson's argument gained unprecedented influence, urban America began to change in ways that are seemingly incomprehensible in light of the story just told: immigrants began flocking to urban regions that purportedly had no place for anyone but the highly skilled. To be sure, many of the immigrants were among the highly educated professionals beckoned to the city by the new, information-based urban economy. Indeed, from a historical standpoint, socioeconomic diversity provides contemporary immigration with its most distinctive feature: yesterday, the newcomers almost always started out at the very bottom; today, many begin at the middle of the job ladder, if not on the upper rungs.

Still, the urban immigrant destinations with which this book is concerned have been receiving immigrants who bear a distinct resemblance to the arrivals of yore—at least in the sense of lacking the baseline skills of the native-born population, a gap particularly glaring when the comparison focuses on the dominant group, native-born whites. As we will note, not every region attracts less-skilled immigrants to the same degree, and there is a good deal of divergence on this axis from place to place. But from the standpoint of the received academic wisdom about urban America, there is something deeply peculiar in the experience of all the key immigrant regions: not only has the foreign-born population burgeoned, these new, less-skilled urban residents are finding a place in the job structure and often working at surprisingly high rates.

If the received diagnosis of the sources of urban distress is correct, then the immigrant pattern represents a significant anomaly. Curiously, immigration experts have not registered much surprise. On the contrary: successful immigrant entry into the economy bears out a crucial tenet of the migration theories elaborated over the past two decades. Whereas we used to think about migrants as "the uprooted," to quote Oscar Handlin's famous immigration history of almost five decades ago, we now describe them as "the transplanted," to cite a slightly less celebrated but no less influential history produced 35 years later.[10] The shifting metaphors of scholarly discourse about migration convey the essence of the new approach: we now understand that migrants do not move as solo adventurers but rather as actors linked to associates here and there, with the ties lubricating and structuring their transition from one society to the next. Rephrased in the jargon favored by the scholarly literature, the connections that span immigrant communities constitute a source of *social capital,* providing social structures that facilitate action—most important, the search for jobs and the drive to acquire the skills and other resources needed to get started in a new world and, with luck, subsequently move up the economic ladder.[11] By contrast, *social isolation* appears to characterize the contemporary urban underclass, its members lacking strong ties to others who have the baseline resources needed for successful insertion into the economy and all the other roles associated with regular work.

As concept, *the underclass* has infiltrated deeply into the vocabulary of contemporary social scientific thinking about urban America and its residents. But its conceptual status seems almost certainly less than scientific: it provides a seemingly neutral label for categorizing undesirables, all the while obscuring interest in the nature of the domination they experience, as clearly implied by the term. After all, there is no underclass without an "overclass," but the latter somehow never gets mentioned in the discussion. Fortunately for them, immigrants enjoy some degree of inoculation from application of the term. The underclass, as concept, has the rhetorical convenience of providing a non-racialized tag for African Americans, a more stigmatized group than immigrants, who occupy a far more accepted role in the American imagination and dream. On the other hand, that more privileged status seems contingent on the willingness and ability, at least among low-skilled immigrants, to continue working at difficult, poorly remunerated jobs and under conditions that most Americans will not accept.[12] For the most part, immigrants appear to be avoiding this danger, although some groups are more marginal to the economy than others, and many commentators have raised a red flag concerning the future of immigrant children. Those worries have already stimulated some analysts to label immigrants as a potential underclass, as suggested by chapter 5 in this book. Anxiety about the prospects for the least-skilled immigrants is far from unreasonable, yet one must note that the availability and application of the underclass category is itself a source of additional liability.

Assimilation

At the top of the immigration research agenda is the question of how the newcomers change after they have arrived. The conventional wisdom, both academic and popular, says that the immigrants *should* change by entering the American mainstream. The concept of assimilation stands as a shorthand for this point of view.

Although it is the point of departure from which almost all scholarly assessments begin, this particular perspective necessitates a skeptical look. "Assimilation" is surely a peculiar scholarly concept, resonating with that normative vision of national life that prescribes a direct relationship between the individual and the nation, unmediated by ties of an ethnic type. Not surprisingly, it sets up an artificial contrast between immigrants depicted as distinctive from the start and a national self, imagined in homogeneous terms—that is, as mainstream—whereas in fact it is riven by all sorts of divisions. That immigrants are surely different is beyond dispute, and yet the concept of assimilation hides the degree to which crucial differences are created through the process of migration and by members of the host group. To mention the most obvious example, farmers and factory owners deliberately and systematically recruit migrant laborers precisely because the latter have different orientations to work than do native-born workers; at the same time, the stigmatized conditions in which migrant workers find themselves generate unfavorable stereotypes that impede subsequent mobility.[13] And the dictionary provides a more expansive definition of assimilation than the social science literature allows—namely, *acceptance,* a condition that implies change on the part of dominants, not just newcomers. However, the scholarly literature on assimilation has yet to conceptualize the mechanisms whereby dominants might exclude immigrants and perpetuate the disadvantages that they experience.

For the purposes of discussion, we might do better by shifting to a more descriptive level and making the terms of discussion more modest. It is probably enough to ask whether immigrants are making progress, though even here complexities of varying sorts quickly arise. In a sense, everyone agrees that newcomers typically begin with a set of liabilities: problems in speaking English, skills or credentials that may not be appropriate to the U.S. labor market, and a lack of exposure to the ways of American society, including the signals and credentials that tell employers that a foreign-born worker can indeed do the job as he or she suggests. Over time, these difficulties are eased. As settlement deepens, immigrants, regardless of skill level, see their earnings and occupational status improve. If we focus on absolute rates of progress, the line is pitched at an upward angle.

But most of the scholarly and policy debate focuses on relative rates of progress, and rightly so. In a sense, all of our social indicators are measures of relative well-being; that a person living below the poverty line in the United States might enjoy considerable comfort as compared to someone from an impoverished Third or Fourth World country is beside the point. Moreover, the very notion of assimilation, problematic as it is, implies a convergence between immigrant and host country expectations: over time, immigrants, and certainly their children, are increasingly likely to aspire to the conditions enjoyed by the average resident of the United States.

In this light, the research consensus has moved from an optimistic to a somewhat pessimistic view. The earliest, most influential view derived from the work of the labor economist Barry Chiswick. Analyzing data from the 1970 census, and thus comparing the very earliest of the "new immigrants" with their counterparts who arrived during the 1950s and earlier, Chiswick found that immigrants began with a disadvantage, but their prospects quickly improved. After the passage of roughly 20 years, immigrants' earnings surpassed those of natives of the same ethnic background. As implied by the terms of comparison, not every group progressed at the same rate; although Mexican immigrants advanced more slowly than newcomers from Europe, over time, they did better than comparable Mexican Americans.[14]

Chiswick's optimistic view was quickly challenged by his fellow economist, George Borjas, who objected on methodological and substantive grounds.[15] Chiswick extrapolated immigrant rates of progress based on an analysis of a cross section of the U.S. population taken at a single point in time. Controlling for other background characteristics, he contrasted immigrants living in the United States for, let's say, 5 years with those residing in the country for longer durations of 10, 15, or more years. But this comparison assumed that the characteristics—both measured and unmeasured—of recent immigrant cohorts would essentially resemble those of their predecessors, making the experience of the earlier immigrants a good predictor of the outcomes of those who arrived later.

Borjas quite reasonably questioned this assumption. Migrations are known to be selective: moving is hardest at the outset, making those with the highest skills, greatest resources, best connections, and greatest propensity for risk the most likely to spearhead a move. Over time, selectivity diminishes, increasing the probability that later arrivals will compare unfavorably with the pioneers who established the initial beachheads. Moreover, the U.S. immigration system changed, starting in the mid-1960s, in ways that lowered the barriers to migration, further reducing selectivity. Thus, contrary to Chiswick's assumption, it seemed unlikely that the trajectories of earlier immigrants would provide a reliable guide to the experience of more recent arrivals.

Although Borjas confirmed that immigrants do indeed move up over time, he also demonstrated that the rate of progress was falling. Analyzing the 1980 census, he showed that the newcomers of the 1970s were moving ahead more slowly than those of the 1960s, who, in turn, were marching forward less briskly than those of the prior decade. Borjas subsequently extended the same analysis, with analogous though still more depressing results, to the 1990 census. Most important, Borjas showed that recent immigrants do not catch up with, let alone surpass, their statistical counterparts among native-born workers. And there is a still more disturbing twist: as the comparison pairs native-born and foreign-born workers of the same ethnicity, it tells us that Mexican immigrants, more than a quarter of all immigrant workers, suffer from a growing gap relative to Mexican Americans, themselves a disadvantaged group.[16]

Borjas's results have been challenged and criticized, but they have largely carried the day,[17] as evidenced by their acceptance and endorsement in the National Research Council's highly influential 1997 report *The New Americans*. As Mark Ellis shows in chapter 4 of this book, consideration of the distinctive regional concentration of the immigrant population puts the basic Borjas finding in a very different light. Immigrants are lagging behind natives, Ellis tells us, not simply because their personal characteristics reduce their competitiveness in the labor market but because of trends in the particular labor markets where immigrants cluster. Nonetheless, Ellis also underscores one of Borjas's most fundamental points: the gap separating new immigrants, especially the low skilled, from natives is growing.

That gap now takes on a dimension not present in the earlier stages of the immigration debate. The new immigration began at the tail end of a period of historically high equality; since then, the distribution of wealth and income has shifted in ways that make the United States a far more unequal society than it once was. For immigrants, that change carries significant peril: real wages among less-skilled workers, of all ethnic stripes, have taken a very sharp hit over the past two decades. Less-skilled immigrants are striving to make it in a labor market oversupplied with poorly educated workers and in which the terms of compensation have shifted sharply against the less skilled.[18] Not all immigrant groups are equally affected by this change; indeed, for some, especially those among whom highly educated, scientific professionals predominate, the burgeoning demand for highly educated labor is good news. But the groups with a more distinctly proletarian cast, most notably the Mexicans, are facing a structure that may well impede their rate of upward movement. The new economy has done nothing to dampen the demand for less-skilled immigrant labor, nor to dislodge less-skilled immigrants from the places that they have established, as we shall see in chapter 3. And immigrants' children may not face pressures of equal severity, as suggested in chapter 8. Still, the facts of the case—high levels of regionally concentrated migration occurring at a time of greater inequality—provide grounds for concern.

Ethnic Persistence

Although the literature on the economic progress of immigrants quickly becomes preoccupied with matters of technical detail—as suggested by the terms of the debate between Chiswick and Borjas described earlier—its substantive concern is quite straightforward. For economists, "assimilation" can be innocently understood as the process by which the economic welfare of immigrants comes to converge with that of natives. Economists certainly understand that any trend toward economic convergence yields related shifts in patterns of residence, association, and self-identity, but their concerns principally involve the dollars and cents of the matter.

The sociological literature casts a wider net. Indeed, the canonical texts on the topic were mainly preoccupied with the social aspects of assimilation, at the expense of the economic dimension. Sociologists now agree that economic progress is the linchpin of assimilation, driving all other shifts in the social structure of ethnicity. Still, it is easy enough to tie together the possible pieces of the package. At the outset, immigrants stick together. Lacking resources and the know-how needed to function beyond the ethnic community, they depend on one another, a dependency that leads newcomers to settle in neighborhoods densely populated with immigrants and to work in the ethnic niches where their compatriots cluster. Over time, the type of economic assimilation described by economists diminishes dependency, as immigrant options increase. As settlers move away from the occupations and neighborhoods of greatest immigrant density, their exposure probabilities change. In turn, they are increasingly likely to encounter out-group members, and in contexts that encourage closer associations. While the immigrants themselves are likely to retain strong in-group attachments, their children are unlikely to share ties of equal intensity. Thus, the social networks of immigrant descendants from the second generation on increasingly cross ethnic lines, leading to new forms of affiliation and identity that eventually replace those characteristic of the original immigrant group.[19]

This volume, in contrast to the earlier work reported in our book *Ethnic Los Angeles,* does relatively little with the sociological interest in these broader dimensions of ethnic change; such important topics as residential integration, intermarriage, and language shifts remain outside of our purview.[20] Rather, we focus, perhaps narrowly, on the labor market aspects of the immigrant experience.

Nonetheless, many of the broader concerns raised by the sociological literature are echoed in the chapters that follow. As noted previously, the traditional approach assumes that immigrants begin in occupational and residential clusters, in which propinquity to coethnics promotes continued interaction within the ethnic circle. However, the search for opportunity soon leads to dispersion along one dimension, if not several, lowering exposure to ethnic insiders. Thus, the established perspective emphasizes the discontinuities that are created as immigrants respond, in individualistic fashion, to options that arise as integration deepens.

But that view reflects the intellectual context in which sociologists have framed and elaborated the concept of assimilation. On the one hand, the canonical account of assimilation emerged in a period very different from today, when immigration had reached its lowest level, and not even the most farsighted of social scientists could imagine the events that would transpire after 1965. Under those circumstances, an effort to illuminate the integration of ethnic groups in American society could be decoupled from a sociology of immigration itself. On the other hand, classical thinking about assimilation bears the clear traces of modernization theory, with its assumption that ethnic ties were culturally based vestiges of older forms of social organization, bound to wither as immigrants acculturated and substituted universal for particular loyalties.

By contrast, the sociology of immigration of the type that has emerged over the past 20 years, with its emphasis on social capital, outlines a trajectory of a very different type. Notwithstanding disagreement over a host of particulars, most scholars now agree that immigration is a fundamentally social process, eased by the connections that link settlers to newcomers. Seedbed newcomers may move without help and tumble into jobs more or less by accident, but they soon find themselves in a position to assist new arrivals. As long as the immigrants are few and their resources limited, only close associates are able to access help. But the buildup of a population inevitably expands and diversifies the types of social networks that an immigrant community includes. Greater numbers then create the basis for institutions, both formal and informal, that bring immigrants together in recurrent, systematic, and more durable ways. The process of migration creates the seeds out of which a new ethnic social structure grows; defensive needs—the awareness of alterability, the hostility displayed by outsiders—further hasten and intensify this development.[21]

Thus, social structures emerge out of migration because of the problems they help the migrants resolve; that they also serve the uses of outsiders with whom the migrants come into contact provides a further fillip. A now massive and familiar body of literature tells us that the embedding of migration in social networks improves the quality of information circulated in immigrant communities and generates trust that serves as social capital among newcomers, who are often deprived and rarely able to access helping mechanisms available to the mainstream.[22] As it happens, the predilections of immigrants match the preferences of employers, who try to reproduce the characteristics of the workers they already have and continue to dip into the immigrant hiring pool. Once established, the social organization and social relations of the immigrant community operate with an independent effect. Consequently, the web of ties linking immigrants to one another shapes and constrains their ability to pursue opportunity, creating information fields and mobility channels that structure the fabric of ethnic life in durable and significant ways. And thus, unlike the older approach of assimilation, with its emphasis on social discontinuity, the newer approach accents those processes leading to social reproduction.

This new perspective appears in the literature in any number of forms, most notably in such concepts as the ethnic enclave, ethnic economy, and ethnic niche, all of which are attempts to understand the characteristics and consequences of the distinctive clusters that immigrants establish in the economy. As discussed in greater detail in chapter 7, most of the sociological work in this vein has focused on those concentrations characterized by high levels of immigrant self-employment. Researchers have been particularly interested in the Cuban ethnic enclave in Miami, where immigrants are not only working on their own account but appear to be employing a considerable number of their coethnics. The various chapters in this volume provide a view of the Cuban ethnic enclave that clashes with much of the literature, a point to which we will return in the concluding chapter. Whatever can be said about the Cuban ethnic enclave, the type of situation that it purportedly represents is relatively uncommon: for the most part, immigrants in business are working on their own with few, if any, nonkin employees. And where entrepreneurship takes spectacular form, as among Koreans, Iranians, or Israelis, for example, the drive to set up one's own business dries up the ethnic labor supply; thus, recourse to nonethnic labor is not an uncommon aspect of the immigrant business scene.[23]

Despite the emphasis on self-employment, it seems reasonable to contend that it represents a single instance of the broader phenomenon denoted by the concept of the ethnic niche. As argued earlier in this chapter, the network-based nature of migration and employment systems funnel and cluster immigrants into specific economic activities. Although these clusters sometimes entail self-employment, they more frequently involve occupational and industrial specializations in which immigrants find themselves working as wage and salaried employees. The lessons revealed by my earlier work on New York and Los Angeles show that the tendency to concentrate in ethnic niches is a distinguishing trait of the immigrant experience, characterizing migrant streams of various types.[24] As in the earlier work, the chapters in this book define an ethnic niche as an occupational or industrial specialization in which a group is overrepresented by at least 50 percent. Chapters 6 and 7 provide ample additional intellectual context, as well as all the details involved in operationalizing the niche concept.

The Second Generation

Migration is an arduous experience, best undertaken by those ready to run risks and prepared to struggle to make it under adverse conditions. For that reason, immigrants have a relatively youthful profile; they arrive as adults but at that stage in adult life when they are either bearing or bringing up young children. Consequently immigration soon yields a second, even more fateful, result: the emergence of the second generation, a population categorized as children of foreign-born parents who are either born in the United States or born abroad and brought to the United States at a very young age.

Questions about the future of the second generation were common early in the twentieth century. At the time, contemporaries lacked the knowledge we now possess; they could not imagine that the children and grandchildren of foreign-born, unskilled workers would eventually climb up the totem pole, helped by the New Deal, the GI Bill, Veterans Administration (VA) mortgages, and a system of high wages and reduced inequality. Rather, the knowledgeable observers of eight to nine decades ago fretted over those developments that they could readily observe: more good jobs required extended levels of education, and the children of immigrant workers seemed unwilling to stay in school.[25]

In the end, those anxieties were for naught: the descendants of the eastern and southern European immigrants who arrived at the turn of the twentieth century have now climbed to the pinnacle of American society, or thereabouts. But our leading researchers think it unlikely that a similar scenario awaits the offspring of the new, late–twentieth-century immigration. In their view, the immigrants of the turn of the twentieth century had the advantage of sharing a common European heritage with the then-dominant white Anglo-Saxon Protestants (WASPs) and that blunted discrimination's edge. The old factory-based economy also allowed for a multigenerational move up the totem pole. Immigrant children could do better than their parents if they stayed in the educational system through high school, after which well-paid manufacturing jobs would await them. The third generation would continue on through college and beyond, completing the move from peddler to plumber to professor, the dirty secret being that the wages of brain work did not always rival the earnings enjoyed in the skilled crafts.[26]

According to the hypothesis of *segmented assimilation,* a term coined by Alejandro Portes and Min Zhou (who has also authored chapter 8 in this book, on the new second generation), the offspring of today's poorly educated immigrants are likely to experience a very different fate.[27] The low-skilled immigrants of the turn of the twenty-first century, visibly identifiable and coming from everywhere but Europe, enter a mainly white society still not cured of its racist afflictions. The immigrants arrive willing to do the jobs that natives will not, but the children want more; not clear is whether the children's careers can live up to "their U.S.-acquired aspirations."[28] The conundrum of the contemporary second generation is heightened by the continuing transformation of the U.S. economy. Although low-skilled jobs persist, occupational segmentation has "reduced the opportunities for incremental upward mobility through well-paid, blue-collar positions." The advent of the hourglass economy confronts the immigrant children with a cruel choice: either acquire the college and other advanced degrees needed to move into the professional and managerial elite or else accept the same menial jobs to which the first generation was consigned. But the immigrants' children may simply say, "no thanks," in which case a new underclass is in the making.

In her chapter Min Zhou draws on a completely new data source to address the educational and employment trajectories experienced by the emerging second generation, and there is no need for me to preempt her message here. But as I dissent from the overall program, a few cautionary words may be in order. On the one hand, one might not have expected the discussions of immigrant children's prospects to have turned so pessimistic so quickly, given the distinctive economic characteristics of the post-1965 immigrants. As I have already noted, socioeconomic diversity is a salient feature of the new immigration, quite in contrast to the situation among the immigrants of 1890–1920, who were concentrated at the bottom of the occupational distribution. In particular, high-skilled immigrants have played a modest but significant role in immigration to the United States since the enactment of the Hart-Celler Act in 1965.

Moreover, there is little question that many, possibly even most, immigrant children are heading upward, as exemplified by the large number of Chinese, Korean, Indian, and other students of Asian origin enrolled in the nation's leading universities, some the children of workers, others the descendants of immigrants who moved right into the middle class. This rapid ascent evokes parallels with the past, most clearly the first- and second-generation Jews who began appearing at City College and then Columbia, Harvard, and other prestigious schools in numbers that discomfited the then dominant WASPs. As Stephen Steinberg pointed out some years ago, it was the Jews' good fortune to have moved to America just when the educational system was expanding and moving away from its classical past and to have converged on the Northeast, where opportunities to pursue schooling were particularly good.[29] But even so, *schleppers* greatly outnumbered scholars, and the proportion of Jews who made their way to Harvard or its proletarian cousin, the City College of New York (CCNY), was dwarfed by those who moved ahead as skilled workers, clerks, or small business owners. In this light, the Asian advance into higher education remains phenomenal; in the Los Angeles region, for example, 18- to 24-year-olds in every Asian group (Vietnamese immigrants who arrived in the United States after the age of 10 included) attend college at a rate that exceeds that of native-born whites, with native-born Asians leagues ahead of native-born whites on this count.[30] And, ironically, the current backlash against affirmative action seems likely to accelerate rather than reverse this trend—quite a different turn of events than that which transpired in the Ivy League 70 years ago.[31]

On the other hand, there is good reason to believe that the children of the immigrant working poor will undergo a rather different and far less brilliant fate. It is not simply the case that the earnings of less-skilled immigrants are lagging behind. One must also remember that their households are often large, containing many children, which depresses per capita income and increases the likelihood that the children will grow up in poverty—bad news, as we know from the large library of research demonstrating that growing up in poverty is associated with decreased school achievement. Even so, the projection of an underclass future seems to involve quite a stretch, and not simply because the underclass concept is of dubious value, as I have already argued. The ghetto underclass may be the result of social isolation, but that term hardly applies to the environments in which the children of immigrants grow up. As we shall see in chapter 3, employment rates among low-skilled immigrants are generally impressive, indeed sufficiently so to make work normative (granted some possible exceptions, such as the Dominicans in New York). The population density of persons with jobs is itself a source of social capital, improving the quantity and quality of job-related information and embedding job seekers in informal networks that transmit skills once jobs are acquired. Is it unreasonable to assume that the deep embedding of immigrant networks in the labor market has no salutary effect on the opportunities available to newcomers' children?

It is also worth recalling that the embedding of immigrant communities in the labor market is, at least in part, a response to employers' favorable views of the work ethic and behavior of the foreign-born; for that reason, one can expect that immigrant children are received quite differently than were the offspring of the African American migrants to the cities of the East and Midwest. The penetration of immigrant networks is also now very deep. To take the Los Angeles case, which I know particularly well, although there are still plenty of immigrant sweepers and sewers, there are also quite a few foremen and skilled workers, which in turn provides the second generation with access to higher-level job opportunities. Because immigration itself generates ample needs for bilingual speakers (whether in hospitals, department stores, or factories), it creates positions for which the children of immigrants are ideally suited. Consequently, anxiety over prospects for second-generation immigrants may be warranted, but the more dire scenarios should be assessed with a good deal of care.

Making It in the Capitals of Immigrant America: An Overview

Having filled in the intellectual background, I use the remainder of this chapter to offer a taste of the topics addressed and arguments advanced in the chapters to follow. Chapter 2, which I have coauthored with Jennifer Lee, further sets the stage by reviewing immigration trends, both in the nation at large and within the five urban regions on which this book focuses. We also highlight the distinctive settlement pattern developed by the immigrants as they have put down roots. We argue that the action takes place in America's five leading immigrant destinations, since the immigrants have become more regionally concentrated over the past several decades. But these key immigrant regions are not of a piece; rather, they differ strikingly in the skill composition of their immigrants, the diversity of their immigrant flows, and the timing of arrival, disparities that are heightened by divergent trajectories of urban economic change. Taking a comparative view of immigrants in their regional concentrations, we highlight similarities and differences entirely ignored by the literature's focus on change at a national level or overlooked by the case study work linked to individual places.

Most of the literature on the transformation of the urban economies studied in this book emphasizes the extraordinary employment difficulties experienced by less-skilled members of native-born minority groups. But immigrants—often poorly educated, recently arrived, and lacking in English fluency—are finding jobs, and doing so at remarkably high rates. Chapter 3 focuses on this paradox and its broader ramifications, emphasizing the importance of comparisons that take into account gender and nativity status. Although less-skilled immigrant men may be more likely to be employed than their African American counterparts they soon discover that finding "adequate employment"—in terms of compensation or hours—is far more difficult. On the flip side, African American men have a more arduous time finding a job but are more likely to find themselves adequately employed once they find one. By contrast, the persons at greatest risk are less-skilled immigrant women, who encounter many more employment problems than their white and African American counterparts and for whom nativity universally depresses employment and often depresses employment adequacy. Thus, immigrants may have ample access to social capital, as the literature suggests, but those resources are not available to all. Even immigrants who benefit from the connections that link them to employers find that those ties work less efficiently in moving them to jobs of adequate quality.

Chapter 4, by Mark Ellis, takes up the same theme and inquires about immigrant progress by comparing wage trends of foreign- and native-born workers in America's five urban immigrant regions. As I have noted, immigration scholars have largely concluded that immigrants are falling behind their native-born counterparts. But as Ellis points out, this consensus rests on analyses done entirely at the national level, whereas the bulk of immigrants are living in the five regions that are the focus of this book. Furthermore, these are places where natives are relatively underrepresented, and the economic structure is shifting in ways quite different from the changes transpiring in the nation as a whole. Ellis finds that the regional comparison reveals a very different portrait of the widening economic bifurcation between the foreign- and native-born than national trends indicate. At a national level, factors related to the national-origin and skill composition of the immigrant population explain much of the gap between the native- and foreign-born. But in the leading immigrant destinations, immigrant disadvantage results mainly from the restructuring of regional economies, making it more difficult for the foreign-born to translate their skills into decent wages. Compared to the native-born, whose wages in these regions are even higher than they are nationally, the disparity between the foreign- and native-born increases dramatically. Ellis points out that the differential change in wage structures implies that the native- and foreign-born work in dual labor markets whose lines of segmentation have cemented over the past decade.

Next we turn to William A. V. Clark's chapter on immigrant poverty and the emergence of an immigrant underclass. Though noting the bifurcated immigrant population of highly educated newcomers working in the high end of the occupational spectrum and their poorly educated and low-skilled counterparts trying to rise out of poverty, Clark argues that immigrant poverty levels are cause for concern. He finds that in the five regions, immigrants overall are doing much better than the native-born black population but worse than the native-born white population, with only four exceptions—Los Angeles, Phoenix, Houston, and Denver—where both native-born populations have lower poverty rates than the foreign-born. Regional differences abound, with the most vulnerable groups varying by place and ethnic origin: Central Americans in Chicago, Mexicans in Miami, and Russians and Southeast Asians in Los Angeles. The critical factor in escaping poverty, Clark finds, is securing employment, a daunting task given immigrants' low skills.

The question of whether and how immigrants affect the employment prospects of African Americans has been a central concern for academics in many disciplines. Chapter 6, by Nelson Lim, investigates this question by comparing African American and immigrant niches over a two-decade period: 1970–1990. In 1970 African Americans and immigrants converged in the same niches, but by 1990 African Americans dominated niches in which immigrants barely penetrated. Did immigrants push African Americans out of some niches, or were they instead pushed up or pulled into better niches by factors bearing little or no relationship to immigration? Lim's chapter argues for the latter of these possibilities, pointing to the endogenous forces that have transformed African American niches in all five immigrant regions, and in remarkably the same way. On the one hand, immigrants made inroads into those African American niches marked by low status and subordination—for example, jobs in the hotel industry or domestic service. By contrast, African Americans made use of their higher levels of education to penetrate better quality niches in the public sector, consequently diminishing the effects of immigrant competition. African Americans have been pulled up, not out.

I continue the analysis of the ethnic niche in chapter 7, coauthored with Claudia Der-Martirosian, in which we switch the focus from African Americans to immigrants. Although the literature has been true to its assimilationist bias, viewing the ethnic niche as a transitional phenomenon limited to new arrivals and low-skilled groups, we find the opposite to be true. Notwithstanding the important differences among the five urban regions, ethnic niches stand out as a characteristic of almost every immigrant group in all five locales—high skilled and low skilled, refugees and entrepreneurial types—with concentration persisting even as immigrant cohorts put down roots. We also take the discussion of niches in a new direction by inquiring into the noneconomic characteristics of ethnic niches, with an emphasis on the cognitive skills required by niche jobs and the physical circumstances under which the jobs get done. We show that although skill sorts immigrants into "good" and "bad" niches, ethnicity works as a fundamental structuring factor, such that groups occupy niches of the same type, regardless of locale. In general, we conclude that concentration, not dispersion, is the road to economic mobility and that the quest for advancement takes a collective rather than an individual form. But we do find one startling exception to the broader pattern: Cubans in Miami, who, contrary to the accepted conventional wisdom, show relatively low levels of ethnic niching and have established niches of exceptionally low quality.

Chapter 8, by Min Zhou, focuses on the prospects of mobility for today's second generation. Zhou poses the following question: Are the offspring of today's immigrant generation facing an unprecedented second generation decline? Most of the second generation has not yet reached adulthood, but significant numbers are now leaving the parental household, with diverse trajectories emerging as young adult immigrant offspring leave school and enter the labor market. In general, the second generation is surpassing the first on a number of indicators including high school graduation rates. Asserting that mobility is not reducible to class differences, Zhou argues that ethnicity seems to be exerting its own effect—accelerating upward progress for some while hindering mobility for others. Whether the second generation's expectations will be met depends on two factors: (1) educational credentials and school-acquired skills and (2) ethnic connections. Zhou's chapter casts doubt on the scenario of second-generation decline since today's second generation is surpassing the first generation's progress. However, she also cautions that the population is diverse, as already manifest in the mobility patterns; Asians are moving up the ranks most rapidly, Mexicans most slowly, and other Hispanics and blacks somewhere in between. What Min Zhou and Carl Bankston find in their work *Growing Up American* is applicable: groups that maintain a distinctive identity and social structures that promote continued cohesion have advantages in getting ahead.[32]

Notes

1. The relationship between immigration and the migration of natives remains a matter of much controversy. In a variety of publications William Frey ("Immigration and Internal Migration 'Flight': A California Case Study," *Population and Environment* 16 [1995]: 353–375; "Immigration and Internal Migration 'Flight' from U.S. Metropolitan Areas: Toward a New Demographic Balkanization," *Urban Studies* 32 [1995]: 733–757) has found a negative correlation between immigration and net internal migration, which he has interpreted as immigration-induced "flight." By contrast, Richard Wright, Mark Ellis, and Michael Reibel have argued that natives' tendency to leave areas of high immigration densities reflects not so much a response to immigration as such but rather to other shifts in the economic structure of those places ("The Linkage between Immigration and Internal Migration in Large Metropolitan Areas in the United States," *Economic Geography* 73, no. 2 [1992]: 232–252). Although the body of literature on this subject is already quite large and rapidly

growing, the basic facts—as opposed to their interpretation—do not seem to be in dispute: America's leading immigrant destinations experience a net outflow of their U.S.-born residents, although the rate of out-migration varies by socioeconomic characteristics.

2. Douglas Massey, Joaquin Arango, Graeme Hugo, Ali Kouaouci, Adela Pelligrino, and J. Edward Taylor, "Theories of International Migration: A Review and Appraisal," *Population and Development Review* 19, no. 3 (1993): 431–466.

3. The Current Population Survey is a monthly survey of a national probability sample of approximately 60,000 households. In light of the limited size of the two populations of interest to us—immigrants, on the one hand, and persons living in the five consolidated metropolitan statistical areas (CMSAs) of interest for this book, on the other—we have sought to increase the size of these target populations by merging the March CPS samples from 1994 through 1998. However, the nature of the CPS precludes use of each year's full CPS sample. The CPS retains respondents during a two-year period, interviewing individuals for four consecutive months, dropping them from the sample for the next eight months, and then reinterviewing them for another four consecutive months, after which they are dropped from the sample completely. Consequently, half of the persons interviewed in any given month reappear in the following year's sample in the same month. To avoid duplicate cases, we retained nonoverlapping halves of the 1994, 1995, 1996, and 1997 samples and included the entire 1998 sample. This procedure tripled the size of the total sample. We used a set of weights developed by Jeffrey Passel of the Urban Institute to adjust for mistakes in the original weights developed by the Bureau of the Census for the 1994 and 1995 March Current Population Surveys. Passel reviews the problems and diagnoses in a document that he kindly made available to us: "Problem with March 1994 and 1995 CPS Weighting," memorandum for CPS Users (Washington, D.C.: Urban Institute, August 21, 1997). A summary of the problems, as well as the procedures implemented by Passel, appears in Jeffrey S. Passel and Rebecca Clark, *Immigrants in New York: Their Legal Status, Incomes, and Taxes* (Washington, D.C.: Urban Institute, 1998), available at http://www.urban.org/immig/immny.html#VII.

4. W. E. B. DuBois, *The Souls of Black Folk: Essays and Sketches* (Chicago: A. G. McClurg, 1903; New York: Johnson Reprint Corp., 1968).

5. Thomas Archdeacon's *Becoming American: An Ethnic History* (New York: Free Press, 1983) provides an admirable history of immigration, as well as of the complicated reactions it has elicited.

6. On the process by which the old "new immigrants" became white, see David Roediger and James Barrett, "Inbetween Peoples: Race, Nationality, and the 'New Immigrant' Working-Class," *Journal of American Ethnic History* 16, no. 3 (1997): 3–44. On the Great Migration, James Grossman's *Land of Hope: Chicago, Black Southerners, and the Great Migration* (Chicago: University of Chicago Press, 1989) is the best recent contribution.

7. See Thomas Sugrue, *The Origins of the Urban Crisis* (Princeton, N.J.: Princeton University Press, 1996).

8. National Advisory Commission on Civil Disorders, *Report* (New York: Bantam, 1968).

9. William J. Wilson, *The Truly Disadvantaged: The Inner City, the Underclass, and Public Policy* (Chicago: University of Chicago Press, 1987); idem, *When Work Disappears* (New York: Alfred A. Knopf, 1996). Over the years, the sociologist John Kasarda has been a particularly influential exponent of the skills-mismatch hypothesis. His chapter "Cities as Places Where People Live and Work: Urban Change and Neighborhood Distress," in *Interwoven Destinies: Cities and the Nation*, ed. Henry Cisneros (New York: W. W. Norton, 1993) provides a particularly succinct and clear expression of his views, which he has elaborated in many publications over the past 15 or so years. For other examples, see "Entry-Level Jobs, Mobility, and Urban Minority Employment," *Urban Affairs Quarterly* 19, no. 1 (1984): 21–40; "Jobs, Mismatches, and Emerging Urban Mismatches," in *Urban Change and Poverty*, ed. M. G. H. Geary and L. Lynn (Washington, D.C.: National Academy Press, 1988), 148–198; and "Structural Factors Affecting the Location and Timing of Urban Underclass Growth," *Urban Geography* 11, no. 3 (1990): 234–264. William J. Wilson liberally cites Kasarda's findings, while endorsing his views, in his various influential books.

10. Oscar Handlin, *The Uprooted* (Boston: Little, Brown, 1953); John Bodnar, *The Transplanted* (Bloomington: Indiana University Press, 1987).

11. For a state-of-the-art review, see Alejandro Portes, "Social Capital: Its Origins and Applications in Modern Sociology," *Annual Review of Sociology* 24 (1998): 1–24. Douglas Massey, Rafael Alarcón, Jorge Durand, and Humberto González, *Return to Aztlan* (Berkeley and Los Angeles: University of California Press, 1987) documents the network-driven nature of U.S.-Mexican migration and the way in which networks can be converted into social capital.

12. For a critique of the "underclass" literature and concept, see Loïc Wacquant, "Three Pernicious Premises in the Study of the American Ghetto," *International Journal of Urban and Regional Research* 21 (June 1997): 341–353.

13. Indeed, as shown in chapter 7, Mexicans, America's overwhelmingly largest immigrant group, are concentrated in jobs that are undesirable on almost all counts, a condition that is likely to set a ceiling on future progress.

14. Barry Chiswick, "The Effect of Americanization on the Earnings of Foreign-Born Men," *Journal of Political Economy* 86 (October 1978): 897–921.

15. George Borjas, "Assimilation, Changes in Cohort Quality, and the Earnings of Immigrants," *Journal of Labor Economics* 3 (October 1985): 463–489.

16. George Borjas, *Friends or Strangers? The Impact of Immigrants on the U.S. Economy* (New York: Basic Books, 1990); idem, *Heaven's Door: Immigration Policy and the American Economy* (Princeton, N.J.: Princeton University Press, 1999).

17. For example, Barry Chiswick, "Is the New Immigration Less Skilled than the Old?" *Journal of Labor Economics* 4 (April 1986): 168–192; Harriet Duleep and Mark Regets, "Measuring Immigrant Wage Growth Using Matched CPS Files," *Demography* 34, no. 2 (May 1997): 239–249.

18. Richard Murnane and Frank Levy, "United States Earnings Levels and Earnings Inequality: A Review of Recent Trends and Proposed Explanations," *Journal of Economic Literature* 30, no. 3 (September 1992): 1333–1381. Borjas, however, concludes that the changes in the wage structure in the United States as a whole account for only a relatively small share of the drop in the immigrant entry wage between 1970 and 1990 (*Heaven's Door*, pp. 36–37); for an alternative interpretation, see chapter 4 of this book.

19. The canonical work on assimilation remains Milton Gordon's *Assimilation in American Life* (New York: Oxford University Press, 1964); for a recent defense of assimilation and review of supporting evidence, see Richard Alba and Victor Nee, "Rethinking Assimilation Theory for a New Era of Immigration," *International Migration Review* 31, no. 4 (winter 1997): 826–874.

20. Roger Waldinger and Mehdi Bozorgmehr, *Ethnic Los Angeles* (New York: Russell Sage Foundation, 1996); see especially chapters 4 and 5.

21. See, for example, Massey et al., *Return to Aztlan*.

22. Alejandro Portes, "Economic Sociology and the Sociology of Immigration," in *The Economic Sociology of Immigration,* ed. Alejandro Portes (New York: Russell Sage Foundation, 1994), 248–281.

23. For a literature review, with ample footnotes, see chapter 7.

24. Roger Waldinger, *Still the Promised City? African-Americans and New Immigrants in PostIndustrial New York* (Cambridge, Mass.: Harvard University Press, 1996); idem, "Ethnicity and Opportunity in the Plural City," in *Ethnic Los Angeles,* ed. Roger Waldinger and Mehdi Bozorgmehr (New York: Russell Sage Foundation, 1996), 445–471; idem, "The Making of an Immigrant Niche," *International Migration Review* 28, no. 1 (1994): 3–30.

25. See Roger Waldinger and Joel Perlmann, "Second Generations: Past, Present, Future," *Journal of Ethnic and Migration Studies* 24, no. 1 (1998): 5–24.

26. Herbert Gans, "Second-Generation Decline: Scenarios for the Economic and Ethnic Futures of the Post-1965 American Immigrants," *Ethnic and Racial Studies* 15, no. 2 (1992): 173–192; Alejandro Portes and Min Zhou, "The New Second Generation: Segmented Assimilation and Its Variants among Post-1965 Immigrant Youth," *Annals of the American Academy of Political and Social Science* 530 (1993): 74–96.

27. Portes and Zhou, "New Second Generation."

28. Ibid., 85.

29. Stephen Steinberg, *The Ethnic Myth: Race, Ethnicity, and Class in America* (New York: Atheneum, 1981).

30. Lucie Cheng and Philip Yang, "Asians: The Model Minority Deconstructed," in *Ethnic Los Angeles,* ed. Roger Waldinger and Mehdi Bozorgmehr (New York: Russell Sage Foundation, 1996), 305–344.

31. For more on the comparison of Jewish and Asian second-generation off-spring, see Joel Perlmann and Roger Waldinger, "Second Generation Decline? Immigrant Children Past and Present—A Reconsideration," *International Migration Review* 31, no. 4 (1997): 893–922.

32. Min Zhou and Carl Bankston III, *Growing Up American: How Vietnamese Children Adapt to Life in the United States* (New York: Russell Sage Foundation, 1998).

Chapter 2

NEW IMMIGRANTS IN URBAN AMERICA

Roger Waldinger and Jennifer Lee

Immigration is again transforming the United States. A renewed immigrant tide stretches back four decades, with newcomers arriving in unprecedented numbers and evidence of a changed America perceptible wherever one goes. Venturing deep into the heartland, one hears foreign accents; looking a little deeper, one encounters the networks that link immigrants and the fledgling institutions that sustain them.

The appearance of immigrants all over the map is not quite an illusion, but it is largely a product of growing immigrant numbers. Small groups filter toward many corners of the country, where observers may note the increased population of newcomers. For the most part, however, immigrants are firmly urban bound. They head to the places where their friends, relatives, and compatriots have already settled, which, for reasons of history, geography, and accident, happen to be the five urban regions whose experience lies at the heart of this book.

Of course, the social science literature takes note of the geographic proclivities of the immigrants, but then usually goes on to other matters, often in ways that are unmindful of immigration's distinctive regional spread. As we will show in this chapter, the geography of the new immigration deserves a good deal more attention than it has received so far. Although immigrants do disperse within the urban regions where they settle, the urban attraction for immigrants has essentially remained unchanged over the past several decades. Moreover, immigrants have converged in urban America in a way that has generated a distinctive hierarchy of immigrant destinations, distinguished not simply by the relative size of the foreign-born populations but by the timing of flows, their skill composition, and the degree of ethnic heterogeneity. This is the story that we will tell in the pages that follow, though we will first set the stage with an overview of immigration trends.

The New Immigration

Home to a relatively sparse group of indigenous peoples, the land that became the United States was peopled by newcomers from abroad: mainly free laborers, who came from Europe, and slaves, who were imported from Africa. While the slave trade was stopped in the early nineteenth century, immigration went on, moving in waves and changing in composition. In the mid–nineteenth century the new arrivals mainly came from England, Ireland, Germany, and elsewhere in western Europe. After 1880 immigrant origins shifted to southern and eastern Europe, and numbers skyrocketed. Following decades of restrictionist agitation, xenophobic alarms eventually won out in the aftermath of World War I, the Bolshevik Revolution, and the Red Scares it produced. In 1924 Congress voted to close the gates, reducing immigration to a trickle and all but barring newcomers from eastern and southern Europe (see figure 2.1).

After four decades of reduced immigration, a more tolerant climate, induced by the civil rights movement of the 1960s, reopened the doors; Congress passed the Hart-Celler Act in 1965, which is the conventional date for the onset of the new immigration to the United States. As we shall see later in this chapter, the seeds of today's new immigration had actually been planted earlier; still, the 1965 reforms exercised a fundamental impact, transforming the immigration system with a few bold strokes.[1] First, it abolished the old country of origin quotas, which had allotted small quotas to southern and eastern Europe and still smaller, almost prohibitively small, quotas to Asia. Second, it established two principal criteria for admission to the United States: family ties to citizens or permanent residents and possession of scarce and wanted skills. Third, it increased the total numbers of immigrants to be admitted to the United States.[2]

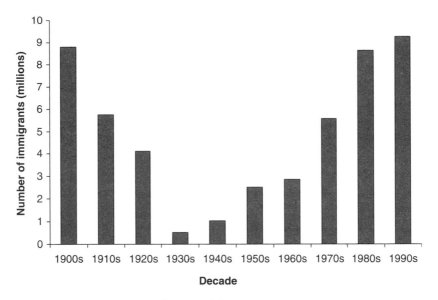

Figure 2.1   Immigration to the United States, 1901–1999

The system established by the 1965 reforms essentially remains in place to this day, despite constant debate and continuous overhauling. But the Hart-Celler Act initiated changes that were entirely different from those intended by its advocates. The reformers thought the new act would keep the size of the immigrant influx to modest proportions, but for various reasons the numbers quickly spiraled: 7.3 million new immigrants arrived in the United States during the 1980s, second only to the peak of 8.8 million newcomers recorded during the first decade of the twentieth century. And between 1990 and 1999, the United States took in newcomers at a clip of 929,000 a year, which means that the intake during the century's last decade exceeded that in the first decade by almost 500,000.

To be sure, at 10 percent immigrants constituted a considerably smaller share of the nation's population in 1999 than in 1910, when 15 of every 100 Americans were foreign-born. Moreover, a glance at the immigration rate—a flow indicator, displayed in figure 2.2, that relates the size of a decade's immigrant cohort to the total population at the end of the decade—indicates that the late-century uptick was decidedly more modest than the early-twentieth-century surge and essentially leveled off during the 1990s. Still, the nation has moved far—and fast—

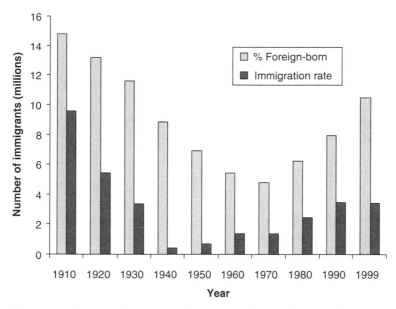

Figure 2.2.   Immigration rate and percentage foreign-born in the United
States, 1900–1999

Source: Data based on immigrants admitted by the INS, 1900–1960; thereafter from
U.S. Census of Population and Current Population Survey. *Statistical Abstract of the
United States,* 2000; U.S. Census of Population, 1970, 1980, 1990.

from the levels in 1970, when the foreign-born share of the U.S. population dropped to its historic nadir.

Along with the unforeseen increase in immigration following the Hart-
Celler Act came a second unexpected twist. The 1965 legislation was tar-
geted principally at eastern and southern Europeans, the groups hardest
hit by the nativist legislation of the 1920s. By the 1960s, however, workers from Italy or Yugoslavia had fallen out of the orbit of transatlantic migration. Instead, the newcomers who took advantage of the newly liberal-
ized system came from Asia, Latin America, and the circum-Caribbean.

What no one anticipated in 1965 was the burgeoning of Asian immigration. The reforms tilted the new system toward immigrants with
kinship ties to permanent residents or citizens. With so little Asian immigration in the previous 50 years, how could Asian newcomers find
settlers with whom to seek reunification? The answer is that kinship
connections were helpful but not essential. The 1965 reforms also created opportunities for immigrants whose skills—as engineers, doctors,
nurses, and pharmacists—were in short supply. Along with students

who were already living in the United States and who enjoyed easy access to American employers, these professionals constituted the first wave of new Asian immigrants, creating the basis for the kinship migration of less well educated relatives.[3] The system was sufficiently flexible for more established groups, such as the Chinese, to renew migration streams, while also allowing entirely new groups—most notably Koreans and Asian Indians—to put a nucleus in place and then quickly expand.[4] The professional route allowed Asian migration to follow a sudden growth curve. For example, between 1940 and 1960 fewer than 400 Indians moved to the United States each year; in the 1960s the legal flow ratcheted up to 2,700 per annum and then increased steadily until it reached the 37,000 per year mark in the 1990s.[5]

By contrast, migration from Latin America and the circum-Caribbean had already swelled to more than a trickle by the time immigration reform occurred. These pioneering immigrants established beachheads in the economy that encouraged newcomers to try their luck as well. A somewhat similar chain of events affected black immigrants from the former British Crown colonies in the West Indies; they had established a sizable community in New York before 1930 but subsequently found their way to the United States blocked by the depression of the 1930s, the advent of World War II, and then new legislative restrictions on colonial immigrants. Once the Hart-Celler Act reopened the front door, newcomers could reactivate the base of kinship connections left by the earlier migrations.[6]

Political developments added substantial and unexpected momentum to the migrant flow. Though the United States had largely closed its doors to refugees fleeing the Holocaust, pressure to admit immigrants fleeing from persecution increased steadily in the years following World War II. Many displaced persons, including survivors of the Holocaust and other Europeans uprooted in the aftermath of World War II, moved to the United States in the late 1940s; the Hungarian Revolution of 1956 produced another smaller but still significant refugee flow. The Cuban Revolution of 1959 caused an exodus of 200,000 persons, who fled to the United States over the next three years.

This backdrop notwithstanding, the 1965 act allowed for only a limited influx of refugees, carefully defined so as to give preference to those fleeing Communist regimes. In the years that followed, unexpected pressures repeatedly forced the United States to greatly expand its admission of refugees. The sudden collapse of the U.S.-supported regime in South Vietnam, followed by Communist takeovers in Cambodia and Laos, triggered a massive, sudden outflow of refugees, many of whom settled on the West Coast. Discontent with conditions in Cuba led to repeated efforts at escape. The most significant migration came in 1980, when Fidel Castro suddenly lowered the barriers to emigration and Cubans fled to the United States in a motley flotilla of fishing boats and any other vessels they could find. While in these instances the United States played the role of reluctant host, U.S. pressure was largely responsible for emigration from the former Soviet Union, which waxed and waned during the 1970s and 1980s in response to changing U.S.-Soviet relations. The collapse of the Soviet Union in 1989 led to a massive outpouring, mainly of Jews but also of Armenians and other minorities.

Thus immigrants who could activate kinship ties to U.S. residents or citizens, who possessed special skills, or who were seeking asylum from Communist regimes were able to pass through the front door opened by the 1965 reforms in a variety of ways. Mexicans and, later on, Central Americans were more likely to come through the back door of unauthorized migration. The immediate roots of unauthorized migration from Mexico lie further back, in the Bracero program begun during World War II to alleviate shortages of agricultural workers. Ostensibly, the Bracero program was to be a short-term solution, and the workers it imported were supposed to head back to Mexico after a stint of temporary labor in the United States. But the influence of agribusiness kept the Bracero program alive until 1964, and with time an increasing number of migrants exited the Bracero stream, heading for better jobs in Los Angeles, San Francisco, and other urban areas. By 1964, when Congress abolished the Bracero program, networks between the United States and villages throughout Mexico's central plateau were already in place, providing all the information and connections needed to keep the migrants coming—with or without legal documents.[7]

Once the ex-Braceros abandoned farm labor, the institutional mechanisms of the 1965 act facilitated the transition to legal status. Marriage to a citizen or legal resident, a change in the legal status of one's sibling, or assistance from an employer eager to retain a skilled and valued hand was enough to eventually transform an undocumented worker into a legal immigrant. Since newly legal immigrants could then bring over immediate relatives still lingering in Mexico, albeit with some delay, the official statistics show steadily expanding legal migration from Mexico.

While Mexicans were drawn by the inducements of American employers, the Salvadorans and Guatemalans who headed for the U.S. border in increasing numbers in the late 1970s and afterward were responding to different factors. Like the Vietnamese, Cambodians, and Laotians, Central Americans were escaping political unrest; unlike their Asian counterparts, however, the Central Americans had the bad fortune to flee right-wing regimes propped up by the U.S. government. Hence, these newcomers mainly moved across the border as unauthorized migrants. During the late 1980s, court battles forced the U.S. government to grant some of these refugees temporary asylum, though the number benefiting from this status has since dwindled and the asylum itself remains a matter of ongoing contention.[8]

Just how many newcomers have arrived without authorization has long been a matter of dispute, with wildly disparate estimates and guesstimates, ranging from 2 to 12 million. However, demographers have now settled on a methodology for counting the uncountable that has yielded estimates on which much of the immigration research community can agree. When first applied, toward the end of the 1980s, this methodology suggested, as of 1980, an undocumented population of about 2 to 4 million, over half of whom had come to the United States from Mexico.[9]

The desire to curtail undocumented immigration has dominated immigration policy debates since enactment of the Hart-Celler Act; with the passage of the Immigration Reform and Control Act of 1986 (known as IRCA), Congress attempted to close the back door and control this unauthorized flow. IRCA had three major provisions: a so-called general amnesty for undocumented immigrants who had resided continuously in the United States since January 1, 1982; a second program, inserted at the behest of agricultural interests and with the help of Pete Wilson (then a senator from California), for agricultural workers who had been in the United States for a minimum of 90 days in the year preceding May 1986; and sanctions against the employers of illegal immigrants. In IRCA, undocumented immigrants found at best a "cautious welcome," as Susan Gonzalez Baker concluded, with countless bureaucratic hurdles and anxiety-provoking administrative rules littering their path to amnesty.[10] In the end, 1.76 million persons applied for general amnesty under the conditions of IRCA, and approximately 1.3 million persons used the Special Agricultural Worker option, a program widely known for its openness to fraud and abuse.[11]

As expected, amnesty diminished the pool of undocumented immigrants. Although Congress designed sanctions and the more stringent border controls adopted in the wake of IRCA to control future unauthorized immigration, evidence suggests that these efforts, while yielding some initial results, in due course failed to curb the flow. Unauthorized migration clearly persists, contributing a net increment of about 275,000 during the mid-1990s. Estimates generated by the Immigration and Naturalization Service suggest that the undocumented population as of 1996 stood somewhere between 4.6 and 5.4 million, an increase of about 1.1 million since 1992. Mexico, the leading source of undocumented immigrants, contributes more than half, followed by El Salvador, Guatemala, Canada, and Haiti.[12]

In its many twists and turns, the country's evolving immigration policy has reshaped the face of immigrant America in varying ways. As noted earlier, numbers are up. Legal immigration has moved well beyond the annual average of 374,000 recorded in the late 1960s; the annual inflow during the years 1990–1997 was 785,000, a figure that excludes the several million persons admitted through the amnesty program, as well as all undocumented immigrants, whether illegal entrants or persons who overstayed the terms of a temporary visa.[13] Large as it is, the legal influx is just part of a broader tide; much to most experts' surprise, the Census Bureau discovered that more people migrated to the United States between 1990 and 1997 than had during the entire decade of the 1980s.

Moreover, European immigration, historically dominant, has been surpassed by migrant flows from all other parts of the world (see figure 2.3). As of the mid-1990s, half of all foreign-born immigrants who had arrived in the United States prior to 1970 originated in either Europe or Canada; among those who arrived in later years the number fell to 13 percent. In their place, immigrants from elsewhere in the Americas emerged as the numerically dominant group, accounting for just over half of the country's foreign-born population; the next largest contingent—at 30 percent—originated in Asia.

Finally, the national origins of the foreign-born population are increasingly diverse, with two important qualifications. First, a single source country dominates, and in ways that were never true before: 28 percent of all foreign-born persons, legal or otherwise, are Mexican, dwarfing the Chinese, the next largest group, at just over 5 percent. Furthermore, the increase in the rate of Mexican immigration, while driven by undocumented arrivals, is fully reflected in the numbers absorbed as legal immigrants, as can be seen in figure 2.4.[14]

Second, and confining ourselves to legal immigrants exclusively, roughly half of the immigrants who move to the United States every year originate in 10 countries. Although Mexico, the Philippines,

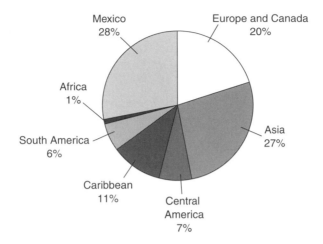

Figure 2.3.   Origins of the foreign-born, mid-1990s

Note: Percentages based on all persons reporting country of birth.
Source: Current Population Survey, 1994–1998.

China, India, the Dominican Republic, and Vietnam generally lead the
pack from year to year, others move in and out of the ranking. In some
cases, political developments lead to sudden changes, as when the former Soviet Union first shut the door on emigration in the early 1980s,
then relaxed, and finally dropped controls in the late 1980s and early
1990s. In other cases, a combination of economic developments at
home and political changes in the United States account for the decisive
shift. Korea, for example, had been a major emigration country
throughout the 1970s and 1980s, but in the 1990s the number of emigrants shrank dramatically, as economic prospects in Korea improved
and potential immigrants became better informed about the problems
that awaited them in the United States.[15] While individual countries
move in and out of the U.S.-bound migration stream, the past two
decades have seen some additions—for example, various countries in
Africa and the Middle East—that have become quantitatively significant
as overall immigration has increased.

Immigrants and the Remaking of Urban America

As in the past, the newcomers to the United States head for the big cities
and their surrounding areas. Compared to the native-born population,

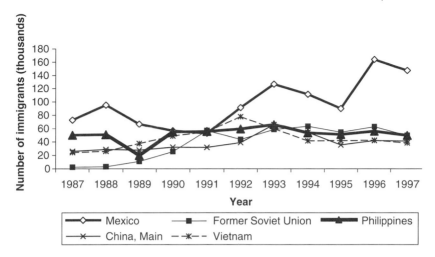

Figure 2.4.   Legal immigration, 1987–1997
Source: Statistical Yearbook of the Immigration and Naturalization Service.

today's immigrants are more likely to live in metropolitan areas, with a still more marked propensity to reside in the 27 largest urban regions of the United States. While an urban concentration of these dimensions is a sign of historical continuity, today's geography takes a very distinct form. Earlier in the century, New York served as the premier port of entry; most newcomers headed on elsewhere, but a disproportionate number found it easier to stay where they had originally landed. Those who moved beyond New York gravitated to cities, mostly in the industrialized areas of the Northeast and Midwest. With the cessation of mass migration in the 1920s, the immigrant populations aged and shrank but never moved far away from the places in which they had originally settled.

An entirely different pattern emerged in the second half of the twentieth century, though as late as 1970 the outline of the new immigrant geography was just barely visible. At that time, as figure 2.5 shows, New York towered over all the other regions; it was still the capital of immigrant America, with almost 25 percent of the country's foreign-born population. Los Angeles, with an immigrant density no greater than San Francisco's, nonetheless followed New York in share of the total U.S. immigrant population, though it had yet to emerge as a truly distinctive immigrant region. The other major areas of concentration—Chicago, San Francisco, Boston, and Philadelphia—had long served as

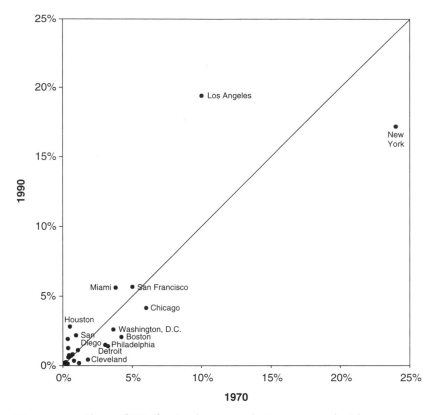

Figure 2.5.   Share of U.S. foreign-born population, 1970 and mid-1990
Source: Census of Population, Public Use Microdata Samples, 1970; Current Population Survey, 1994–1998.

destinations for immigrants; the sole exception to this historical rule was Miami, which, as figure 2.6 shows, had already gained the distinction as being the most densely populated immigrant region, thanks to the Cuban refugee inflow that began in 1959. Otherwise, as can be seen from figure 2.6, immigrant population densities tended to be higher in older urban America, which meant that Cleveland, Milwaukee, Detroit, and Pittsburgh, along with the leading immigrant destinations just mentioned, still retained sizable immigrant populations.

The center of gravity then shifted. The newcomers stayed away from the troubled, older metropolitan centers of the Midwest, and regions such as Houston and Dallas, which had never before held much attraction for the foreign-born, suddenly acquired large immigrant populations. More-

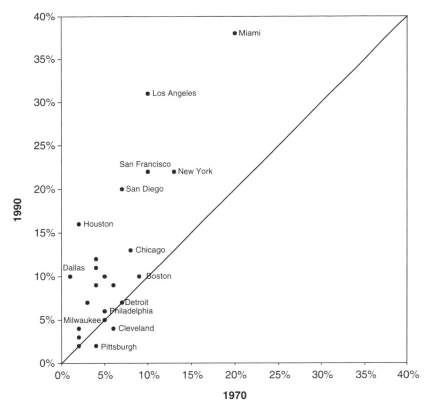

Figure 2.6.   Percentage foreign-born, 1970 and mid-1990

Source: Census of Population, Public Use Microdata Samples, 1970; Current Population Survey, 1994–1998.

over, the migration took a distinctly southern and southwestern tilt: the share of the total U.S. foreign-born population living in Los Angeles, San Francisco, Miami, and Houston rose, while the proportion residing in New York, Chicago, and Boston dropped, as can be seen in figure 2.6.

The key development during this period, however, was the channeling of immigration toward the five places that form the focus of this book, a tendency that grew more pronounced as immigrant numbers increased. Because continued immigration has been slow to produce meaningful geographic dispersion, with the foreign-born more likely today than in 1960 to live in Miami, Los Angeles, New York, San Francisco, and Chicago, the impact of immigration has diverged. Immigrant densities are sharply up in the key destination regions; in the rest of the United States, one notes an uptick in the proportion of foreign-born,

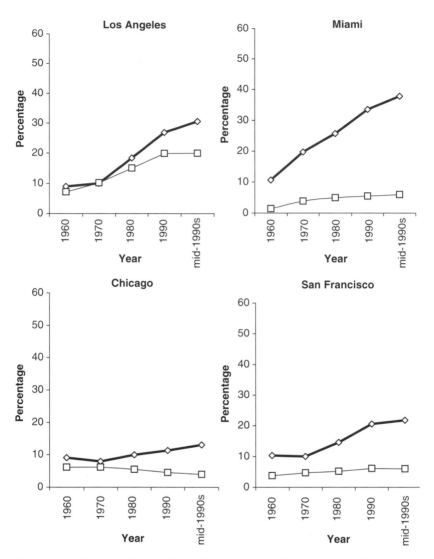

Figure 2.7.   Immigration trends: major immigrant destinations and the rest of the United States, 1960 through the mid-1990s

Source: U.S. Bureau of the Census, *Census of population: 1960;* Census of Population, Public Use Microdata Samples, 1970–1990; Current Population Survey, 1994–98.

but the shift takes off from a low base and involves a change of a very modest degree, as shown in figure 2.7.

Convergence on a limited number of places has generated a clear hierarchy of immigrant regions. At the top, as indicated in figure 2.8,

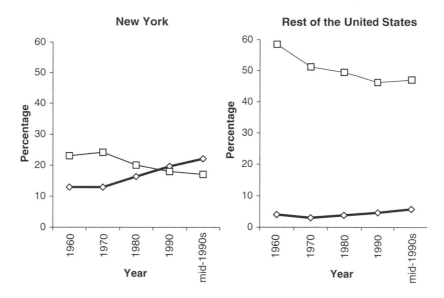

Figure 2.7.   *(continued)*

stand two mega–immigrant regions: Los Angeles and New York. Los
Angeles has now replaced New York as the capital of immigrant America, and both regions, together, contain almost 40 percent of the immigrant population. Next, though at a much smaller scale, come three
gateway regions—Miami, the densest immigration region, with 6 percent of the immigrant population; San Francisco, also with 6 percent;
and Chicago, with 4 percent. Five other regions—Boston, Dallas, San
Diego, Washington, and Houston—are minor entryways, with Houston home to 3 percent of the foreign-born and the rest to 2 percent
each. At the bottom of the hierarchy are places varying greatly in both
size and foreign-born population densities.

In general, the immigrants' settlement pattern reveals a preference
for larger regions over smaller ones. Nonetheless, the relationship between size of region, on the one hand, and size of the immigrant population, on the other, is modest indeed; while New York and Los Angeles are the largest American regions, their importance for immigrant
geography is of a totally different order. Moreover, location and history exercise an independent influence, as best indicated by the extraordinary magnetism of Los Angeles and Miami. The larger urban regions
contain a disproportionate share of the native-born population; how-

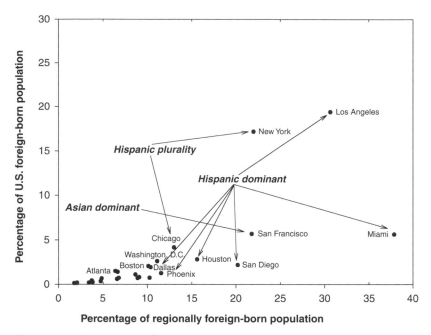

Figure 2.8.   Immigrant urban regions
Source: Current Population Survey, 1994–1998.

ever, the correlation with the foreign-born share is modest, in part because immigrants reveal a far stronger propensity for clustering in the
largest urban regions and in part because the natives take off when the
immigrants arrive. From this view, Miami emerges as an immigrant region of a very particular type, the only lesser metropolis among the
leading immigrant destinations.

Regardless of what factors account for immigrants' locational
spread, the resulting configuration stands at some variance from the ge-
ography of the native-born African American population. Immigrant
densities tend to build up away from the areas of greatest African
American concentration: Atlanta, Detroit, St. Louis, Cleveland, and
Philadelphia all stand out for their feeble attraction to the foreign-born.
In quantitative terms, the leading immigrant centers contain significant
African American populations. But in contrast to their disproportionate concentration of the foreign-born, Los Angeles, San Francisco, New
York, and Miami have African American population densities hovering
around the national average, with Los Angeles and San Francisco con-

siderably lower, New York just a shade above the national mean, Miami considerably higher, and Chicago a good deal higher still (although it is also a place of much lower immigrant population density). And our urban focus actually overstates the degree of geographic overlap between the two groups, since, in comparison to immigrants, African Americans are at once less urbanized, far more likely to live in the South, and more apt to reside in smaller metropolitan regions.

If sheer numbers fundamentally distinguish the immigrant regions from one another, compositional considerations point to other axes of variations. The key regions are linked to different flows that make for considerable diversity in national and ethnic origins. We categorize regions by the degree of categorical diversity, distinguishing between situations of numerical dominance, in which just one of the census ethnoracial categories accounts for 60 percent or more of the foreign-born population, and plurality, in which a single ethnoracial category simply outnumbers all others without attaining a numerical majority.

As figure 2.8 shows, 5 of the top 10 urban regions—Los Angeles, Houston, Dallas, San Diego, and Miami—have more Hispanic immigrants than any other ethnoracial group. Within this broad category, Miami stands out as the only region where Cubans form the overwhelmingly largest group and where Mexicans are virtually unrepresented. It also happens to be the one leading immigrant region that has yet to attract an Asian migration of any note, a factor of some consequence for the skill distribution of its immigrant population. In the other regions dominated by Hispanics, national origins reflect proximity to the U.S.-Mexico border; there, Mexicans predominate but are accompanied by sizable, though much smaller, Central American populations. New York and Chicago are regions of Hispanic plurality; although roughly equivalent in the Hispanic share, the origins of their Hispanic immigrants and the overall diversity of their foreign-born populations vary widely. Mexicans, first drawn to Chicago in the 1910s and 1920s by the region's massive industrial complex, greatly outrank all others, numbering over a third of all immigrant Chicagoans. By contrast, Dominicans top the list of immigrant New Yorkers but account for only 1 out of every 10 of the region's foreign-born. Other newcomers in the nation's number two immigrant destination are an extraordinarily diverse lot; Russians, at 5 percent, are the second largest immigrant group. San Francisco qualifies as the only region with an Asian majority in the immigrant population, though in this case the diversity of its Asian immigrants—Filipinos, Chinese, Vietnamese, and Indians,

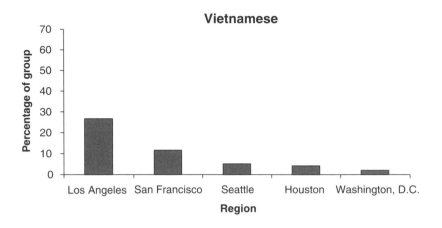

Vietnamese

Percentage of group

Los Angeles San Francisco Seattle Houston Washington, D.C.

Region

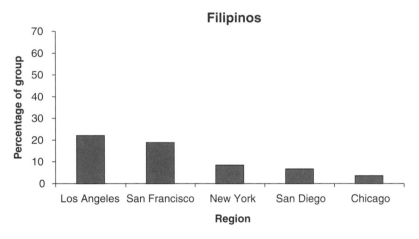

Filipinos

Percentage of group

Los Angeles San Francisco New York San Diego Chicago

Region

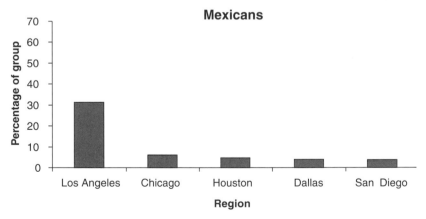

Mexicans

Percentage of group

Los Angeles Chicago Houston Dallas San Diego

Region

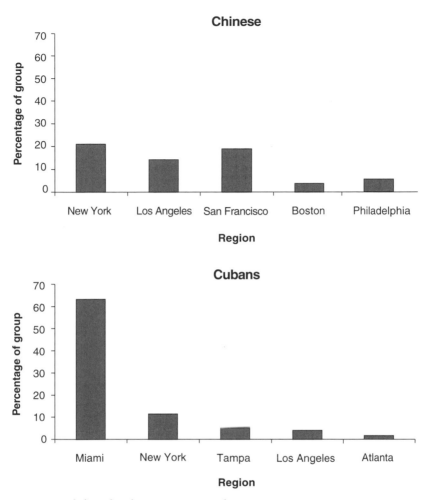

Figure 2.9 *(left and right).*   Locations of major immigrant groups (percentage of group in region)

Source: Current Population Survey, 1994–1998.

to name only the top nationalities—prompts a reminder that *Asian* denotes a category rather than a group. Washington can be characterized as a region of Asian plurality but just barely; this newly emerged immigrant region lacks any group that nears the 10 percent level. Only Boston retains a plurality of immigrants of European origin; this pattern reflects the continuing influence of the past, because the advent of mixed Asian and Hispanic populations is yielding a very different but pluralistic immigrant population.

Looking at immigrant geography from the standpoint of the groups, as we do in figure 2.9, opens another window onto the nature and sources of diversity among regions. Regional concentration is a by-product of a variety of factors. Cities have always been havens for the least skilled; immigrants with the fewest resources—whether measured in terms of capital or specialized know-how—prove the most dependent on migration networks and therefore converge on the largest urban centers. For the more skilled, formal education offers a way up and a way out: the higher the level of formal schooling, the greater the access to national labor markets, which in turn produces greater geographic dispersion. And while social class influences the degree of concentration, other considerations—most notably, the proximity between country of origin and target region and the inertial effects exercised by earlier migration histories—influence the particular destinations on which immigrants converge. Consequently, the leading immigrant groups differ greatly, in the degree of clustering and in the particular concentrations that they establish, as can be seen by surveying the geographic dispersion of the top five immigrant populations—Mexicans, Filipinos, Cubans, Chinese, and Vietnamese.

Let's begin with the well-known Cuban case. South Florida had been a place to which Cubans traveled for business and pleasure well before the advent of a sizable refugee flow in 1959. Not all refugees were able to head to Miami when the Cuban Revolution erupted, largely because the federal government tried hard to scatter the refugees, in the hope of diminishing negative reactions and potentially negative effects. Over time, however, the immigrants opted to settle where they wanted, which, for the most part, meant Miami.[16] By planting themselves so firmly in the Miami region, Cubans have ended up far more concentrated in a single place than any other group; consequently, they are also unlikely to live in most of the other leading immigrant destinations, and their absence is particularly noticeable in the immigrant centers of the West and Southwest.

By contrast, the roots of contemporary Mexican migration extend to the Bracero program, which brought Mexicans to work in farms and fields. Many immigrants left the program and headed for the largest metropolitan areas, where their presence influenced the next wave of newcomers, many of whom made a beeline for the city, avoiding a rural beginning altogether. In large measure, this description fits the Mexican immigrant history in Los Angeles, whose emergence as the most significant Mexican destination also reflects its employers' adaptation to the growing availability of Mexican immigrant labor. Nonetheless, the older pattern created by the Bracero program persists; Mexicans are more likely than other immigrant groups to live outside metropolitan areas, and a sizable proportion settle in smaller cities. Consequently, the geography of Mexican immigration has assumed a bimodal form: Los Angeles is the foremost destination, with almost a third of the nation's Mexican immigrants; the remaining 26 urban regions contain a roughly equal number, which leaves just over a third of the Mexican immigrant population in smaller metropolitan and rural areas.

Asians, of whom we profile here the three largest groups (Filipinos, Chinese, and Vietnamese), are far more likely than Mexicans to head for the largest urban regions. Though none of these leading Asian groups gravitate to a single place in quite the same way as the Mexicans converge on Los Angeles, the California connection is particularly noticeable. Almost half of all Filipinos live in the Los Angeles, San Francisco, San Diego, and Chicago regions (listed in order of importance); New York, the only other area of notable concentration, houses less than one-tenth of this group. The same regions in California contain 40 percent of the Vietnamese, who have not yet moved to New York or Chicago in large numbers and who also maintain a presence in smaller areas, thanks to federal resettlement efforts. Though California holds no small attraction for the Chinese, this group's geographic pattern takes a unique form, in that it is the only Asian group whose chief locational concentration is on the East Coast, in New York. Large numbers have also put down roots in Los Angeles and San Francisco; together these three regions alone contain almost 60 percent of all immigrants from China, Taiwan, and Hong Kong. Conspicuously absent from the list of favored Asian destinations is Miami, made distant from the U.S.-bound Asian streams by geography and history but also lacking in the high-skilled employment clusters that could activate a new flow.

Origins may not be destinies, but they are certainly influential. National origins matter most because of their strong association with class. Socioeconomic diversity can reasonably qualify as the distinguishing characteristic of the new immigration. Arriving with no capital, few useful skills, and—Jews excepted—limited literacy, the southern and eastern European predecessors of the 1880–1920 period moved into the bottom rungs: servants, laborers, longshoremen, *schleppers* all. Today's immigrants, however, are quite likely to have completed college and perhaps postgraduate studies; rates of college completion among Indians, Koreans, Taiwanese, Chinese, Iranians, and others considerably surpass the native norm, yielding a similar gap between these foreign- and native-born workers in attainment of upper white-collar employment. Substantial low-skilled contingents accompany these high-skilled immigrants, though, and the very least skilled are also the overwhelmingly largest group—namely, the Mexicans.

Some experts have looked at the educational characteristics of the foreign-born to conclude that the "quality" of America's immigrant streams has gone down.[17] They have found that the educational and skill backgrounds of the immigrants no longer compare as favorably with those of natives as they did in the relatively recent past.[18] Indeed, a comparison of educational attainment for those between the ages of 25 and 64 years shows that immigrants compare unfavorably with native-born persons. The sharpest disparities show up at the lower end of the educational spectrum: whereas 97 percent of all U.S.-born adults had received at least some secondary schooling as of the mid-1990s, only 78 percent of the foreign-born population had completed elementary school (see figure 2.10).

But comparisons of this sort miss the point, given the extraordinary educational differences among various immigrant groups. Highly educated professionals and managers dominate some streams—most notably those from the Middle East, from Africa, and from southern and Southeast Asia. Among many of these groups, median levels of schooling are far higher than those of America's native white workers. Populations with refugee origins tend to be internally diverse; high levels of education are characteristic of the early arrivals, and low levels are more common among those who emigrate in later years. Manual workers with little schooling predominate among other groups—Mexicans being the most conspicuous such example—and the contribution of low-skilled workers to America's immigrant pool has risen substantially in recent years. Thanks to these variations in the immigrant streams, educational attainment is more likely to be bimodal among the foreign-born than among natives; among immigrants, a large contingent of highly educated individuals is balanced by a sizable group with levels of schooling that fall far below the native-born norm. Restricting the purview to immigrants from all countries except Mexico, the foreign-born look much like the natives, especially in the proportion of those with education beyond high school, and immigrants hold a lead at the very top of the educational spectrum. On the other hand, among those

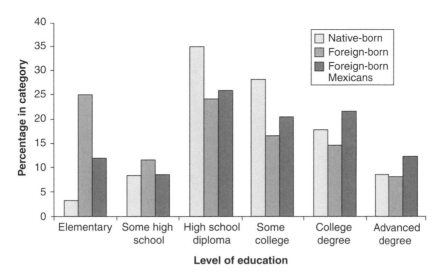

Figure 2.10.   Education of foreign- and native-born (ages 25 to 64 only)

with a high school degree or less, the foreign-born are far more likely than the native-born to be clustered at the very bottom.

Consequently, education forms another axis of variation distinguishing the key immigrant regions. More educated immigrants are likelier to disperse, as can be seen from figure 2.11, which displays the ratio of college-educated immigrants to those without a high school degree. Immigrant-dense regions tend to accumulate less-skilled immigrants, and these regions possess sizable foreign-born contingents with schooling levels far below native norms. Nonetheless, not all immigrant regions fall out alike on this crucial dimension. The least-skilled immigrants outnumber the most skilled in 6 of the top 10 immigrant regions, 5 of which also fit the earlier characterization as predominantly Hispanic. With twice as many low-skilled as high-skilled immigrants, America's leading immigrant region, Los Angeles, falls at the very bottom of the list, a position it shares with Houston. For the most part, the unfavorable skill balance of these predominantly Hispanic regions has little to do with selectivity within streams: the Mexicans who move to LA or Houston are no more and no less educated than those who head elsewhere in the United States. Roughly the same generalization holds for all the other groups. LA, Dallas, Houston, San Diego, and Chicago differ simply in the overrepresentation of those immigrant groups that arrive with the least education. Much the same can be said for Miami,

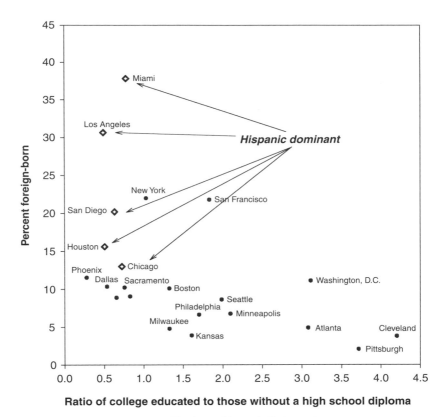

Figure 2.11.   Destinations of high- and low-skilled immigrants
Source: Current Population Survey, 1994–1998.

whose relatively unfavorable skill distribution is a product not of Mexican migration—which is virtually absent from the region—but rather the influx of a sizable group of poorly educated Caribbeans.

Though generally a region of yawning inequalities, New York's parity stands out on this dimension; high-skilled and low-skilled immigrants are roughly equal in numbers. Only San Francisco, among the most important immigrant regions, exhibits a skill distribution clearly tilted toward the upper end. In the Bay Area, college-educated immigrants outnumber their least-skilled counterparts by almost two to one, a pattern reflecting the educational background of the Asian immigrants who flock to this region in disproportionate numbers. Washington and Boston, the most heterogeneous of immigrant regions, also attract a more skilled group, a characteristic likely related to both diversity of national origin and the distinctive mix of jobs in these regions.

Thus, today's immigration has infused urban America with new residents whose low skills ensure that they start out at the very bottom. Moreover, the places that have attracted the immigrants have also seen the characteristics of native-born residents undergo the greatest change: the less skilled among them have voted with their feet, moving to other locations; those who remain in the big city or gravitate there from elsewhere are ever more likely to boast increasing levels of education. Consequently, newcomers and natives are tending toward divergence; the growing gap between native and immigrant skill levels indicates the distance immigrants must traverse if they are to get ahead, and it is a theme to which we will return frequently in this book. First, however, we take a close look at the five urban regions at the heart of our inquiry.

America's Leading Immigrant Places

Miami

We begin with Miami, since it was here that the sudden influx of refugees escaping the Cuban Revolution signaled the advent of what would later be recognized as the new immigration.[19] Miami is the newest of our five urban regions; founded in the late 1890s as a wintertime escape for the rich and idle, it quickly lost any exclusivity as the growth of the middle class expanded the market for leisure activity. The region simultaneously gained a more diverse population than its founders, with their socially constricted vision, had initially anticipated. New York and other northern Jews enjoyed the southern clime. Proximity drew Cubans, both the rebellious sort, for whom Miami served as a convenient outpost for exile politics, and the well-to-do, who came mainly on the tourist circuit but also discovered business opportunities in southern Florida. While Bahamians were also present from the beginning and remained in the city, Miami soon attracted a large population of African Americans from Georgia and northern Florida; for the first half of the twentieth century, this group was mostly left with menial work and the provision of tourist services.

But the post–World War II years found Miami slumbering, until it was suddenly woken up by the large, abrupt exodus from Cuba. Migration from the island took an erratic form over the following decades, the tension between the United States and the Castro regime providing each party with reasons to periodically open and then close the door. The initial wave of roughly 200,000, which was heavily tilted toward the middle-class elements of prerevolutionary Cuba, lasted until the Cuban missile crisis of 1962. Though a trickle of migrants arrived in 1964 and 1965, the flow then spurted again in 1966, eventuating in a wave that deposited more than 250,000, until 1973, when Cuba again stanched the outward flow. It kept the doors shut through the rest of the 1970s, but when emigration pressures became intolerable, potential migrants were suddenly allowed to leave in a 1980 outflow from the port of Mariel, from which 120,000 people migrated to the United States during a six-month period. Flows tailed off during the rest of the 1980s and more so in the 1990s, until the 1995 Balsero crisis, in which a possible reprise of the Mariel experience finally led to an agreement between the United States and Cuba that allowed the orderly entry of 20,000 immigrants a year.[20]

Though the capital of Cuban America, Miami also evolved into a different and more diverse type of immigrant region than one might have anticipated from the trends at work up through the early 1970s. Cuban migration dropped sharply after 1973, but other streams expanded. The Haitians arrived in small numbers; the first boatload of Haitians came in 1962, and the second major landing did not follow until the early 1970s. However, numbers began growing substantially in the late 1970s, with many arriving illegally, bringing little education and encountering substantial stigmatization. By the mid-1990s, Haitians constituted Miami's second largest immigrant group, though the Cuban population was still far higher.[21]

Violence in Central America launched another outflow, and antagonists to the Nicaraguan Sandinistas decided that Miami would serve as a suitable home. Though this refugee stream shared some characteristics with the early Cuban exodus, the Nicaraguans came with fewer resources and received far less government support.[22] Meanwhile, Miami also attracted growing numbers of West Indians, who spoke English and had some skills but were far less educated than the Asians who flocked to New York or the West Coast centers.[23]

Perhaps it is equally important to take note of the immigrants Miami has failed to attract. Despite the hype that seeps into the social science literature, Miami does not quite rate its frequent accolades of most globalized or most cosmopolitan metro.[24] As an immigrant region, Miami is the wrong place to look for globalization, because it never managed to attract an Asian population of any note. "Caribbeanization" would be the more appropriate label, because Miami has attracted immigrants almost exclusively from the region of which it is a part. It is thus unique among America's top immigrant destinations.

The Miami that has emerged after the past four decades of mass migration is dramatically different from the region the first Cuban refugees encountered. For one thing, it boomed, benefiting from the broader regional redistribution of jobs and people to the South and to Florida in particular. But Miami's prosperity was certainly related to the presence of the Cubans and especially those early migrants who came with skills and capital. Miami became an entrepôt for the entire Caribbean region, which itself underwent considerable restructuring, as many islands were transformed into low-cost manufacturing centers and major continental cities added an industrial base of impressive dimensions. With changes in the region motivating U.S. and foreign banks and multinational companies to set up large-scale operations or regional headquarters within the United States but in close proximity to emerging Latin American and Caribbean markets, the presence of the highly skilled, Spanish-speaking Cuban refugees drew these new jobs to Miami.[25] Good economic times and the maturation of an ethnically self-conscious, highly organized Cuban community also bred a lively ethnic economy, though one of limited importance given the modesty of Cuban self-employment rates.[26]

The Miami of the twenty-first century contains a dynamic, diverse economy occupying an important node in the market linking the United States with Latin America and the Caribbean; still, one should be wary of exaggerating the extent of the economic change, as well as the similarity to the other key immigrant regions that stand at the top of the urban hierarchy. First, Miami's manufacturing base essentially remains what it always was: weak. From the beginning, Miami lacked the assets—natural resources, population base, and proximity to either final markets or raw materials—that would have generated rapid development of an industrial base; its off-center location has been a persistent factor in reducing its appeal to manufacturing, whether of the runaway or start-up kind. Second, Miami may be the capital of the Caribbean, but that status leaves it far from the global city standing enjoyed by the other key immigrant regions. Consequently, the region lags behind in the development of those new economic activities—whether in the production of goods or in the transmission and creation of information—that require higher-level skills.[27] Finally, the region's economy still bears the traces of its earlier specialization as vacation paradise, as evidenced by the disproportionately large contingent of low-level service workers.

In part, the new Miami reflects the old: in particular, the presence of a large, relatively poor, relatively low-skilled African American population that has been displaced from its former role as servant class but has yet to find a fully adequate place in this immigrant-dominant metropolis (though chapter 6 will highlight the distinctive and important niche that better educated black Miamians have established). But the explanation for Miami's distinctiveness also involves the adaptations made to the extraordinarily large number of immigrants living there. These newcomers, after all, are a relatively low-skilled group, and homogeneously so. Recall that Miami remains largely outside the ambit of those high-skilled migratory currents, largely from Asia and the Middle East, that are so prominent in the other leading immigrant destinations. Whatever the precise causal nexus between immigration and the evolution of the region's economic base, Miami has been badly outpaced by the larger immigrant centers in the shift toward jobs employing highly qualified workers. In a sense, this is good news, because it implies a better match between the (low) skills of the immigrant workforce and the modest requirements of Miami's employers. On the other hand, as we shall see in chapter 4, an economy based on low-skilled workers generally also delivers low wages; given Miami's continued dependence on lower-valued services and the continuing absorption of poorly educated immigrants, the fit between the economy and the newcomers seems such as to slow, if not prevent, progress upward.

Los Angeles

For most of its modern existence, Los Angeles has attracted newcomers who were mainly white and mainly native-born. In 1920, just before the close of the last great immigration wave, only 17 percent of Angelenos had been born abroad, as compared to 35 percent of their contemporaries in New York.[28] The next decade witnessed the arrival of a substantial Mexican inflow, but the movement northward stopped with the onset of the depression, and the politics of the times led to deportations—often regardless of legal status—that further diminished the Mexican presence. In any case, immigrants were replaced by internal migrants in search of the California dream, made all the more attractive by the prosperity of the war and postwar years. These native-born newcomers were not all of a piece ethnically: the period between 1940 and

1970 saw a large-scale arrival of African Americans, attracted by the region's relatively hospitable race relations climate and its burgeoning economy. Still, the arrival of domestic migrants en masse, combined with the emergence of the second and third generations linked to earlier Asian and Mexican migrations, seemed to place immigration firmly—and permanently—in the region's past.[29]

Or so it seemed as of 1960. The foreign-born population, which had dropped steadily since 1920, then constituted a relatively small and dwindling presence. Roughly 150,000 of the immigrants, comprising less than 2 percent of the region's 7.6 million residents, were Mexican-born. Although the region's Mexican-origin population was sizable, it was a largely second- or third-generation group, with the foreign-born making up a relatively small and graying mass. And matters seemed destined to stay that way, as noted in *The Mexican-American People,* an encyclopedic and landmark study published in 1970, but based on research conducted during the mid-1960s, a time when no one could imagine how quickly the tables would turn and how far-reaching the change would be.[30]

Just beneath the surface, the face of the future was already taking shape. The Bracero program, begun during World War II, had rekindled the outflow of migrants from Mexico's central plateau; its abolition in 1964 forced the migrants into an illegal status but left the factors that pushed and pulled them to California unchanged. As time passed, agricultural workers left farm labor for better-paid pursuits, which in turn led them to the city. By 1970 LA already registered an uptick in the share of its population that was foreign-born, in contrast to the rest of the United States, which saw the population fall to its historic nadir.

For the next two decades, the influx of newcomers to LA ratcheted upward in a far more radical way as the LA-bound immigration rate grew steadily out of line with that of the rest of the nation. The immigration simultaneously diversified, and Los Angeles attracted large numbers of newcomers from Asia and the Middle East. The latter two source areas also served as the launching pad for sizable refugee movements—most notably, the exodus from Southeast Asia. For the most part, Asian and Middle Eastern newcomers were successful professionals and entrepreneurs who moved right into the middle class.[31] Quite a different fate awaited the immigrants who flocked to Los Angeles from Central America; though they moved to the United States in search of safe haven, the Cental Americans were fleeing right-wing regimes, which is why they never qualified for refugee status. Instead, these newcomers mainly moved across the border as unauthorized migrants, a factor that, when combined with their low skills, made it harder for Central Americans to move up the socioeconomic scale.[32]

Scholars, journalists, and publicists have widely touted immigrant Los Angeles as the exemplar of multiethnic America—indeed, so many times that the reader perhaps need not be reminded of just how many languages are spoken in Los Angeles schools (more than 125). Although immigrants from all over the world call LA home, the great majority come from a handful of places. As of the mid-1990s, a single source country, Mexico, accounted for almost half of the region's foreign-born residents; El Salvador and Guatemala collectively contributed another 10 percent. The remaining seven countries supplying the most immigrants—all but one located in Asia—along with the three mentioned earlier accounted for 78 percent of all foreign-born Angelenos. In the rest of the country, by contrast, newcomers from Mexico, El Salvador, and Guatemala made up only a quarter of the foreign-born population. And as a total, immigrants hailing from the same countries of origin that make the top 10 list in Los Angeles account for less than half of the foreign-born persons living elsewhere in the United States. Since, as we noted earlier, national origins matter because of the skill differences among migration streams, low-skilled persons greatly overshadow highly educated immigrant Angelenos, even if the latter constitute a quantitatively significant component of the immigrant population.

The immigrant advent has occurred in the context of a rapidly changing regional economy. For most of the twentieth century, the Los Angeles region was home to a fabulous job machine. To be sure, the region's economy did not diversify quite as quickly or as extensively in the 1910s and 1920s as its kingpins in real estate and commerce had wished. But the heavy industrial base that developers and business interests so badly coveted arrived in the 1930s, in the form of branch plants exported by the tire, steel, and auto giants of the time. The advent of World War II then unleashed a fury of growth and, more important, transplanted the nascent aerospace industry from the East to the West Coast. The onset and continuation of the cold war did the rest; thanks for the robust growth of southern California's high-technology complex belonged almost entirely to the Department of Defense.[33] Though natural resources, tourism, and Hollywood—"*the* industry*,*" in local parlance—helped, the region's emergence as the nation's premier concentration of manufacturing jobs accounts for its history of stupendous growth.

A new pattern emerged in the late 1970s and 1980s. On the growth side, the Reagan-era defense buildup kept the defense complex alive and well up until the late 1980s. The regime of easy money and the region's attraction to foreign, especially Japanese, capital made for an extraordinary burst of office development. As with other metropolitan areas, the service and finance sectors enjoyed the greatest growth. For a while, Los Angeles seemed poised to emerge as an international finance complex, smaller than but still rivaling New York. Not all of the region's sectors, however, enjoyed equally favorable times: the older manufacturing base in high-paying, non-defense-related durables had begun to crumble in the 1970s and by the early 1990s was barely standing.

The end of the cold war signaled a downturn in defense contracts. In the early 1990s that change triggered the most severe economic recession that southern California had experienced since World War II; engineers and skilled aerospace workers were let go by the droves, major banks closed their doors, and the negative effects were felt far and wide. The recession hit hard and lingered long, but by the late 1990s the region's economy had turned around, largely on the strength of a greatly expanded and diversified entertainment industry, a revived high-technology sector, a reengineered defense economy that had found new markets and products, and a buoyant low-wage sector that had largely survived the recession unscathed.

This restructured economy provided ample room for the immigrants, largely because Los Angeles long functioned as a growth machine for jobs of all types. While job gains were disproportionately concentrated near the top between 1970 and 1990, LA also generated new jobs for the low skilled, in contrast to the paradigmatic postindustrial centers of New York and San Francisco.[34] Thus even as the passage from 1970 to 1990 generated plenty of top-drawer jobs, it also yielded a bulge in employment for workers in the least-schooled categories—those with some high school, those with a primary school education or less, and even those with virtually no schooling at all.

Los Angeles has thus been different from the other immigrant regions, in ways that have opened the door to less-skilled immigrants. In part, the Los Angeles factor rests on the strength of its manufacturing sector. For all the loose talk about southern California's rust belt, visits to a few industrial parks will confirm what the statistics suggest: manufacturing may have been down in the 1990s but it was still a colossus—alive, reasonably well, and providing ample employment. Moreover, the distress of LA's manufacturing sector hastened the outflow of its native workers, creating a game of musical chairs in which immigrants could pick up jobs by taking the place of the departing natives.

The structure of LA's economy has created a place for low-skilled newcomers. While the region's established residents are at best ambivalent about the immigrants, its employers know a good deal when they see one: an incessant flow of job seekers willing to do any job at bargain-basement rates. The Los Angeles economy has adapted to the availability of low-skilled help by expanding portals to workers with few if any formal skills, as evidenced by the increases in such immigrant-absorbing, low-skilled occupations as janitors, gardeners, and domestics; the number of such positions practically doubled between 1980 and 1990. One indicator shows how thoroughly the newcomers have been integrated into the production systems of the region's low-cost manufacturing and service complexes: of the 83 manufacturing industries with 1,000 employees or more identified by the U.S. Census in 1990, 53 employed Mexican immigrants at disproportionately high levels.[35] Thus, the factory or office of the future notwithstanding, the reality of immigrant Los Angeles remains closer to the work world of the past, with plenty of jobs for poorly educated but manually proficient workers.

Of course, the focus on the modal group—LA's low-skilled immigrants—necessarily pushes the experience of the high-skilled newcomers out of view. Indeed, the hidden story of today's immigration is the many newcomers who find themselves at a far more elevated status than their low-skilled compatriots. In contemporary Los Angeles, coveted occupations in medicine, dentistry, and various engineering and computer specialties have become immigrant niches. And business—of the small and large sort—also contains a noticeable immigrant presence. In particular, Chinese immigrants, mainly from Taiwan, have established an extraordinary "ethnoburb" in the San Gabriel Valley west of downtown Los Angeles, complete with upmarket retail complexes and a vast array of ethnic export-import firms, high-tech establishments, and producer service organizations, all of which employ a mainly foreign-born workforce.

New York

New York began the twentieth century as the capital of immigrant America, a role it has lost to California and the Southwest. New York remains an immigrant stronghold, though, and large numbers of immigrants settled there in the second half of the twentieth century. Indeed, migration streams are so deeply embedded in the region's social fabric that the numbers of newcomers kept increasing during the protracted slowdowns experienced during the mid-1970s and again during the early 1980s and early 1990s.[36]

In New York, as in Miami and Los Angeles, the new immigration began before 1965, though it was noticed by only the most perceptive observers, who still had no inkling of how drastically the situation would soon change. The stirrings in the Caribbean—notably the rise of Fidel Castro and the assassination of the Dominican dictator Trujillo—sparked movement to New York in the early 1960s, when the newest arrivals rejoined small clusters of pioneers who had arrived years, if not decades, before.[37] The Cuban influx to New York City was of short duration; most, as noted previously, headed for Miami, though a sizable group settled in a series of old New Jersey towns just west of the Hudson River.[38] By contrast, migration from the Dominican Republic produced a steadily growing population that gravitated to New York City and stayed there, eventually becoming the region's single largest immigrant group.[39]

Although the Dominicans top the list of migrants from the Caribbean, the entire region has fed into the post-1965 boom. Anglophone West Indians have a long history in New York, but the depression of the 1930s and restrictions imposed by immigration legislation passed in 1952 largely choked the flow. However, migration quickly resumed once the Hart-Celler Act reopened doors in 1965. Moreover, specific labor market shifts—most important, the rising demand for health care workers and a shortage of skilled nurses—combined with the availability of an English-speaking, literate, and well-trained population for whom opportunities on the islands were either declining or growing too slowly eased the West Indians' route into New York's economy. While emigration from Jamaica, Trinidad, and Barbados, countries with a prior history of migration to the United States, was renewed, new sources—most notably, Guyana and Haiti—also opened up.[40]

Its distance from the main West Coast centers of the nation's Asian population notwithstanding, the New York region has seen its Asian population burgeon. Historically, New York had attracted Chinese immigrants but few other Asians in significant numbers, quite unlike San Francisco and Los Angeles, with their proportionately larger and more diverse Asian populations. After 1965 Chinese migration to New York mushroomed as New York City became the most popular destination for Chinese newcomers. Though their numbers increased rapidly, the Chinese soon found themselves only one component of a rapidly growing and diverse Asian population. Indians, Koreans, Filipinos, and others, who 30 years before had only small, almost invisible, communities dominated by students and a handful of businessmen and professionals, established a visible presence by the late 1970s and became increasingly prominent in the last two decades of the twentieth century. Unlike the movement to Los Angeles, which included a large, quite affluent Taiwanese contingent, Chinese immigration to New York stemmed mainly from Hong Kong and the People's Republic; these immigrants of more modest origins ended up converging on New York City. Other Asians were more likely to come with more skills and from relatively higher-class backgrounds, a characteristic reflected in their tendency to opt for suburban residential locations instead of New York City.[41]

To these new sources must be added a series of reactivated or new streams from the Old World. At the top of the list stand the Russians, who began to appear in the 1970s, found exit doors shut in the 1980s, and then began flooding out of the disintegrating Soviet Union starting in 1989.[42] Other eastern Europeans began to show up in growing numbers around the same time, thanks to repression in Poland, the collapse of the Soviet empire, and disturbances in the Balkans. Most surprisingly, Irish immigration was reactivated in the 1980s, as the slowdown in the Irish economy led an increasingly educated population of newcomers to follow the time-honored path to seek alternatives in New York.[43]

Thus, the New York pattern of immigration stands in great contrast to that in either Los Angeles or Miami. Though the latter are certainly both diverse, their foreign-born populations are dominated by a single group (even more so in Los Angeles than in Miami). By contrast, New York's newcomers retain a bewildering diversity, its very largest source area, the Caribbean, itself extraordinarily variegated culturally, linguistically, and ethnically. Moreover, the new continues to mingle with the old; New York, like Chicago, is an immigrant region where arrivals from Europe have significantly influenced the growth of the foreign-born base. And the diversity in the national origins of the immigrants further implies a significant degree of heterogeneity in their skills. Though in relative terms the least educated represent a larger contingent among immigrants than among natives, New York's least-skilled newcomers tend to arrive with higher levels of education than the Mexicans who predominate in LA. And as we have noted previously, highly educated immigrants flock to New York, thus producing a foreign-born population more closely matched with the region's changing skill structure than that found in Los Angeles.

Of course, that structure changed greatly, just as the region's immigrant base was utterly transformed. As late as the 1950s, the New York region was seen as a stronghold of manufacturing, but the goods production sector had already begun to falter by then, and it has never stopped shrinking. The region's mix of manufacturing industries spelled problems for manufacturers who were still trying to make it in New York. The labor-intensive industries that made up the cornerstones of the local manufacturing sector—apparel, electronics, and other forms of light manufacture—found themselves under severe and unending wage pressure. Manufacturing came under greatest strain within New York City and the other older, smaller cities around it; in the suburbs, pharmaceuticals, aerospace, and high technology—in the form of IBM—remained strong through the 1980s, when they, too, began to feel considerable stress.

The region's economy found other ways to grow, mainly through the development of a globally oriented information economy, which evolved substantially and uncertainly during the same years that immigration burgeoned. Corporate headquarters—long a major player in New York's regional economy—slid into sharp decline after the 1960s. However, the corporate headquarters complex of banks, law, accounting, and security firms, advertising agencies, and other business services continued to flourish and even expand because of the intensifying demand for information services. With its already large buildup of information services, New York was ideally positioned to benefit from the rapid growth of services in the 1980s and 1990s. Globalization yielded similar effects, since large corporations with heavy foreign involvements found themselves more dependent on their external providers of business services, which were disproportionately based in large, diversified urban areas such as New York. And the stock market booms of the 1980s and 1990s—influenced by both globalization and the takeoff of the information economy—furnished plenty of work for the region's providers of advanced services. To be sure, the stock market had its ups and downs; a very long low period between 1987 and 1993 yielded a crushing blow whose severity was compounded by downsizing in the defense sector and a national recession.

Though the New York region's economy grew far more sluggishly than either Miami's or LA's, it experienced a more fundamental overhaul; that change, in turn, involved a pronounced shift toward the upper end of the occupational spectrum and jobs for which college or advanced degrees were expected. Consequently, this new New York looked very different from the region in its earlier heyday as the immigrant capital. True to its roots, though, it found a way to absorb the immigrants. To a considerable extent, the immigrants eased the transition from the old New York to the new, providing a willing labor force for the manufacturing industries that were in decline but not yet ready to expire. That clothes are still made in New York—at low wages and under deplorable conditions, when they should be fabricated in Sri Lanka—illustrates the way in which immigration and the region's economic trajectory are thoroughly intertwined. The same is true for the region's concentration of petty retailers, who continue to do business in small stores on old, crowded city streets, as in years gone by, but have had their ranks replenished by the new arrivals from abroad. The fabulous incomes earned in the stock market and in the related advanced service industries—reflecting the polarized job structure of the metropolis, as discussed in chapter 4—have created jobs for immigrants employed in helping the new and old affluent manage the chores of daily life. Of course, the foreign-born are also employed in the region's export sectors, most notably the huge and highly sophisticated health care sector. So, too, has the corporate headquarters complex found ways to make good use of the large pool of highly educated immigrants, with their high-level, heterogeneous skills.

San Francisco

California's social cleavages are almost as prominent as its physical fractures. No divide looms quite so large as the division between north and south, though the contest between stately San Francisco and its nouveau riche cousin to the south no longer stirs the same passions as before, now that the weight of political and economic gravity has definitively passed to LA.

Los Angeles played an insignificant role in the giant immigration wave of the early twentieth century. Its civic consciousness, such as it was, never made much room for the Mexican immigrants who converged on Los Angeles beginning in the 1920s. By contrast, San Francisco has always been an immigrant town and so it remains today. In the Bay Area—which for our purposes includes the cities of San Francisco, Oakland, and Berkeley and their environs, as well as the San Jose metropolitan area—the old and new in immigration come together as nowhere else. Due to San Francisco's location and history they do so with an unusual twist.

In San Francisco, the new immigration of the late twentieth century was actually the reactivation of a much older stream. Prior to the opening of the transcontinental railroad in 1869, San Francisco's geographic location impeded access to European immigrants, as well as to U.S.-born Euro-Americans. Consequently, many of the original forty-niners lured by the mid–nineteenth-century gold rush came from countries around the Pacific Basin; most significant were the Chinese immigrants, who came in search of gold and with every intention of returning home. The Chinese, who served as an important source of cheap and docile labor in railroad construction, manufacturing, mining, and agriculture, soon ran into nativist hostility, which turned to violence during the 1870s and eventually resulted in the passage of the Chinese Exclusion Act in 1882.[44] But California farmers and industrialists needed low-wage labor and their eyes turned toward the Pacific again; Japanese immigration soon followed, as did yet another nativist reaction, which choked off this flow in 1907. Though relatively short-lived, these two immigration waves left San Francisco with a sizable Asian population that never completely severed the ties to the home countries. Among the Chinese, in particular, those connections rekindled the migration networks to southern China that had lain dormant until the gates began to slowly open after World War II.[45]

Large-scale immigration of Europeans to San Francisco took place in the late nineteenth century, with Ireland, Germany, and Great Britain at the head of the pack, ensuring that San Francisco would possess a large foreign-born population, even if the flows from Asia were greatly reduced. Although significantly outnumbered by the Irish, Germans, and British before the turn of the century, by 1920 Italians were the largest foreign-born ethnic group in San Francisco; their influence was symbolized by the evolution of the immigrant-founded Bank of Italy into that kingpin of California finance, the Bank of America. Though European immigration to San Francisco tailed off after the 1920s, as it did elsewhere, the Bay Area long retained the immigrant imprint, as preserved in ethnic enclaves such as North Beach and emblazoned in the radical politics that long animated its labor movement.

If the roots of contemporary immigrant LA can be traced to the Bracero program, the advent of an immigrant San Francisco seems more directly tied to the 1965 reforms of the immigration act. After all, the 1965 legislation had its greatest influence on immigration from Asia, which had been largely barred until the postwar period and thereafter was allowed in very limited numbers. And immigrants from Asia have constituted the largest group of newcomers to the Bay Area, which, as noted earlier, has emerged as the only immigrant region with an Asian majority.

Though outstripped by the large increase in Asian numbers, immigrants from Mexico and Central America also have a noticeable presence. Mexican immigration began from a much lower base in San Francisco than in Los Angeles, and the rate of growth has been only slightly faster than the increase in foreign-born numbers for the region as a whole; thus Mexicans remain an important but secondary immigrant population, in contrast to their dominance in LA. Central Americans, especially from El Salvador, gravitated to the Bay Area in disproportionately large numbers. Though overshadowed by Mexicans, they are a relatively more important component of the Latino population in the Bay Area than they are in Los Angeles.

Today's immigrants have positioned themselves in a changing economic structure led by three important trends.[46] First, like the other urban centers in this study, San Francisco is increasingly dependent on its service sectors, particularly business services. Second, the economy is characterized by a new manufacturing base in which deindustrialization in traditional "smokestack" durable goods is offset by the growth in high-technology manufacturing in computers, electronics, instruments, and defense. Third, these changes have produced a unique economic structure in San Francisco; there, high levels of manufacturing employment persist yet the labor force has shifted to a pattern in which highly skilled and educated workers outnumber their less-skilled cohorts as nowhere else.

Behind this engine of growth lies Silicon Valley, geographically positioned in the northern part of Santa Clara County. Silicon Valley has captured global attention as the leading high-technology center of the world. Between 1962 and 1987 the San Francisco region saw employment increase by 116 percent, California's growth measured 105 percent, and the job base for the nation as a whole expanded by only 71 percent. The decade of the 1970s marked enormous job expansion in the region, with 800,000 new jobs created at a rate of 4 percent growth per year. The increase did not stop in the 1980s, when another 550,000 jobs were added at a rate of 2 percent growth per year. And the 1990s saw another tremendous burst in job growth, with employment growing by 23 percent in Santa Clara County, a clip well above the 15 percent gain experienced statewide.[47]

The tremendous surge in immigration furnished the labor needed to fulfill the growing demands of the region's economy. As in other urban centers, the immigration flow was not monolithic: professionals and highly educated workers were meeting the demand for engineers and scientists, and unskilled immigrants had become the "proletarian servants in the paragon of post-industrial society."[48] Both categories of immigrants have been pivotal in supporting the Bay Area's economic growth.

On the one hand, highly trained Asian immigrant engineers have come to dominate the occupational niche for global programming in the region. Most notably, Asian Indian and Taiwanese immigrants are hired by Silicon Valley's high-tech firms, which insist that their continued competitiveness requires access to the best and brightest scientists and engineers around the globe.[49] Not surprisingly, high-tech companies have effectively lobbied for immigration policies that provide both permanent and temporary migration for highly skilled scientists and engineers. The Asians' presence in these firms is quite remarkable; their skills and education position them to follow the employment patterns of native-born whites.[50]

While Silicon Valley and the Bay Area more generally have been able to successfully integrate highly skilled immigrants into their professional ranks, San Francisco has been equally able to incorporate those who come from more modest origins. Situated toward the bottom of this upwardly tilting class structure is the emergence of a new working class that supports the region's growing cadre of aspiring and arrived nouveaux riches.[51]

This new working class is composed of two distinct labor pools: native-born, white female office workers and new Central American and Mexican immigrants, whose occupations are bifurcated along gender lines. Foreign-born immigrant women perform assembly-line work in the factories that manufacture goods related to the microelectronics industry. Not surprisingly, as one of the lowest paid categories within the high-technology industry, the assembly labor force contains an extremely high concentration of low-skilled immigrant women. Latino immigrant women also pick up the domestic work that the native-born have chosen to outsource, such as baby-sitting and housekeeping, at low wages. Although Mexican immigrant men are moving away from agriculture, they are still heavily concentrated in low-wage jobs as factory operatives, laborers (e.g., janitors, construction workers, gardeners), and service workers in restaurants and hotels, where they are joined by the burgeoning Central American population.[52] The increasing flexibility of Silicon Valley's labor market has also given rise to a flourishing informal economy that includes subcontracting of unskilled Mexican labor and small-scale vending.[53]

Chicago

The Windy City has always been home to a rich diversity of immigrants. Immigration streams from Europe in the late nineteenth and early twentieth centuries and the Great Migration of African Americans from the South simultaneously transformed Chicago into one of the most ethnically diverse—and one of the most segregated—cities in the nation. Contemporary migration from Latin America and Asia is remaking Chicago's landscape once again, though at a distinctly slower pace and in a somewhat different way than in the other key immigration regions.

Present-day immigrant Chicago is largely shaped by the past. From the late nineteenth century through the 1920s, the region's rapidly expanding industrial sector offered European immigrants plenty of opportunities in blue-collar skilled and unskilled industries such as steel, construction, and packing plants.[54] Slavic immigrants, in particular, gravitated toward the region's heavy manufacturing complex, proving far more likely to head to Chicago than to New York, quite in contrast to the other major groups of the time.[55] Chicago's factory sector also found room for Mexicans, who began arriving in considerable numbers by 1910. Most were young, single men drawn to Chicago by recruiters seeking laborers for the railroads, steel mills, and packinghouses and were used as strikebreakers during the labor disputes in 1916 and again in 1919. Migration from Mexico accelerated in the 1920s, when nativist legislation robbed Chicago's manufacturers of their source of cheap, European labor. Later, in the 1930s, immigration and welfare agencies from the state of Illinois and the city of Chicago collaborated to return Mexican residents—regardless of citizenship—to their homeland.[56] The Mexican presence nevertheless remained firmly established, albeit on the bottom rungs, among the region's production workers.[57]

In the main, today's immigrants represent the continuation of these two historic streams. Chicago remains a significant destination for eastern European immigration, thanks to the region's historic concentration of Slavs and continuing unrest and trouble in the eastern European homelands. The communities established at the turn of the century were first renewed in the late 1940s by a wave of refugees displaced by the turbulence and forced migrations of World War II and the immediate postwar period; these refugees solidified the Slavic presence on the shop floor but also included a middle-class and professional contingent. A new flow began in the 1960s, with numbers burgeoning as the Communist regimes began to crack in the 1970s and 1980s. Unlike the earlier peasant migrants, these recent immigrants were largely middle class, urbanized, and educated, reflecting the twentieth-century transformations that had occurred in eastern Europe. Lacking credentials, English-language facility, and the appropriate know-how, they were often forced to begin at the bottom, though with time they appear to be edging back toward the occupational range they knew before migration.[58]

Chicago's role as a destination for Slavic, eastern European migration makes it distinctive among America's key immigrant regions. But in other respects, it deviates only slightly. Immigrant Chicago is most heavily dominated by the region's large Mexican contingent; at 40 percent of the region's total foreign-born, the group is almost as important a presence in Chicago as it is in LA, albeit in the context of a much smaller immigrant population overall.[59] Here, too, we see historical continuity, though the circumstances of incorporation are not identical with those of the past, because many of the old-time immigrant-employing industries are either gone—as in the case of meatpacking—or severely eroded—as with steel. However, the networks linking Chicago to the key sending communities in the Mexican central plateau were never entirely severed. And with contacts in place, new arrivals have been able to find a niche not so much in traditional manufacturing but rather in downgraded manufacturing and low-wage service work.[60]

Like all of the other regions except Miami, Chicago's Asian population is expanding rapidly, although, as elsewhere, Asian is a cover-all category of limited sociological meaning that includes a diverse group of nationalities dominated by none. Still small, the Asian population grew 43 percent between 1980 and 1990 alone. Unlike New York, San Francisco, or even Los Angeles, the proletarian contingent is of particularly modest dimensions. For the most part, Asian immigrant Chicagoans belong to an emergent professional or petit bourgeois group. Filipinos and Indians, the third and fourth largest, respectively, of the region's immigrant groups, and far less numerous than the Mexicans, exemplify the former type; Koreans, who have established a small business niche with some distinctive regional peculiarities, are examples of the latter.[61]

The immigrant advent has occurred at a time of profound regional economic restructuring. Like the rest of the industrial heartland, Chicago was deeply struck by the sharp hike in foreign competition that began in the early 1970s and the wave of disinvestment and corporate restructuring that ensued. The region's antiquated plants made it difficult to compete, and the presence of militant unions provided a convenient means for corporations—on the hunt for sources of cash and increasingly oriented toward the next quarter—to close facilities where efficiency was not quite up to standard. Between 1967 and 1987 Chicago lost 60 percent of its manufacturing jobs.[62]

After two decades of churning, the region's economy remained strongly tilted toward manufacturing, complete with a revived and more competitive industrial sector. Nonetheless, the change had come about at a price—most notably, extensive labor shedding and a shift from older plants in the inner core to newer green-field sites in the suburbs and exurbs. At the same time, much like New York, downtown Chicago gained jobs during the 1980s and became a magnet for advanced services; employment in the rest of the city of Chicago sagged, the heavy shoulders profiled by Carl Sandburg no longer much in need.[63]

Employment deindustrialization in the urban core, coupled with the accelerated formation of edge cities that have acquired an ever greater share of Chicago's employment prospects, altered the pathways by which newcomers entered the region. Today's new immigrants are following the emerging job opportunities, frequently bypassing settlement in the traditional port-of-entry neighborhoods that house the city's poorest residents. Between 1980 and 1990 the geographic center of Chicago's immigrant population shifted decidedly northwest, as it headed in the same general direction as the city's white population and its employment opportunities.[64]

The social consequences of the region's economic transformations have garnered much social science attention, largely thanks to the influential work of William Julius Wilson.[65] In Wilson's view, the shift from manufacturing to services dashed the prospects for the region's less educated African Americans, whose ties to the labor market were sundered by the collapse of the inner-city factory sector. Whatever the merits of Wilson's arguments—and the evidence presented in chapter 6 of this book suggests that his depiction of the importance of manufacturing for African American employment in Chicago is at best questionable—they hardly allow for the phenomenon in question here—namely, the emergence of immigrant Chicago. On the one hand, low-skilled Mexican immigrants—far less educated than their African American counterparts—have secured a niche at the bottom of the manufacturing and service sectors. As we shall see in chapters 3 and 4, the jobs are low paying, and, as chapter 7 shows, the conditions of work and the skills required leave much to be desired. Nonetheless, Mexican immigrants remain strongly attached to Chicago's labor market and more securely so than their better educated African American counterparts.

On the other hand, the region's diverse economy has provided portals for better educated Asian immigrants. To some extent, the story reads much the same as elsewhere: the potential to replace the aging Euro-American petite bourgeoisie as shopkeepers servicing inner-city poor and their yuppie neighbors generates opportunities for the newest ethnic entrepreneurs. But the region's concentration of industrial facilities, complete with extensive research and development staff; its complex of technical universities; and the concentration of producer and health services at the core have all created openings for highly educated Asians who build careers around the human capital accumulated at home or through some education in the United States.

Conclusion

Immigration is remaking America, but not everywhere and not at the same rate. Outside of a handful of key regions, the foreign-born presence is modest and only recently felt. But travel to New York or Los Angeles or Miami or San Francisco or Chicago, and the sounds are those of the Tower of Babel and the faces are those of a cross section of humanity, the likes of which America has not seen for quite some time. In the capitals of immigrant America, we seem to have returned to the turn of the twentieth century. Amidst the dawn of a technologically different, we hesitate to say *new*, age, the numbers tell us that immigrant America has returned.

If there is something deeply familiar about America's reemergence as an immigrant country, there is something bewildering about it as well.

Last time around, there seemed to be a fit between the evolving economy and the types of immigrants we received. The American economy on the brink of the twentieth century was growing at a rapid clip. In a tight labor market, employers wanted no more than brawn and a willingness to work hard—just what the newcomers provided.

In some ways, contemporary immigration has turned the entire process around. The hidden story of today's immigration is that of the many newcomers who arrive here with considerable advantages and quickly accumulate more. Well-educated, entrepreneurial, and entering the professions in great and growing numbers, these newcomers are making American history, fitting into the new economy by eschewing the bottom and entering at or near the top.

The story of the highly educated immigrants who supply the skills the new world order requires is, however, but half the tale. Somehow, urban America is also making room for many immigrants who are not simply recently arrived, unfamiliar with American ways, and unable to make do in English. These immigrants also lack the basic rudiments of formal schooling that nearly all U.S.-born adults—regardless of ethnic background—now take for granted. Our urban economies, shedding manufacturing jobs and adding positions for persons specializing in the production and transmission of information, should have no place for these people, arriving, as they do, with no more sophistication than the Europeans of a century ago. The puzzle is that these immigrants with little schooling seem to possess traits that employers want. Regardless of what economic experts might predict, they are working, often holding jobs at enviable rates. And though the hard-working immigrant fits right into the iconography of American life, this time around there is a good deal of ambivalence, influenced by concern that new immigrants are taking jobs that might otherwise be held by less-skilled U.S.-born workers, people who have enough problems without the threat of immigrant competition.

As newcomers to urban America, the immigrants share the common fate of entering regions that differ substantially, in economic and demographic structures, from the rest of the country and thus offer a distinctive mix of opportunity and constraint. Yet the key immigrant regions themselves vary as well, not just in the histories of migration but in the particular migration streams to which they are linked. And so the urban worlds transformed by immigration take multiple forms. Just how urban America has changed under immigration's influence and how, in turn, urban structures have shaped immigrant trajectories are the questions to which the rest of this book attends.

Notes

1. In retrospect, revocation of the Chinese Exclusion Act in 1943 might mark the beginning of the new immigration era. This measure, to be sure, had little practical importance in the short term, because it allowed for the influx of only 105 Chinese immigrants a year. But it also indicated that immigration decisions were sensitive to foreign policy considerations, as would often be the case in years to come. Those same factors, which would affect Hungarians, Cubans, Indochinese, and others, also helped expand the scope of Chinese immigration in the immediate postwar years.

2. David Reimers, *Still the Golden Door: The Third World Comes to America* (New York: Columbia University Press, 1985).

3. Because the number of foreign students began to mount significantly as of the mid-1950s, the seeds of high-skilled Asian immigration were probably planted prior to the enactment of the 1965 legislation itself.

4. For an overview of Asian immigration, see Herbert Barringer, Robert B. Gardner, and Michael J. Levin, *Asian and Pacific Islanders in the United States* (New York: Russell Sage Foundation, 1993), a comprehensive though already outdated volume. Other groups—various Middle Easterners and Africans—followed the same trajectory, and the immigrant population thus diversified to groups that had never previously made the United States their home.

5. Calculated from the *Statistical Yearbook of the Immigration and Naturalization Service* (Washington, D.C.: U.S. Government Printing Office, various years).

6. On the background of West Indian migration, see Ira DeA. Reid, *The Negro Immigrant: His Background, Characteristics, and Social Adjustment, 1899–1937* (New York: Columbia University Press, 1939); and Philip Kasinitz, *Caribbean New Yorkers* (Ithaca, N.Y.: Cornell University Press, 1992).

7. Ernesto Galarza, *Merchants of Labor: The Mexican Bracero Story* (Santa Barbara, Calif.: McNally & Loftin, 1964); Douglas Massey, Rafael Alarcón, Jorge Durand, and Humberto González, *Return to Aztlan* (Berkeley and Los Angeles: University of California Press, 1988).

8. David Lopez, Eric Popkin, and Edward Telles, "Central Americans: At the Bottom, Struggling to Get Ahead," in *Ethnic Los Angeles,* ed. Roger Waldinger and Mehdi Bozorgmehr (New York: Russell Sage Foundation, 1996).

9. Robert Warren and Jeffrey Passel, "A Count of the Uncountable: Estimates of Undocumented Aliens Counted in the 1980 United States Census," *Demography,* 24, no. 3 (1987): 375–393.

10. Susan Gonzalez Baker, *The Cautious Welcome: The Legalization Programs of the Immigration Reform and Control Act* (Santa Monica, Calif.: RAND Corporation, 1990).

11. IRCA enabled two groups of illegal aliens to become temporary and then permanent residents of the United States: aliens who had been living illegally in the United States since January 1982, technically known as legalization applicants, and aliens who were employed in seasonal agricultural work for a minimum of 90 days in the year preceding May 1986 (Special Agricultural Workers [SAW] applicants). As of 1992, the Immigration and Naturalization Service had received 1,759,705 legalization applications and an additional 1,272,143 SAW applications.

12. Barry Edmonston and Jeffrey Passell, "The Future Immigrant Population of the United States," in *Immigration and Ethnicity: The Integration of America's Newest Arrivals,* ed. Barry Edmonston and Jeffrey Passell (Washington, D.C.: Urban Institute, 1994), chapter 11; Immigration and Naturalization Service, Statistics Division, "Illegal Alien Resident Population," June 28, 1998, available at http://www.ins.usdoj.gov/graphics/aboutins/statistics/illegalalien/index.html.

13. Calculated from *Statistical Yearbook of the Immigration and Naturalization Service,* various years.

14. Among the confusions attending any discussion of legal immigration is that a large portion of each year's legal immigrants consists of people already living in the United States, a category described in Immigration Service parlance as "adjusters," as opposed to "new arrivals." The adjusters are a motley group: some are persons who legally entered the country and remained here on temporary but long-term visas, as students, temporary workers, or businesspersons; others came as tourists, neglected to return home, and then married a U.S. citizen or were sponsored by U.S. employers; still others crossed the border illegally but managed to obtain legal status through one of the mechanisms just mentioned or some other means. As one might expect, given the magnitude of the illegal flow of Mexican immigrants, a substantial portion of Mexican immigrants are classified as adjusters; nonetheless, the rate is only somewhat greater than that of persons coming from other sources. In 1996 68 percent of Mexican immigrants and 51 percent of persons from all other countries were classified as adjusters. Calculated from *Statistical Yearbook of the Immigration and Naturalization Service, 1996,* table 7.

15. In 1988 almost 35,000 Koreans immigrated to the United States; by 1997 the total had dropped to just over 14,000. Although the impact of the Korean economic collapse—ongoing as we write—may well lead to a reversal of course, at this point future trends are a matter of speculation.

16. Maria Christina Garcia, *Havana USA: Cuban Exiles and Cuban Americans in South Florida, 1959–1994* (Berkeley and Los Angeles: University of California Press, 1996), chapter 1.

17. See George J. Borjas's book *Friends or Strangers* (New York: Basic, 1990), in which he argues that educational levels among immigrants have declined over the past several decades.

18. For a further discussion of this matter, see chapter 4 in this book, by Mark Ellis.

19. The literature on Miami is extensive. In addition to Garcia's *Havana USA,* important sources include Alejandro Portes and Alex Stepick III, *City on*

the Edge (Berkeley and Los Angeles: University of California Press, 1993); Guillermo Grenier and Alex Stepick III, eds., *Miami Now! Immigration, Ethnicity, and Social Change* (Gainesville: University Press of Florida, 1992); Sheila Croucher, *Imagining Miami: Ethnic Politics in a Postmodern World* (Charlottesville: University of Virginia Press, 1997); a variety of articles by the historian Raymond Mohl, notably, "An Ethnic Boiling Pot: Cubans and Haitians in Miami, *Journal of Ethnic Studies* 13, no. 2 (1987): 51–74; and the series of articles in the special issue of the *Pacific Historical Review*, May 1999.

20. Larry Nackerud, Alyson Ouellette, Christopher Larrison, and Alicia Isaac, "The End of the Cuban Contradiction in U.S. Refugee Policy," *International Migration Review* 33, no. 1 (1999): 176–192.

21. Alex Stepick III, "The Refugees Nobody Wants: Haitians in Miami," in *Miami Now! Immigration, Ethnicity, and Social Change,* ed. Guillermo Grenier and Alex Stepick III (Gainesville: University Press of Florida, 1992), chapter 4.

22. See Portes and Stepick, *City on the Edge,* chapter 7.

23. Marvin Dunn and Alex Stepick III, "Blacks in Miami," in *Miami Now! Immigration, Ethnicity, and Social Change,* ed. Guillermo Grenier and Alex Stepick III (Gainesville: University Press of Florida, 1992), chapter 3, especially pp. 48–50.

24. See, for example, Jan Nijman, "Globalization to a Latin Beat: The Miami Growth Machine," *Annals of the American Academy of Political and Social Sciences* 551 (May 1997): 165.

25. Ibid., 164–177; Ramon Grosfoguel, "Global Logics in the Caribbean City System: The Case of Miami," in *World Cities in a World-System,* ed. Paul Knox and Peter Taylor (Cambridge: Cambridge University Press, 1995), 156–170.

26. The importance of the "ethnic enclave" is a theme developed by Alejandro Portes. Portes's claims about the beneficial aspects of enclave employment, a matter of much controversy, are revisited in chapter 7 of this book.

27. Jan Nijman, "Breaking the Rules: Miami in the Urban Hierarchy," *Urban Geography* 17 (1996): 5–22.

28. The data for Los Angeles apply to the region; in Los Angeles County, the foreign-born share of the population was half a percent higher.

29. The literature on immigrants in Los Angeles, though growing, remains underdeveloped, especially in comparison to the corpus available for New York. Our earlier book, *Ethnic Los Angeles,* edited by Roger Waldinger and Mehdi Bozorgmehr (New York: Russell Sage Foundation, 1996), provides the most comprehensive overview, though largely—possibly excessively—based on the information to be gleaned from the U.S. Censuses of Population, up to 1990. Much of the remaining section draws on this work, as well as an updating by Roger Waldinger, "Not the Promised City? Los Angeles and Its Immigrants," *Pacific Historical Review* 68, no. 2 (1999): 263–272. For another overview, from a geographic perspective and more oriented toward spatial matters, see James Allen and James Turner, *The Ethnic Quilt* (Los Angeles: California State University Northridge, 1997). Thomas Mueller and Thomas Espenshade's book, *The Fourth Wave* (Washington, D.C.: Urban Institute, 1985), represents an early and now dated though still valuable effort to assess LA's immigrant transformation.

A number of recent edited collections contain additional valuable material on the region's history, with some attention to matters of immigration and ethnicity; most notable are Allen Scott and Edward Soja, eds., *The City: Los Angeles and Urban Theory at the End of the Twentieth Century* (Berkeley and Los Angeles: University of California Press, 1996); and Michael Dear, H. Eric Schockman, and Greg Hise, *Rethinking Los Angeles* (Thousand Oaks, Calif.: Sage Publications, 1996). The monographic literature and studies of individual ethnic groups remain in a state of bad repair, with a few exceptions. Korean immigration has received valuable treatment, most notably from Ivan Light and Edna Bonacich, *Immigrant Entrepreneurs: Koreans in Los Angeles, 1965–1982* (Berkeley and Los Angeles: University of California Press, 1988); and Pyong Gap Min, *Caught in the Middle: Korean Communities in New York and Los Angeles* (Berkeley and Los Angeles: University of California Press, 1996). The Chinese settlement in Monterey Park has also been the subject of considerable work; John Horton's book, *The Politics of Diversity* (Philadelphia: Temple University Press, 1996), provides the best treatment. Amazingly, Mexican immigration has been relatively neglected, perhaps because the size of the group and the complexity of its experience make study of the recent Mexican immigrant experience a daunting task. Valuable material can be found in the Mueller and Espenshade book; George Sanchez's *Becoming Mexican American: Ethnicity, Culture, and Identity in Chicano Los Angeles, 1900–1945* (New York: Oxford University Press, 1993) is essential but limited to the earlier period. A key reference for the current period is Vilma Ortiz, "The Mexican-Origin Population: Permanent Working-Class or Emerging Middle-Class?" in *Ethnic Los Angeles,* ed. Roger Waldinger and Mehdi Bozorgmehr (New York: Russell Sage Foundation, 1996), chapter 9.

30. Leo Grebler, Joan Moore, Ralph Guzman, Jeffrey L. Berlant, Thomas P. Carter, Walter Fogel, C. Wayne Gordon, Patrick H. McNamara, Frank G. Mittelbach, and Samuel J. Surace, *The Mexican-American People: The Nation's Second Largest Minority* (New York: Free Press, 1970).

31. Lucie Cheng and Philip Yang, "Asians: The 'Model Minority' Deconstructed," in *Ethnic Los Angeles,* ed. Roger Waldinger and Mehdi Bozorgmehr (New York: Russell Sage Foundation, 1996), chapter 11; Mehdi Bozorgmehr, Georges Sabagh, and Claudia Der-Martirosian, "Middle Easterners: A New Kind of Immigrant," ibid., chapter 12.

32. David Lopez, Eric Popkin, and Edward Telles, "Central Americans: At the Bottom, Struggling to Get Ahead," in *Ethnic Los Angeles,* ed. Roger Waldinger and Mehdi Bozorgmehr (New York: Russell Sage Foundation, 1996), chapter 10.

33. Allen J. Scott, *Technopolis: High-Technology Industry and Regional Development in Southern California* (Berkeley and Los Angeles: University of California Press, 1993), 13–14.

34. Allen Scott, "The Manufacturing Economy: Ethnic and Gender Divisions of Labor," in *Ethnic Los Angeles,* ed. Roger Waldinger and Mehdi Bozorgmehr (New York: Russell Sage Foundation, 1996), chapter 8.

35. Roger Waldinger, "Ethnicity and Opportunity in the Plural City," in *Ethnic Los Angeles,* ed. Roger Waldinger and Mehdi Bozorgmehr (New York: Russell Sage Foundation, 1996), chapter 15.

36. For a more complete treatment of New York's immigrant transformation, see Roger Waldinger, *Still the Promised City? African-Americans and New Immigrants in PostIndustrial New York* (Cambridge, Mass.: Harvard University Press, 1996) and the sources cited therein. Other overviews include Elizabeth Bogen, *Immigration in New York* (New York: Praeger, 1987); City of New York, Department of City Planning, *The Newest New Yorkers: An Analysis of Immigration into New York City during the 1980s* (New York: Department of City Planning, 1992); and Ellen Percy Kraly, "U.S. Immigration Policy and the Immigration Populations of New York," in *New Immigrants in New York,* ed. Nancy Foner (New York: Columbia University Press, 1987), 35–78.

37. Eugenia Georges, *The Making of a Transnational Community: Migration, Development, and Cultural Change in the Dominican Republic* (New York: Columbia University Press, 1990), 37–43, 79–81.

38. Eleanor Meyer Rogg, *The Assimilation of Cuban Exiles: The Role of Community and Class* (New York: Aberdeen Press, 1974).

39. Sherri Grasmuck and Patricia Pessar, *Between Two Islands: Dominican International Migration* (Berkeley and Los Angeles: University of California Press, 1991).

40. For further background, see Reid, *Negro Immigrant,* and Kasinitz, *Caribbean New Yorkers,* as well as the sources cited in Waldinger, *Promised City,* chapter 4.

41. On Asian immigration to New York, the following works provide an overview of the major groups: Min Zhou, *Chinatown: The Socioeconomic Potential of an Ethnic Enclave* (Philadelphia: Temple University Press, 1992); Illsoo Kim, *The New Urban Immigrants: Korean Immigrants in New York* (Princeton, N.J.: Princeton University Press, 1982); Pyong Gap Min, *Caught in the Middle* (Berkeley and Los Angeles: University of California Press, 1996); and Johanna Lessinger, *From the Ganges to the Hudson* (Boston: Allyn & Bacon, 1996).

42. Fran Markowitz, *Community in Spite of Itself: Soviet Jewish Emigres in New York* (Washington, D.C.: Smithsonian Institution, 1993).

43. Mary Corcoran, *Irish Illegals: Transients between Two Societies* (Westport, CT: Greenwood Press, 1993).

44. In 1884 a federal court ruling took this nativist stance one step further, prohibiting the entry of the wives of the Chinese laborers and thus greatly restricting the immigration stream from China. This ruling coupled with the antimiscegenation laws that prevented Chinese males from intermarrying with Europeans led to the creation of a "bachelor society" during the nineteenth century characterized by very large, segregated, and institutionally complete Chinatowns.

45. On the Chinese, see Victor Nee and Brett de Barry Nee, *Longtime Californ'* (New York: Pantheon, 1973).

46. For reviews of the role of immigrants in the Bay Area's economy, see Rafael Alarcón, "From Servants to Engineers: Mexican Immigration and Labor Markets in the San Francisco Bay Area" (Chicano/Latino Policy Project working paper, Berkeley, Calif., 1997); Michael Teitz and Philip Shapira, "Growth and Turbulence in the California Economy," in *Deindustrialization and Regional Eco-*

nomic Transformation: The Experience of the United States, ed. Lloyd Rodwin and Hideniko Sazanami (Boston: Unwin Hyman, 1989, 81–103); Dick Walker and the Bay Area Study Group, "The Playground of US Capitalism? The Political Economy of the San Francisco Bay Area in the 1980s," in *Fire in the Hearth: The Radical Politics of Place in America,* ed. Mike Davis, Steven Hiatt, Marie Kennedy, Susan Ruddick, and Michael Sprinker (New York: Verso, 1990), 3–82.

47. Calculated from U.S. Bureau of the Census, County Business Patterns, July 2000, available at http://www.census.gov/epcd/cbp/view/cbpview.html.

48. Roger Rouse, "Mexican, Chicano, Pocho, La Migración Mexicana y el Espacio Social del Postmodernismo," *Uno Mas Uno,* December 31, 1988.

49. Alarcón, *From Servants to Engineers;* Kanjanapan Wilawan, "The Immigration of Asian Professionals to the United States: 1988–1990," *International Migration Review* 29, no. 1 (1995): 7–32.

50. Alarcón, *From Servants to Engineers.*

51. Ibid.; Walker et al., "Playground of U.S. Capitalism?"000000

52. Wayne A. Cornelius, Richard Mines, Leo R. Chávez, and Jorge G. Castro, "Mexican Immigrants in the San Francisco Bay Area: A Summary of Current Knowledge" (Research Report Series 40, Center for U.S.-Mexican Studies, University of California, San Diego, 1982); Cecilia Menjívar, "Immigrant Kinship Networks and the Impact of the Receiving Context: Salvadorans in San Francisco in the Early 1990s," *Social Problems* 44, no. 1 (February 1997): 104–123; Steven P. Wallace, "The New Urban Latinos: Central Americans in a Mexican Immigrant Environment," *Urban Affairs Quarterly* 25, no. 2 (December 1989): 239–264.

53. Christian Zlolniski, "The Informal Economy in an Advanced Industrialized Society: Mexican Immigrant Labor in Silicon Valley," *Yale Law Journal* 103, no. 8 (June 1994): 2305–2334; Christian Zlolniski and Juan-Vicente Palerm, "The Working Poor in the Restructured California Economy: An Ethnographic Study of a Mexican Immigrant Barrio in San Jose" (California Policy Seminar, Berkeley, 1995).

54. William Cronon, *Nature's Metropolis: Chicago and the Great West* (New York: W. W. Norton, 1991); Humbert S. Nelli, *Italians in Chicago, 1880–1930: A Study in Ethnic Mobility* (New York: Oxford University Press, 1970).

55. Ira Katznelson, *Black Men, White Cities: Race, Politics, and Migration in the United States, 1900–30, and Britain, 1948–68* (New York: Oxford University Press, 1973); Thomas Lee Philpott, *The Slum and the Ghetto: Immigrants, Blacks, and Reformers in Chicago, 1880–1930* (Belmont, Calif.: Wadsworth, 1991).

56. Louise Año Neuvo de Kerr, "The Chicano Experience in Chicago, 1920–1970" (diss., University of Illinois, Chicago, 1976); Louise Año Neuvo de Kerr, "The Urban Frontier: Chicago," in *The Ethnic Frontier,* ed. Melvin G. Holli and Peter Jones (Grand Rapids, Mich.: William B. Eerdsmans, 1977), 269–299.

57. Joanne M. Belenchia, "Latinos and Chicago Politics" (Chicago Politics Papers, jointly sponsored by the Center for Urban Affairs, Northwestern Uni-

versity, and the Institute of Government and Public Affairs, University of Illinois, 1979); John J. Betancur, Teresa Cordova, and Maria de los Angeles Torres, "Economic Restructuring and the Process of Incorporation of Latinos into the Chicago Economy," in *Latinos in a Changing U.S. Economy,* ed. Rebecca Morales and Frank Bonilla (Newbury Park, Calif.: Sage, 1993), 109–132; Felix M. Padilla, *Latin American Consciousness: The Case of Mexican Americans and Puerto Ricans in Chicago* (Notre Dame, Ind.: University of Notre Dame Press, 1985); Julián Samora and Richard A. Lamanna, "Mexican-Americans in a Midwest Metropolis: A Study of East Chicago," in *Forging a Community: The Latino Experience in Northwest Indiana 1919–1975,* ed. James B. Lane and Edward J. Escobar (Chicago: Calumet Regional Archives and Cattails Press, 1987), 215–250.

58. Helena Lopata, *Polish Americans: Status Competition in an Ethnic Community* (Englewood Cliffs, N.J.: Prentice-Hall, 1976); William Kornblum, *Blue-Collar Community* (Chicago: University of Chicago Press, 1974); Mary Patrice Erdmans, *Opposite Poles: Immigrants and Ethnics in Polish Chicago, 1976–1990* (College Park: Pennsylvania State University Press, 1998); Mary Patrice Erdmans, "Illegal Home Care Workers: Polish Immigrants Caring for American Elderly," *Current Research on Occupations and Professions* 9 (1996): 267–292.

59. Richard Greene, "Chicago's New Immigrants, Indigenous Poor, and Edge Cities," *Annals of the American Academy of Political and Social Science* 551 (May 1997): 178–190; Kevin E. McHugh, "Hispanic Migration and Population Redistribution in the United States," *Professional Geographer* 41, no. 4 (1989): 429–439.

60. Maria de Lourdes Villar, "Changes in Employment Networks among Undocumented Mexican Migrants in Chicago," *Urban Anthropology* 21 (1992): 385–397; idem, "Rethinking Settlement Processes: The Experience of Mexican Undocumented Migrants in Chicago," *Urban Anthropology* 19 (1990): 63–79.

61. On Koreans in Chicago, see In-jin Yoon, *On My Own* (Chicago: University of Chicago Press, 1996); and Erick Howenstine, "Ethnic Change and Segregation in Chicago," in *EthniCity: Geographic Perspectives on Ethnic Change in Modern Cities,* ed. Curtis C. Roseman, Hans Dieter Laux, and Günter Thieme (Lanham, Md.: Rowman & Littlefield, 1996), 31–49.

62. Jeffrey D. Morenoff and Marta Tienda, "Underclass Neighborhoods in Temporal and Ecological Perspective," *Annals of the American Academy of Political and Social Science* 551 (May 1997): 59–72; William Julius Wilson, *When Work Disappears* (New York: Alfred A. Knopf, 1996).

63. Morenoff and Tienda, "Underclass Neighborhoods"; and Wilson, *When Work Disappears.*

64. Greene, "Chicago's New Immigrants."

65. William Julius Wilson, *The Declining Significance of Race* (Chicago: University of Chicago Press, 1980); idem, *The Truly Disadvantaged* (Chicago: University of Chicago Press, 1987); idem, *When Work Disappears.*

Chapter 3

UP FROM POVERTY?

"Race," Immigration, and the Fate of Low-Skilled Workers

Roger Waldinger

Immigration has transformed America's largest urban places in ways that even the casual observer of cities cannot help but notice. Yet we have made little progress in pursuing the intellectual implications of the new metropolitan demography, mainly because our understanding of today's urban reality remains deeply embedded in older frameworks, never adequate to begin with and now badly outdated.

The "urban problem" of the past half century was framed by a preoccupation with race and the difficulties African Americans encountered in their attempts to get ahead. Although the literature offered a plethora of explanations for these problems, the most influential emphasized the mismatch between the requirements of employers and the skills of black residents. African Americans entered the American metropolis as the least skilled of all workers and, owing to the problems of urban schools, stayed at the end of the hiring queue. Consequently, they found themselves vulnerable to the steady accretion in skill requirements that has systematically put less-schooled workers at risk, no matter where they live. For African Americans, however, place mattered because they were disproportionately concentrated in and around cities. The factory sector crumbled faster and more profoundly in cities than anywhere else; moreover, the new sources of urban economic growth provided little place for the less skilled. The same general trends hit the suburbs, but not nearly so hard; African

Americans, however, found that suburban economic health and job diversity did little to alleviate their situation, since housing discrimination and distance from urban centers made suburban jobs almost impossible to get.[1]

The story enjoys the ring of plausibility, mainly because it links the fate of black city dwellers to the extraordinary, visible economic changes that American cities have undergone. Note the themes that the narrative strikes, emphasizing obstacles entailed in securing employment while glossing over matters of occupational and income advancement among the employed—questions that it largely neglects. Equally instructive is the way in which conventional wisdom attends to a central element in the explanation: it identifies the skills deficiencies of blacks as the original source of the problem but then fails to note the subsequent considerable educational upgrading by African Americans. If the problem hinges on the diminishing demand for less-skilled workers, then the educational changes experienced by African Americans over the past several decades should have greatly reduced their vulnerability. Persons with a high school degree or less may still be in trouble, but as of the late 1990s that group constituted a relatively small proportion of the urban black population, reflecting a substantial improvement in comparison to earlier decades.

Of course, that generalization cannot be applied to the most recent group of newcomers to have descended on America's urban centers: the immigrants. As noted earlier, socioeconomic diversity stands out as the distinguishing characteristic of the new immigrants, an observation of particular use when trying to understand the differences between past and present immigrant experiences. But immigrant diversity involves an important twist, since the immigrant population stretches across the entire skills spectrum in ways that the native-born population no longer does. The immigrant group includes a large number of professionals but also a disproportionate number who fall at the very lowest levels of the educational distribution. Today's least-skilled urban workers are overwhelmingly foreign-born, and the schooling gap that separates them from the native-born is substantial, far greater than the disparity that earlier divided African Americans from whites.[2]

Immigrants line up at the tail end of employers' hiring queue. And yet their labor market experience is one for which urban analysis has not prepared us: however poorly schooled, or recently arrived, or unfamiliar with American ways, or lacking in English fluency, the immigrants are working, and at remarkably high rates.[3] The urban observer might wonder at the paradox of high employment in a metropolis long said to suffer a shortage of jobs suited to workers of today's immigrant type. But the students of immigration have not tarried over this issue and instead furnish an explanation that illuminates how immigrants find jobs: theirs is the story of the inexorable and progressive implantation of immigrant networks.[4] Instability at the bottom of the labor market creates vacancies that immigrants, impelled by a different set of tastes and expectations than natives, are especially likely to obtain. Immigrant ranks quickly proliferate, as veterans tap the newest arrival to fill each subsequent vacancy; the process consolidates once the most established among the immigrants moves up the pecking order and gains influence over hiring decisions, a factor further opening the door to kith and kin. As the immigrant network expands and immigrant niches proliferate, immigrants are only mildly penalized for the little they know and rewarded instead for whom they know. In the memorable phrase coined by Douglas Massey and his collaborators, landless Mexican *campesinos* "may be poor in financial resources, but they are wealthy in social capital, which they can readily convert into jobs and earnings in the United States."[5]

Thus, unskilled immigrants, with far less education than the least schooled among urban blacks, find jobs that, were the received wisdom of the past 40 years substantiated, either should not or do not exist. Granted, no one has yet figured out how to dispense with dishwashers and sweepers. But the immigrant phenomenon is of a totally different scale; the massive infusion of immigrants into the urban regions studied in this book provides evidence that immigrants have found a role well beyond a small cluster of static manual jobs. As long as we are willing to shelve questions relating to the demand for low-skilled labor, we can accept network theory as a powerful explanation of how immigrants secure entry-level positions. We then confront a different question: Even if immigrants do well in finding a way into urban economies, can they then move ahead?

This question is one to which research on immigration has yet to provide a clear, unambiguous answer. Though "no" would probably be a stretch, "with great difficulty" is a conservative assessment for which the literature furnishes ample support, as Mark Ellis demonstrates in chapter 4. Clearly, the least-skilled immigrants are in trouble, not so much because they cannot find work but because the jobs they secure do not provide adequate reward. Although immigrants are progressing, the rate at which wages have improved has decelerated among succeeding waves. As Ellis shows, the least skilled are bearing the brunt of the slowdown. Their problems stem from the steadily downward wage pressure experienced by all less-schooled workers, regardless of ethnic background; the pressure takes an intensified form among the foreign-born, owing to the intraimmigrant competition that occurs as newcomers converge on a narrow tier of the labor market in a limited number of urban areas.

So the literature produces two very different framings of the urban problem, each one at odds with the other. The traditional view, developed as an effort to understand the situation of African Americans, accents the barriers that keep blacks out of the labor market altogether. By contrast, the newer view tacitly assumes the workings of inclusive forces that bring immigrants into the labor market, neglecting the conditions that might impede access to the better jobs lying beyond those positions with which the immigrant networks connect.

The two understandings appear contradictory, but only if one insists that social exclusion in the metropolis takes a single form. I argue, instead, that ethnic differences among the less-skilled residents of America's largest urban centers are associated with distinctive forms of labor market vulnerability. Less-skilled African Americans face a penury of jobs; those whose educational levels fall too far below the white average pay the price in the form of extrusion from the job market. By contrast, immigrants, the least skilled of whom are far less schooled than the most poorly educated of African Americans, find an abundance of jobs but at pitifully low wages. For the newcomers, lack of skills imposes a penalty of a different sort, impeding progress beyond the easy-entry, low-wage positions in which the immigrant networks are so deeply embedded.

Complications

The accounts summarized frame their explanations in universal terms. Lack of the appropriate skills generates the problems bedeviling African Americans, implying that jobs are filled in ways that are indifferent to the person and that an abstract set of proficiencies provide the principal criterion on which hiring decisions are made. Access to the network, by contrast, is characterized as an attribute of community membership; being part of the group ensures availability of the resources generated by the connections that tie immigrant communities to workplaces.

Appearances notwithstanding, neither story deals in universals. Each one, instead, provides a deeply gendered account. The skills-mismatch hypothesis is fundamentally concerned with the fate of black men. That preoccupation can be readily understood: after all, it is black men whose participation in the urban economy has steadily and so severely declined over the past several decades. But the object of explanation then assumes an underlying causal mechanism that the intellectual framework precludes: a fundamentally social structuring process that works in such a way as to sort categorically distinctive people among jobs. Thus the possibility that men, and not women, are adversely affected by the upgrading of employers' requirements assumes that the match between jobs and people involves more than the simple matter of skills.

Network theory similarly emphasizes processes that are seemingly gender neutral. One would be hard-pressed to imagine how the underlying mechanisms, which relate to the role of preexisting social connections in generating trust and reducing uncertainty, could be specific to men or women. But the social ties of men and women are gendered, as are the expectations of behavior appropriate to those connections. Even if labor market information and support were to flow freely between immigrant men and women, other factors—most notably, the sex typing of jobs and gender segregation at work—would sort men and women into different types of positions and for that reason yield unequal access to jobs. And because the resources unlocked by networks are contingent on membership in a community, prevailing community expectations about the appropriate economic roles of men and women are bound to influence labor market experiences.

Advancing an explanation for these gender differences in labor market experiences goes beyond the scope of this chapter, but it is still possible to make gender central to the description and analysis. Focusing on differences across two dimensions—ethnicity and gender—yields a very different story than forecast by either of the conventional narratives. As I shall show, the disparities between men and women of the same ethnic group can often be as great as the interethnic differences among men that have been the subject of so much attention. To anticipate, the extrusion of less-skilled blacks from employment is principally a phenomenon that applies to men; among less-skilled immigrants the converse generalization applies: high employment rates are a phenomenon specific to men. But gender differences modulate in examining the factors associated with access to better jobs; chances for these jobs are equal among black men and women, though not among immigrants.

Subthemes

Ethnic Niches, Economies, and Enclaves

As I and others shall discuss in much greater detail elsewhere in this book (see, especially, chapters 6, 7, and 9), groups of categorically distinctive workers tend to converge on particular occupations or industries; if employment then builds up, this process of concentration eventuates in an ethnic niche. The existence of an ethnic niche can lower the barriers to employment for coethnics with minimally required skills because (1) ethnic concentration increases the likelihood that news about job openings will leak out first to other members of the group and (2) employers' common preference for hiring workers who resemble the existing workforce gives a leg up to those with connections. Workers who find jobs in ethnic niches can also find that concentration has benefits in terms of wages and the acquisition of skills, since connections to established coethnics both facilitate on-the-job training and provide the motivation to obtain the proficiencies needed to move ahead.

The ethnic niche is one of a series of related concepts that have gained popularity among students of the economic aspects of ethnicity; analysts have coined other similar concepts, most notably ethnic economy and ethnic enclave, to cover concentrations in which ethnics have established a significant base in self-employment. In my view, the ethnic niche is the concept of greatest generality, covering any sort of ethnic concentration, whether in government, self-employment, or simple wage and salary work. The crucial point, however, has to do with the consequences of ethnic clustering; whether labeled ethnic niches, economies, or enclaves, these concentrations are hypothesized to change employment outcomes in just the way described earlier.[6]

This chapter offers an opportunity to assess that hypothesis in the case of a particularly celebrated ethnic niche—the Cuban concentration in Miami. Hailed as an immigrant success story of an extraordinary sort, the Cuban experience is regularly attributed to the dense layer of Cuban-owned firms that has developed over the past three decades. While business itself offers an avenue for immigrants to get started and move ahead, researchers have spilled much ink trying to determine whether the existence of this business concentration has yielded positive spillover effects for the rest of the community. Much of the scholarly work has focused on the fate of the employed, an issue that I will revisit as I examine the conditions that affect the likelihood of obtaining full-time jobs that pay significantly above the poverty wage. But I will also inquire into the logically prior questions that, so far, researchers have not yet asked: Does the existence of this niche improve Cubans' prospects of holding a job, pure and simple? And how does the pattern differ, if at all, between men and women?[7]

Blacks: Immigrants Contrasted with Natives

Among the various immigrant groups present in the urban regions under study, few garner as much fascination as the English-speaking West Indians, whose numbers are particularly notable in New York. As immigrants who are categorized as blacks (and therefore as members of a particularly stigmatized group), Caribbeans provide a natural case study in the relative importance of "race" as compared to ethnicity. The issue has long been with us, gaining an initial academic airing with the publication of Ira DeA. Reid's now-classic book *The Negro Immigrant* (1939) but coming to broader intellectual attention with Glazer and Moynihan's *Beyond the Melting Pot* (1963), which noted the significant advantages apparently enjoyed by West Indians over their U.S.-born black counterparts. For Glazer and Moynihan (and for Ivan Light, who picked up and greatly elaborated on the observations made by Glazer and Moynihan), the West Indian difference was mainly of historical importance.[8] But the unexpected renewal of West Indian immigration, beginning in the 1960s and continuing uninterrupted ever since, has brought the issue front and center. Some scholars continue to detect a notable West Indian lead over their African American counterparts, concluding (1) that "race"—by which they mean racial discrimination—is not all-determining of the life chances of "black-skinned" people, especially (2) when the latter possess some set of resources—having to do with expectations, self-understanding, group organization—that mitigate the effects of "race." Other researchers find for the contrary: that on most if not all counts, West Indians experience the same fate as their African American counterparts, a conclusion pointing to the pervasiveness of racial discrimination, notwithstanding the signals that might differentiate West Indians from their U.S.-born counterparts and any distinctive group resources that the immigrants possess.[9]

This chapter is unlikely to provide closure to that controversy, especially because resolution largely depends on outcomes observable only when examining patterns across the generations. However, we can revisit the question in a novel way. While West Indians have succeeded in expanding their economic presence in New York's economy at a time when African Americans have seen their role diminish, some portion of the West Indian success may result from this group's relatively high educational levels; we do not know how the less skilled among both African Americans and West Indians have been faring. And the clearest evidence of West Indian advantage has to do with the unusually high levels of job holding, which, as I have noted, may not necessarily translate into movement out of the poverty-level jobs with which immigrants so often start.

Concepts, Explanatory Factors, Groups, and Analysis

Concepts

This chapter focuses on two crucial issues. First, what accounts for differences in the rates at which men and women, of varying ethnic and national backgrounds, hold jobs of any quality at all? This question is standard in sociological and economic investigations; the population of interest includes all adults, ages 25 to 64; the contrast is between the employed and the unemployed, an aggregate that includes jobless persons looking for work and those who are out of the labor force altogether. But as suggested by the profusion of such concepts as "disguised unemployment," the "working poor," and "structural underemployment," the category of employed is too global. For my purposes, employment encompasses workers of very different types: those who can be considered underemployed, either because they work at part-time jobs when full-time work is desired or because they labor full-time but at a poverty wage, are placed under the same rubric as workers employed at jobs of greater adequacy. As I contended earlier, the conditions affecting access to employment as such may differ significantly from those that allow workers to move up from jobs at the very bottom, a matter of particular importance when considering the labor market situation of less-skilled African American and immigrant workers. For these reasons, I draw on the "labor force utilization" framework, largely developed by the sociologists Teresa Sullivan and the late Clifford Clogg, to inquire into a second question: What accounts for the differences in the rates at which job holders gain access to full-time jobs that pay 50 percent or more of the poverty rate for a household of one person?[10]

Explanatory Factors

The motivation for this chapter came from the understanding that urban employers—like all employers anywhere, but even more so—are increasingly on the lookout for workers with higher skills. This transformation threatens to marginalize workers who find themselves at the lower end of the educational distribution. Stated somewhat differently, upgrading puts all less-schooled workers at risk, regardless of ethnic or national background. For that reason, the situation of white, native-born workers with a high school degree or less provides an appropriate benchmark by which to assess the skill-based disadvantages confronted by all other groups, since we can reasonably assume that the problems of less-skilled native whites have to do with their lack of school-based or school-acquired proficiencies and nothing else. As I shall show, less-skilled native whites do pay a price for their lack of the requisite proficiencies—as measured in lower employment rates and in lesser access to adequate employment—though modestly.

It is certainly possible, though unlikely, that the price of low skills is essentially the same among all persons of all groups, provided we stick to the same educational category. "Race" may impose no penalty on the job prospects of less-skilled African Americans; likewise, any disadvantages associated with immigrant status per se may disappear with time spent in the United States. However, as long as low skills exact a penalty, then these groups will be more profoundly affected than native whites, simply because a larger proportion of the former fall in the lower end of the educational distribution, a tendency particularly marked among the foreign-born. For this reason, I structure this discussion around the less-schooled persons among all groups, although noting that immigrants are likely to fall a good dealer lower on the schooling spectrum than any of the native groups; I also provide data on outcomes at all levels of the educational distribution.

The immigration literature reports that immigrants move ahead with time spent in the United States, an outcome usually described as evidence of immigrant assimilation.[11] However, scholarship provides no certainty as to whether time affects all immigrants in the same way; in particular, much (though not fully definitive) evidence suggests that more recent arrivals are progressing at a slower pace than those who came earlier, all factors controlled. Unfortunately, my analyzing data from a single cross section in time precludes the option of tracking an immigrant cohort from one period to the next. In any case, the net effect of time depends on the staging of migration flows. Given the volume of recent migration to all the urban areas under examination, relatively few immigrants will qualify as well settled, which implies that recency of arrival should have a depressing effect on the outcomes of interest.

Of course, the impact of any variable of theoretical interest is mediated by the effect of the other background characteristics with which it may be correlated. The analysis in this chapter controls for a variety of standard background variables, all of which are listed in the appendix to this chapter.

Groups

The multicultural metropolis of the early twenty-first century contains myriad immigrant groups, an embarrassment of riches so great as to strain our capacity to make sense of the patterns. To keep the analysis tractable, this chapter mainly focuses on three sets of groups in each of the five urban regions, multiplied by two to include men and women. In each region, I have chosen the largest of the immigrant groups for which the average level of schooling falls below the average for the region at large. Not surprisingly, this procedure profiles the Mexicans, at once the overwhelmingly largest and also the least educated among today's immigrants; I examine Mexicans in Los Angeles, Chicago, and San Francisco. The same procedure, however, yields a different target group in two other immigrant regions: in Miami I focus on Cubans, who predominate at all ranks, including the least skilled; and in New York I examine Dominicans, who are at once the largest group and also the most sizable group among the least skilled. In New York I also add black immigrants from the Anglophone countries of the Caribbean to further examine the interplay of race and ethnicity.

Analysis

Thus, this chapter focuses on two outcomes. I first estimate the likelihood of employment, regardless of a job's quality or its full- or part-time status. Focusing just on employed persons, I then estimate the likelihood that an employed person holds a position that meets my criterion for adequate employment: a full-time job that pays 50 percent or more of the poverty rate for a household of one person. Each outcome represents a dichotomy: one is either employed or not, and, similarly, one is either adequately employed or not. For that reason, I use a statistical technique known as logistic regression, which is the appropriate choice when analyzing dependent variables of this type. In each urban region, I conducted two separate analyses, one for the total population of men and women ages 25 to 64 and a second for all those persons in the same age category who are employed. The results of the regressions, with standard errors, appear in tables 3.1 and 3.2 as an appendix to this chapter.

Although it is the correct statistical technique, logistic regression yields coefficients that resist intuitive interpretation. Consequently, I have converted the results to probabilities, which I have in turn graphed to facilitate understanding.

The Changing Structure of Skills

Over the past 25 years, the economies of urban regions have shifted from the making of things to the processing, creation, and transmission of information, a change that greatly altered the structure of skills required. In 1970 workers' skills were scattered across the educational distribution, with the single largest group of workers in every region clumped right smack in the middle; in each of the five regions, high school graduates accounted for a third of all employed persons. As for workers above and below the median, the distribution varied modestly from one region to the next. In Miami, New York, and Chicago the skills structure tilted slightly toward the low end; in Los Angeles and especially in San Francisco it tilted the other way.

By the mid-1990s, however, the center of gravity had shifted toward higher skills, a pattern most evident in San Francisco, where workers holding a college degree or more also constituted the largest class. By the mid-1990s, however, the new pattern was not as uniformly distributed as had been the old. San Francisco's job structure showed the sharpest tilt toward skill intensity; in New York and Chicago, the skill structure was also weighted toward jobs that required a college education or more. Miami and Los Angeles both looked quite different, with a larger complement of very-low-skilled workers and a substantially smaller share of those with extended formal schooling.

By the late twentieth century, workers in the five regions clustered at the high end rather than the middle of the skill structure; even so, the middle had hardly disappeared, and jobs for the high school educated remained abundant. Indeed, employment of high school–educated workers increased in all five regions and by sufficient quantities so that employment/population rates for this category rose in every place as well—the sagging industrial complex of Chicago and the postindustrial complex of New York included. Change since 1970 was chiefly concentrated at the very low end, with sharp declines for the least-skilled workers in every region except Los Angeles, where the large influx of very-low-skilled Mexican and Central American immigrants yielded an adaptation in employers' requirements, as reflected in a sizable increase in the number of jobs available for persons with only an elementary school education. Moreover, the number of jobs for the less skilled declined faster than the number of low-skilled persons, depressing employment to population rates for low-skilled categories in almost every region. Los Angeles again deviated from the norm, as did San Francisco, though for opposite reasons, since in LA the low-skilled population grew less slowly than the number of low-skilled jobs, whereas in the Bay Area, the low-skilled sector shrank less radically than did the available pool of low-skilled workers. Regardless of the interregional differences, a basic pattern emerges: urban economic trends in the early twenty-first century have put low-skilled workers at risk, a shift that heightens the disadvantages of workers already suffering from any vulnerability associated with nativity or racial prejudice. However, employment and employment/population rates have remained relatively stable for high-school graduates—a matter of particular import for the contrast between immigrants and African Americans, as already underscored.

Intergroup Differences

White Men

Since the most influential themes in urban analysis emphasize the disabilities associated with low skills, I begin by examining workers who enter the labor market with no disadvantages other than low skills: white males. Of course, this group does not quite fit the usual descriptors; the segment with the lowest skills has virtually disappeared, making high school graduates the group at risk. Even so, most adult white men in the urban centers of interest have accumulated at least some college training, leaving only a minority—barely one-quarter—in the now anomalous situation of possessing no more than a high school degree.

But these considerations apart, the patterns appear much as conventional analysis would suggest. Although the point estimates vary somewhat from place to place, the shape of the overall relationship between education, on the one hand, and employment and employment adequacy, on the other, differs little. Education yields its predictably salutary effect: the proportion of white men at work rises more or less monotonically as one moves from one broad educational category to the next (e.g., high school degree to some college to college degree), although the advantages of education beyond the bachelor's degree do not emerge convincingly. Having more schooling also increases the likelihood of being adequately employed, because education's immediate influence on the quality of a job is greater than its impact on employment as such.

However, as shown in the leftmost column of graphs in figure 3.1, which displays probabilities of employment for whites evaluated at age 35, lower levels of education hardly yield a disaster among the least-skilled white men. While not quite equaling the pattern displayed by persons with 16 years or more of schooling, employment probabilities for white high school graduates appear impressively high; indeed, in all five regions, a very modest gap separates white high school graduates from their ethnic counterparts who either completed college or continued for postgraduate work. The contrast sharpens when we turn to employment adequacy (see figure 3.2), where the gap between workers with a high school education and those with a college degree or more widens. Still, the probability of holding a job that qualifies for employment adequacy appears high for the relatively small portion of white men who hold only a high school degree.

Less-Skilled Men: Immigrants versus African Americans

Although low skills adversely affect outcomes among workers whose ethnic attributes should otherwise improve employability, the impact proves relatively modest. But the same factors work quite differently when one looks at workers farther back in employers' hiring queues,

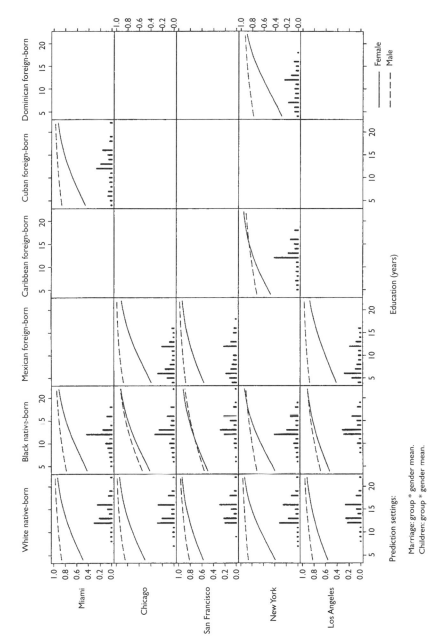

Figure 3.1. Effect of education on predicted probability of employment (at 35 years old) for the native-born and pre-1980 immigrants, by gender; at bottom, a histogram showing the distribution of years of education

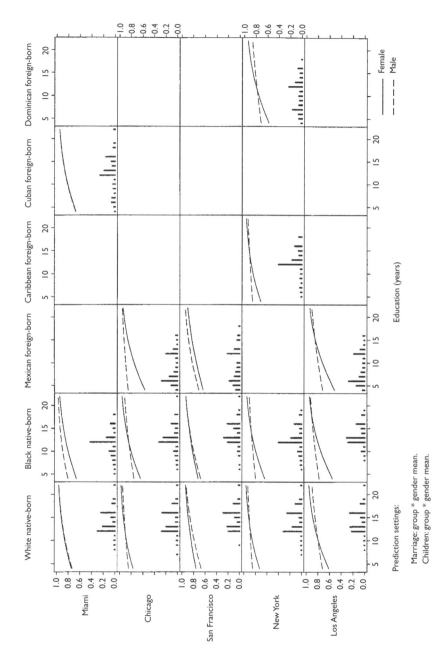

Figure 3.2. Effect of education on predicted probability of adequate employment (at 35 years old) for the native-born and pre-1980 immigrants, by gender; at bottom, a histogram showing the distribution of years of education

and gender almost completely alters the story. Regardless of place, African American high school graduates are less likely to hold jobs than their white counterparts; more surprisingly, they are also less likely to hold jobs than the least-skilled men. The experience of Mexican immigrants provides a contrast, highlighted by comparing the patterns displayed in the second and third columns of figures 3.1, 3.3, and 3.5. In Chicago, as one might have predicted from a reading of the works of William Julius Wilson, low-skilled African Americans confront an experience of job scarcity. But Mexican immigrants residing in the very same place have a radically different fate; the least-skilled Mexican immigrant men have employment probabilities comparable to those of college-educated African American men. And the liabilities of African American men reappear in the very different economic context of Los Angeles, where Mexican immigrants with only a primary school education enjoy employment probabilities that compare favorably with all but the most educated African American men.

Insofar as the foreign-born do worse than native-born whites, the disadvantage is almost entirely reducible to skills; immigrants with a high school degree have employment patterns similar to, if not better than, those of their white counterparts. Greater time in the United States does not hurt, but it does not significantly increase employment levels. Recent arrivals are clearly at a great disadvantage when it comes to holding a job. But after the first decade or so, settlement has little effect on the likelihood that an immigrant will be employed; this finding implies that foreign birth as such does not reduce the job-holding chances of immigrant men. On the contrary, some bundle of attributes associated with the immigration process itself—most likely the dense set of networks that connect the foreign-born to one another and to their employers—systematically improves job-holding prospects. That male immigrants are not working at higher rates boils down to their lacking the skills that employers most want.

Clearly, some powerful set of non–skill-based factors—or non–school-based skills—attach less-educated immigrants to the labor market. But the same circumstances that propel immigrants into employment do not serve equally well in the quest for jobs of adequate quality, although the patterns differ from place to place. With few exceptions, most notably that of well-settled Mexicans in Chicago, immigrants without a high school diploma find that lower levels of schooling yield a disproportionately severe impact on levels of adequate employment

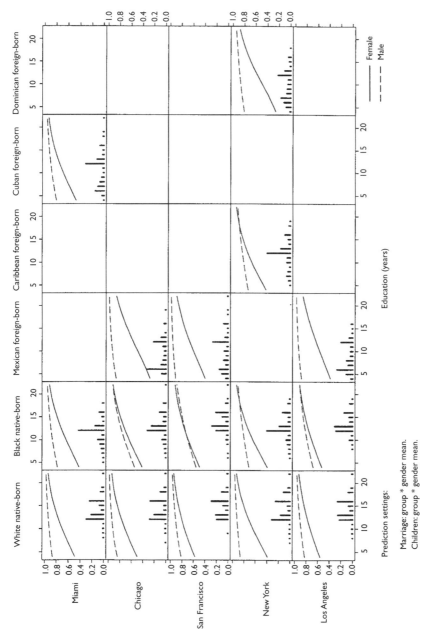

Figure 3.3. Effect of education on predicted probability of employment (at 35 years old) for the native-born and immigrants of the 1980s, by gender; at bottom, a histogram showing the distribution of years of education

(see figures 3.4 and 3.6). One notch higher in the educational pecking order and the foreign-born do better in every region. Education among immigrants does not generate the same quality of employment as it does among whites, largely because access to adequate employment is heavily driven by settlement (which may also serve as a proxy for English-language facility). While high school–educated Mexican men living in Los Angeles and Chicago approach their native-born white counterparts in the probability of attaining adequate employment, the great majority of Mexican men have much less education.

For the less skilled, time in the United States helps but does not fully even out the immigrant disadvantage. The same recent arrivals who find jobs at surprisingly high rates discover that the likelihood of finding adequate employment is low. Longer-settled immigrants fare better but remain penalized for their low skills in all regions. According to the literature, different immigrant cohorts may well follow varying trajectories, with more recent arrivals progressing at a slower rate than those who immigrated earlier; however, the most optimistic interpretation of the data presented here indicates that even veteran immigrants confront significant obstacles in the search for jobs of adequate quality.

The pattern of progress shows both considerable complexity and variation by region. Dominicans in New York conform best to the hypothesis sketched out earlier in this chapter; they have reduced access to adequate jobs because of nativity, low skills, and protracted period of settlement. The latter two factors work to the detriment of LA's Mexicans, but in this case group membership has a positive effect. In San Francisco neither nativity nor ethnicity is a cause for distress; rather, the problem is lack of skills in the most educationally advanced regional economy. As a result, the new cohorts show distressingly low levels of employment adequacy, and immigrants of greater vintage show limited evidence of movement into better-paying jobs.

Despite anticipated differences among the various regions, a consistent generalization emerges: low-skilled male immigrants are highly likely to find a job but rather less likely to find a job that proves adequate in terms of hours and compensation. By contrast, in every region, African American men with high school degrees—a better educated but relatively low-skilled group—are less likely than their white counterparts to hold jobs. In Los Angeles finding a job is the chief difficulty, but African American men with jobs have a better chance of obtaining

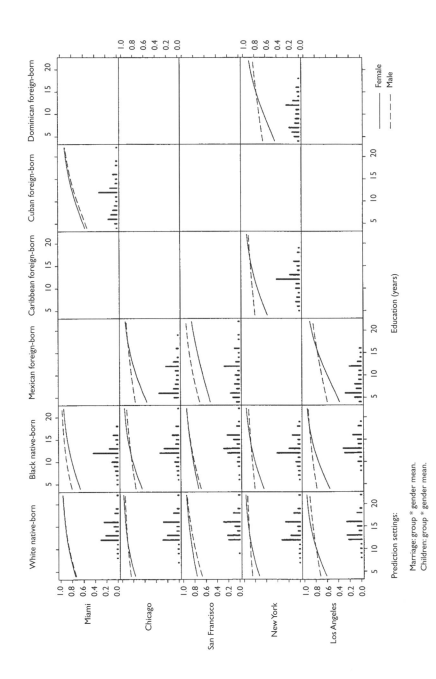

Figure 3.4. Effect of education on predicted probability of adequate employment (at 35 years old) for the native-born and immigrants of the 1980s, by gender; at bottom, a histogram showing the distribution of years of education

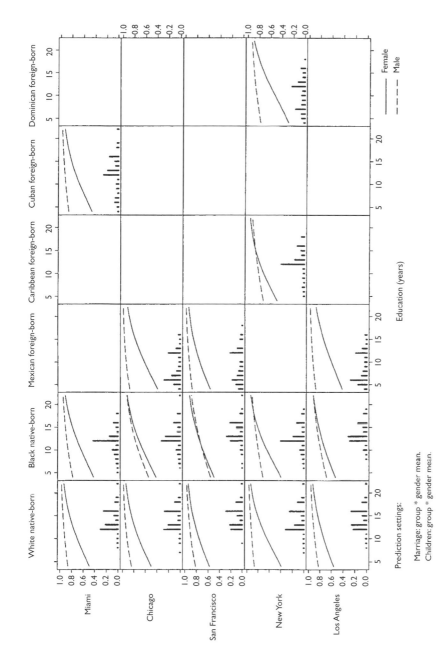

Figure 3.5. Effect of education on predicted probability of employment (at 35 years old) for the native-born and immigrants of the 1990s, by gender; at bottom, a histogram showing the distribution of years of education

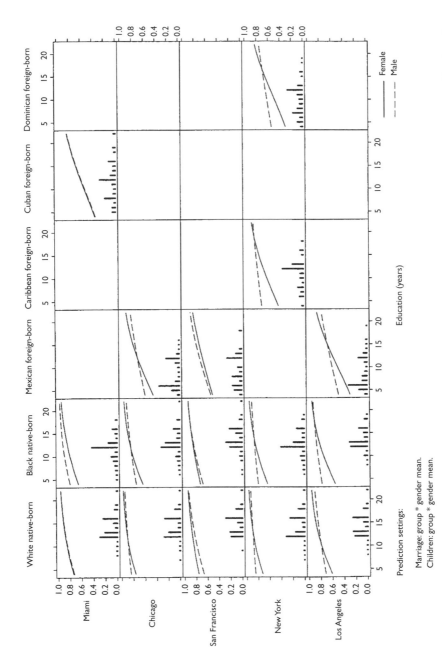

Figure 3.6. Effect of education on predicted probability of adequate employment (at 35 years old) for the native-born and immigrants of the 1990s, by gender; at bottom, a histogram showing the distribution of years of education.

adequate employment than their white counterparts. In Chicago and New York, African Americans are disadvantaged, relative to their white counterparts, on both counts, although I note regional particularities. In Chicago, as in Los Angeles, access to employment constitutes the central vulnerability, whereas in New York employed African Americans are also less likely to work at jobs of adequate quality, as compared with their native white counterparts.

In the end, then, at-risk African American and immigrant men differ along two dimensions; the latter are more likely to hold jobs, and the former are more likely to obtain adequate employment once they land a job. More needs to be said, because a bottom-line assessment should consider both groups in their entirety. In this perspective, the differences cancel out: a high job-holding rate and low employment adequacy rate ensures that, as a totality, less-skilled immigrant men have a relatively low probability of having a full-time job that yields earnings 50 percent or more above the poverty line. Among less-skilled African Americans, a low probability of holding a job accompanied by a high rate of employment adequacy among the employed generates a similar pattern. But the terms of the comparison shift if one examines a somewhat more settled or somewhat more educated group among the immigrants—in which case a net African American disadvantage appears more sharply.

Less-Skilled Women: Immigrants versus African Americans

As I noted earlier, this chapter engages in a debate framed in strikingly gendered terms. For a variety of reasons, far too complicated to untangle in this chapter, the great bulk of research on African Americans has been explicitly focused on the conditions of black men. Scholarship on immigration has been less self-consciously preoccupied with the fate of immigrant men than that of immigrant women, but its concern generally zeros in on the fault line between the foreign-born and the native-born, yielding little substantive interest in how these differences might vary by gender. Whatever the explanation for this focus, its gendered nature is problematic for a variety of reasons; one issue is the contrast in interethnic differences between men and women, and the other involves the explanatory frameworks, which do not allow for the possibility just mentioned.

When one expands the comparison to women, the patterns described in the previous sections on men appear dramatically different. Gender exercises its most direct impact on the likelihood of having a job, and it does so just as one would suspect: women of all ethnic (and educational) backgrounds who have children are less likely than their male counterparts to hold jobs; because the comparison in this chapter involves married persons with children, the disparity is that much greater. This gap between men and women varies among the regions, generally showing the greatest compression in San Francisco and the widest divergence in Miami. More important than region, however, is the effect of education, with each increment of schooling yielding a greater impact on women than on men; at the top of the educational spectrum, the difference in employment rates for men and women is reduced to a very slender divide.

Once women are employed, the likelihood of the job qualifying as adequate employment appears greatly improved, quite in contrast to the situation for men, among whom the relationship between employment and employment adequacy took the opposite form, with the latter generally less likely than the former. In several regions and among numerous groups, women with more education are actually more likely than their male counterparts to hold jobs that qualify as adequate. To some extent, the reversal is an artifact of my definition of employment adequacy, in which persons working part-time on a voluntary basis qualify for the adequacy criteria. Not surprisingly, women are significantly more likely than men to voluntarily work part-time.

Although a distinctive contrast obtains between men and women of all groups, the intragroup differences are no less notable. Most important, gender differences among African Americans are far more modest than those among native whites. Relative to men, African American women bear much less disadvantage in comparison with native whites, and the lead is sometimes actually reversed, depending on region and indicator.

The tables turn when one shifts the comparison to the foreign-born. Immigrant men have a high probability of employment, especially remarkable among those who are either recently arrived or have little schooling. Their female counterparts, however, enjoy no such good fortune. Employment probabilities are uniformly and substantially lower among less-skilled immigrant women than among their white or black counterparts. More striking, perhaps, is the case of newly arrived Dominican women in New York who lack a high school degree or their Mexican counterparts in Chicago, among whom employment probabilities fall at the .3 level or below. Although time in the United States matters, it does not carry tremendous weight: immigrant women of earlier vintages show employment probabilities still well below the levels of whites and African Americans. And it is worth recalling the substantial effect associated with education and the penalty of low skills, whose distribution varies substantially between native- and foreign-born workers. Employment probabilities for Mexican foreign-born women in Los Angeles are depressed for all three immigration cohorts, especially in the modal category of persons with 6 years of schooling or less. By contrast, the modal African American woman in Los Angeles has completed 13 years of schooling, a point in the educational distribution where the gap between men and women is sharply eclipsed.

Low employment probabilities go hand in hand with obstacles that impede access to adequate employment. In no case do less-skilled immigrants approach their white or black counterparts in the likelihood of access to jobs that meet my criteria of adequacy. However, the relative disparity is in part a matter of definition. As noted, my definition of employment adequacy creates an artifactual impression of parity among men and women at large, since an "adequate" job may be one in which an individual is voluntarily employed part-time. The same characteristic yields a different effect when the focus is restricted to women. Immigrant women are far less likely than their native-born counterparts to voluntarily work on a part-time basis; white women consistently lead all others in the rate of voluntary part-time work. Consequently, a different, possibly more stringent, definition of employment adequacy would reduce the interethnic differences along these dimensions.

More important, though, the generally low levels of employment for immigrant women ensure that adequate employment, even under my liberal definition, is unlikely. Under the best circumstances, involving high school–educated women residing in the United States for at least 20 years, one out of every two immigrant women might be employed under conditions of adequacy; under less favorable and also more common conditions, probabilities of employment adequacy hover between the .2 and .3 levels.

Drawing out the full implications of these patterns would be a daunting task. On the one hand, the much lower level of voluntary part-time employment among immigrant women—a one to three difference when comparing Mexican or Dominican to white women—suggests that the absence of adequately paying jobs may be the crucial factor depressing immigrant women's employment rates. If the available positions for less-skilled immigrant women overwhelmingly are poor paying and irregular, as in the garment industry or any form of household service, then the benefits of paid employment may simply not outweigh its costs, especially when there are young children not yet in school who require full-time care. On the other hand, differences in employment probabilities almost certainly bear a direct relationship to the potential for income packaging. For less-skilled immigrants, in particular, the possibility that husband and wife could have combined earnings sufficient to lift a household substantially above the poverty level would seem severely constrained; the combination of depressed female employment rates and low levels of employment adequacy among men makes it hard for households to escape poverty.

The Cuban Case

Unlike Mexicans and Dominicans, on whom I have focused so far, Cuban refugees who have flocked to Miami can also look for work among their coethnics, an option that results from the buildup of a large, apparently prospering concentration of Cuban-owned business. The literature has not yet opened a debate on the health or size of the Cuban ethnic economy, a matter this book questions (as fully explored in chapter 9). Until now, however, scholarly controversy has surrounded the contention that, among Cubans in Miami, working for one's own kind significantly improves either access to employment or access to good jobs.

At the very least, as figures 3.1, 3.3, and 3.5 show, the presence of a Cuban business sector does nothing to depress employment opportunities among immigrant men. Low-skilled and relatively recent Cuban immigrants fare no differently than white high school graduates in the likelihood of holding a job. But the ethnic enclave hypothesis, as well as the related ethnic economy and ethnic niche hypotheses, make grander claims, asserting that the availability of coethnic employment should speed movement up from the bottom. From that perspective, however, the employment niche occupied by Miami's Cubans is not particularly impressive. Working Cubans are a good deal less likely than low-skilled whites to hold adequate jobs, which in turn generates a wide gap between Cuban men and comparable white natives in the probability of adequate employment. Though Cuban men are more likely than their

African American counterparts to be working, the terms of the comparison switch when the focus narrows to the employed; in that category black workers are more likely than Cubans to be adequately employed. And recent arrivals are about as likely as their Mexican, West Indian, and Dominican counterparts elsewhere to be adequately employed, a finding hard to reconcile with the notion that Miami offers Cubans a distinctive mode of entry into the U.S. economy.

Rather than profiling the singular character of the Miami case, consideration of women's experience only recalls the patterns evident in the other regions. Compared with native whites, Cuban women have a significantly lower probability of holding a job, and the gap between immigrants and whites widens when one examines the probability of adequate employment. As with Dominican and Mexican immigrant women, low employment probabilities have a deeply depressing effect and ensure that adequate employment is far less likely for all Cuban women than for comparable white women.

Defenders of the ethnic enclave and related hypotheses will rightly contend that my analysis does not distinguish a likely Cuban ethnic sector from the so-called mainstream economy and thus logically fails to capture the effects of the Cuban ethnic economy as such. Perhaps, but if an ethnic economy does indeed alter employment outcomes, it is hard to imagine that a concentration as large as Miami's is purported to be would have no distinct impact on access to jobs. The structure of Miami's economy should improve employment prospects for all immigrants, because it has a large low-skilled sector that has remained remarkably solid over the past 25 years. Cubans should fare particularly well in this context, since, in relative terms, Miami's Cuban population is better established and longer settled than either LA's Mexicans or New York's Dominicans. And yet the comparison to the other immigrant regions underlines the similarities in the labor market experiences of Miami's Cubans, not the distinctiveness so often emphasized in the literature. Further hints as to the origin of this lack of adequate employment emerge from chapter 7, which provides a rather different picture of the Cuban ethnic economy than that conventionally portrayed.

"Race" and Immigrant Status: Black Immigrants in New York

Although West Indian immigrants have not received quite as much attention as Cubans, social science interest in the West Indian experience began earlier. The source of fascination with the two groups is much the same: the perception that the group's lot is somehow different from another with which it shares other salient characteristics—in this case, the perception of racial distinctiveness and the accompanying package of prejudice and discrimination. Some researchers have pursued the matter through comparisons constructed on a national level, but most have focused on New York, which is where the bulk of the black immigrant population has converged.

The results of my analysis come down squarely on the side of those skeptical of claims of immigrant distinctiveness: for all practical purposes, black American and black immigrant New Yorkers experience strikingly similar outcomes, as can be seen from figures 3.1 through 3.6. Indeed, no appreciable difference appears on either indicator, regardless of gender. Caribbean immigrants of the greatest vintage—those residing in the United States for more than 20 years—appear to hold a very slight advantage over their African American counterparts, though, as I have already noted, what such differences in the cross section imply for later cohorts is open to question. Although later cohorts might progress at a rate similar to that of their predecessors, the more recently settled Caribbean New Yorkers appear to have less favorable educational characteristics than their predecessors, which would impede advancement. On the other hand, rough parity with African American natives is not an unimpressive attainment because it puts New York's Caribbean immigrant women well ahead of the Dominican, Mexican, and Cuban women I have discussed thus far. To a lesser extent, the same generalization holds for New York's Caribbean immigrant men, who exhibit the highest rates of employment adequacy among the foreign-born.

Conclusion

Explaining the economic experience of the minority workers who have congregated in America's cities has been an enduring social science preoccupation. The work since the middle of the twentieth century has taken the form of a series of master narratives, organized around the competing themes of race, class, and, most recently, social capital. In a sense, each of these narratives can point to considerable success, their longevity signaling their notable persuasive power. Nonetheless, all of the narratives seem increasingly unsatisfactory, in light of the economic and demographic transformations of American cities and the welter of seemingly anomalous, unexpected developments at work. To be sure, it is hard, perhaps impossible, to kill a theory with facts. But the findings of this chapter do point to the need for a new, more complex, understanding of the opportunities and obstacles confronted by minority workers in America's key urban regions.

The central problem is simply that none of the grand explanations covers the range of experiences represented by the groups in question. Low-skilled white men are more likely to work than comparable black men, highlighting the continuing importance of "race" in labor market outcomes. Once employed, the gap between white and African American men is not nearly as impressive or pervasive, suggesting that the effects associated with "race" have to do with employability; African Americans who are working—whether because of access to jobs, skills unmeasured by my data, or a greater willingness to work at the going wage—are only slightly different from whites in the likelihood of holding adequate jobs. In itself, this finding suggests a strong labor supply effect, amplified by the strong impact that marriage and children exercise on both employment and employment adequacy. Since African American men are so much less likely both to be married and to have children than white men, household characteristics widen the net differences between blacks and whites. The causal linkages are deeply clouded—Is it the lack of jobs that reduce marriage rates or low marriage rates that depress employment?—but the comparison to immigrants, who are less skilled, often much less skilled, adds weight to a labor supply interpretation.

The pattern among immigrant men makes little sense from the standpoint of conventional analysis, with its emphasis on the baneful consequences of low skills. The low skills of immigrant men depress employment rates, but the immigration literature would suggest that something about the immigration process works in the opposite direction. The group effect does not take hold instantaneously, and thus recent arrivals have trouble finding jobs. Still, the penalties associated with recency wear off quite quickly, so that in three of the regions in question the arrivals of the 1970s are at parity with comparable white natives.

By comparison, immigrant social capital works less efficiently in moving immigrant men to jobs of adequate quality. However, it occasionally yields some helpful effect and the harmful consequences of recency of arrival eventually wear off. Some groups in some regions—in particular, Dominican men in New York—are at especially high risk of inadequate employment. In other cases, as in San Francisco, the settlement process facilitates labor market integration, but the penalties associated with immigrants' low skills narrowly circumscribe the potential for progress.

My most striking set of findings involves a theme only orthogonally related to the prevailing stories of race, class, and social capital: the pronounced effect of gender. One can view these results as confirming theories of double or triple jeopardy, but to leave the conclusion there would simplify greatly while providing only limited illumination. For white women, outcomes vary by gender; women are less likely than men to be employed but as likely (or no less likely) to hold jobs that qualify as adequate employment (though my criteria allow for a significant labor supply effect). African American women are only slightly less likely than their white counterparts to hold jobs and, if employed, to work in positions of adequate quality. The persons at greatest risk are immigrant women, for whom nativity universally depresses employment and frequently depresses employment adequacy. This factor, when coupled with the employment-depressing effects associated with marriage, children, low skills, and recency of arrival (where relevant), yields the largest gaps among groups observed in this chapter.

The proliferation of differences by ethnicity and gender makes a single conclusion elusive. In the end, it is clear that low-skilled urban residents— whether immigrants or African Americans—are running into trouble in the quest for economic mobility. On balance, the picture probably looks somewhat better for immigrant men, given the high employment probabilities and the evidence that longer time in the United States reduces dependence on jobs of inadequate quality. However, my measure of employment quality is not terribly demanding; full-time work in jobs that pay 50 percent above the poverty line still leaves one below the median earnings in any of the regions in question. The low skills of the immigrant population make it doubtful that a high proportion of the immigrant male earners will eventually cluster around the median, even under the best of conditions. And thus the progress denoted by the concept of immigrant integration necessarily involves labor force participation of at least two household members. But the low levels of employment among immigrant women, retarded undoubtedly by the presence of children for whom public day care provision is essentially nonexistent, will make such progress hard to achieve. Further word on that topic awaits another chapter.

TABLE 3.1. COEFFICIENTS FROM LOGISTIC REGRESSIONS
OF SELECTED INDEPENDENT VARIABLES ON EMPLOYMENT

	Women only				
	Los Angeles Is Employed	New York Is Employed	San Francisco Is Employed	Chicago Is Employed	Miami Is Employed
Age of person	0.120	0.096	0.183	0.138	0.025
	(0.026)**	(0.022)**	(0.059)**	(0.037)**	(0.051)
Age squared	−0.001	−0.001	−0.002	−0.002	0.000
	(0.000)**	(0.000)**	(0.001)**	(0.000)**	(0.001)
School years	0.125	0.168	0.137	0.153	0.149
	(0.010)**	(0.010)**	(0.026)**	(0.017)**	(0.021)**
Marital status	−0.387	−0.240	−0.504	−0.605	−.395
	(0.069)**	(0.058)**	(0.156)**	(0.107)**	(0.137)**
Any children	−0.721	−0.905	−0.809	−0.563	−0.602
	(0.075)**	(0.060)**	(0.164)**	(0.109)**	(0.145)**
Black native-born	−0.192	−0.037	−0.277	−0.449	−0.307
	(0.150)	(0.093)	(0.293)	(0.129)**	(0.243)
Hispanic native-born	−0.112	−0.344	−0.124	−0.316	0.344
	(0.103)	(0.085)**	(0.235)	(0.173)*	(0.261)
Immigrated in 1970s	0.113	0.301	−0.227	1.087	−0.473
	(0.143)	(0.146)*	(0.444)	(0.285)**	(0.254)*
Immigrated in 1980s	0.022	0.164	−0.689	0.453	−0.131
	(0.141)	(0.134)	(0.414)*	(0.275)*	(0.240)
Immigrated in 1990s	−0.623	−0.528	−1.884	−0.021	−0.706
	(0.161)**	(0.144)**	(0.446)**	(0.298)	(0.266)**
Other immigrants	−0.373	−0.337	0.778	−0.694	0.131
	(0.144)**	(0.119)**	(0.397)*	(0.224)**	(0.252)
Mexican foreign-born	−0.429		0.252	−1.088	
	(0.145)**		(0.429)	(0.274)**	

(continued)

TABLE 3.1. (continued)

Women only

	Los Angeles Is Employed	New York Is Employed	San Francisco Is Employed	Chicago Is Employed	Miami Is Employed
Caribbean foreign-born		0.051 (0.187)			
Dominican foreign-born		-0.588 (0.159)**			
Cuban foreign-born					0.047 (0.236)
Constant	-2.155 (0.546)**	-2.610 (0.450)**	-3.283 (1.222)**	-2.922 (0.794)**	-0.616 (1.072)
Observations	5,587	8,274	1,450	2,987	1,490

Men only

	Los Angeles Is Employed	New York Is Employed	San Francisco Is Employed	Chicago Is Employed	Miami Is Employed
Age of person	0.078 (0.038)*	0.088 (0.031)**	0.138 (0.076)*	-0.020 (0.059)	0.164 (0.075)*
Age squared	-0.001 (0.000)*	-0.001 (0.000)**	-0.001 (0.001)	0.000 (0.001)	-0.002 (0.001)*
School years	0.090 (0.015)**	0.076 (0.013)**	0.102 (0.030)**	0.129 (0.027)**	0.096 (0.031)**

	(1)	(2)	(3)	(4)	(5)
Marital status	(0.113)**	0.706 (0.096)**	0.725 (0.232)*	0.534 (0.182)*	0.420 (0.227)
Any children	−0.119 (0.113)	0.089 (0.099)	0.060 (0.244)	0.550 (0.193)**	0.621 (0.247)**
Black native-born	−0.652 (0.188)**	−0.788 (0.135)**	−1.165 (0.328)**	−1.393 (0.193)**	−0.587 (0.397)
Hispanic native-born	−0.003 (0.155)	−0.714 (0.129)**	−0.461 (0.309)	−0.953 (0.254)**	−0.278 (0.371)
Immigrated in 1970s	0.109 (0.226)	−0.327 (0.229)	0.159 (0.519)	−0.381 (0.464)	0.111 (0.447)
Immigrated in 1980s	0.245 (0.223)	−0.136 (0.216)	0.532 (0.495)	−0.346 (0.461)	−0.279 (0.384)
Immigrated in 1990s	−0.570 (0.240)**	−0.648 (0.219)**	−0.082 (0.520)	−0.487 (0.472)	−0.229 (0.414)
Other immigrants	−0.512 (0.219)**	−0.122 (0.198)	−0.653 (0.440)	−0.578 (0.402)	−0.408 (0.403)
Mexican foreign-born	0.242 (0.229)		0.227 (0.586)	0.339 (0.471)	
Caribbean foreign-born		−0.716 (0.264)**			
Dominican foreign-born		−0.332 (0.268)			
Cuban foreign-born					−0.130 (0.395)
Constant	−0.766 (0.794)	−0.852 (0.649)	−2.424 (1.577)	0.935 (1.241)	−2.544 (1.597)
Observations	5257	7118	1470	2702	1319

Note: Standard errors in parentheses
*significant at 5 percent level; **significant at 1 percent level.

TABLE 3.2. COEFFICIENTS FROM LOGISTIC REGRESSIONS
OF SELECTED INDEPENDENT VARIABLES ON EMPLOYMENT ADEQUACY

	Women only				
	Los Angeles	New York	San Francisco	Chicago	Miami
Age of person	0.010	-0.070	-0.043	0.051	0.001
	(0.036)	(0.035)*	(0.081)	(0.056)	(0.064)
Age squared	0.000	0.001	0.000	-0.001	0.000
	(0.000)	(0.000)*	(0.001)	(0.001)	(0.001)
School years	-0.147	0.134	0.090	0.137	0.122
	(0.014)**	(0.015)**	(0.034)**	(0.027)**	(0.027)**
Marital status	0.107	0.336	-0.096	0.246	0.296
	(0.091)	(0.087)**	(0.196)	(0.150)	(0.166)*
Any children	0.086	-0.080	-0.064	-0.058	-0.115
	(0.100)	(0.092)	(0.211)	(0.165)	(0.181)
Black native-born	-0.228	-0.308	-0.192	-0.528	-0.342
	(0.197)	(0.139)*	(0.406)	(0.190)**	(0.345)
Hispanic native-born	0.011	-0.419	0.391	-0.132	-0.460
	(0.148)	(0.139)**	(0.376)	(0.300)	(0.323)
Immigrated in 1970s	-0.251	-0.134	-0.091	-0.685	-0.292
	(0.207)	(0.236)	(0.485)	(0.443)	(0.327)*
Immigrated in 1980s	-0.764	-0.687	-0.565	-0.670	-0.608
	(0.202)**	(0.213)**	(0.456)	(0.455)	(0.296)*
Immigrated in 1990s	-1.126	-1.287	-0.576	-0.985	-1.518
	(0.238)**	(0.230)**	(0.562)	(0.490)*	(0.336)**
Other immigrants	-0.082	-0.180	0.139	-0.221	-0.292
	(0.208)	(0.199)	(0.421)	(0.391)	(0.326)
Mexican foreign-born	-0.246		-0.512	-0.309	
	(0.207)		(0.501)	(0.468)	

	Los Angeles	New York	San Francisco	Chicago	Miami
Caribbean foreign-born		0.071			
		(0.280)			
Dominican foreign-born		-0.518			
		(0.253)*			
Cuban foreign-born					-0.177
					(0.311)
Constant	-0.437	1.660	1.911	-0.420	0.652
	(0.769)	(0.726)*	(1.718)	(1.226)	(1.360)
Observations	3710	5747	1130	2205	1101

Men only

	Los Angeles	New York	San Francisco	Chicago	Miami
Age of person	0.043	0.050	-0.011	0.020	-0.102
	(0.031)	(0.032)	(0.066)	(0.055)	(0.071)
Age squared	-0.001	-0.001	0.000	0.000	0.001
	(0.000)*	(0.000)*	(0.001)	(0.001)	(0.001)
School years	0.072	0.052	0.104	0.069	0.123
	(0.011)**	(0.012)**	(0.025)**	(0.024)**	(0.025)**
Marital status	0.371	0.455	0.236	0.452	0.419
	(0.094)**	(0.096)**	(0.195)	(0.170)**	(0.200)*
Any children	0.013	-0.060	-0.055	-0.080	-0.054
	(0.090)	(0.094)	(0.194)	(0.170)	(0.195)
Black native-born	0.383	-0.280	0.088	-0.503	0.390
	(0.216)*	(0.155)*	(0.401)	(0.212)**	(0.440)
Hispanic native-born	0.330	-0.007	0.386	0.076	-0.218
	(0.136)**	(0.153)	(0.319)	(0.303)	(0.324)
Immigrated in 1970s	-0.037	-0.436	0.299	0.565	0.451
	(0.182)	(0.222)*	(0.429)	(0.417)	(0.361)

(continued)

TABLE 3.2. (continued)

Men only

	Los Angeles	New York	San Francisco	Chicago	Miami
Immigrated in 1980s	-0.560	-0.656	0.216	-0.133	-0.444
	(0.177)**	(0.203)**	(0.395)	(0.377)	(0.296)
Immigrated in 1990s	-0.933	-1.037	-0.480	-0.794	-1.149
	(0.205)**	(0.212)**	(0.436)	(0.382)*	(0.307)**
Other immigrants	-0.143	-0.012	-0.150	-0.354	-.211
	(0.179)	(0.188)	(0.350)	(0.331)	(0.315)
Mexican foreign-born	-0.037		-0.073	-0.440	
	(0.181)		(0.436)	(0.376)	
Caribbean foreign-born		0.281			
		(0.297)			
Dominican foreign-born		-0.513			
		(0.247)*			
Cuban foreign-born					-0.483
Constant	-0.321	0.270	0.608	0.697	2.584
	(0.659)	(0.657)	(1.391)	(1.147)	(1.513)*
Observations	4,666	6,330	1,331	2,476	1,195

Note: Standard errors in parentheses.
*significant at 5 percent level; **significant at 1 percent level.

Notes

1. For the most recent exposition of this point of view, see William J. Wilson, *When Work Disappears* (New York: Alfred A. Knopf, 1996) and the references therein; I have presented a more extensive critique of the skills-mismatch hypothesis in *Still the Promised City? African-Americans and New Immigrants in PostIndustrial New York* (Cambridge, Mass.: Harvard University Press, 1996). See also Harry Holzer, *What Employers Want: Job Prospects for Less-Educated Workers* (New York: Russell Sage Foundation, 1996).

2. James Smith and Barry Edmonston, eds., *The New Americans* (Washington, D.C.: National Academy Press, 1997); the diversity of today's immigrant flows is a central theme sounded in Alejandro Portes and Rubén Rumbaut's *Immigrant America: A Portrait*, 2d ed. (Berkeley and Los Angeles: University of California Press, 1996).

3. As I note in *Promised City*, especially chapter 2.

4. Touchstones of this literature include Alejandro Portes, introduction to *The Economic Sociology of Immigration* (New York: Russell Sage Foundation, 1995); Douglas Massey, "Theories of International Migration: A Review and Reappraisal," *Population and Development Review* 19, no. 3 (1993): 431–466; idem, "Continuities in Transnational Migration: An Analysis of 19 Mexican Communities," *American Journal of Sociology* 99, no. 6 (1994): 1492–1533; and the numerous references found in these various sources.

5. Douglas Massey, Rafael Alarcón, Jorge Durand, and Humberto González, *Return to Aztlan* (Berkeley and Los Angeles: University of California Press, 1987), 170–171.

6. Chapter 7 supplies an extended, if somewhat idiosyncratic, review of the relevant literature. Ivan Light and Steven Gold's *Ethnic Economies* (San Diego: Academic Press, 2000) provides an alternative point of view and in much greater depth.

7. The basic references are Alejandro Portes and Robert Bach, *Latin Journey* (Berkeley and Los Angeles: University of California Press, 1985); and Alejandro Portes and Alex Stepick, *City on the Edge* (Berkeley and Los Angeles: University of California Press, 1993). For further discussion, see chapter 7 of this book and the references cited therein.

8. Ira DeA. Reid, *The Negro Immigrant: His Background, Characteristics, and Social Adjustment, 1899–1937* (New York: Columbia University Press, 1939); Nathan Glazer and Daniel P. Moynihan, *Beyond the Melting Pot* (Cambridge, Mass.: MIT Press, 1963); Ivan Light, *Ethnic Enterprise in America* (Berkeley and Los Angeles: University of California Press, 1972).

9. Thomas Sowell, in "Three Black Histories" (in *Essays and Data on American Ethnic Groups,* ed. Thomas Sowell [Washington, D.C.: Urban Institute, 1978]), makes the case for West Indian advantage; Suzanne Model, in "Caribbean Immigrants: A Black Success Story?" (*International Migration Review* 25, no. 2 [1991]: 248–276), argues the contrary. Mary Waters's forthcoming book, *Black Identities: West Indian Immigrant Dreams and American Realities* (Cambridge, Mass.: Harvard University Press, 1999), is likely to be

the definitive statement; her extraordinarily subtle analysis suggests that the balance is likely to fall on the negative side.

10. Clifford Clogg, Scott Eliason, and R. J. Wahl, "Labor-Market Experiences and Labor-Force Outcomes," *American Journal of Sociology* 95, no. 6 (May 1990): 1536–1576; Daniel Lichter, D. J. Landry, and Clifford Clogg, "Measuring Short-Term Labor Force Mobility with the Labor Utilization Framework," *Social Science Research* 20, no. 4 (December 1991): 329–354; Teresa Sullivan, *Marginal Workers, Marginal Jobs: The Underutilization of American Workers* (Austin: University of Texas Press, 1978).

11. Barry Chiswick, "The Effect of Americanization on the Earnings of Foreign-Born Men," *Journal of Political Economy* 86, no. 5 (1978): 897–921; George Borjas, *Friends or Strangers? The Impact of Immigrants on the U.S. Economy* (New York: Basic Books, 1990).

Chapter 4

A TALE OF FIVE CITIES?
Trends in Immigrant and Native-Born Wages

Mark Ellis

Americans entertain any number of anxieties about contemporary immigration to the United States. Among the more rational reasons for concern, evidence of the widening economic gap between the native- and foreign-born should rank high on the list. Whether the indicator involves wages, poverty (see chapter 5), or access to full-time, well-paying jobs (see chapter 3), the signs all point in the same direction: immigrants to the United States are falling farther behind the native-born on a range of basic measures of economic well-being.[1]

Most of the interest, naturally enough, has focused on wages.[2] The typical approach involves a comparison of national samples of immigrants and natives, contrasting the two groups first at one point in time and then some years later to determine how each falls out in the wage distribution and how those positions change over time. Although researchers disagree about how to interpret the data, there seems to be little disagreement about the broad trend: on a national level, post-1965 immigrants are failing to catch up with the native-born in terms of wages. Moreover, the gap between immigrants and natives is growing; compared to natives, the most recent arrivals enter the labor market at lower wage levels than did those newcomers who arrived just two decades ago. Thus, the prospects for economic assimilation appear to be getting bleaker still for those immigrants who have just started to work in the United States.

This story—one of a widening wage gap between immigrant and native workers—derives from the results of research conducted on a national level. National-level comparisons are of unquestionable significance for the overall picture they provide, but they implicitly assume that the geography of immigration matters little. They also mask the fact that contemporary immigration to the United States primarily involves migration to a limited number of states and urban regions, most important the five city-regions of New York, Los Angeles, Chicago, San Francisco, and Miami that serve as the focus of this book.[3] If the characteristics of these particular destinations exercise little effect on immigrants' economic success, then the exclusively national focus of most research conveys the correct picture. But if contexts of reception affect the economic outcomes for immigrants and if these contexts are expressed not at the national but rather at the subnational level, such as in these city-regions, then trends in the wages of natives and immigrants may also vary from one immigrant destination to another.

Indeed, the literature provides convincing evidence that the ability of immigrants to make economic gains depends on conditions in the places where they settle, not just on the individual characteristics they bring with them or acquire while in the United States. For example, Alejandro Portes and Robert Bach found that differences in individual characteristics, such as education and English-language ability, explained only half of the income disadvantage of Mexican men relative to Cuban men.[4] The disparity between Cubans and Mexicans, they suggest, derives from differences in the contexts of reception, a concept they coined to denote a variety of features of the destination community, including the resources of the absorbing ethnic community, the robustness of the local labor market, and the policies of the receiving government.[5] Others have made similar arguments about the importance of conditions in the place of settlement affecting immigrant economic success. Charles Tilly compared emigrants from one small town in southern Italy to four cities in different countries (Lyon, Toronto, New York, and Buenos Aires).[6] This unique sample controls for variation in migrant characteristics and isolates conditions in the place of settlement as the probable cause of differences in economic success. Similarly, Jeffrey Reitz, in his book comparing immigrants in the United States, Canada, and Australia, has argued that the social and institutional structures of destination societies, rather than immigrant characteristics, largely account for the higher economic inequality between immigrants and natives in the United States than between those in either Australia or Canada.[7]

Thus place-specific conditions are likely to matter, in part because immigrants gravitate to particular places and not others, but for other reasons as well. Most important, wage levels and wage trends for all workers—native- and foreign-born alike—typically vary within countries across regions. Those variations are likely to be accentuated when economic restructuring also affects regions in very distinctive ways—as has been the case for America's leading immigrant destinations.

Each of the five major centers of immigration in the United States experienced distinctive economic transformations in the 1970s and 1980s. New York lost much of its manufacturing employment and developed further as a center of advanced financial services. Through 1990 Los Angeles emerged as the premier manufacturing region in the country—based on electronics, aerospace, and a reinvigorated low-technology base of garments and furniture—and it expanded its dynamic entertainment sector. Typical of other Midwestern cities, Chicago experienced considerable restructuring and job loss in its traditional heavy and consumer-oriented manufacturing industries. The San Francisco region boomed largely because of the electronics and computer-related industries in Silicon Valley to its south. And Miami solidified its position as a financial and tourist center for Latin America and the Caribbean.[8] Other regions of the country also experienced singular economic transformations, but the key point is that these shifts occurred in labor markets in which immigrants played a very modest role.

Thus, immigrants disproportionately made their way to regions whose economies evolved in ways that were at once distinctive and at variance from the pattern captured by the national average. Consequently, the best framework for understanding the source of differences between immigrants and natives involves a contrast of foreign- and native-born wages by the city-region in which both live. A comparison of this sort yields a measure of immigrant disadvantage—or advantage, whatever the case may be—relative to natives working under labor market conditions that both groups actually experience. National analyses compare immigrants and natives who live in a mix of regions with different economic structures and variable concentrations of immigrants. But, as noted in chapter 1, a large proportion of the native population lives in parts of the United States where immigrants are particularly unlikely to settle. Furthermore, those places that hold little attraction to the foreign-born are also likely to experience different wage changes and economic pressures than those at work in the regions that have attracted the most sizable immigrant inflows. If the wages of natives in regions of immigrant settlement differ from those of the natives who live elsewhere, then the national relative wage will differ from the relative wage measured in the places where immigrants actually live. Moreover, because of distinctive regional economic transformations, changes in the wages of natives and immigrants may take a different path in regions of immigrant settlement than they do nationally. If this is the case then national assessments of the economic assimilation of immigrants may not reflect the actual progress of native- and foreign-born workers in those places where immigrants actually live and work.

Thus, in this chapter I argue that regional labor markets centered on the city-regions in which immigrants live provide better units than the United States as a whole in which to compare the wages of native- and foreign-born workers. Furthermore, national-level comparisons of immigrant and native wages obscure significant variation in relative wages across major centers of immigrant settlement.

The remainder of this chapter investigates changes in the wage levels of native-born and immigrant men and women between 1980 and 1990 in five major city-regions of immigrant settlement: New York, Los Angeles, Chicago, San Francisco, and Miami. The focus on men *and* women remains relatively unusual, as the literature on the economic adjustment of immigrants has mainly concerned itself with the experiences of men, even though immigrant women now constitute over 40 percent of all immigrant workers in the United States.[9] As such, the chapter builds on a small but growing body of literature reporting on the labor force activity and assimilation trajectories of immigrant women, and in so doing has found both differences and similarities in the experiences of immigrant men and women.[10]

The initial parts of the analysis present descriptive evidence on the relative wage of immigrants and natives by metropolitan region and on differential changes in the relative wage by region between 1980 and 1990. Later sections consider the extent to which characteristics of immigrants and natives explain differences in relative wages between city-regions and whether shifts in these characteristics are sufficient to explain changes in the relative wage in each region in the 1980s. I start with an overview of what is known about immigrant and native wages in the 1980s at the national level and then proceed to the presentation of data and models for the city-regions.

Wages, Skills, and the New Immigration

The 1980s began and ended with national recessions, but the years 1982–1989 witnessed a continuous period of economic expansion. Despite this prolonged expansionary phase, real wages for all men in 1990 fell below their 1980 level. In contrast, wages for women climbed during the decade, albeit modestly.[11] Thus the gender wage gap closed somewhat, but by decade's end women's wages remained substantially lower than men's. These trends in mean national wages camouflage significant changes in the wage distribution during the 1980s, most notably the increase in income inequality, particularly among men.[12] There seems little question that the income distribution widened to a certain degree, as those in the upper part of the distribution experienced income growth while those at the bottom experienced substantial declines in wages.

The literature contains a variety of explanations for the new pattern, the most popular of which contends that the job market of the 1980s reflected the shift to a high-tech, information services economy. In this view, employers placed an increased premium on skill, benefiting those with advanced levels of education and relegating those with a high school degree or less to poorly paid jobs with few prospects for advancement.[13] Other explanations have also surfaced, most notably the contention that the erosion of union membership beginning in the late 1960s and the associated rising power of employers reduced the bargaining power of less-skilled workers—an account that can be accepted without excluding the first.[14] Whatever the precise reason for a shift to a more unequal pay structure, observers developed a grab bag of phrases, including "income polarization" and "the declining middle class," to describe the social changes wrought by these developments.[15]

The period between 1980 and 1990 was also a decade of immigration; the 1980s witnessed the arrival of more than 8 million persons, many of whom had few skills and poor ability in English and ended up in low-paying jobs. As described at greater length in chapter 6, this influx has been a prominent target in the search for causes of the worsening job prospects of the unskilled native-born. The evidence for an immigration effect, however, is not strong; it suggests that there may be a minor immigration-induced reduction in wages of perhaps 1 to 2 percent at most among competing native-born workers—those with a high school degree or less.[16] Most important, any such impact looks small relative to the overall real decline in wages experienced by those with modest levels of education. Real annual earnings for male high school dropouts fell by 13 percent between 1973 and 1987; for high school graduates they fell by 8 percent.[17]

The increased premium paid to skilled workers and the fact that recent immigrants are relatively unskilled compared to natives undoubtedly help explain the widening gap in hourly wages between immigrants and the native-born. In 1970 the earnings of immigrant women and men stood at roughly the same level as native-born workers of the same sex. But relative earnings then slipped among immigrants, especially men. By 1980 male immigrants' hourly wages had fallen 9.9 percent behind the hourly wages of native men; 10 years later, the gap widened still further, reaching 14.4 percent in 1990. The patterns for women show a similar but less extreme trend: immigrant women's hourly wages were 1.6 percent below those of native women in 1980 and a little more than 4.4 percent below those of native women in 1990.

In part, immigrants have fallen behind natives for reasons that have to do with the shift in immigration source countries that followed the 1965 immigration act (as described at greater length in chapter 1 of this book). In 1970 immigrants from today's principal sending regions—Asia, Mexico, Central America, and the Caribbean—still constituted a minority of the foreign-born labor force. At the time most immigrant workers were European-born and also older and relatively skilled to boot; consequently, their relative wages were high.

By 1990, however, the tide had turned. Immigrants from nontraditional source regions were the majority of foreign-born workers, and relative wages began to slide. *The New Americans,* the National Research Council's influential study of immigration, attributed almost all of the 1970–1990 decline in the relative wage of immigrant men, and about 75 percent of the drop in the relative wage of immigrant women, to change in the national-origin mix of immigrants.[18]

One simple fact accounts for this overwhelming source country effect: the arrivals of the past two decades came predominantly from countries with poorer educational systems than that of the United States. Despite this education gap the skills of immigrants, as measured by mean years of education, percentage of high school dropouts, and percentage with a college degree, actually improved slightly between 1970 and 1990.[19] Thus one should not interpret the effect of national-origin mix on relative wages as an indication of a decline in immigrant quality. Rather, the source country effect reflects the relatively rapid improvement in the education of the native-born and the approximately equivalent increase in the educational qualifications of immigrants from Europe. Thus if the national-origin mix of immigrants in 1990 resembled that of 1970 (i.e., had it remained predominantly European) it would not only generate a much more skilled immigration stream than we find today but one that would compare favorably with the distribution of immigrant skills as of 1970. The key points, therefore, are twofold: (1) today's immigrants are, on average, of higher quality than in 1970, but (2) they enter the American labor market at lower wages relative to the native-born than earlier settlers did because their skills are now considerably inferior to those of the native-born.

Trends in Wages in Five Immigrant City-Regions

With few exceptions, the scholarly debate about the gap in wages and skills between natives and immigrants has focused on national-level comparisons. As we shall see, the story in the five major regions of immigrant settlement diverges considerably from this account of changes at the national level.

Men

Nationally, the data confirm the well-known story to which we have already referred: real hourly wages for men declined during the 1980s, as can be seen from figure 4.1, which displays trends in mean hourly wages for native- and foreign-born men for the United States and for each of our five immigrant regions, further subdivided by major ethnoracial group.[20] The comparison to natives puts the deterioration in the immigrant wage situation in sharper relief; although immigrants fell farther behind natives during the period in question, that decline took place in a context in which the wages for native workers were also eroding. Not all groups did equally poorly: the wages of Asian American men and white immigrants stood still; those of black immigrants actually improved; and those of all others, both native- and foreign-born, declined.

Thus, trends at the national level looked grim, with immigrants' lag behind natives widening even as native wages deteriorated. But the pattern looked quite different in the capitals of immigrant America. The wages of native-born workers increased in San Francisco, in Los Angeles, and, most dramatically, in New York, where native men earned a

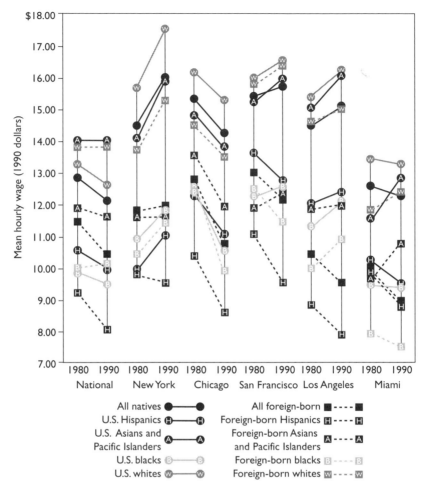

Figure 4.1.   Men's wages, 1980–1990

Note: Wage data are restricted to men (ages 25 to 64) who have wage and salary income, work in the civilian sector and are not self-employed, and do not live in group quarters. The reported means are the antilogs of the mean of log hourly wages.

little under two dollars an hour more in 1990 than in 1980. Moreover, the gains were shared by a broad, though not full, spectrum of native workers: native-born whites, blacks, and Asians enjoyed growth in wages in all three city-regions; earnings among native-born Hispanics similarly improved in Los Angeles and New York but slipped in San Francisco. A full account of this change exceeds the scope of this chapter, but several factors seem likely to have been important: all three city-regions experienced continuing transformation of their economic bases in the 1980s, shifting from manufacturing and traditional services to financial, professional, information, and entertainment services. As they moved to service-based economies, these regions also generated large numbers of well-paying jobs for workers with sufficient skills—typically at least a college education.

High-wage job growth also came with a flip side—in this case, expansion in low-wage support services in offices and restaurants and in personal services, which have increasingly come to be performed by immigrants.[21] Reflecting this division of labor, the real wage of immigrant men declined in Los Angeles and San Francisco and increased modestly in New York.

Beneath the aggregate trends lie variations among groups; most important, one trend separates Hispanics from all others. In New York and Los Angeles, the wages of white, black, and Asian immigrants grew; the same held true for whites and Asians in San Francisco, though not for the area's very small number of foreign-born blacks. In all three places, by contrast, the wages of Hispanic immigrants declined.[22] Consequently, where Hispanic immigrants were of disproportionate importance and Hispanics' wages dropped precipitously, as in Los Angeles and San Francisco, average wages for all male immigrants were pulled down as well. By contrast, because Hispanics' wages also dropped in New York but at a much slower rate than in Los Angeles and San Francisco, the economic performance of Hispanics acted as a brake on the growth of total male immigrant wages in New York rather than causing them to decline.

Miami is a rather different story altogether. Figure 4.1 alerts us to a central characteristic of Miami that has somehow been neglected in the immigration literature: it is a low-wage town. Native-born workers do worse in Miami than in any other of the regions with which we are concerned; native-born black workers do particularly poorly, as might be expected in this southern city-region, but U.S.-born whites compare unfavorably with their counterparts elsewhere as well. Asian men, both U.S.- and foreign-born, were the only winners during the 1980s, but, as pointed out in chapter 1, the relative absence of an Asian population is one of Miami's distinctive traits as a leading immigrant destination.

Like native men, immigrant male Miamians suffered wage erosion during the 1980s. Notwithstanding the presence of the established Cuban population, Hispanics saw their wages drop. But in Miami, unlike all the other immigration regions, immigrant Hispanics stood one rung up from the very bottom of the wage structure. That honor, instead, fell to immigrant blacks; in Miami, this heavily undocumented, highly stigmatized, effectively marginalized population did a good deal worse than their counterparts in New York, the only other region with a sizable foreign-born black population.

In relative terms, however, male Chicagoans, both natives and immigrants, did the worst of all, although the wage erosion among the latter was steeper, in both proportional and absolute terms. These changes shifted Chicago's position in the wage structure, relative to the other city-regions: in 1980 the wages of Chicago's native- and foreign-born men ranked second, after those of San Francisco's; by 1990 native-born men had fallen behind their counterparts in San Francisco, New York, and Los Angeles, and foreign-born Chicagoans had dropped behind immigrants in both New York and San Francisco.

Women

Wages for women followed a rather different trajectory than that of men and also hewed to a different pattern, as can be seen by comparing figure 4.1 with figure 4.2, which displays the wage data for women, broken down in the same fashion as in figure 4.1. Of course, the spread in wages, and any changes therein, occurs within a different range: women's wages rank lower than men's, a generalization that holds for all groups and all places in question and at both times studied. That said, the ways in which the wage structure and its evolution differ by gender stand out.

First, and unlike the case among men, women's wages rose, at least at the national level. Second, the gap separating immigrant women from their native-born counterparts was a good deal smaller than that separating immigrant and native men. Indeed, at the national level, native and immigrant women in 1980 enjoyed almost equal wages. Some inequality between native and immigrant women emerged by 1990, but the disparity came nowhere near the gulf separating native- and foreign-born men. Third, all groups, except for Hispanics, made more in 1990 than they did 10 years before.[23]

Women's wages acted much in New York, Los Angeles, San Francisco, and Miami as they did in the nation at large; in all four city-regions both native and immigrant women experienced rising wages, although native women's wages grew faster. In New York all ethnoracial groups of women experienced wage growth; native blacks, whites, and Asians topped the absolute increases, earning about two dollars an

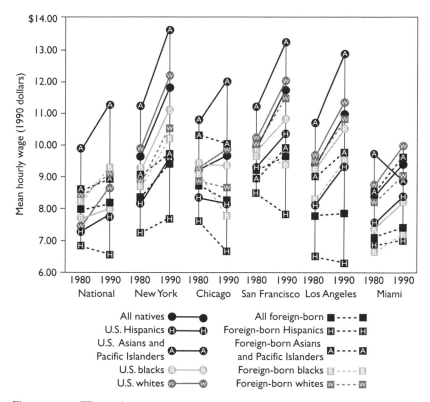

Figure 4.2.   Women's wages, 1980–1990

Note: Wage data are restricted to women (ages 25 to 64) who have wage and salary income, work in the civilian sector and are not self-employed, and do not live in group quarters. The reported means are the antilogs of the mean of log hourly wages.

hour more in 1990 than in 1980. The same native-born groups did well in San Francisco and Los Angeles, though the rate of increase did not match the trend in New York.

In contrast, all groups of foreign-born women did not fare equally well. In Los Angeles immigrant Hispanic women's wages declined slightly; in San Francisco the wages of both Hispanic and black immigrant women fell, although the latter constitute a very small fraction of the city-region's foreign-born population. As with men, the relatively large pockets of Hispanic immigrants in Los Angeles and San Francisco dragged down the average for all foreign-born women in these two places. Unlike men, however, the decline in wages of immigrant Hispanic women did not cause erosion in immigrant women's wages overall;

rather, it diminished wage growth by muting the impact of the rapid wage increase among other groups of foreign-born women.

As for Miami, it is no less a low-wage region for women than for men. Nonetheless, the picture for female Miamians was somewhat brighter than for their male counterparts; women's wages rose during the 1980s, although the rates of growth generally paled in comparison to the trends in New York, Los Angeles, and San Francisco.[24] Moreover, wage growth for Miami's single largest foreign-born group, Hispanics, took a particularly anemic form, sufficiently so that immigrant Hispanic women actually followed immigrant black women, taking up the bottommost position in Miami's wage structure.

Finally, as with men, women's wage trends in Chicago stand out from those of other cities and the nation as a whole. Not every group of female Chicagoans fared poorly; U.S.-born Asians and whites saw their wages improve, and the decline among U.S.-born black and Hispanic women was not sufficiently steep to pull the native-born average down. But only in Chicago did the foreign-born wage average drop, driven largely by the decline in wages for Hispanic immigrant women, whose situation in Chicago deteriorated even more than it did in Los Angeles or San Francisco.

Summary of Trends

Figures 4.1 and 4.2 suggest three additional observations that apply to both men and women. First, the gap between the wages of natives and immigrants widened during the 1980s, both nationally and in each city-region. Second, wage differences between the native- and foreign-born loom larger in all five city-regions than they do nationwide. Consequently, national comparisons of immigrant and native wages understate the true wage disadvantage that immigrants experience in the regional labor markets in which they work.

Third, trends in native- and foreign-born wages in each city-region vary from the national picture, a divergence most noticeable among men. Nationally, the wages of both native and immigrant men fell in the 1980s, but the wages earned by the latter group underwent a steeper decline. Similar trends—declining native- and foreign-born wages but the latter dropping at a faster rate—also occurred in Chicago and Miami. The gap between the wages of immigrant and native men also widened in New York, Los Angeles, and San Francisco, but here the underlying trends took a different form. In Los Angeles and San

Francisco the wages of native-born men grew, while those of foreign-born men declined. In New York both native and immigrant wages grew, but the latter increased only slightly. For women the trend in four of the five city-regions conforms with that observed nationally: wages rose for both native and immigrant women but at a faster rate for the former group. In Chicago native women's wages grew during the 1980s but foreign-born women's wages were lower in 1990 than in 1980.

Thus the wage trends responsible for the widening gap between immigrant and native wages varied across city-regions. In some instances, increased inequality emerged in the context of growing native and immigrant wages—the situation for men in New York and women in all cities but Chicago. In others, a widening gap in the wages of immigrants and natives stemmed from either rising native and falling immigrant wages or situations in which both native- and foreign-born wages fell but at unequal rates.

Relative Wages and the Ethnoracial Mix of Immigrants

That immigrants make less than natives is to be expected. Less predictable are the facts that I have just revealed: that the size of the gap varies from place to place and within places by gender and, furthermore, that the pattern of change takes not one but several forms, depending on the particular place. In this section, I inquire into the source of these variations.

I begin by focusing on 1990. As figure 4.3 indicates, the gap in wages between natives and immigrants exceeds the disparity at the national level in each of the five cities, a generalization that holds for both men and women. Although women do not trail quite as far behind their native-born counterparts as men, the same pattern holds for both genders: places with the lowest relative wage for men (Los Angeles and Miami) are also places with the lowest relative wage for women.

Could differences in national origins matter? As noted in chapter 1, America's key immigrant destinations are linked to migration streams that differ both in national origins and in skill composition, such that some regions receive immigrants of disproportionately low skills and others attract a more highly skilled group. Breaking down the immigrant population into the four mutually exclusive categories of white, black, Hispanic, and Asian highlights the regional distinctiveness.[25] (The index of dissimilarity provides a convenient way of measuring the

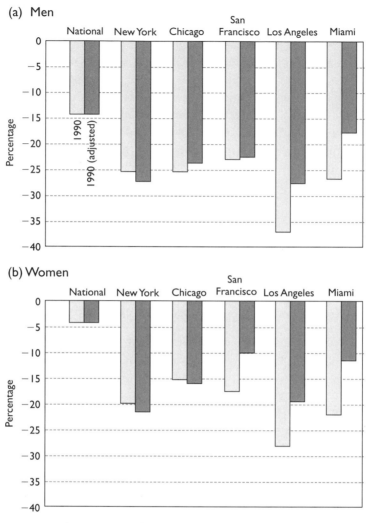

Figure 4.3. Relative wages of immigrant (a) men and (b) women, 1990: adjusting regions by national foreign-born ethnoracial composition

degree to which each region's mix compares to the nation's [see table 4.1].) Using this categorization, New York's and Chicago's mix differs somewhat from the nation's but only to a modest degree. On the other hand, the newer immigration regions of San Francisco, Los Angeles, and Miami have attracted a foreign-born population of rather different background. Each also contains a particular mix: the first is heavily

TABLE 4.1.   INDEX OF
DISSIMILARITY: REGION
VERSUS UNITED STATES

	1980	1990
New York	9	9
Chicago	4	7
San Francisco	23	25
Los Angeles	21	19
Miami	42	39

tilted toward Asians; the second is heavily tilted toward Hispanics, though it has also absorbed a sizable Asian contingent; and the third is overwhelmingly tilted toward Hispanics. Hispanic immigrants, regardless of gender, as we have just seen, fall at the bottom of the wage hierarchy in almost every place; they also arrive with very low skills, as noted in chapter 1. Therefore, if compositional factors were driving inequality between natives and immigrants in particular places, statistically altering the ethnoracial mix of each region so that local ethnoracial proportions equal the nationwide pattern should reduce the gulf between the wages of natives and immigrants.[26]

Figure 4.3 presents the results of just such an exercise. Standardizing for ethnoracial composition does little to affect the relative wages of immigrant men or women in New York, Chicago, or San Francisco. But the same procedure substantially reduces the gap in wages between natives and immigrants in Miami and Los Angeles. Standardization also changes the disparities among places: given the same ethnoracial proportions, immigrant men in New York and Los Angeles fall an equal distance behind natives whereas the existing mix makes for much greater inequality in Los Angeles than in New York. Standardization also reorders rankings among cities: immigrant men in Miami have the second worst relative wage before standardization, but afterward they have the best relative wage; the same procedure moves women in New York from third to last in the relative wage rankings.

Thus standardization reduces variability in relative wages across city-regions. However, it fails to reduce relative wages to the national level in any city-region, and immigrants' wages remain far below those enjoyed by their native counterparts, a pattern particularly noticeable in New York and Los Angeles. What accounts for this gap?

One answer might be that immigrants make less in the leading immigrant destinations than they do nationwide, but that possibility is precluded by the patterns observed in figure 4.1: while immigrant wages vary across city-regions they hover at roughly the same level as the national immigrant wage. The better answer, rather, is that native workers in the five city-regions earn more than their counterparts elsewhere. Immigrants live disproportionately in places at the top of the urban hierarchy, which in turn entails a concentration of high-level management and information services jobs. Natives who live in these regions therefore enjoy disproportionate access to these same positions, which also happen to be the highest-paying jobs in the country. Thus, when measured in the context of labor markets that generate high-paying employment, immigrant wage performance is a good deal worse than it appears to be at the national level.

Concluding that the characteristics of the key immigrant destinations account for the distinctively large wage gap between natives and immigrants solves only part of the puzzle, since we also want to know why that gap grew during the 1980s. Once again, composition offers a likely lead: any shift in migration streams during the 1980s, so that they delivered a larger flow of less-skilled Hispanic immigrants and a smaller flow of more-skilled Asian and white immigrants, could have increased wage inequality between the native- and foreign-born in just the fashion that I have observed. To assess that hypothesis, I performed another standardization exercise, this time giving each place the same ethnoracial mix in 1990 that it had in 1980.

Figure 4.4 confirms what I noted at the outset of this chapter: nationally, changes in ethnoracial composition in the 1980s explain almost all of the decline in relative wages for immigrant men and a majority of that for immigrant women; with 1980 immigrant fractions immigrant men would have remained approximately 9 percent behind native men and immigrant women about 2 percent behind native women.[27]

But the same factor serves much less well in explaining the deterioration in relative wages in the city-regions. Giving the immigrant men of 1990 the same ethnoracial characteristics possessed by immigrant men residing in the same place in 1980 accounts for 70 percent of the decline in San Francisco but only 33 percent of the decline in New York. In the other three city-regions the percentage decline in relative wage explained by the change in ethnoracial mix varies between these limits. In women's case the picture is even more varied. More than 60 percent of the decrease in relative wages during the 1980s in Los Angeles is accounted for

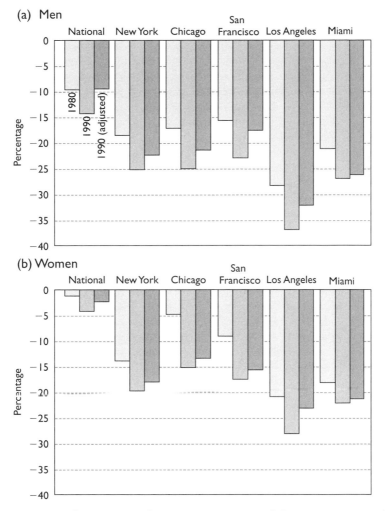

Figure 4.4.   Relative wages of immigrant (a) men and (b) women, 1990: adjusting by 1980 foreign-born ethnoracial composition of regions

by change in ethnoracial composition. By contrast, ethnoracial change is responsible for a quarter or less of the decline in relative wages in Chicago, San Francisco, and Miami. In New York standardizing wages using ethnoracial composition in 1980 actually widens the wage gap between native and immigrant women by 10 percent. Thus change in the ethnoracial composition of New York's immigrant population during the 1980s improved the relative wage of foreign-born women.

Variation in Immigrant Skills across City-Regions

Change in ethnoracial composition serves as a surrogate for change in immigrant skills. In this section I tackle the issue of skills directly and explore differences in levels and trends in immigrant and native educational qualifications across city-regions during the 1980s; these differences may help explain both interregional variation in immigrant relative wages and the disparities in the rate at which the immigrant relative wage has declined.

Immigrants fall behind natives in educational attainment nationwide, in all five city-regions, and at both times studied. One can find an exception here and there: a greater percentage of immigrant men and women in Chicago in 1980 had college degrees than did natives of the same sex, and in San Francisco in 1980 immigrant men were slightly more likely to have college degrees than were native men. Otherwise, natives hold a consistent lead in attainment of education, although skills improved for both natives and immigrants in all locations and regardless of whether one looks at mean years of education, percentage with a college degree, or percentage with an eighth-grade education or less.

Although they lag behind natives on a national level, immigrants do not experience the same level of disadvantage in relative skills in each of the primary metropolitan centers of settlement. The greatest disparities are found in Los Angeles and Miami, where the gulf between the wages of natives and immigrants was at its widest in both years and where immigrant men were farther behind their native-born counterparts than were immigrant women. Immigrant men in Miami and Los Angeles share the dubious honor of possessing the lowest mean years of education, the highest percentages with an eighth-grade education or less (Los Angeles in particular stands out on this measure), and the lowest percentage to have completed four years of college. In contrast to these two cities, immigrants in San Francisco constitute a relatively well-educated group. In this case, the lag is strictly of a regional nature: Bay Area immigrants are much better educated than the average U.S. immigrant, but they simply do not reach the educational level of the unusually well-educated natives in that city-region. By contrast, the educational attainment of immigrants in New York and Chicago is not quite so impressive, as it essentially resembles the pattern that holds for immigrants nationally (though New York is home to a much smaller proportion with very low levels of education).

Immigrants are becoming more skilled everywhere, but some argue that this advancement may matter little. In this view, the important question involves not so much the absolute trends in immigrant skill levels but the immigrant skill level relative to that of the native-born.[28] If relative standing is what counts and if the improvements in native educational attainment in recent decades have outpaced those of immigrants, foreign-born workers may increasingly find themselves unable to compete for any but low-wage jobs.

However, empirical evidence for slippage in the relative skills of immigrants during the 1980s turns out to be mixed (see figure 4.5). In this respect, the pattern nationwide and in each city-region has changed in roughly similar ways: for the most part, the relative years of education of immigrants (the percentage differential between immigrants and natives in mean years of education) lessened. Only in two cases—men in San Francisco and women in Los Angeles—did immigrants fall farther behind natives on this measure. Immigrants also gained ground on another indicator: the difference in the percentage of immigrants and natives with an eighth-grade education or less declined. But immigrants are falling behind, regardless of where they live, in the relative size of the college-educated group. Although the percentage of immigrants with four or more years of college increased dramatically between 1980 and 1990, that gain took even more dramatic form among natives, nationally and in all five city-regions. Thus, at the top of the skills spectrum, the relative gap between immigrants and natives increased.

To a limited degree these differences in skill accord with the pattern in relative wages observed earlier (see figure 4.3a). For example, in Los Angeles immigrant male wages were almost 37 percent less than those of native men in 1990, whereas in San Francisco this gap was only 23 percent; as we have just seen, Los Angeles is home to a particularly low-skilled group of immigrants and San Francisco, a particularly high-skilled contingent. Similar patterns are observable among immigrant women, whose relative wage is lowest in Los Angeles and highest in Chicago (see figure 4.3b). As with men this contrast matches the extremes in relative educational attainment: the college education gap for women is lowest in Chicago, and the percentage difference in eighth-grade education is greatest in Los Angeles.

Nonetheless, the principal impression gained from figure 4.5 is of the similarity in relative skills from place to place and between each of the five city-regions and the nation as a whole. This rough resemblance in the relative skills of immigrants in each place has no parallel in relative

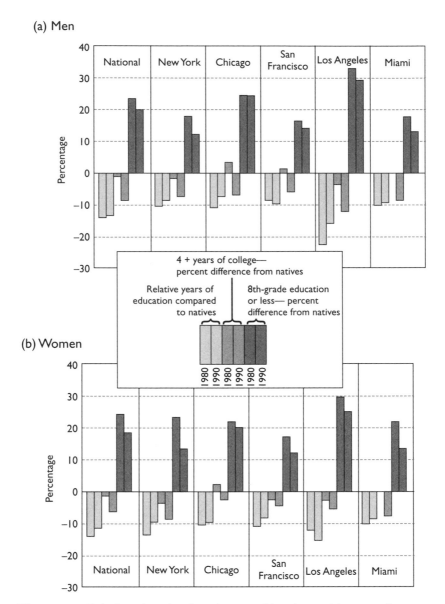

Figure 4.5.   Relative educational attainment of immigrant (a) men and
(b) women

wages: relative wages for immigrant men and women fall below the national level in each city region (figure 4.3). One can readily understand why relative wages are lower for immigrants in Los Angeles, where immigrants are less educated relative to natives than in the nation as a whole. But how is one to explain the situation in San Francisco, where the relative education levels of immigrants surpass the national norm but the wage gap separating foreign- from native-born San Franciscans greatly exceeds the comparable disparity that holds nationwide?

One possible explanation for this anomalous situation is the large supply of well-educated labor in the San Francisco region. Because 40 percent of native men and 36 percent of native women have at least four years of college education, employers in the region have a much richer pool of talent to draw on than do employers elsewhere. Those who live in San Francisco with less than these qualifications—a greater proportion of whom are immigrants than are natives—may find themselves unable to get good jobs even though they have better qualifications than immigrants elsewhere. At a national level there is less crowding of those with at least four years of college, so that immigrants and natives with a high school diploma or some years of college education can get better jobs and thus are farther from the bottom of the wage distribution. A similar but less extreme version of this process could be occurring in other city-regions where the relative educational attainment of immigrants is better than it is nationally but relative wages are worse.

A Multivariate Analysis of Changes in Native and Immigrant Income

The relative wages of immigrants are falling, an erosion correlated with a widening divide in the skill levels of natives and immigrants. Both generalizations hold at national and city-regional levels, with an occasional modification as noted previously.

As I have already pointed out, two likely factors emerge as explanations for these trends: one relates to changes in the personal characteristics of workers, both native- and foreign-born; the second relates to the wage structure—that is, shifts in the premiums paid to the high skilled and penalties levied against the low skilled. Clearly, these two changes are not mutually exclusive; given what we know about both immigrants and shifts in the labor market more generally, it is a safer bet to assume that both factors were in play during the period in question. If that is the case, then the situation of immigrant workers is even more parlous than suggested so far: not only have they fallen farther behind native workers than they were earlier, but they have done so at a time when the remuneration of low-skilled workers is under attack. Indeed, much of the research, conducted at the national level, suggests that changes in the wage structure explain most of the trend in relative immigrant wages.[29]

In this section I inquire into the relative importance of changes in personal characteristics, as opposed to changes in the wage structures, as factors affecting the relative wage of immigrants. I do so with a series of wage regressions, pooling the 1980 and 1990 samples from the Census Bureau Public Use Microdata Samples, running separate regressions for native- and foreign-born men and native- and foreign-born women, nationally and in each city-region. The models deployed involve log-wage regressions based on standard sets of independent variables.[30] Following this well-established procedure, I multiply all variables by a dummy variable, indicating whether the observation was drawn from the 1990 census. The resulting model yields estimated coefficients for 1980 and shifts, if any, in these coefficients between 1980 and 1990. Much of the discussion will focus on the results for these interactions. I have listed the coefficients for men in table 4.2 and those for women in table 4.3. I limit my discussion of the results to the most relevant variables, which are shaded for ease of viewing.

Education Effects

Comparison of the size of the coefficients for education *(years of education)* reveals that natives experienced a greater return on schooling than did immigrants, regardless of gender or location. But examination of the coefficients that multiply education by the 1990 census dummy *(years of education*90)* points to significant changes during the course of the decade. For native men, the return on education increased everywhere, as would be expected given employers' increasing premium on skills. In contrast, a look at the same coefficient reveals no such consistent pattern of increase for immigrant men. Immigrants received a slightly higher premium for education nationally and in Miami and San Francisco but not in Chicago or New York; the trend was reversed in Los Angeles. Just how to account for these results is not quite clear, but the literature immediately suggests one possibility: immigrant men in Chicago, New York, and particularly Los Angeles are disproportionately concentrated in industries in which natives are also underrepresented and where wages are likely to be low and employment either falling or stagnant.[31]

As for women, the premium for schooling increased everywhere but in Los Angeles, a region where native women's return on years of education grew but immigrant women's return remained unchanged. As with their male counterparts, immigrant women in Los Angeles appeared to be cut off from the trend toward an increased premium on skill. In this respect, foreign-born women in Los Angeles may simply be suffering from the consequences of their distinctive employment concentrations, as they are clustered in industries whose wage patterns and structural features severely restrict the potential for advancement.[32]

Duration of Residence Effects

Immigrants' earnings rise with time spent in the United States, as the foreign-born gain skills and experience relevant to the U.S. workplace. The regressions show that immigrant men and women earn more the longer they live in the United States, regardless of city-region. This effect of duration of residence, measured by a series of dummy variables for years spent in the United States *(6–10 years, 11–15 years, 16–20 years, 21 + years),* seems to be more pronounced in the city-regions under focus than it is nationally. The premium on length of residence appears to be particularly strong in Los Angeles.

But the effects of duration of residence changed during the 1980s in ways that affected both genders and in all locations. As can be seen by inspecting the coefficient interacting 6–10 years in the United States with the 1990 census dummy, a modest amount of time spent in the United States proved less beneficial in 1990 than it had 10 years before. Simply put, the wage gap between immigrants who arrived in the first and second halves of the 1980s (measured in 1990) was smaller than that between immigrants who arrived in the first and second halves of the 1970s (measured in 1980). In contrast, the wage differential between long-settled immigrants—those who have been in the United States for more than 20 years—and the most recent arrivals in each census grew over the decade (see the coefficients for *21 + years*90*). Thus those who came in the 1980s find themselves farther behind long-settled immigrants than did arrivals of the 1970s. This finding accords with what we know of trends in the economic progress of recent immigrants: those who have arrived recently are starting farther behind in their earnings than those who came just two decades ago.[33] Whether

TABLE 4.2. LOG-WAGE REGRESSIONS FOR NATIVE- AND FOREIGN-BORN MEN

	National		Chicago		Los Angeles		Miami		New York		San Francisco	
	NB	FB	NB	FB	NB	FB	NB	FB	NB	FB	NB	FB
Intercept	-1.15	1.36	1.59	1.55	1.26	1.52	1.23	1.58	1.13	1.40	1.39	1.57
Ethnoracial effects												
Black	-0.16	-0.22	-0.17	-0.08	-0.22	-0.24	-0.18	-0.24	-0.21	-0.20	-0.17	-0.17
Asian	0.03	-0.13	-0.10	-0.09	-0.04	-0.13	-0.17	-0.17	-0.05	-0.16	-0.05	-0.24
Other	-0.13	-0.21	-0.12	-0.33	-0.14	-0.20	-0.09	-0.47	-0.22	-0.27	-0.08	-0.21
Hispanic	-0.09	-0.21	-0.13	-0.15	-0.12	-0.25	-0.16	-0.16	-0.23	-0.20	-0.06	-0.21
Education effects												
Years of education	0.06	0.05	0.05	0.04	0.06	0.04	0.06	0.03	0.07	0.05	0.05	0.04
Work experience effects												
Experience	0.04	0.02	0.03	0.02	0.04	0.02	0.03	0.01	0.04	0.02	0.04	0.02
Experience squared	0.00	0.00	0.00	0.00	0.00	0.00	0.00	0.00	0.00	0.00	0.00	0.00
Language effects												
English very well		0.06		0.05		0.10		0.08		0.05		0.08
English well		0.01		0.05		0.07		-0.02		-0.05		0.05
Other personal characteristics												
Married	0.18	0.14	0.21	0.12	0.19	0.13	0.23	0.17	0.21	0.13	0.22	0.17
Disability	-0.17	-0.14	-0.15	-0.10	-0.17	-0.07	-0.15	-0.19	-0.16	-0.10	-0.14	-0.12
Duration of residence effects												
6–10 years		0.14		0.14		0.16		0.15		0.10		0.18
11–15 years		0.21		0.23		0.28		0.19		0.17		0.25
16–20 years		0.25		0.26		0.34		0.30		0.21		0.32
21+ years		0.25		0.30		0.37		0.29		0.25		0.32
1990	-0.33	-0.09	-0.47	-0.24	-0.13	0.09	-0.23	-0.20	0.07	0.08	-0.18	-0.05

Ethnoracial effects												
Black*90	0.00	**0.05**	**-0.06**	**-0.13**	0.01	0.01	-0.02	-0.03	-0.02	0.03	-0.02	-0.03
Asian*90	**0.06**	0.01	0.03	-0.04	0.03	-0.04	**0.09**	**0.06**	0.01	**-0.05**	0.02	0.04
Other*90	-0.02	-0.03	0.00	0.00	-0.04	-0.13	-0.01	-0.02	0.05	0.03	-0.04	-0.08
Hispanic*90	0.01	**-0.07**	-0.01	**-0.06**	-0.01	**-0.15**	-0.02	**-0.11**	-0.01	**-0.07**	**-0.05**	**-0.05**
Education effects												
Years of education*90	**0.02**	0.00	**0.02**	0.01	**0.01**	0.00	**0.02**	**0.01**	0.00	0.00	**0.02**	**0.01**
Work experience effects												
Experience*90	0.00	0.00	0.00	0.00	0.00	**-0.01**	0.00	0.00	0.00	**-0.01**	0.00	**-0.01**
Experience squared*90	0.00	0.00	0.00	0.00	0.00	0.00	0.00	0.00	0.00	0.00	0.00	0.00
Language effects												
English very well*90		0.03		0.01		0.03		0.05		0.01		0.02
English well*90		0.02		-0.04		0.06		0.06		0.03		-0.02
Other personal characteristics												
Married*90	-0.01	**0.03**	**0.04**	**0.07**	**0.03**	**0.06**	0.01	**0.04**	**0.03**	**0.08**	0.00	**0.04**
Disability*90	-0.01	0.02	**-0.05**	0.05	**-0.04**	**-0.08**	-0.05	**0.12**	0.00	0.05	-0.03	-0.05
Duration of residence effects												
6–10 years*90		**-0.07**		**-0.06**		**-0.05**		**-0.06**		**-0.05**		**-0.06**
11–15 years*90		**-0.03**		-0.02		-0.03		0.00		-0.01		0.02
16–20 years*90		-0.01		**0.07**		-0.01		**-0.05**		-0.02		0.01
21+ years*90		**0.03**		**0.11**		**0.08**		**0.06**		**0.04**		**0.09**
Adjusted r²	0.16	0.22	0.16	0.19	0.17	0.24	0.17	0.16	0.21	0.18	0.16	0.21

Note: **Bold** denotes significance at p < .05. NB, native-born; FB, foreign-born.

TABLE 4.3. LOG-WAGE REGRESSIONS FOR NATIVE- AND FOREIGN-BORN WOMEN

	National		Chicago		Los Angeles		Miami		New York		San Francisco	
	NB	FB	NB	FB	NB	FB	NB	FB	NB	FB	NB	FB
Intecept	0.96	1.45	1.23	1.55	1.12	1.53	1.01	1.60	1.15	1.46	1.31	1.64
Ethnoracial effects												
Black	0.03	0.04	0.08	0.06	0.00	-0.09	-0.01	-0.08	0.04	0.04	0.03	0.00
Asian	0.13	0.02	0.09	0.12	0.06	-0.01	0.10	-0.01	0.04	0.03	0.08	-0.06
Other	-0.02	-0.03	-0.04	0.12	-0.03	-0.11	0.16	-0.13	0.06	0.03	-0.02	-0.14
Hispanic	0.06	-0.08	0.10	-0.02	-0.01	-0.18	-0.05	-0.15	0.02	-0.12	-0.04	-0.06
Education effects												
Years of education	0.08	0.04	0.07	0.04	0.07	0.04	0.08	0.03	0.08	0.04	0.06	0.03
Work experience effects												
Experience	0.01	0.00	0.01	0.00	0.02	0.00	0.02	0.00	0.01	0.01	0.02	0.00
Experience squared	0.00	0.00	0.00	0.00	0.00	0.00	0.00	0.00	0.00	0.00	0.00	0.00
Language effects												
English very well		0.07		0.03		0.06		0.14		0.08		0.06
English well		0.00		0.00		0.01		0.03		0.00		0.02
Other personal characteristics												
Married	-0.03	-0.01	-0.04	0.00	-0.02	0.01	0.00	0.03	-0.04	-0.03	-0.02	0.03
Disability	-0.14	-0.08	-0.14	-0.15	-0.14	-0.09	-0.05	-0.10	-0.15	-0.04	-0.10	-0.06
Fertility	-0.03	-0.02	-0.04	-0.01	-0.04	-0.01	-0.03	-0.01	-0.05	-0.02	-0.03	0.00
Duration of residence effects												
6–10 years		0.12		0.20		0.13		0.12		0.12		0.17
11–15 years		0.18		0.26		0.23		0.12		0.20		0.22
16–20 years		0.16		0.25		0.22		0.22		0.20		0.28
21+ years		0.17		0.27		0.24		0.17		0.21		0.27
1990	-0.30	-0.19	-0.29	-0.35	-0.07	0.02	-0.12	-0.29	-0.06	-0.09	-0.08	-0.20

	(1)	(2)	(3)	(4)	(5)	(6)	(7)	(8)	(9)	(10)	(11)	(12)
Ethnoracial effects												
Black*90	-0.02	0.05	-0.05	**-0.11**	-0.03	0.05	-0.05	**0.06**	-0.02	0.04	**-0.06**	**-0.12**
Asian*90	0.05	0.01	0.01	0.01	0.00	-0.03	**-0.06**	0.05	0.02	-0.05	-0.01	-0.01
Other*90	-0.03	-0.02	-0.03	**-0.39**	-0.05	**-0.13**	-0.03	0.07	**-0.12**	**-0.11**	**-0.08**	0.03
Hispan*90	-0.01	-0.05	**-0.11**	-0.07	-0.03	**-0.11**	-0.02	-0.04	-0.07	-0.03	-0.05	**-0.13**
Education effects												
Years of education*90	**0.02**	**0.01**	**0.02**	**0.01**	**0.01**	0.00	**0.01**	**0.01**	**0.01**	**0.01**	**0.01**	**0.01**
Work experience effects												
Experience*90	0.00	0.00	0.01	0.00	0.00	0.00	0.00	0.00	0.00	-0.01	0.00	0.00
Experience squared*90	0.00	0.00	0.00	0.00	0.00	0.00	0.00	0.00	0.00	0.00	0.00	0.00
Language effects												
English very well=90	0.02	0.02		0.02		**0.07**		**0.06**		0.01		**0.03**
English well=90	0.00	0.00		-0.03		0.00		**0.04**		0.01		0.01
Other personal characteristics												
Married*90	0.01	0.02	**0.03**	0.02	**0.04**	**0.04**	**0.03**	0.00	**0.03**	**0.04**	**0.03**	0.00
Disability*90	0.01	0.01	0.00	**0.07**	-0.01	0.01	**-0.08**	**0.06**	0.02	0.00	**-0.07**	-0.03
Fertility*90	-0.02	-0.01	-0.01	0.00	-0.01	-0.01	0.00	-0.01	0.00	-0.01	-0.01	-0.01
Duration of residence effects												
6–10 years*90	-0.02	-0.02	**0.05**	**0.05**	-0.02	-0.02	-0.02	-0.02		-0.03	-0.03	0.01
11–15 years*90	**0.04**	**0.04**	**0.14**	**0.14**	0.02	0.02	**0.11**	**0.11**		0.00	0.00	**0.12**
16–20 years*90	**0.11**	**0.11**	**0.22**	**0.22**	0.02	**0.10**	0.02	0.02		**0.08**	**0.08**	**0.12**
21+ years*90	**0.11**	**0.11**	**0.23**	**0.23**	**0.17**	**0.16**	**0.17**	**0.17**		**0.10**	**0.10**	**0.16**
Adjusted r²	0.13	0.13	0.10	0.13	0.11	0.20	0.12	0.15	0.15	0.15	0.10	0.14

Note: **Bold** denotes significance at p < .05. NB, native-born; FB, foreign-born.

they will ever catch up is difficult to assess from these estimates because the models do not control for cohort effects.[34] Nevertheless, at the very least, the results suggest that the most recent arrivals face a more daunting economic challenge than those who came but 10 years before them.

English-Language Effects

As with time spent in the United States, facility in English tends to improve earnings. The census asked those respondents who spoke a language other than English to rate their facility in English, according to one of four categories—very well, well, not well, and not at all. I omitted the latter two categories so that the coefficients for the effects of speaking English either well or very well are relative to those who speak it poorly or not at all. Speaking English very well yields the expected outcomes in all locations for immigrant men and women, except in Chicago, where it has no significant effect on wages. Language ability became more important during the 1980s in Los Angeles for men and women and in Miami for women.

Ethnoracial Effects

The four mutually exclusive ethnoracial categories of white, black, Hispanic, and Asian do not identify groups as such but serve to designate populations that are likely to be treated in different ways by both employers and coworkers. Consequently, I seek to assess both the effects associated with any particular category and the changes in those effects. Because these effects vary widely across cities and are different for men and women and for natives and immigrants, I draw out only the most essential patterns and trends.

In general, with all other things equal, white men, whether native- or foreign-born, tend to earn higher wages than men in other groups. Native-born Asian men are the only exception to this rule; they make more per hour than native white men, but only when compared at a national level. Among natives, the largest negative effects are associated with black men, a pattern that shows up at the national level and in all of the five city-regions except New York. Foreign-born black men vie with foreign-born Hispanics for the largest negative effect among immigrants. Immigrant Asian men generally do better than black or Hispanic male immigrants, except in San Francisco, where their hourly wage is worse, all other things being equal.

Although some groups of men improved their wages relative to whites during the 1980s and others did worse, depending on location, two points deserve particular mention. First, the hourly wages of native black men held steady in relation to native white men everywhere except Chicago, where they fell. Second, immigrant Hispanic men did worse everywhere, especially in Miami and Los Angeles.

Group effects for women show a markedly different pattern. All other things being equal, black, Hispanic, and Asian native-born women had higher hourly wages in 1980 than did white women. Similarly, black and Asian immigrant women earned more per hour in 1980 than did immigrant white women. Immigrant Hispanic women's wages, however, were lower than those of foreign-born white women, and this gap was largest in Los Angeles, Miami, and New York. The 1980s saw native black and Hispanic women's advantage slide relative to native white women, particularly in Chicago and New York. Foreign-born Hispanic women's wages increased in most places, but especially in Los Angeles and San Francisco.

Unraveling the Causes of the Declining Immigrant Relative Wage

The coefficients in tables 4.2 and 4.3 show that the wage structure changed in the 1980s in ways that favored workers with skills, though not all comparably skilled workers were positively affected by this shift. Most important, native-born workers saw the return to education increase, but immigrants experienced little positive change. Thus the declining relative wage for immigrants may derive from changes in the wage structure, which simultaneously improved the rewards for skilled workers but also did so in ways that principally worked to the benefit of those skilled workers who happened to have been born in the United States.

Alternatively, the source of change may lie in differences in the rate at which native and immigrant workers have upgraded their skills. From this point of view, the wages of native workers have pulled ahead of the wages of immigrants, because natives have also pulled ahead in terms of schooling; change in the rate at which those with more education are paid was a factor of little importance. In other words, relative wage decline derives from decline in immigrant quality, either absolute or relative, rather than from changes in the wage structure.

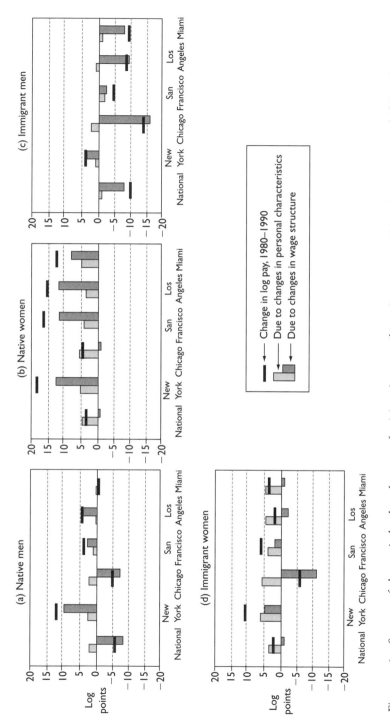

Figure 4.6. Sources of change in log hourly wages for (a) native men, (b) native women, (c) immigrant men, and (d) immigrant women

Note: These are log points multiplied by 100, which are approximately equivalent to percentages.

To assess these two alternatives, I have carried out a standard decomposition of the log-wage regressions reported previously, apportioning changes in the wages of immigrants and natives either to shifts in the wage structure or to individual characteristics.[35] In essence, the procedure involves two statistical experiments: first, asking what would have happened to the wages of immigrants and natives if the wage structure had not changed over the 1980s (i.e., workers received the same premium on skill in 1990 as in 1980), and, second, asking what would have happened to both groups' wages in 1990 had their personal characteristics remained the same as in 1980. I conducted these decompositions for all five city-regions and for the United States; the results are summarized in figure 4.6.

Men

In general, men's pay in the 1980s was influenced more by changes in the wage structure than by shifts in characteristics, but the relative strength and direction of the two effects varied between natives and immigrants and across city-regions. Nationally, shifts in the wage structure had an approximately equal negative effect on native and immigrant men. Whereas native men's skill characteristics improved, those of immigrants worsened; consequently, the decline in native men's pay slowed at the same time as the decline in immigrant men's pay accelerated.

The causes of wage change take a different form in each city-region, and variations distinguish one place from another and from the nation overall. In Chicago the characteristics of native and immigrant men improved by similar amounts between 1980 and 1990, but Chicago's wage structure grew spectacularly more unfavorable for immigrant men than for natives; in that city-region, then, all of the difference between the two groups in wage decline was due to changes in the wage structure. Miami resembled Chicago in that both native and immigrant men's wages fell during the 1980s (although the former fell only slightly), but the underlying cause of that change stemmed from a different source. The attributes of native men remained unchanged and the wage structure they faced was stable. However, the wage-earning characteristics of immigrant men in Miami declined, and, most important, they confronted a much more negative wage structure in 1990 than they had a decade earlier.

Los Angeles and San Francisco exhibited similar wage trends in the 1980s: native men's wages grew while immigrant men's wages fell. The wage trends in Los Angeles were caused largely by changes in the wage structure rather than changes in personal characteristics. Thus while native and immigrant men's attributes remained constant between 1980 and 1990 the wage structure improved for the former but worsened for the latter. Unlike the situation in Los Angeles, San Francisco's wage changes were more of an equal function of changes in worker characteristics and wage structures. Changes in worker attributes and wage structure together positively influenced wages for natives in San Francisco but negatively influenced those for immigrants.

Only in New York did changes in both the characteristics of workers and the local wage structure prove beneficial for both native and immigrant men. The wage structure accounted for most of the improvement in the wages of both groups, although it exercised a considerably stronger effect on the wages of natives. Likewise, the positive impact of change in characteristics did more to boost the earnings of native than of immigrant workers.

Women

Compared to men, changes in personal characteristics yielded a larger effect on women's wage trends, although shifts in wage structure were still responsible for much of women's wage increase—particularly for the native-born. At a national level, native- and foreign-born women both enjoyed wage increases in the 1980s as a result of shifts in their personal characteristics. Changes in the wage structure were nominally negative for native women and a little more negative for immigrant women. Consequently, native women's wages outgrew those of the foreign-born, but not by much.

In each city-region the changes in native and immigrant women's personal characteristics were approximately equal in their positive effect on wages. Although the magnitude of the effects of personal characteristics varied across city-regions (largest in New York and smallest in Los Angeles), the essential point is that native and immigrant women's wage growth during the 1980s would have been similar in each city-region had the wage structure remained the same as in 1980. In all five city-regions, however, native women's wage change outstripped that of immigrant women because the wage structure encountered by the former became either more positive or less negative by 1990 than it did for immigrants. For instance, in Chicago, the wage structure for native women in 1990 was similar to that in 1980, but for immigrant women it was much worse by 1990 than it had been a decade earlier. In the other four city-regions the change in wage structure during the 1980s positively affected native women's wages, with New York's native women enjoying the most improvement from this effect. But immigrant women's wage structure deteriorated in two of the city-regions, Los Angeles and Miami, and the improvement in wage structure for immigrant women was much less than that for native women in the other two city-regions, San Francisco and New York.

Changes in Wage Structure and the Deterioration of Relative Wages

The clearest way to see the significant effect of differential changes in wage structure on the widening wage gap between immigrants and natives is to calculate predicted relative wages in 1990 using the characteristics of workers in 1990 but the wage structure in 1980.[36] The results of this exercise are shown in figure 4.7.

For immigrant men, using the 1980 wage structure marginally slows the decline in relative wages in the United States as a whole. Thus change in wage structure is not responsible for the majority of the decline in immigrant men's relative wages when measured nationally. Presumably, most of the national decline in relative wages stems from changes in the characteristics of immigrants and natives. The situation is much different in four of the five immigrant city-regions—New York, Chicago, San Francisco, and Los Angeles—where almost all of the drop in immigrant men's relative wages is explained by shifts in the local wage structure. In other words, in these four city-regions immigrant men's relative wages would have been almost identical in 1980 and 1990 if the wage structure had stayed the same. Miami is an exception; application of the 1980 wage structure removes only half of the decline in immigrant men's relative wages. Changes in individual characteristics play a larger role there than in the other four city-regions.

Application of 1980 coefficients yields a similar effect on change in the relative wages of immigrant women, with one major exception: the distinction between the nation and the city-regions disappears. Wage structure accounts for almost all of the decline in immigrant women's relative wages nationally and in all five city-regions.

Together these results suggest two important conclusions. First, changes in wage structure and not shifts in the characteristics of immigrant or native workers largely account for the declining relative wages of immigrant men and women. In fact, change in the personal charac-

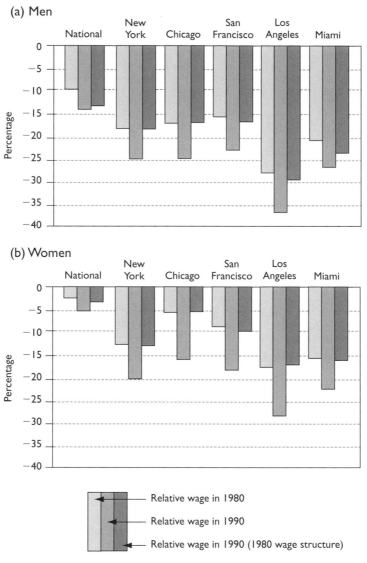

Figure 4.7. The effect of changes in wage structure on relative wages for immigrant (a) men and (b) women

teristics of immigrants between 1980 and 1990 had generally positive effects on immigrant wage change, especially among women. Second, focusing on the city-regions in which immigrants live rather than the nation as a whole more clearly demonstrates the negative impact of the change in wage structure, particularly for men. Analysis at a national level obscures the effects of wage structure for men, and thus interpretations of the decline in relative wage get deflected to other causes, especially immigrant quality.

Conclusions

In this chapter, I have sought to compare trends in the wages of immigrants and natives across the major centers of immigrant settlement. As such, the chapter stands in contrast to the bulk of analysis that compares the wage performance of immigrants and natives at a national level. As I argued at the outset, focusing on the key immigrant destinations produces comparisons of natives and immigrants in the regions in which immigrants actually live and work. By contrast, national-level comparisons include natives who live in areas far from the regions of immigrant concentration. Although the statistical analyses typically control for region, they do so without controlling for the possibility that wage structures might also vary from place to place; nor do they control for the possibility that the pattern of change in wage structures may differ across regions.

The empirical evidence presented here lends considerable support to the idea that the economic position of immigrants and the forces changing that position over time look different when measured in the city-regions in which immigrants live rather than in the United States as a whole. Such a regional perspective matters because most U.S. immigrants live in the five city-regions under analysis in this chapter. In two of these immigrant destinations, New York and Los Angeles, the wages of native men and women were considerably higher than they were in the rest of the country in 1980. Moreover, the wages of native men and women grew in these cities during the 1980s but declined for men or grew relatively slowly for women in the United States as a whole. In contrast, immigrant wages in New York and Los Angeles were not markedly different from immigrant wages elsewhere in the United States in 1980. Moreover, the wages of immigrants in New York and Los Angeles either grew more slowly than those of natives or actually declined during the 1980s, mirroring more closely the performance of immigrants nationally than natives in the same city-region. Simply put, many immigrants live in places in which natives have access to jobs at above the national average wage but they themselves work at wage rates comparable to those of immigrants nationally. And although the economic fortunes of natives in New York and Los Angeles improved considerably over the decade reviewed, little if any of this good fortune filtered down to immigrants. Thus a comparison of wages in the two most significant centers of immigrant settlement actually paints a bleaker picture of the widening economic gulf between immigrants and natives than does a national comparison.

The description of the situations in New York and Los Angeles also applies in San Francisco. But in the other two city-regions—Chicago and Miami—the wage pattern is different. To be sure, relative wages for immigrant men and women in Chicago and Miami are lower than they are nationally, much as they are in the other three immigrant centers. And, as in New York, Los Angeles, and San Francisco, immigrants' relative wages fell in the 1980s. But what distinguishes Miami and Chicago, at least for immigrant men, is that the relative wages of immigrant men fell in the context of declining rather than rising wages for natives. Chicago is also distinctive because it is the only city-region in which immigrant women's hourly wage fell between 1980 and 1990.

Thus the decline in immigrant relative wages in some city-regions is underpinned by the same wage trends seen nationally, but in others the widening gap between wages for immigrants and natives is the result of regional wage trends at odds with national wage trends. However, an analysis of the causes of change in immigrants' and natives' wages reveals a broad similarity among all five city-regions and draws a sharp contrast between them and the nation as a whole. The first clues come from standardizing ethnoracial composition to its 1980 mix in each location. At a national level change in ethnoracial composition explains almost all of the decline in immigrant men's relative wage in the 1980s and a large portion of the decline for immigrant women. In contrast, shifts in ethnoracial composition account for a much smaller portion of the decline in relative wages in most of the city-regions.

The regression models and decomposition analysis help explain why ethnoracial compositional change accounts for relatively little of the deterioration of immigrant relative wages in the city-regions. The national models indicate that most of the increasing wage gap between natives and immigrants results from growing differences in their personal characteristics, including their ethnoracial mix and skills. Shifts in native and immigrant wage structure account for little of the decline in national immigrant relative wages, especially for men.

The city-region models point to substantially different reasons for declining immigrant relative wages: the wage structure for natives generally improved, whereas that for immigrants worsened or changed very little. In a nutshell, had the wage structures of each city-region remained the same in 1990 as they were in 1980, relative wages would not have decreased. Instead, the labor markets of the places in which immigrants settle became more disadvantageous for immigrants, particularly for immigrant men; simultaneously, conditions in these same labor markets became more advantageous for natives. Even though each city-region witnessed improvements in immigrant skills between 1980 and 1990, the labor markets of these places make it more difficult than ever for the foreign-born to translate what increased skills they now possess into decent wages.

Thus the spatial scale of analysis fundamentally affects conclusions about the causes of the decline in immigrant relative wages. A national analysis draws attention to the role of immigrant characteristics. In contrast, analysis of the city-regions emphasizes differential change in wage structures, implying that native and immigrant labor work in dual labor markets and that the lines of segmentation hardened in the 1980s.

Notes

1. G. J. Borjas, "Assimilation and Changes in Cohort Quality Revisited: What Happened to Immigrant Earnings in the 1980s?" *American Economic Review* 77 (1995): 531–553; J. P. Smith and B. Edmonston, eds., *The New Americans: Economic, Demographic, and Fiscal Impacts of Immigration* (Washington, D.C.: National Academy Press, 1997).

2. G. J. Borjas, "Assimilation, Changes in Cohort Quality, and the Earnings of Immigrants," *Journal of Labor Economics* 3 (1985): 463–489; G. J. Borjas, "The Economics of Immigration," *Journal of Economic Literature* 32 (1994): 1667–1717; B. R. Chiswick, "The Effect of Americanization on the Earnings of Foreign-Born Men," *Journal of Political Economy* 86 (1978): 897–921.

3. These are approximately equivalent in area to consolidated metropolitan areas, as defined by the U.S. Bureau of the Census in June 1990.

4. A. Portes and R. Bach, *Latin Journey: Cuban and Mexican Immigrants in the United States* (Berkeley and Los Angeles: University of California Press, 1985).

5. A. Portes and R. Rumbaut, *Immigrant America: A Portrait,* 2d ed. (Berkeley and Los Angeles: University of California Press, 1996).

6. C. Tilly, "The Weight of the Past on North American Immigration" (Research paper no. 189, University of Toronto, Centre for Urban and Community Studies, Toronto, 1994).

7. J. G. Reitz, *The Warmth of the Welcome: The Social Causes of Economic Success for Immigrants in Different Nations and Cities* (Boulder, Colo.: Westview, 1998).

8. Job growth varied considerably among the five cities in the 1980s. The Chicago city-region added 7 percent more jobs overall, but its employment in manufacturing fell by 23 percent (almost 250,000 jobs). Similarly, New York's total employment grew by 13 percent, but it also lost 23 percent of its manufacturing jobs (400,000 jobs). San Francisco's employment growth was a more solid 24 percent, and its number of manufacturing jobs also increased by 5 percent. Miami and Los Angeles had the most spectacular total job growth of 39 and 37 percent, respectively, and both saw their manufacturing employment base increase by more than 8 percent. Thus manufacturing's percentage share of employment fell at different rates in each city-region, and the regional balance of manufacturing jobs shifted from New York and Chicago to Los Angeles. Consequently, by 1990 Los Angeles led the nation in manufacturing employment (1,437,403 jobs compared to 1,327,240 in New York, 801,900 in Chicago, 587,758 in San Francisco, and 169,703 in Miami). *Source:* 1980 and 1990 Public Use Microdata Samples, U.S. Bureau of the Census, Washington, D.C.

9. R. F. Schoeni, "Labor Market Outcomes of Immigrant Women in the United States: 1970 to 1990," *International Migration Review* 32 (1998): 57–77.

10. K. F. Butcher and J. DiNardo, "The Immigrant and Native-Born Wage Distributions: Evidence from United States Censuses" (Working paper 6630, National Bureau for Economic Research, Cambridge, Mass., 1998); W. A. V. Clark, *The California Cauldron* (New York: Guilford, 1998); H. O. Duleep and S. Sanders, "The Decision to Work by Married Immigrant Women," *Industrial and Labor Relations Review* 46 (1993): 67–80; J. E. Long, "The Effect of Americanization on Earnings: Some Evidence for Women," *Journal of Political Economy* 88 (1980): 620–629; R. F. Schoeni, "Labor Market Assimilation of Immigrant Women," *Industrial and Labor Relations Review* 51 (1998): 483–504.

11. L. A. Karoly, "The Trend in Inequality among Families, Individuals, and Workers in the United States: A Twenty-Five Year Perspective," in *Uneven Tides: Rising Inequality in America,* ed. S. Danziger and P. Gottshalk (New York: Russell Sage Foundation, 1993), 19–97.

12. G. Burtless, "Earnings Inequality over the Business and Demographic Cycles," in *A Future of Lousy Jobs? The Changing Structure of US Wages,* ed. G. Burtless (Washington, D.C.: Brookings Institution, 1990), 77–117; L. A. Karoly, "Trend in Inequality"; F. Levy, *Dollars and Dreams: The Changing American Income Distribution* (New York: W. W. Norton, 1988); P. Ryscavage and P. Henle, "Earnings Inequality in the 1980s," *Monthly Labor Review* 113 (December 1990): 3–16.

13. M. L. Blackburn, D. E. Bloom, and R. B. Freeman, "The Declining Economic Position of Less Skilled American Men," in *A Future of Lousy Jobs? The Changing Structure of US Wages,* ed. G. Burtless (Washington, D.C.: Brookings Institution, 1990), 31–67; C. Jun, K. M. Murphy, and B. Pierce, "Wage In-

equality and the Rise in Returns to Skill," *Journal of Political Economy* 101 (1993): 411–442; K. M. Murphy and F. Welch, "Industrial Change and the Rising Importance of Skill," in *Uneven Tides: Rising Inequality in America*, ed. S. Danziger and P. Gottshalk (New York: Russell Sage Foundation, 1993), 101–132.

14. R. B. Freeman, "How Much Has De-unionization Contributed to the Rise in Male Earnings Inequality?" in *Uneven Tides: Rising Inequality in America*, ed. S. Danziger and P. Gottshalk (New York: Russell Sage Foundation, 1993), 133–163.

15. B. Harrison and B. Bluestone, *The Great U-Turn: Corporate Restructuring and the Polarizing of America* (New York: Basic Books, 1988); S. Sassen, *The Global City: New York, London, Tokyo* (Princeton, N.J.: Princeton University Press, 1991).

16. Borjas, "Economics of Immigration"; R. M. Friedberg and J. Hunt, "The Impact of Immigrants on Host Country Wages, Employment, and Growth," *Journal of Economic Perspectives* 9 (1995): 23–44. Most analyses of interactions between immigrant and native wages use cross sections of metropolitan areas to estimate competition effects. This method may understate the immigrant impact on native wages if natives respond by migrating, either through increased out-migration from or reduced in-migration to regions of immigrant concentration. The evidence for such a migration response is mixed (compare W. Frey, "Immigration and Internal Migration 'Flight' from US Metropolitan Areas: Towards a New Demographic Balkanization," *Urban Studies* 32 [1995]: 733–757, and R. Wright, M. Ellis, and M. Reibel, "The Linkage between Immigration and Internal Migration in Large Metropolitan Areas in the United States," *Economic Geography* 73 [1997]: 234–254). To help avoid these problems alternative methods either focus on different spatial scales (states and census regions) to minimize the migration effect (G. J. Borjas, R. Freeman, and L. F. Katz, "Searching for the Effect of Immigration on the Labor Market," *American Economic Review* 86 [1996]: 246–251) or take a national approach using what is called the factor proportions method (G. J. Borjas, R. Freeman, and L. F. Katz, "On the Labor Market Effects of Immigration and Trade," in *Immigration and the Work Force*, ed. G. J. Borjas and R. Freeman [Chicago: University of Chicago Press, 1992]; G. J. Borjas, R. Freeman, and L. F. Katz, "How Much Do Immigration and Trade Affect Labor Market Outcomes?" *Brookings Papers on Economic Activity* 1 [1997]: 1–90). These studies find larger immigration impacts on the wages of competing groups (a 5 percent reduction in the wages of high school dropouts) than do the cross-sectional approaches.

17. M. L. Blackburn, D. E. Bloom, and R. B. Freeman, "The Declining Economic Position of Less Skilled American Men," in *A Future of Lousy Jobs? The Changing Structure of US Wages*, ed. G. Burtless (Washington, D.C.: Brookings Institution, 1990), 31–67.

18. Smith and Edmonston, *New Americans*.

19. Ibid.

20. The wage data used throughout this chapter come from the 1980 and 1990 Public Use Microdata Samples (PUMS) (U.S. Bureau of the Census,

Washington, D.C.) but are measured for the year before each census—1979 and 1989. I refer to them by census year throughout the chapter. The wage data are restricted to those who have wage and salary income and are between the ages of 25 and 64, do not live in group quarters, and are not self-employed. The means displayed in figures 4.1 and 4.2 are the antilogs of the mean of log hourly wages. As such, they are equivalent to geometric means.

21. S. Sassen, *The Mobility of Labor and Capital: A Study in International Investment and Labor Flow* (New York: Cambridge University Press, 1988); R. Wright and M. Ellis, "Nativity, Ethnicity, and the Evolution of the Intra-urban Division of Labor in Los Angeles," *Urban Geography* 18 (1997): 243–263; R. Waldinger, "Black/Immigrant Competition Re-assessed: New Evidence from Los Angeles," *Sociological Perspectives* 40, no. 3 (1997): 365–386.

22. The wages of foreign-born black men declined in San Francisco, but this population is a very small percentage of San Francisco's total foreign-born population.

23. Thus, the differences between men's and women's wage trends observed here accord with the findings of Butcher and DiNardo, whose analysis showed that the wage differentials separating native- and foreign-born women were smaller than those distinguishing their counterparts among men. See Butcher and DiNardo, "Immigrant and Native-Born Wage Distributions."

24. The only anomaly is native-born Asian women, whose wages declined rapidly in the 1980s. The Asian population of Miami is small, so this trend should be treated with caution because it may reflect sample-size problems as much as the changing economic fortunes of this group.

25. However, this particular categorization obscures intracategorical differences (such that Dominicans who head to New York and Mexicans who converge on Los Angeles both appear under the Hispanic rubric).

26. The adjusted immigrant wage in each city-region is calculated using the following formula: $\overline{W}_{sr} = \Sigma q_{is} w_{isr}$, where $\overline{W}_{sr}$ is the mean wage of immigrants of sex s in city-region r, q_{is} is the probability an immigrant worker is of sex s in ethnoracial group i nationally, and w_{isr} is the mean wage of those immigrants in city-region r. Standardized relative wages are calculated using this adjusted immigrant wage.

27. This finding accords with the National Research Council reports, which noted that the relative wage of immigrant men and women would hardly have changed between 1970 and 1990 if the national-origin mix of immigrants in 1990 replicated that in 1970. Smith and Edmonston, *New Americans*.

28. Ibid.; G. J. Borjas, *Friends or Strangers? The Impact of Immigrants on the US Economy* (New York: Basic Books, 1990).

29. Butcher and DiNardo, "Immigrant and Native-Born Wage Distributions"; E. Sorensen and M. E. Enchautegui, "Immigrant Male Earnings in the 1980s: Divergent Patterns by Race and Ethnicity," in *Immigration and Ethnicity: The Integration of America's Newest Arrivals*, ed. B. Edmonston and J. Passel (Washington, D.C.: Urban Institute, 1994), 139–161.

30. For natives these include years of education, experience (age minus years of education minus 5) and experience squared, fertility or number of chil-

dren ever born (women only), two dummy variables for marital status (married = 1) and disability status (disabled = 1), and four dummy variables for ethno-racial group (white is the reference category). Immigrants have these same variables plus four dummy variables for duration of U.S. residence (6–10 years, 11–15 years, 16–20 years, and 21 or more years); under 5 years is the reference category. Immigrants also have two dummies for language ability that equal 1 if the immigrant speaks English well or very well.

The PUMS variable for years of education is different in 1990 than in 1980. The following transformations were applied to the 1990 data: grades 1–4 = 4 years of education, grades 5–8 = 8, 12th grade no diploma = 12, high school diploma = 12, some college = 13, associate degree = 14, bachelor's degree = 16, master's degree = 18, professional or doctoral degree = 22. The 1980 variable for years of education records years of education directly.

The models follow the procedure developed in Sorensen and Enchautegui, "Immigrant Male Earnings in the 1980s."

31. M. Ellis and R. Wright, "The Industrial Division of Labor among Immigrants and Internal Migrants to the Los Angeles Economy," *International Migration Review* 33 (1999): 26–54; R. Wright and M. Ellis, "Immigrants and the Changing Racial/Ethnic Division of Labor in New York City, 1970–90," *Urban Geography* 17 (1996): 317–353; Wright and Ellis, "Nativity, Ethnicity, and Evolution."

32. R. Wright and M. Ellis, "The Ethnic and Gender Division of Labor Compared among Immigrants to Los Angeles," *International Journal of Urban and Regional Research* 24, no. 3 (2000): 583–601.

33. Borjas, "Assimilation and Changes in Cohort Quality Revisited"; Smith and Edmonston, *New Americans*.

34. The measurement of economic assimilation has been the subject of methodological disagreement—most notably between Chiswick and Borjas. Chiswick examined the earnings of immigrants by duration of residence using a sample measured at a single point in time. He concluded that immigrants will catch up with natives (Chiswick, "Effect of Americanization"). Borjas claimed the labor market experience of long-settled immigrants is a poor guide to the economic fortunes of more recent arrivals because of declines in the relative skills of immigrants in recent decades. He traced the earnings of arrival cohorts (groups of immigrants who arrive at the same time) over multiple censuses and reached the conclusion that recent immigrants are unlikely to reach economic parity with natives (Borjas, "Assimilation, Changes in Cohort Quality, and Earnings").

35. The apportionment of change in immigrant and native wages to either shifts in the wage structure or to changes in individual characteristics is a matter of first estimating separate log-wage regressions for 1980 and 1990, using the variables listed in tables 4.2 and 4.3, for each city-region and nationally. Then the coefficients and variables from these models are input into an Oaxaca-Blinder decomposition (R. Oaxaca, "Male-Female Wage Differentials in Urban Labor Markets," *International Economic Review* 14 [1973]: 693–709; A. S. Blinder, "Wage Discrimination: Reduced Form and Structural

Variables," *Journal of Human Resources* 8 [1973]: 436–455) of the following form:

$$\overline{\ln w}_{90ijk} - \overline{\ln w}_{80ijk} = \beta_{80ijk} (\overline{X}_{90ijk} - \overline{X}_{80ijk}) + \overline{X}_{90ijk} (\beta_{90ijk} - \beta_{80ijk}),$$

where $\overline{\ln w}_{90ijk}$ and $\overline{\ln w}_{80ijk}$ are the mean log hourly wage in 1990 and 1980, respectively, for nativity group i (native or foreign-born), sex j, and region k; $\overline{X}_{90ijk}$ and $\overline{X}_{80ijk}$ are the means of the vectors of independent variables in 1990 and 1980; and β_{90ijk} and β_{80ijk} are the estimated coefficients for 1990 and 1980. The first component, $\beta_{80ijk} (\overline{X}_{90ijk} - \overline{X}_{80ijk})$, measures changes in log wages due to changes in personal characteristics. The second component, $\overline{X}_{90ijk} (\beta_{90ijk} - \beta_{80ijk})$, measures changes due to shifts in the wage structure.

It is possible to decompose the regression results using the 1990 coefficients and 1980 mean values as weights instead, as do Sorensen and Enchautegui (in "Immigrant Male Earnings in the 1980s"). However, as Butcher and DiNardo (in "Immigrant and Native-Born Wage Distributions") argue, it seems more intuitive to ask the question what would have happened to the wage gap between natives and immigrants if the wage structure had been stable between 1980 and 1990. Regardless, using either set of weights does not change the decomposition results noticeably.

36. This involves calculating 1990 wages using 1990 characteristics and 1980 regression coefficients. That is: $\ln w_{90ijk} = \beta_{80ijk} X_{90ijk}$.

Chapter 5

THE GEOGRAPHY OF IMMIGRANT POVERTY
Selective Evidence of an Immigrant Underclass

William A. V. Clark

While some immigrant households are experiencing severe hunger as the federally mandated cuts in food stamps go into effect, others celebrate their successful entry into the labor market.[1] At one extreme, California Food Policy Advocates reported that 50 percent of the households in which at least one member lost food stamps in Los Angeles County were experiencing hunger and that the hunger rate in Los Angeles County was four times higher than that in the United States as a whole.[2] At the other extreme, a substantial number of immigrant households in the high-technology centers of Silicon Valley have incomes much greater than the California average.[3]

The emergence of an immigrant poverty population, often dependent on food stamps, at the same time that other immigrants are moving up the ladder of success only serves to underscore a bifurcation in the foreign-born population that mimics that of the society as a whole. Chapter 3 demonstrated that although new immigrants are securing employment, too many of them are finding jobs that pay very low wages, a problem compounded when there is only one member of the household bringing home a paycheck. These immigrant families, living at low incomes and headed by persons with little schooling, will likely have great difficulty in escaping poverty and moving up in what we think of as the traditional immigrant trajectory. The analysis of poverty in this chapter reveals that, when immigrant origin and immigrant gender are taken into account, some groups are already falling into serious poverty, with long-range implications for the success of their children and the generations to follow.

In the past, the debate about poverty and its implications focused primarily on African American households. A large body of literature has examined the extent to which inner-city poverty for black households was creating an "underclass" of poor and dysfunctional black families. The explanations for the emergence of a black underclass involved a triplicate of arguments about the disconnection between black residential locations and black jobs (the spatial-mismatch hypothesis), the culture of poverty, and the inability of black households to generate the human capital to move into the economic mainstream. The last argument, we will see, is relevant for the future of the immigrant poverty population as well.

Now the debate about skills and poverty has been enlarged to include other minorities and rural as well as urban communities. Metropolitan areas are not the only communities showing evidence of increasing poverty populations; new research suggests that rural communities in California have levels of deprivation similar to those of the crowded inner-city communities of large metropolitan areas.[4] Overall, the immigrant community now accounts for a significant proportion of the poverty population in many states, and much of the increase in Aid to Families with Dependent Children (AFDC; now Temporary Assistance to Needy Families [TANF]) is occurring in the immigrant community. While most states experienced a decline in AFDC outlays between 1980 and 1990, California, Texas, and Florida witnessed a substantial increase in AFDC payments. Between 1980 and 1990 these three states accounted for almost all of the increase in AFDC families.[5] California alone accounted for half of the increase in AFDC households.

Although some immigrant households are increasing their incomes and moving ahead in their new society, many, especially those from Mexico and Southeast Asia, are falling behind the native-born population.[6] While immigrants who arrived between 1965 and 1970 earned about 17 percent less than the native-born, by 1990 immigrants who had arrived in the previous five years earned about 32 percent less. The average hourly piece rates for U.S. agricultural workers declined from $8.41 in 1989 to $7.24 in 1995. The wages were even lower in 1993 but made a modest recovery.[7] Not surprisingly, the percentage of immigrant households in poverty in the United States increased from 18.8 percent in 1970 to about 25 percent in 1990.[8]

The increase in poverty among immigrant groups is particularly relevant because of its long-term impact on the children and grandchildren of the foreign-born. The question posed in this chapter is not just about immigration in general but about the outcomes that will arise from the future social and economic paths of these new citizen children. New citizen children who grow up in poverty will likely face many obstacles to their future success in the labor market. In this chapter I argue that an increase in the poverty status of the foreign-born is likely and will have significant and deleterious effects for their children. The recent significant influx of low-skilled, low-income migrants, who also have relatively high fertility rates, has the potential to create a dependent and economically segregated population because their children will be unable to follow the path of earlier immigrant arrivals. Thus, the nature and extent of poverty are critical because of the long-term implications for future generations of immigrants.

This study is designed to document and explain the way in which immigrant poverty varies across metropolitan areas within the United States, using data from the Current Population Survey, as in other chapters of this book.[9] Poverty among new immigrants is an increasingly critical element in immigrant transformation of the large entry-point cities, but we still do not fully understand its extent and variation across immigrant groups, metropolitan areas, or gender. Although we have some knowledge of foreign-born poverty in national terms, the local level is where the implications of poverty are played out, in higher school dropout rates and lower academic achievement levels for immigrant children than for native children. In addition, in a society that has substantially changed the social safety net, local communities increasingly bear the burdens of caring for the poverty population. Finally, localized concentrations of poverty populations hint at the possibility of creating new distressed inner-city neighborhoods, a foreign-born parallel to the already significant black poverty population in the inner cities of large metropolitan areas.

This chapter has two broad objectives. First, I describe the geography of immigrant poverty—defined as a household characteristic—and examine the sources of variation across metropolitan areas and within groups. Second, I explore the factors that account for immigrant poverty in the five major immigrant regions that serve as the focal point of this book. In doing so, I take immigration as a given; my concern, rather, is to explain its consequences in those particular locations on which the newcomers converge.

Understanding Poverty

Two important conceptualizations underpin the research presented in this chapter; the first relates to the effects of low income and poverty on achievement, and the second relates to the changing work opportunities available to new immigrants. The points are interwoven, of course, because the lack of opportunities in turn leads to probable underemployment or unemployment, which in turn leads to inadequate family resources and poverty.

There is substantial evidence that family income is a critical variable in school achievement for children and for later outcomes in child development and occupational success.[10] Parental income has a positive and significant effect on how well children will do later in the labor market. Haveman and Wolfe concluded in their review of several studies that growing up in a poor family appears to have a particularly negative effect on later success in the workforce and on earnings.[11] It also appears that the negative effects are greater when low family income occurs in early childhood rather than in later years.[12] Specific studies of the linkage between poverty and achievement have also shown place and locality effects and that attending a school with a high concentration of poor students is strongly negatively associated with student achievement in reading and mathematics.[13] Overall, the literature suggests that low incomes carry with them high risks of reduced access to education, information, and training.[14] Parents in poverty cannot give their children the opportunities for better health, education, and the associated skills to improve their situation. In addition, Myers draws an important distinction in the path of assimilation between those who tend to learn English rapidly and become citizens and those who have much lower levels of language skills. Low levels of schooling and poor language skills may limit immigrants' potential for successful adjustment and in turn their ability to participate in the economy.[15]

It is not simply that poverty has increased but that concentrated poverty and social exclusion in a few neighborhoods have dramatic effects on the population, including children, living in those neighborhoods. O'Hare points out that children living in distressed neighborhoods are likely to be part of a minority group and foreign-born, as many new immigrants are concentrated in inner-city neighborhoods. This concentration of poverty has the potential to decrease the future opportunities of immigrant children.[16]

The issue of changing occupational opportunities is also important in this evaluation because the prospective job trajectories of immigrant children are central to understanding the future of immigrant populations in general. Those who argue that immigrants will follow the path of earlier immigrants and successfully adapt to the new environment and eventually participate fully in the host economy see a convergence of immigrant and native-born characteristics. However, if the old paths are no longer available or are available only with difficulty to the less well educated new immigrants, then the opportunities for employment have changed and the pattern of the past cannot be repeated. In fact, there is substantial evidence that economic restructuring is at least part of the explanation for low success levels among new immigrants.[17] Jobs that used to be the mainstay for low-skilled workers may be disappearing, and the creation of an under- or unemployed class filling only low-skilled, nonprofessional occupations may result. At the moment many immigrants are apparently still able to enter the low end of the labor market, but it is unclear whether they will be able to step up the labor market ladder. The evidence from chapter 3 suggests that low-skilled city dwellers are "running into trouble in the quest for economic mobility." The consequence of lack of employment, in the case of the black population, is the creation of a socially excluded population unable to participate in the evolving social structure of modern society.[18] More recent evidence from Frey and Fielding suggests that the changing structure of the economy is already concentrating poverty and unemployment among other racial minorities.[19]

Research in Europe has also emphasized the role of social exclusion and its ramifications and has addressed the question of whether new immigrant groups are excluded and hence more likely to live in poverty. The studies note that although immigrant concentrations encourage networking and function as immigrant enclaves, they also lead to separation from mainstream society. This separation, especially where ethnicity and poverty overlap and where participation in the labor market is marginal, leads to social separation and marginality.[20] Researchers emphasize the emergence of a fragmented society in which the less-privileged groups—migrants, the unemployed, women, and the elderly—are excluded from education, employment, housing, and health and other social services. Whether the findings of these studies conducted in Europe apply also in the United States is as yet unclear.

There is in fact a lively debate about whether the underclass concept applies to Latino households. Moore and Pinderhughes argue that the pathology of the black ghetto of which Wilson writes—of single-parent families headed by women, declining marriage rates, illegitimate births, and welfare dependency—is not replicated in inner-city barrios. They suggest that poverty is not as concentrated, that many of the inner-city communities still provide jobs (albeit low-wage service jobs), and that a strong informal sector exists among Latinos in inner cities. Thus, the arguments focus attention on the importance of employment as the most critical factor in countering the marginalization of disadvantaged groups.[21]

If poverty negatively influences the employment opportunities for the native-born, this pattern is likely exacerbated for immigrants and the children of immigrants, who are even less skilled and have fewer years of basic education. The problem is further exacerbated by an employment structure in which job opportunities are decreasing and in which the skills required for occupational success are increasing. A close link thus emerges among poverty, large-scale immigration, and trajectories of failure within localized concentrations in large U.S. cities. Immigrant poverty matters because children from households living in poverty have low education gains, which lead to low skills, which in turn may lead to low levels of employment and thus continuation of the cycle of low income and poverty.

A U.S. Perspective on Immigrant Poverty

Some national studies have documented the impact of immigration on poverty. Frey and Fielding found that much of the growth of the poverty population in inner cities and metropolitan areas in general in the United States was due to immigration.[22] Frey reports that the number of poor international migrants exceeded the net flow of poor internal migrants in 34 states between 1985 and 1990. Furthermore, this imbalance tends to be spatially concentrated; for example, California gained about nine times more poor migrants than it lost through migration to other states, and approximately 20 percent of the growth of the poverty population in Los Angeles was due to immigration.[23]

An additional critical dimension involves the growing isolation of the U.S. poverty population in general that has occurred over the past decades. For example, Kasarda and Abramson and Tobin draw attention to the increased separation of the poverty population from mainstream society between 1970 and 1990, noting that the isolation of the poor in general increased by 9 percent.[24] Although the poor are not as isolated as some ethnic or racial groups, distressed neighborhoods and concentrations of poverty create a negative context for new immigrants. Good jobs may not be available within reasonable distances of the poverty concentrations, schools are likely to face considerable stress in providing adequate services for their special-needs populations, and crime and drugs may make the neighborhoods unsafe. A specific analysis of the general distressed population using measures of poverty, joblessness, number of single-parent families headed by women, welfare receipt, and teenage dropout rates ranked Los Angeles and New York near the top of the most distressed cities.[25]

Research by economists, demographers, and geographers has established that recent immigrants to the United States are doing worse than earlier arrivals; work at the metropolitan level has also shown that recent immigrants are likely to live in poverty.[26] Although individual immigrants may be doing better in the United States than in their countries of origin and some will succeed much as earlier migrants did, most immigrants struggle.[27] Research in New Jersey suggesting that immigrants are less likely to live in poverty and a study of Latino entry into the middle class only serve to emphasize the potential for a bifurcation of the foreign-born population.[28]

The data for the United States as a whole reveal that the gap between the native-born and immigrants in the mean number of years of education is increasing. The differential between the earnings of the native- and foreign-born is more negative for immigrants who arrived in the late 1980s than for those who came earlier.[29] Whereas between 1970 and 1990 the average number of years of education for the native-born population increased from 11.5 to 13.2, that number increased by less than a year for immigrants. As a result, the mean educational attainment of immigrants slipped against that of the native-born. Similarly, the relative wages of immigrants fell between 1970 and 1990. By 1990 immigrants who entered the United States between 1985 and 1990 were, on average, earning almost one-third less than the native-born population. Most relevant to this study, the foreign-born population living in poverty has been increasing over the past three and a half decades, especially among women. In 1970 the proportions and numbers of foreign-born living in poverty were modest; by 1990 the percentages were approaching 25 percent for foreign-born women and the total numbers had almost tripled.

But there are as many questions as answers in the analyses to date. First, as I have emphasized, the research is largely national in scale, with some limited regional analyses. Second, the research compares the immigrant population with the native-born population without disaggregation of immigrants by ethnic origins. Such approaches fail to consider that national origin plays a critical role in understanding the variations in poverty among immigrants. Third, very few of the previous studies examined gender as a critical dimension of changing levels of poverty.

Metropolitan Outcomes

Variations across the United States

We can examine the immigrant population living in poverty with two measures that, together, provide a context of the intersection of the foreign-born population and the poverty population. In this way we can begin to disentangle the contribution of the foreign-born population to poverty in metropolitan areas. One measure captures the proportion of the foreign-born population living in poverty, and the other captures the proportion of the poverty population that is foreign-born.

The percentage of the foreign-born population living in poverty varies from a high of more than 30 percent in Houston, Phoenix, and Sacramento to lows of 5 to 7 percent in Norfolk, Virginia, Cincinnati, and Cleveland (table 5.1). What do these variations mean? Clearly, the entry-point cities and cities along the border with Mexico have high proportions of the foreign-born living in poverty, largely because of the disadvantaged position of the new Mexican and Central American immigrants in these cities. At the same time, Midwestern cities such as Denver, Kansas City, and Minneapolis have high proportions of the foreign-born living in poverty as well, evidence of the increasing redistribution of migrants across the U.S. metropolitan landscape. In particular instances, large numbers of relatively disadvantaged migrants, the Hmong in Milwaukee and the Twin Cities and the Somalis in Minneapolis, have transformed the social structure of the minority population in the cities in which they live and have created new special-needs populations.

The data in table 5.1, ordered by percentage of the foreign-born population living in poverty, provide a new perspective on the patterns

TABLE 5.1.   PERCENTAGE IN POVERTY
BY CITY AND ETHNIC STATUS

City	Foreign-born	White	Native-born black	Hispanic
Phoenix	34.4	7.8	29.4	27.4
Sacramento	30.5	11.0	34.9	24.8
Houston	30.1	8.0	26.8	27.5
Los Angeles	27.2	7.4	23.4	29.7
Milwaukee	26.8	4.3	41.8	22.1
Tampa	26.6	9.5	34.4	29.8
San Diego	26.3	6.4	38.8	29.7
Seattle	23.7	7.3	28.7	9.7
Miami	21.9	8.1	35.3	19.5
Denver	21.7	6.5	20.8	23.0
Dallas	20.7	6.3	22.2	16.3
Kansas City	20.7	8.4	27.4	12.0
New York	20.4	5.9	30.5	36.8
Minneapolis	18.6	6.0	31.3	39.2
Detroit	16.4	7.8	33.5	27.4
Philadelphia	15.8	6.2	32.3	37.2
Portland	15.8	9.4	31.8	25.3
St. Louis	15.2	6.2	26.3	—
Chicago	14.9	4.3	33.6	22.6
Boston	14.3	6.2	29.7	38.5
San Francisco	11.9	5.7	19.4	12.0
Washington, D.C.	11.3	5.8	22.0	8.6
Atlanta	9.3	6.4	23.9	14.0
Pittsburgh	9.1	10.3	31.0	—
Cincinnati	7.5	6.8	25.8	—
Clevcland	7.2	13.3	31.9	57.4
Norfolk	5.2	8.2	19.0	20.5

Note: The five metropolitan case studies are underlined

of native-born poverty. The poverty rate is low among native-born white citizens but, strikingly, is higher among native-born Hispanics than immigrants, across a wide range of metropolitan areas. This finding hints at what we may expect to result from large-scale Hispanic immigration. Included later in this chapter is a breakdown of poverty by ethnic origin that emphasizes the ways in which Hispanic foreign-born populations are contributing to the very high levels of poverty among the foreign-born.

I am also interested in the foreign-born population living in poverty relative to the total foreign-born population. Is the percentage of the

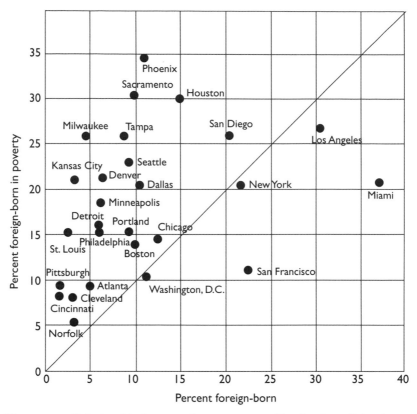

Figure 5.1.   Relationship between the percentage of foreign-born living in poverty and the percentage of foreign-born overall

foreign-born living in poverty greater than the percentage of the foreign-born living in the United States? A plot of 27 U.S. urban regions shows a significant number of regions with disproportionate percentages of their foreign-born populations living in poverty (figure 5.1). Phoenix provides the most extreme case, but high percentages of the foreign-born live in poverty in Sacramento, Houston, and Tampa as well. Three of the five entry-point regions that are the focus of more detailed study later in this chapter are near a one-to-one ratio (represented by the diagonal line in the figure), and Miami and San Francisco have lower percentages of immigrants living in poverty than might be expected. Thus the most severe poverty rates are not in the largest entry-point regions, though of course they do have the greatest number living in poverty.

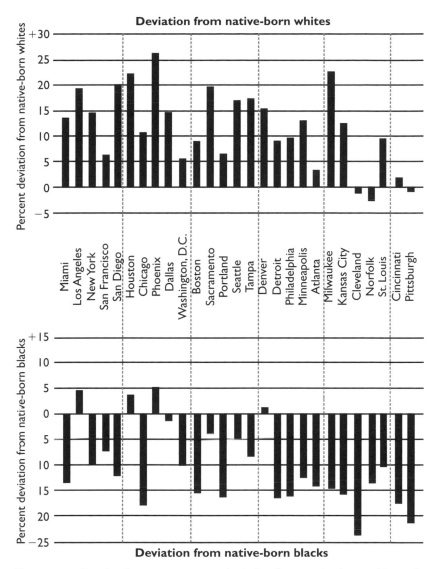

Figure 5.2.   Foreign-born poverty rate: deviation from native-born white and black poverty rates (arranged by population density of immigrants)

An alternate picture of the patterns of foreign-born poverty is created by comparing the poverty levels of the foreign-born population and the native-born white and black populations. Not unexpectedly, these comparisons generate strikingly different images (figure 5.2); the foreign-born population as a whole is doing much worse than the native-born white population but much better, on average, than the African American population. At the same time, there is a great deal of variation across metropolitan areas.

As we saw in figure 5.1, Phoenix had the highest proportion of the foreign-born living in poverty; figure 5.2 show that it is also the place where the gap between immigrants and native whites in the proportion in poverty takes its widest form. While distinctive, Phoenix is not alone on this count. In seven other regions—Houston, Los Angeles, Sacramento, Seattle, Tampa, San Diego, and Milwaukee—the proportion of immigrants living in poverty stands at 15 percent or more above the level for native whites (figure 5.2). The differences can be grouped into West Coast entry-point regions (Los Angeles and San Diego), Midwestern regions that are receiving internal flows from entry-point regions (Minneapolis and Milwaukee), and East Coast entry-point regions. In general, the West Coast entry-point locations—Los Angeles, Sacramento, Seattle, Phoenix, and San Diego—show considerably greater levels of poverty among immigrants than among native whites. Milwaukee is an outlier because of its high foreign-born and low native-born white poverty rates.

The variations between the foreign-born and black poverty rates contrast with those between the foreign-born and the native-born white poverty rates. For example, the foreign-born poverty rates are not much different from the native-born white poverty rates in Cincinnati and Cleveland, but their differences from the black poverty rates in these cities are among the largest in the distribution.

Overall, the foreign-born are doing much better than native-born blacks and worse than native-born whites, with five notable exceptions. In Los Angeles, Dallas, Denver, Phoenix, and Houston, both white and black natives are doing better than the foreign-born. This anomaly is a function in part of the overall poverty levels of the foreign-born population and in part of the success of the white and black populations.

Focusing on the composition of the poverty population itself and determining the ways in which its foreign-born segment varies across the major metropolitan areas add an important dimension to the analysis of the poverty population (figure 5.3). In Los Angeles and Miami almost half of the poverty population is foreign-born. In contrast, in cities with large black populations—Cleveland, Detroit, and Atlanta, for example—a much smaller proportion of the poverty population is foreign-born. In the entry-point cities in general the foreign-born population makes up a much larger segment of the poverty population (as expected) than in Midwestern cities. However, it is striking that the poverty population in

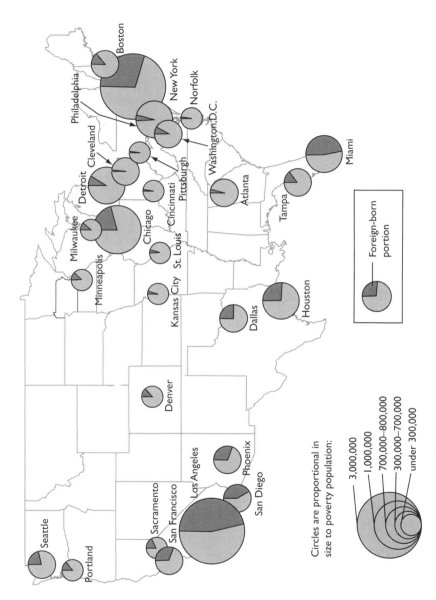

Seattle
Portland

Sacramento
San Francisco
Los Angeles
San Diego

Denver

Phoenix

Minneapolis

Milwaukee
Chicago
St. Louis
Kansas City

Dallas

Houston

Detroit
Cleveland
Cincinnati
Pittsburgh

Philadelphia
Boston
New York
Norfolk
Washington,D.C.

Atlanta
Tampa

Miami

Foreign-born
portion

Circles are proportional in
size to poverty population:

3,000,000
1,000,000
700,000–800,000
300,000–700,000
under 300,000

Figure 5.3.   Percentage of the poverty population that is foreign-born

almost all of the coastal entry-point cities is now 25 percent or more foreign-born. Even Chicago is approaching the one-quarter mark, but Los Angeles, San Diego, and Miami stand out with the highest percentages of foreign-born in their poverty populations.

In general northern entry-point cities have the lowest proportions of immigrants in their total poverty populations, and entry-point regions in California, Arizona, and Texas have the greatest proportions of immigrants in their total poverty populations, again an expected finding. Clearly the large influx of poorly educated Mexican and Central American immigrants is creating strongly negative poverty trends in the accessible border states. Of course, the foreign-born proportion of the poverty population is related to the overall size of the foreign-born population in a particular region.

Five Immigrant Regions

The five urban regions that serve as the focus of this book stand out for their concentrations not only of the foreign-born but also of the poor. For the purposes of this chapter, these five regions are sufficiently well represented in the sample to examine poverty characteristics by both ethnic origin and gender.

As can be detected from table 5.1, foreign-born poverty is high in Los Angeles, New York, and Miami and moderate in San Francisco and Chicago. In every city but Los Angeles African American poverty levels are higher and in every city but Miami—where we see the Cuban effect—native-born Hispanic poverty levels are higher than foreign-born poverty levels. Only in San Francisco is the poverty rate of the foreign-born moderate and the difference among groups modest. The high levels of poverty in the Hispanic native-born populations are suggestive of the inability of these groups to move up the ladder; if true, the situation bodes poorly for new Hispanic immigrants.

As expected, in all five regions the recently settled foreign-born are much more likely to live in poverty than their longer-settled counterparts. In Los Angeles and Miami nearly two-fifths of those immigrants who arrived after 1990 live in poverty, levels that are remarkably high and represent rates that stand significantly above those for migrants who entered as recently as the 1980s (figure 5.4). Overall, the rates have increased by one-third to one-half in the past few years and have jumped dramatically in Miami. Whereas only 10 percent or so of pre-1980 arrivals are now living in poverty, the percentage among those

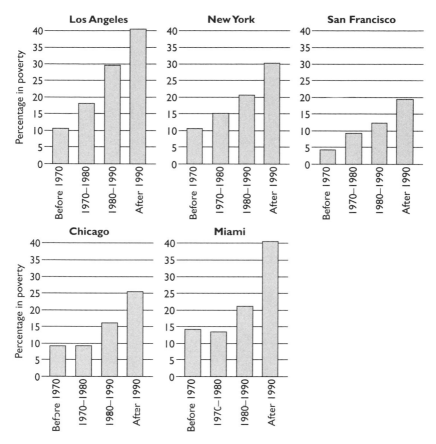

Figure 5.4.   Percentage of immigrants living in poverty by year of arrival

who settled after 1980 is much higher. Recent immigrants are likely to need social services at a time of significant cutbacks in these areas, and their sheer numbers may frustrate the attempts of cities and community agencies to provide the basic services needed to ensure a transition into mainstream society. The result may be that sizable groups of foreign-born or foreign-origin individuals never are able to escape poverty and so begin to form a socially excluded and marginal population.

Gender and Poverty

Poverty varies not only by city and ethnic origin but also by gender. One of the important new findings in this area is that immigrant

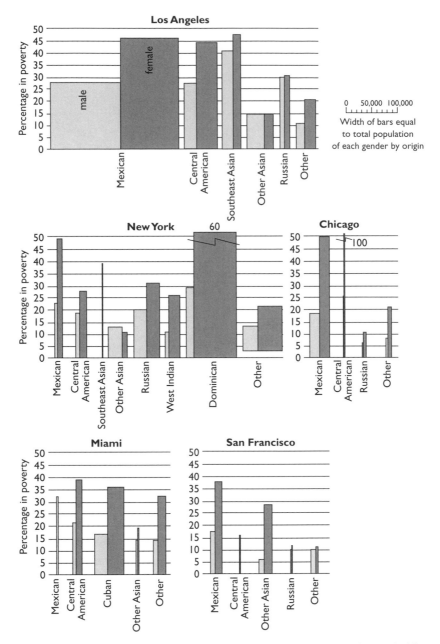

Figure 5.5. Poverty by country of origin and gender for heads of households

women who are heads of households are highly likely—in fact, much more likely than immigrant men who are heads of households—to be living in poverty (figure 5.5). The figure is designed to provide information on ethnic origin and gender and is weighted by the size of the foreign-born population. The graphs reveal the overwhelming dominance of Mexican and Central Americans in Los Angeles and of Dominicans and immigrants not otherwise classified in New York. New York and Los Angeles are clearly more dominant immigrant entry points than San Francisco, Chicago, and Miami. However, Cubans dominate Miami in the same way as Mexicans dominate Los Angeles. New York has a much greater variety in the national origins of its foreign-born, as exemplified in the large number of immigrants categorized as "other."

Although Asian immigrants (other than refugees) in Los Angeles have similarly low poverty levels for men and women and Russian immigrants have similarly high poverty levels, almost all other national-origin groups show marked differences in the poverty rates of men and women. The poverty rates of women are nearly always a third higher than those of men, and sometimes the rate of women living in poverty is more than twice that of men, as for Mexicans in Chicago. The poverty rate for Dominican women is 60 percent, more than twice that of Dominican men. Even in San Francisco, where the poverty rates are in general much lower than in other metropolitan areas, both Mexican and Other Asian (mainly Filipino and Chinese) women are two to four times more likely than their male counterparts to live in poverty. This finding supports my contention that the poverty levels of certain groups, in particular locations, have long-term effects on the future paths of the foreign-born population. It appears that difficulties in language and education are creating problems, especially for single Hispanic mothers, in moving off welfare and into mainstream economic activities.

Predicting Poverty

It is important to couch the descriptive and observational findings from earlier sections of this chapter in an analytic framework and to provide some context for understanding the probability of immigrants living in poverty. I begin by analyzing the odds of living in poverty given a range of variables that measure education, involvement in the labor market,

TABLE 5.2. LOGISTIC COEFFICIENTS FOR THE PROBABILITY
OF LIVING IN POVERTY: IMMIGRANTS VERSUS NATIVE-BORN WHITES

Variable	Los Angeles	New York	San Francisco	Chicago	Miami
Number of earners	-1.039**	-1.185**	-.798**	-.944**	-.950**
Less than high school education	1.141**	.957**	.633*	.758**	1.135**
High school graduate	.515**	.543**	.430	.302	.297
Under hours	1.967**	1.862**	1.944**	2.482**	1.987**
Under income	2.229**	2.600**	2.381**	3.184**	2.054**
No jobs	1.371**	.937**	1.777**	1.694**	.261
Subunemp	2.679**	1.285**	3.361**	2.315*	1.154
Nilf	1.383**	1.755**	1.784**	1.942**	1.377**
Retired	.681**	1.000**	1.075**	1.819**	1.240**
Child under 18	.842**	1.024**	.960**	1.433**	1.474**
Mexican	.540**		.242	.525	.409
Central American	.280				
Dominican		.658**			
Cuban		.135			.317
Other Hispanic					.334
Southeast Asian	.972**				
Other Asian	-.138		.443		
West Indian		-.055			-.020
Russian	.561	.420*		-.511	
Immigrated in 1970s	.509**	.401**	.502	.125	.023
Immigrated in 1980s	.906**	.689**	.169	1.135**	.281
Immigrated in 1990s	1.251**	.722**	1.176*	1.050*	1.017**
U.S. citizen	-.270	.279*	-.066	.364	.352
Not U.S. citizen	.237	.789**	.372	.813*	.705*
Not married	.684**	.898**	1.148**	1.004**	.919**
Female	.089	.192*	.122	.679**	.020
Constant	-3.374**	-4.011**	-4.315**	-5.161**	-3.902**
Pseudo R_2	.34	.36	.27	.36	.31

*Significant at .05 level; **Significant at .01 level.

country of origin, period of immigration, and a variety of indexes of citizenship, family status, and gender.

The model simply analyzes the likelihood of living in poverty versus not living in poverty as a function of specific measures of socioeconomic status. I computed the models for the contrast between native-born whites and the foreign-born (table 5.2).[30] The models are constructed for each metropolitan area, and the fits, as measured by the pseudo-R^2, are reasonable, with the variance explained ranging from the .27 to the .36 level. Clearly, the reasons for foreign-born poverty are complicated and have dimensions beyond the measured variables in this analysis. Individual circumstances probably interact with particular places to generate different outcomes for different ethnic origins, and there is considerable variability even within groups as to who falls into poverty.

The logit model coefficients reveal the critical role of labor force participation in determining the likelihood of poverty. Moore and Pinderhughes (as well as chapter 3 in this volume) emphasize the importance of being employed, and they argue that being even marginally involved in the labor market is central to escaping poverty. However, as we will see, marginal involvement in the labor market is not enough. The number of earners in a household is consistently important in assessing the probability of living in poverty. Human capital, measured by high school education, is equally important. Individuals with lower levels of education and thus lower levels of human capital are more likely to live in poverty. However, the levels of employment are at the center of the most critical argument.

In the regression equations, two sets of variables measure specific characteristics of the foreign-born. Countries of origin are used to assess the likelihood of specific groups living in poverty compared to the native-born white population, native-born black population, and Hispanic population. Duration measures assess the impact of time of arrival on the likelihood of living in poverty. Not all countries of origin are represented in all metropolitan areas; for example, Dominicans, Cubans, and West Indians are not present in significant numbers in San Francisco or Chicago.

Ethnic origins and poverty are positively correlated for almost all groups and all cities; that is, poverty increases with foreign-born status across the board. However, Asians (other than refugee groups) in Los Angeles and New York and Russians in Chicago are not associated with poverty. (We observed this finding in figure 5.6.) Interestingly,

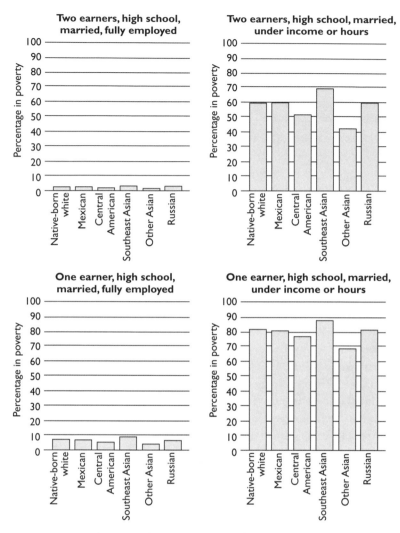

Figure 5.6. Probability of living in poverty for foreign-born versus native-born white earners, controlling for education, marital status, and employment status in Los Angeles

Southeast Asians in Los Angeles are more likely than both whites and blacks to live in poverty. The smaller positive coefficients in New York and Miami suggest that ethnic origin is less critical in understanding the likelihood of living in poverty in these cities than in others; rather, measures of employment alone account for much of the variation in poverty.

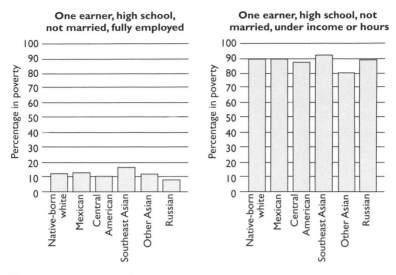

Figure 5.6.   *(continued)*

Time of arrival makes a difference in all cities but has the least effect in New York. In Los Angeles earlier settlers are less likely than recent arrivals to live in poverty, and in San Francisco the real difference is between the most recent arrivals and those who came before 1990. The results of the analysis of this variable and the earlier analysis of country of origin suggest that outcome is strongly dependent on ethnic origin and location. Measures of citizenship, family composition, and gender have expected relationships with poverty.[31]

Although the logit models clearly establish employment as the critical underlying dimension in determining level of poverty, an alternative presentation provides additional and possibly more transparent interpretations of the role of employment in combination with measures of marital status and education levels. In this manner it is possible to examine just how employment affects different foreign-born groups of different socioeconomic status.

The method computes the probabilities of living in poverty for each ethnic group in comparison with the native-born white population. The results for Los Angeles reveal the impact of not being able to find sufficient work or having to take a low-wage job. The probabilities reflect the likelihood of living in poverty across the number of earners in the household, marital status, education levels, and employment levels (figure 5.6). Three findings are striking. First, the likelihood of living in poverty is not dramatically different for the foreign-born and native-born white populations *if* the foreign-born are adequately employed. The real gap appears when employment levels drop. Second, lack of employment increases the probability of living in poverty by a factor of 10 to 12. Third, the proportion living in poverty increases significantly when the number of earners in a household decreases from two to one.

A summary of the results for Los Angeles and the other five entry-point regions in the study shows the generalizability of the findings for Los Angeles (figure 5.7). I aggregated the probability of living in poverty for all foreign-born groups and compared it with the probability of native-born whites living in poverty. I found that if the foreign-born can attain full employment they are no more likely than natives to live in poverty. Thus the importance of jobs and entry into the job market is reiterated as a critical dimension of the progress of immigrants. There is, however, an important variation across the five metropolitan areas. In Los Angeles and New York native-born whites are, on average, doing better than the foreign-born. In San Francisco there is little difference between the two groups, although the results vary according to the specific type of household; in Chicago and Miami the foreign-born are less likely than the native-born to live in poverty.

The findings tell a compelling story about the importance of obtaining employment. In fact, the relatively small differences in probabilities of poverty across the foreign-born categories suggests that if the foreign-born can get adequate employment, then the likelihood of poverty is low. In effect, however, the modal categories for most foreign-born groups are not two earners with high school education—or, for that matter, adequate employment.

To illustrate the interrelationship of poverty, employment, and marital status I evaluated the levels of poverty for the modal categories of selected immigrant groups. That is, I determined the poverty rate for the most likely combination of employment, marital status, and ethnicity. In this analysis I did not distinguish adequacy of employment. The modal analysis compared native-born white heads of households with the heads of households for the foreign-born group with the highest proportion living in poverty. Thus, I compared Mexicans in Los Angeles, San Francisco, and Chicago, Dominicans in New York, and Cubans in Miami.[32] I also included average household size for the selected groups and cities; clearly, the larger the household, the greater the likelihood of poverty.

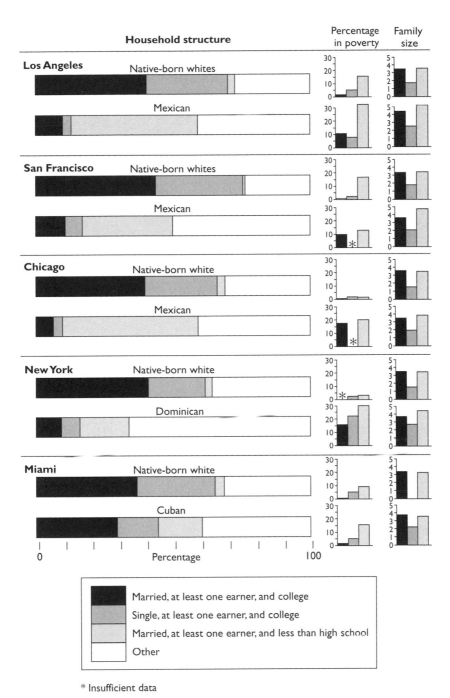

Figure 5.7. Poverty and household size by modal groups

For all cities for the native-born white groups the modal category is married, at least one earner, and college education. For the three cities in which the foreign-born group is Mexican, the modal group is married, one earner, and less than a high school education. For example, 41.8 percent of the Los Angeles native-born white households consist of a married couple with one earner and a college education. In contrast, 46.4 percent of Mexican households consist of a married couple with at least one earner but less than a high school education. In New York for Dominicans the modal group is not employed, which shows up as low percentages of households with at least one earner, regardless of marital status. In Miami the modal category is married, at least one earner, and college education for both native-born whites and Cubans. Miami also has significant proportions of households headed by college-educated single individuals and married couples with less than a high school education.

As one would expect the poverty levels for the college-educated households are extremely low. The levels are higher for the college-educated foreign-born, but the real contrast is the very high rates of poverty in the foreign-born modal groups. For the Mexican modal group, the percentages living in poverty by city are 32 percent in Los Angeles, 21 percent in Chicago, 20 percent in Miami, and almost 30 percent in New York. The rate is much lower in San Francisco, a place effect I noted earlier in the chapter. The analysis using modal categories disentangles the poverty effect across groups and explains why the overall poverty rate is so high for the foreign-born. The study also reiterates the critical role of human capital in escaping poverty.

An additional plot line of the story is the substantial variation in household size between the foreign-born and native-born white groups, also displayed in figure 5.7. Overall, household sizes for the foreign-born groups are 30 to 50 percent larger than for the native-born white groups. Household size is 3.4 for the native-born white modal category in Los Angeles but 5.2 for the Mexican modal category. The difference is not as great in Chicago, San Francisco, and New York. However, household poverty appears to be more likely in larger households. Revealingly, household size is almost the same for the modal categories of the various groups in Miami.

In some sense the findings from the logit models and the probability presentation are expected. Even so, they highlight an issue of concern for the foreign-born in general and for recent immigrants in particular. Adequate employment is the critical factor in avoiding poverty. The inability to find jobs, particularly jobs with sufficient hours and income, leads to a high likelihood of poverty. The employment factor cuts across ethnic groups. In addition, hidden in the analysis is the importance of human capital. In San Francisco, where an expanding high-tech industry provides jobs for new highly educated immigrants, rates of poverty are low in general and the coefficients indicate that immigrant group membership is only weakly, though positively, correlated with poverty. Only Central Americans and Southeast Asians, groups with the lowest human capital, are not participating in the overall gains in the San Francisco region.

Observations and Conclusions

We are on the brink of fundamental changes in the social fabric of America's urban immigrant regions, approaching a point at which inner-city black poverty may be replicated by a new pattern of foreign-born poverty. The story sketched out in the preceding pages suggests that many immigrants live in poverty, that they are unable to find jobs with sufficient hours or income to escape poverty, and that the very recent foreign-born arrivals are the most disadvantaged. In addition, although human capital is the key to future success, the foreign-born are neither achieving high levels of human capital nor pursuing it aggressively.

A related issue involves the implications of poverty and growing up in poverty. The findings on the effect of low income in early childhood and the health research that demonstrates that hunger can cause serious short- and long-term health consequences emphasize the ramifications of poverty in the immigrant community. Children suffering from hunger are more likely to perform poorly in their academic work, and young hungry children may have long-lasting nutrition-related health problems. In these situations, minor policy changes such as restricting food stamp eligibility can have dramatic effects at the margin. These changes further increase the likelihood of poor performance in school and decrease the chances of acquiring the human capital essential for job seeking and entry into the mainstream labor market.

Finally, the high levels of poverty among foreign-born women bring us back to the earlier observations that immigrant women are employed at strikingly low levels and that the lack of employment is translated into low household incomes. Given a vanishing, or at least much reduced, safety net, the future of the inner-city concentrations of the foreign-born, perhaps disproportionately foreign-born women, is not likely to follow the upward paths of earlier immigrants. Indeed, a new immigrant underclass, struggling for the ever scarcer resources available from local cities and counties, may emerge.

Notes

1. A. Portes and R. Rumbaut, *Immigrant America: A Portrait,* 2d ed. (Berkeley and Los Angeles: University of California Press, 1996).

2. California Food Policy Advocates, *Impact of Legal Immigrant Food Stamp Cuts in Los Angeles and San Francisco* (San Francisco: California Food Security Monitoring Project, 1998). The hunger rate is based on data from the U.S. low-income sample from the Current Population Survey.

3. W. A. V. Clark, *The California Cauldron: Immigration and the Fortunes of Local Communities* (New York Guilford Press, 1998).

4. E. Taylor, P. Martin, and M. Fix, *Poverty amidst Prosperity: Immigration and the Changing Face of Rural California* (Washington, D.C.: Urban Institute, 1997).

5. W. A. V. Clark and F. Schultz, "Evaluating the Local Impacts of Recent Immigration to California: Realism vs. Racism," *Population Research and Policy Review* 16 (1997): 474–491.

6. Clark, *California Cauldron*; George J. Borjas, "The Economics of Immigration," *Journal of Economic Literature* 32 (1994): 1667–1717.

7. U.S. General Accounting Office, Government Printing Office, 1997. Quoted in the *Wall Street Journal,* May 20, 1998.

8. Clark, *California Cauldron.*

9. In this chapter I rely on a merged sample of the Current Population Survey for 1994–1997.

10. G. J. Duncan, W. J. Yeung, and J. Brooks-Gunn, "Does Childhood Poverty Affect the Life Chances of Children?" (paper presented at a meeting of the Population Association of America, New Orleans, La., May 9, 1996).

11. R. Haveman. and B. Wolfe, "The Determinants of Children's Attainments: A Review of Methods and Findings," *Journal of Economic Literature* 33 (1995): 1829–1878.

12. Duncan et al., "Childhood Poverty."

13. U.S. Department of Education, *Prospects: The Congressionally Mandated Study of Educational Growth and Opportunity* (Washington, D.C.: U.S. Department of Education, 1993).

14. Isabel Sawhill, "Poverty in the United States: Why Is It So Persistent?" *Journal of Economic Literature* 26 (1988): 1073–1119.

15. D. Myers, "The Changing Immigrants of Southern California: Los Angeles" (Research report no. LCRI-95-04R, University of Southern California School of Urban and Regional Planning, University of Southern California, Los Angeles, 1996).

16. W. O'Hare, "3.9 Million Children in Distressed Neighborhoods," *Population Today* 22, no. 9 (1994): 4–5.

17. Susan Fainstein, Ian Gordon, and Michael Harloe, *Divided Cities* (Oxford: Basil Blackwell, 1992); Roger Waldinger and Mehdi Bozorgmehr, *Ethnic Los Angeles* (New York: Russell Sage Foundation, 1996).

18. William Julius Wilson, *The Truly Disadvantaged* (Chicago: University of Chicago Press, 1987).

19. W. Frey and E. Fielding, "Changing Urban Populations: Regional Restructuring, Racial Polarization, and Poverty Concentration," *Cityscape* 1 (1995): 1–66.

20. S. Musterd, "A Rising European Underclass," *Built Environment* 20 (1994): 185–191.

21. Joan Moore and Raquel Pinderhughes, eds., *In the Barrios: Latinos and the Underclass Debate* (New York: Russell Sage Foundation, 1993).

22. Frey and Fielding, "Changing Urban Populations."

23. W. Frey, "Immigration and the Changing Geography of Poverty," *Focus* 18, no. 2 (1996–1997): 24–28.

24. John Kasarda, "Inner-City Concentrated Poverty and Neighborhood Distress: 1970–1990," *Housing Policy Debate* 4 (1993): 253–302; A. Abramson and M. Tobin, "The Changing Geography of Metropolitan Opportunity: The Segregation of the Poor in U.S. Metropolitan Areas, 1970–1990," *Housing Policy Debate* 6 (1995): 45–72.

25. Kasarda, "Inner-City Concentrated Poverty."

26. Clark, *California Cauldron.*

27. Clark and Schultz, "Evaluating Local Impacts"; Kevin McCarthy and Georges Vernez, *Immigration in a Changing Economy: California's Experience* (Santa Monica, Calif.: RAND Corporation, 1997).

28. Thomas Espenshade, ed., *Keys to Successful Immigration: Implications of the New Jersey Experience* (Washington, D.C.: Urban Institute, 1997); Gregory Rodriguez, *The Emerging Latino Middle Class* (Los Angeles: Pepperdine University, Institute for Public Policy, 1996).

29. Clark, *California Cauldron.*

30. I have also computed models for the contrast between native-born blacks and Hispanics and the foreign-born. I have not included the results here because of space constraints, but the patterns are consistent with the conclusions drawn in this chapter.

31. Versions of the model with age did not change the overall coefficients. It appears that age is subsumed by time of arrival.

32. The group is the largest numerical group in poverty, not the group with the highest rate of poverty.

Chapter 6

ON THE BACK OF BLACKS?
Immigrants and the Fortunes of African Americans

Nelson Lim

"On the back of blacks?" asked Toni Morrison in a recent essay, contemplating the role of "race talk" in the assimilation of newcomers into a racially stratified society such as ours.[1] The same question naturally arises in the context of today's immigration debate, having served as a fulcrum of controversy among scholars and advocates of varying stripes for more than two decades. The reasons for disquiet are not difficult to discern. Immigrants are getting a toehold in the American economy and many are "making it" at a time when progress for too many African Americans seems stalled.[2] While the boom of the 1990s has reduced poverty, a disturbingly large number of African Americans—and, especially, African American men—have not yet found their life chances improved. Under these circumstances the nation's burgeoning immigrant population emerges as a likely cause of the persistent problems affecting less-skilled African Americans.

Competition with immigrants is only one of many possible causes invoked to explain persistent levels of poverty and unemployment among African Americans. Researchers subscribing to individualistic theories of social behavior have tended to emphasize those factors that allow jobless African Americans to choose leisure over work. They contend that high levels of African American unemployment result from choosing alternative income sources, such as welfare benefits or criminal activities, over work.[3] Others argue that African Americans are more likely to be jobless because they are less willing to seek out whatever low-paying jobs might be available. Researchers attribute this unwillingness to a so-called psychology of poverty or simply to wage expectations that are unrealistically high, given the relatively low schooling level of less-skilled African American males.[4]

But the dominant tendency in social science research has emphasized those factors that make it difficult for less-skilled African Americans to find work. The most influential point of view involves the dual-mismatch hypothesis. Its proponents argue that economic restructuring lies behind the stubbornly high jobless rates experienced by less-skilled city dwellers, especially African Americans. From this perspective, African Americans are mismatched with the urban job structure because of two simultaneous shifts: on the one hand, manufacturing jobs have been drifting away from cities to suburban areas, and, on the other hand, educational requirements for those jobs that remain in urban areas have been increasing. Hence, cities have become inhospitable places for job seekers with limited schooling, who do not qualify for the jobs that are nearby and cannot easily commute to the jobs for which they would be most likely to be hired.[5]

In its emphasis on the changing skill structure of urban economies and the geographic redistribution of people and jobs, the mismatch hypothesis captures a salient and undeniable aspect of today's urban reality. But the advent of an immigrant population raises doubts as to the causal chain invoked by mismatch proponents. If a mismatch between the requirements of urban employers and the skills of less-educated workers explains persistently high rates of African American unemployment, then African American workers should stand at the very tail end of the skill structure. That generalization once held true but no longer does, as shown in figure 6.1, which displays data for adult urban residents. In 1950 four out of every five African Americans had not earned a high school degree; that proportion subsequently slipped, so that by 1970 only three out five were not high school graduates, and by 1990 only one out of every five fell into this group of least-skilled workers. Low levels of education similarly predominated among the foreign-born at the start of this period. As with African Americans, the relative size of the adult population lacking a high school degree declined substantially after 1950. By 1990, however, there were relatively more immigrants than African Americans who lacked a high school

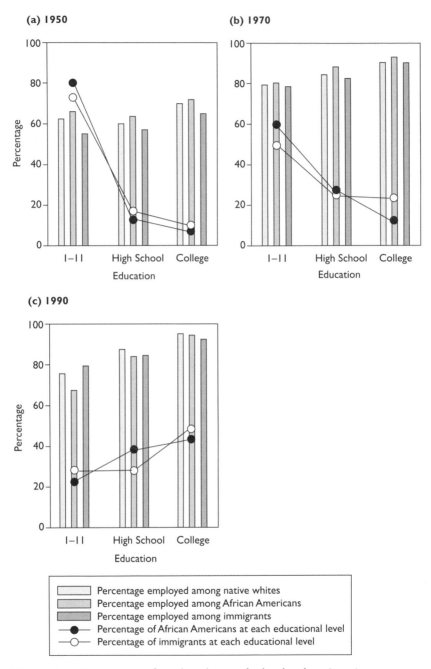

(a) 1950

(b) 1970

(c) 1990

Percentage employed among native whites
Percentage employed among African Americans
Percentage employed among immigrants
—●— Percentage of African Americans at each educational level
—○— Percentage of immigrants at each educational level

Figure 6.1. Percentages of employed, out-of-school, urban Americans, ages 24 to 65, grouped by educational levels in (a) 1950, (b) 1970, and (c) 1990

degree—a disparity that would widen were we to focus on Mexicans or exclude some of the high-skilled, Asian immigrant streams.

If skill deficiencies made some groups of urban residents more vulnerable to economic changes than others, immigrants—not African Americans—should top the list of groups in trouble. But, as figure 6.1 shows, immigrants do not. In 1950 African Americans were the least well educated of urban residents, but their paucity of formal school did not make them more vulnerable than others to unemployment; indeed, the least-skilled African Americans were more likely to work than comparable immigrants or native-born whites. By 1990 the patterns had reversed, and the least-skilled African Americans—a much smaller population than before—were the least likely to work of all. Thus, by the end of the twentieth century, urban African Americans seemed much less mismatched with their environment than immigrants were. And yet African American fortunes were clearly at low ebb.

Faced with this comparison, the importance of structural changes no longer seems quite so compelling. Rather, the crucial question becomes the issue posed by Vroman and Peterson: "If employers are looking for better educated workers, and the lack of jobs in the manufacturing sector explains the pressure on black employment, what accounts for the strong demand for immigrant Hispanic workers, who on average have less schooling and fewer skills?" To that query one can respond with any variety of possibilities, some of which are explored in chapter 3 of this book. In this chapter, I will pursue only one line of argument: the contention that the influx of immigrants, rather than any decline in the demand for less-skilled workers, lies behind the economic difficulties of urban blacks.

Toward that end, I will tackle the argument that immigrants may have pushed African Americans out of jobs by focusing on the chief African American employment concentrations in America's leading immigrant destinations. I will invoke the concept of ethnic niche to refer to the principal African American clusters, which I will identify as industries in which African Americans are employed at 150 percent of their share of total employment in any one place, at one time. The analysis involves a contrast between 1970 and 1990, the former year capturing immigration at a relatively low level, soon after the inception of the "new immigration," and the latter year capturing a situation of much greater immigrant density.

The logic of inquiry is straightforward. First, I seek to determine whether immigrants have converged on those same activities toward which African Americans have also gravitated. Second, after mapping shifts in the industries in which African Americans have concentrated,

I assess whether those changes might be due to displacement from immigrants or to some other set of factors. I focus on regions with an above-average foreign-born population, but they nonetheless vary considerably on this dimension as well as others, most notably the class and national-origin composition of the immigrants in question and the history and size of the African American population.

In effect, my methodology searches for *patterns* in the African American response to immigrants across places that vary along a variety of relevant dimensions. This contrast allows me to determine whether (1) the exogenous forces that vary across places lead to changes in African American employment patterns, in which case we should expect persistent, possibly growing intermetropolitan diversity in the characteristics of African Americans over time, or (2) change is due to factors endogenous to African Americans, in which case we should find growing similarity across these varying places, implying that immigration exercises at best a marginal influence on the outcomes of interest.[6] Now I return to the scholarly debate over immigrant competition, to set the intellectual context for the analysis that will follow.

Immigrant Competition Hypothesis

Research on the economic incorporation of immigrants and their impact on native workers has been an ongoing activity for much of the past two decades, with no sign that interest in the question is beginning to flag. Indeed, the question of competition loomed especially large in the deliberations of a special panel of the National Research Council convened to assess immigration's impact on the nation.[7] The commission's report, issued in 1997, has already come to be seen as the definitive statement on the issue. As one of its main conclusions, the panel offered the following assessment of the controversy over job competition between blacks and immigrants: "While some have suspected that blacks suffer disproportionately from the inflow of low-skilled immigrants, none of the available evidence suggests that they have been particularly hard-hit on a national level. Some have lost their jobs, especially in places where immigrants are concentrated. But the majority of blacks live elsewhere, and their economic fortunes are tied largely to other factors."[8]

Unambiguous and forthright as the statement may be, it is unlikely to be the last word uttered on this issue, in part because the literature provides too many contradictory conclusions. For instance, another, more recent, major collective project specifically designed to study the impact of immigrants on African Americans offers a different assessment: "Recent immigration to the United States appears to have exerted small negative effects on the economic situation of African Americans. Each of the effects uncovered by the individual research projects is small. If viewed in isolation, none of them would be thought to constitute strong evidence about adverse effects from immigration on African Americans. As a group, however, they add up to more compelling documentation that the positive effects of immigration ... are substantially less likely to extend to African Americans."[9]

What is more, quantitative researchers, mostly economists and social demographers, and qualitative researchers, mostly sociologists, approach the problem in quite distinct ways that in turn yield different conclusions. Surprisingly, though, each group's conclusions stand at some variance with the research programs within which they work. Quantitative researchers, who subscribe to the tenets of neoclassical economic theory, begin with theoretical predictions that forecast negative impacts, to be exerted by immigrants on native-born workers; yet the empirical studies undertaken by the same economists almost never find the predicted effect.

By contrast, qualitative researchers, working within the "new economic sociology," find evidence that immigrants hinder the life chances of natives by monopolizing the labor supply of the industries and occupations in which they concentrate. But the new economic sociology begins with the fundamental assumptions that (1) racial and ethnic lines fragment the labor market and (2) jobs get allocated through social networks, not the competitive process. Hence, this conclusion is logically inconsistent with sociological conceptualizations of how labor market processes work.

Quantitative Studies

Quantitative studies of immigration's impact on the labor market are the province of economists and social demographers. As noted, most economists work within the theoretical framework of neoclassical economics; most of the social demographers, by contrast, rarely explicate their theoretical perspective, yet their analyses are virtually identical to those of the former. A typical theoretical work in neoclassical economics begins with a small set of common assumptions. First, the number of workers employers are prepared to hire falls as the wage rate increases. Second, an increase in the number of workers caused by immigration will not induce an increase in demand for labor, since it is assumed that the prevailing wages and the level of hiring are fixed independently of the level of immigration. Third, the labor market is a perfectly competitive homeostatic market. Fourth, natives and immigrants are perfectly substitutable. Fifth, the host economy is a closed system with no international trade.[10]

These assumptions and the basic neoclassical model of the labor market can be concisely depicted by a simple figure, as in figure 6.2, which contains two types of curves. The downward-sloping curve shows the demand for labor in the market, with the number of workers employers are willing to hire declining as wages increase. In contrast, upward-sloping curves depict the supply of labor; here the number of workers who want to work rises as the wage increases. The intersection of these curves (B and C) determines the "equilibrium" wages (W1 and W2). This model depicts the labor market just as it would any other commodity market in which prices freely fluctuate until the market is clear. As is true in all other markets, whoever can sell at the cheaper price wins.[11]

Armed with this analytical model of the labor market, a neoclassical economist deduces that an inflow of immigrants will cause the income of the natives to fall. With falling wages, some natives may choose not to work for the lower wages and drop out of the labor market. The process of wage cuts and new hiring continues until jobs are provided for all the immigrants and natives who want them. The simple theoretical analysis predicts that immigrants will have negative effects on native workers by placing downward pressure on their wages.

Then the story gets more complicated. At the new equilibrium, production levels rise; in turn, higher production in a situation of falling wages increases the return for capital. Hence, immigration yields a hidden effect, entailed in the transfer of income from workers to capitalists. As George Borjas notes, "Immigration . . . generates a sizable redistribution of wealth in the economy, reducing the incomes of natives who are now competing with immigrant workers in the labor market and increasing the incomes of capitalists and other users of immigrant services."[12]

In short, the simple theoretical model predicts that immigrants will harm native workers, especially low-skilled workers, by reducing their wages and increasing the income inequality in the country. Further,

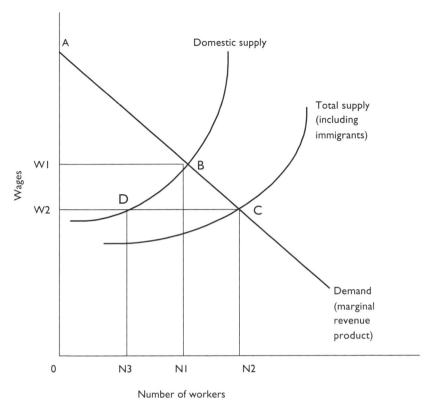

Figure 6.2.   Labor market demand and supply changes as a result of immigration

given the racial distribution of capital, this result implies that any benefits derived from immigration will more likely be reaped by European Americans than by African Americans.[13] To be sure, these conclusions are heavily shaped by the assumptions, which can legitimately be criticized as highly unrealistic. Yet not all of the assumptions listed prove equally necessary, and relaxing a number of assumptions leaves the conclusions generated by the simple model essentially unchanged.[14]

   Although researchers can agree on the direction of the impact, its magnitude is debatable. Based on a model of this generic type, George Borjas, Richard Freeman, and Lawrence Katz deduced that about 42 to 47 percent of the overall increase in the gap between the earnings of high school dropouts and those of high school graduates in the 1980s can be attributed to immigration and trade.[15] Thus, the combined effect of immigration and trade seems quite substantial, although more recent work, using somewhat similar theoretical simulations, suggests that the effect associated with immigration alone turns out to be a good deal smaller.[16]

A fuller range of neoclassical models yields roughly the same predictions about immigration's negative effects. Yet empirical research, whether conducted by economists or social demographers, produces a rather different view: so far, the empirical studies show that immigration has little if any economic impact on the wages and employment opportunities of natives, whether classified as unskilled, low paid, or members of racial minorities.[17]

Among the more influential studies is David Card's work on Miami, which exploited the natural experiment that transpired when Mariel refugees from Cuba suddenly arrived in Miami in September 1980, increasing the labor force by 7 percent almost overnight, after a decade with relatively little immigration. Were neoclassical theory to hold, such an exogenous "shock" should yield clear traces of either employment displacement or a drop in wages, and yet Card found no discernible effects on outcomes of either type.[18]

Similarly, using the 1970 and 1980 censuses, Robert LaLonde and Robert Topel studied the effects of immigration in 119 standard metropolitan statistical areas. They found that immigration had only a slight effect on earnings, such that a 100 percent increase in immigration to a city would cause only a 3 percent decline in the earnings of immigrants themselves and a 1 percent decline in the earnings of African Americans and Latino residents.[19] In another study Joseph Altonji and David Card reported on findings of a more ambiguous sort.[20] Looking at labor market outcomes among less-skilled natives in 120 major metropolitan areas in 1970 and 1980, they found a modest degree of competition between immigrants and less-skilled natives. While some of their statistical tests failed to reject the null hypothesis that there is no impact of immigration on the employment and earnings of low-skilled residents, others showed statistically significant results. Thus, Altonji and Card concluded that their estimates of the effect of immigration on native wage rates were so sensitive to the choice of specification and estimation procedure that it was hard to conclude definitively for displacement or against.

Bringing the analysis closer to the present, Butcher and Card used data from Current Population Surveys administered in 1979, 1980, 1988, and 1989, with a focus on 24 major cities, 10 of which involved the highest level of immigrant density and 14 of which had stable boundaries, had relatively large sample sizes, and were geographically comparable to the high-density immigrant cities but otherwise had relatively small immigrant populations. Again, they found that differences in immigrant density or changes in immigrant density had no significant effects on either low- or high-paid workers.[21]

Motivated, perhaps, by the failure of empirical research to behave as theory commands, a number of prominent labor economists have argued that the basic analytic strategy involved in these intermetropolitan comparisons has been flawed from the start.[22] To begin with, Borjas, Freeman, and Katz have argued, most extant studies have assumed that an increase in the fraction of immigrants in the city represents a net increase in the supply of labor in the local labor market. This assumption may be unwarranted, however, since those natives who are most affected by the immigration may migrate out of the city, reducing the impact of immigration on the overall wage restructure. Second, immigrants are more likely to settle in cities with growing economies and tight labor markets, a pattern that might bias the estimated correlation between immigrant inflows and native wages upward. Third, since cities are open economies, intercity trade may have diffused the impact of immigration to the local supply of labor. Finally, the studies ignore the skill differentials that exist in both the native and immigrant populations across metropolitan areas; instead, they lump all immigrants into one group and study the correlation between the fraction of immigrants in the labor market and the native wage. For these reasons, Borjas and his colleagues speculate, the findings accumulated by empirical researchers in economics remain highly suspect.

In response, Card, using the 1990 census, produced a new study designed to take into account internal migration flows among natives and heterogeneity among immigrants.[23] Instead of dividing natives into only two groups—low-skilled and high-skilled groups—Card tries to identify natives and immigrants who are most likely to compete in the labor market. He groups workers with "similar expected wage rates," assuming that workers who share the same predicted wage decile are most likely to compete in the labor market. Consequently, he divides up the sample into 10 skill groups, focusing the analysis not on the effect of the overall inflow of immigrants but on the "net number of people in a given skill group added to a city's population when an immigrant moves in."[24]

After identifying workers who are most likely to compete in the labor market, Card carefully proceeds to answer the objections leveled against the existing quantitative studies. First, he investigates "whether immigrant inflows to particular labor markets result in significant out-migration of natives."[25] He finds that the inflow of recent immigrants tends to increase the net outflow of immigrants who arrived before 1985 from the respective city, but it has no net negative effect on na-tives. He writes:

> The estimated effects of recent immigrant inflows on the raw or adjusted outflow rates of natives . . . are uniformly negative, and are relatively similar across specifications. The effects on the outflow rates of pre-1985 immi-grants are also uniformly negative, although there is more variation in the point estimates across specifications. With respect to inflow rates, the esti-mated effects are close to zero for natives, but are negative and statistically significant for pre-1985 immigrants. For natives, the estimated effects of re-cent immigrant inflows on *net* migration (inflows minus outflows) are there-fore positive, while for pre-1985 immigrants the effects on net migration are negative. *These findings suggest that inflows of recent immigrants generate some offsetting net out-migration among earlier cohorts of immigrants, but no such response among natives.*[26]

After investigating the claim that the nonfinding of the negative im-pact of immigrants is due to the internal migration of native workers, Card estimates the local labor market impacts of immigration. He fails to find any substantive support "for the notion that inflows of immi-grants depress the entire wage structure of a city."[27] In fact, the results indicate that "immigrant inflows actually attract significant numbers of natives and older immigrants. Moreover, simple cross-city comparisons of wages for particular skill groups with the overall inflow rate of recent immigrants show that, if anything, immigrant inflows are associated with higher wages."[28] Thus, the latest, most sophisticated treatment by a neoclassical economist concludes for the often-replicated nonfinding: that immigration yields little effect on less-skilled native workers, even in a period of such greatly accelerated immigration as the 1980s.

Searching for the elusive negative effect, however, continues. Sum-marizing the studies that appear in their edited volume on the economic impact of immigration on African Americans, a book published subse-quent to the *New Americans* study, the labor economist Daniel Hamer-mesh and the sociologist Frank Bean contend that immigration has had a modest but clearly identifiable negative effect on less-skilled African American workers.[29] The reports in the Hamermesh and Bean book, just like Card's work, belong to a new generation of empirical studies that try to overcome the shortcomings associated with the "area approach," identified by Borjas, Freeman, and Katz. For instance, the chapters by both Reimers and Butcher avoid the common pitfall of constructing seemingly similar but in reality quite heterogeneous groupings, as, for example, when all immigrants are grouped into cohorts regardless of educational levels or workers get divided into two simple groupings of high and low skilled.[30] Moreover, they show great creativity in their use of the statistical methods employed for specifying the effect of immigration as distinct from other potentially confounding factors related to local labor market characteristics or regional growth rates. As a result of refinements, Reimers arrives at a nuanced conclusion at some variance with the rest of the literature: low-skilled immigrants put a small but visible downward pressure on the hourly wages of native non-Hispanic white and black high school dropouts but have a positive impact on the wages of native-born Mexican American male dropouts. She also shows that the negative effect is greater for natives with higher "expected" wages, since "at the eightieth percentile of the wage residuals of native black and white non-Hispanic dropouts, a 1-percent-point increase in the share of unskilled recent immigrants in the local labor force during the 1980s (such as that experienced by Los Angeles, Houston, and Dallas–Fort Worth) reduced wages by over 4 percent."[31] Similarly, Butcher finds a small but "significant impact" of immigration on the change in the gap in annual earnings between whites and blacks. Thus the controversy bubbles on, all the high-profile efforts at closure notwithstanding.

Qualitative Studies

After more than a decade of work, quantitative researchers have yet to find conclusive evidence showing that immigration substantially harms the jobs or livelihoods of native-born workers. By contrast, qualitative researchers have found evidence of a sort obscured by econometric research, indicating that an inflow of immigrants does yield negative consequences for native workers, especially for African Americans.

Qualitative researchers, mostly sociologists, work within the conceptual framework of the new economic sociology. Unlike neoclassical economics, the new economic sociology lacks a deductive structure. It consists, instead, of a cluster of highly abstract concepts loosely tied together, although the recent efforts by Tilly and Tilly have improved the cohesiveness of this research program, especially as regards its application to the labor market.[32]

The notion of "embeddedness" provides the conceptual cornerstone of the new economic sociology.[33] Alejandro Portes defines embeddedness as a concept referring to "the fact that economic transactions of the most diverse sorts are inserted in overarching social structures that affect their form and their outcomes."[34] In practice, embeddedness simply means that "the economic action of individuals as well as larger economic patterns, like the determination of prices and economic institutions, are affected by networks of social relationships."[35]

Consequently, those labor mechanisms responsible for the creation and maintenance of social inequalities in society are influenced not just by such "objective" factors as quality or efficiency but also by other, intangible, factors including social networks, culture, and history.[36] As Tilly and Tilly argue, "Much of what passes for prejudice, discrimination, and preferential treatment in an individual perspective actually consists of differential connections among relations of production and nonproduction networks that are segregated by gender, race, ethnicity, age, schooling, and neighborhood."[37] Thus, the new economic sociology directs attention to the ways in which social networks affect individuals' socioeconomic outcomes. Most important for the question at hand, this sensitivity leads sociologists to focus on social differences in the processes that attach workers from different groups to jobs of disparate kinds.

Sociologists have pursued this interest in job-matching processes through case studies, focusing on the industries in which competition between immigrants and natives is most likely to occur and studying the mechanisms by which the typical entry-level job is filled. Research conducted in this tradition finds that employers typically fill jobs by relying on connections that link existing employees to their associates outside the workplace. Network hiring proves so common not just because it is cost-effective but because it also functions as a form of social control: new employees' social obligations to their sponsors at work effectively compel them to work hard. Using the existing employees as filters also ensures the reproduction of a workforce willing and able to work under the prevailing work conditions. As employers told Roger Waldinger, "I find that employees will only refer qualified applicants. Because that applicant they're referring, they're putting their name on, so they're at stake too. And the employee has a good understanding [of the business]—can communicate what the job, the pay, etc. are really like."[38]

In some cases employers further seek a racially and ethnically homogeneous workforce as a way of reducing friction on the job. This practice is especially common in environments in which series of jobs are interdependent in the production. As one employer said, "In the back of the house the most important thing is interaction with co-workers. There's limited space. You don't want guys who don't like one another. Everyone has to help one another. They have to get along. You don't want friction."[39]

The consequence of network hiring is "a tendency toward social closure, removing those workers not connected to incumbents from the effective labor supply. [Hence,] . . . blacks were the most likely to be tacitly excluded, though in some cases reliance on Mexican networks barred Central Americans, and vice versa."[40]

The perpetual use of network hiring balkanizes the labor market along ethnic lines. Sociologists explain the creation and maintenance of racial and ethnic balkanization using the concept of path dependency or cumulative causation. Portes explains:

> Cumulative causation operates in this case through the entry and successful performance of "pioneers" in certain branches of employment and their subsequent referral of kin and co-ethnics for other job openings. Later arrivals are compelled to work diligently not only to fulfill personal obligations to those who found them jobs but also because they are being monitored by the entire ethnic community (enforceable trust). These employees open the way for others until the ambiance of the work place acquires the cultural tones of the group. Once this happens, outsiders find it increasingly difficult to overcome entry barriers, while those in co-ethnic networks are granted privileged access.[41]

By implication, the advent of immigration has segmented the labor market along ethnic lines, as those activities into which immigrants have gravitated get turned into ethnic niches, which in turn reduces job opportunities for natives, especially low-skilled African Americans.

From this point of view, native workers have trouble finding jobs not because they lack the necessary human capital but because they lack social capital, another key concept invoked by the new economic sociology. "Social capital refers to the capacity of individuals to command scarce resources by virtue of their membership in networks or broader social structures."[42] In practice, however, social capital means much more. For instance, Model identifies an additional aspect of social capital involving the "widespread belief that members of a particular group are well suited to their niche jobs and poorly suited for alternatives."[43] But there is another side of the same coin to these favorable group-specific perceptions: the expectation that out-groups lack the ability or productivity needed to do the job in the appropriate way. For instance, Kirschenman and Neckerman and William J. Wilson found that Chicago employers view immigrants as willing to take jobs with "harsher conditions, lower pay, fewer upward trajectories, and other job related characteristics that deter native workers, and thereby exhibit a better 'work ethic' than others."[44] And an excerpt from one of Waldinger's interviews with Los Angeles employers provides further amplification:

> Yes, the immigrants just want to work, work long hours, just want to do anything. They spend a lot of money coming up from Mexico. They want as many hours as possible. If I called them in for 4 hours to clean latrines, they'd do it. They like to work. They have large families, a big work ethnic, and small salaries. The whites have more, so they're willing to work fewer hours. Vacation time is important to them. They get a play and want to get 2 months off. They want me to rearrange a schedule at a moment's notice. These guys in the back would never dream of that. They would like to go back to Mexico every four years for a month which I [let them] do. The back of the house workers take vacation pay and then work through their vacations. I try to get them to take off a week once a year. But most of them plead poverty. The kids [who are natives] in the front of the house are still being taken care of by their parents. I'm not trying to disparage them, but they're spoiled.[45]

Similarly, Katherine Newman's recent study of fast-food workers in Harlem shows just how employers' preference for hiring through contacts *combined* with their group-specific preferences yields devastating results: employers in this low-skilled industry were significantly less likely to hire blacks than others, more likely to hire immigrants than U.S.-born persons, and more likely to hire persons who had a contact with an existing employee.[46]

The importance of social capital implies that not all workers are perceived as interchangeable in the market for all the available jobs, at least in the short run. Consequently, the sociological conceptualization of labor market functioning differs fundamentally from the neoclassical view. In the sociological perspective, labor market processes are governed by two queues: a job queue, arraying the available jobs according to their relative desirability to workers, and a labor queue, ordering the available worker groups according to their relative desirability to employers. Those at the beginning of the queue are the most desirable employees: first to get hired and last to get fired. Those at the end of the queue are last hired and first fired.[47]

Recruiting agents determine who gets to the front of the labor queue, using a variety of sorting criteria to pick and choose among groups—

most notably, socioeconomic background, place of residence, educational credentials, and, unfortunately, the race and ethnicity of the worker. For some agents, any ethnic preference in hiring reflects an antipathy toward some out-group, or a taste for discrimination, as Gary Becker puts it.[48]

Alternatively, recruiters may rely on signs of ethnic group membership, but not for reasons at all related to preferences as such. Instead, ethnic traits may be important because they function as substitutes for other, unavailable, forms of information. After all, reliable information about a potential worker's possible productivity is costly, if even feasible, to obtain. Because workers surely have better knowledge of their own habits and abilities than do employers, the relationship between buyers and sellers is one of "asymmetric information," which in turn implies that efficient, "competitive" market conditions are unlikely to apply. Facing a "hidden information" problem in the labor market, recruiting agents may conclude that ethnicity serves as "a good statistic for the applicant's social background, quality of schooling, and general job capabilities."[49] Familiarity with the work habits of the dominant ethnic group in the workplace will generate further reason to favor applicants whose ethnicity is similar to those of the dominant incumbents.

If hiring agents use group membership as a proxy for an applicant's productivity, they may also be motivated by other considerations—most important, the possibility that recruiting coethnic workers is a way of generating social control. In effect, the employer is in search of what Portes has labeled "enforceable trust," since the new employee brought in through networks to incumbents will be motivated to comply as a result of the social obligation owed to his or her sponsor at work.

The role of ethnic networks in the labor market thus tends to lock any given set of employers to some categorically distinctive set of workers; for this reason, the sociological perspective on labor markets suggests that immigrants and natives will act as noncompeting groups in the labor market in any given period, each group serving as the favored, if not monopolistic, supplier of labor for its economic niche.

Appraisal

Thus, we arrive at a central paradox: sociologists work with a conceptual apparatus that emphasizes the noncompetitive nature of the labor market and use it to draw the conclusion that the deteriorating socioeconomic conditions of low-skilled native workers, and especially African Americans, result, in part, from the inflow of immigrants. Neoclassical economists conceptualize the labor market as a competitive and naturally self-adjusting entity, but they cannot find any substantial effects on native wages or employment produced as a result of immigration.

One source of the problem may be disciplinary bias—most notably, the highly abstract nature of the formal theoretical and econometric work. For instance, as careful as he is, Card's conceptualization of "skill" is wanting. As stated previously, he uses the expected wage rate, measured by predicted wage deciles, as a proxy for the skill level of workers. This procedure lumps together sales representatives and electricians into a homogeneous skill group, members of which are expected to compete against each other in the labor market, since they earn very similar hourly wages. But that grouping, which follows by definition, is otherwise not very plausible.[50]

In addition, the average impact of immigration may well be slight. Nonetheless, averages are misleading, especially since the immigrant population is concentrated in just a handful of metropolitan areas, many of which have seen a rapid and massive buildup of the immigrant population, of a scale and at a pace sufficient to produce a large impact. In Los Angeles, for example, the immigrant population increased by 550 percent between 1960 and 1990. Based on the estimate by Robert LaLonde and Robert Topel, cited earlier, this rapid increase could have caused a 15 percent decline in the earnings of immigrants and a 5.5 percent decline in the earnings of African American and Latino residents of Los Angeles.[51] True, the declines are not of overwhelming magnitude, but from the standpoint of groups already standing at the bottom of the totem pole, they are hardly trivial.

Finally, the deductive-nomological model of explanation practiced by economists who study immigration also provides little, if any, insight into the actual process by which immigrants affect the labor market, because it reveals little about how the preferences, recruitment techniques, and organization practices of employers enter into the equation.[52]

Qualitative studies suffer from shortcomings of a different type. Although intuitive and yielding insights into the actual labor processes, the evidence furnished by these studies too frequently involves "systematically" selected anecdotes. The case study approach employed by sociologists has its own problems. Case study research concentrates on one or, at best, a few strategically chosen industries at a time, and the narrow range of selection is likely to influence the results. Typically, the relevant studies single out cases in which immigrants are substitutes for rather than complements of natives. Consequently, studies of immigrant-dense industries cannot preclude the possibility that any competition the researchers observe is outweighed by new opportunities created by immigration in other sectors of the economy. As Waldinger concludes an essay in which he argues that immigrants displaced blacks from the restaurant and hotel industries in Los Angeles, "To be sure, I've uncovered no smoking gun and the small size of the sample leaves any conclusions less than decisive."[53]

Moreover, the conclusion that African American workers have been displaced by immigrants implies that immigrants and natives are seeking the same jobs. But the data provided by the sociological research almost never address this issue. The research is lacking in this regard because most of the information comes from employers, not from workers, who are the most appropriate source of information regarding the jobs they prefer and seek. In any case, the hints supplied by the qualitative studies suggest divergent, not convergent, labor supply paths. Waldinger writes:

> Previous research . . . emphasize[s] the importance of network recruitment as one of the mechanisms that block blacks' access to entry-level jobs. . . . But hotels and restaurants do a considerable amount of hiring from the workers who simply come in off the street looking for jobs. And what was striking about my interviews was the sense that black workers—not unlike white—have fallen out of the labor force most available to fill the lowest, entry-level positions, with the notable exception of front-of-the-house restaurant jobs which remain dominated by whites. "There are very few blacks among the walk-ins," noted the personnel manager in a hotel where, indeed, very few blacks were employed.[54]

Finally, the argument that blacks have lost jobs due to immigrant displacement assumes that the quantity and quality of jobs in the economy are independent of the existence of immigrant labor. But many of the jobs held by immigrants may be the by-product of immigration itself, as, for example, when immigration creates demand for the products and services that immigrants themselves consume. In this case, one could no longer argue that immigrants displace natives but rather that natives find themselves excluded from the economic sectors benefiting from immigration-driven job creation. Any such conclusion, however, implies that the current composition of jobs would change if the inflow of immigrants were limited or if immigration were reduced as a result of some other development. Were immigration to cease, the jobs created as a result of past immigration might shift over to the native-born. But conditions in the global and globalizing economy make such prospects doubtful; far likelier is the possibility that capitalists will relocate their investments abroad, resulting in the wholesale disappearance of the jobs once filled by immigrants. It is not just that "immigrant" jobs could go abroad, a scenario whose direct effects would be limited by the fact that only about 25 percent of the jobs held by immigrants are in the manufacturing sector and are thus most at risk of relocation. More broadly, these immigrant-dense production activities are linked to other jobs in services, trade, design, and so on, which means that the ripple effects associated with the out-migration of jobs now held by immigrants are likely to be greater still.

African Americans and Immigrants in America's Leading Immigrant Destinations

Rather than provide yet another foray into assessments of an econometric or qualitative type, in this chapter I opt for intermediate ground, working inductively and focusing on concrete employment patterns in the nation's leading immigrant destinations. I begin with the assumptions of the new economic sociology, that categorically different groups of workers get sorted into distinctive places in the labor market, yielding concentration in particular activities; this concentration is denoted by the concept of ethnic niche. If immigrants have displaced African American workers, we should see immigrant incursion into those activities in which African American workers played a disproportionately important role, at least until the recent inflow of immigrants. Insofar as the structure and characteristics of African American niches might either facilitate or impede immigrant entry, we can draw reasonable inferences about the potential for displacement. Likewise, changes in the industries in which black workers concentrate provide the basis for drawing inferences about competition or its absence.

From the standpoint of a sociologically oriented understanding of labor market competition, as I have already argued, institutional and group-specific factors reduce the potential for displacement. None of the groups of interest—neither immigrants nor African Americans—is allocated across labor markets on the basis of skill or training alone. Rather, the pattern is affected by the historically contingent balance of forces pushing toward exclusion, on the one hand, and expansion of opportunities, on the other; the embeddedness of employment networks thus leads to a high degree of path dependence.

Moreover, one wants to distinguish between employment concentration as a phenomenon and the specific clusters on which groups converge at any one point in time. Both may be variable, and the growing influence of either market forces or assimilation could lead to declines in both the overall level of concentration and concentrations in niches of any particular kind. But concentration may well persist over an extended period of time, during which the specific lines of concentration get greatly overhauled. This dynamic and uncertain relationship complicates the problem of identifying competition. A shift from one set of niches to another may be impelled as much by factors endogenous to the group, such as the changing expectations of younger generations, as by exogenous factors, including a decline in discrimination.

In any case, region-specific factors, such as those reviewed in chapter 1, naturally influence the types of niches in which groups can cluster. The nature of the Miami economy is such that manufacturing, of any type, is unlikely to provide room for ethnic niches of any significant size. Chicago's very different industrial mix, oriented toward goods production, has the potential for yielding the opposite effect. On the other hand, some functions reappear from region to region: personal service industries, such as hotels or domestic service or government employment. Region-specific histories, including the specific circumstances under which groups entered an urban area, and the other contending parties with whom they had to deal are also influential factors, accentuating interregional differences in the mix of any group's niches. By contrast, effects that are endogenous to African Americans, regardless of place, work in the opposite direction, narrowing rather than widening interregional differences and producing largely the same patterns of economic concentration. Thus, convergence or divergence of niche structure across regions provides a key indicator of immigration's impact or lack thereof.

In 1970 African American employment concentrations gave evidence of both regional particularities and group effects. As can be seen from figure 6.3, black workers were heavily concentrated in niches in all five regions, though with noticeable differences from place to place: almost half of black workers clustered in niches in Miami (47 percent) and San Francisco (45 percent); by contrast, niches employed just over one-third of black workers in New York and Chicago and just under one-quarter in Los Angeles.

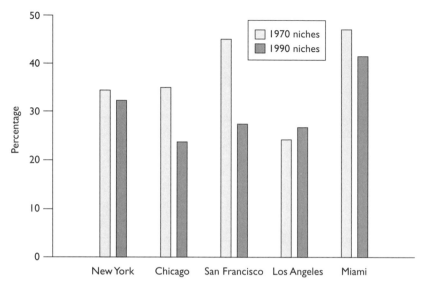

Figure 6.3.   Percentage of African Americans employed in niches, 1970 and 1990

Regardless of the overall level of concentration, African Americans were likely to converge on a similar set of industries in all five places, as can be seen at the sectoral level, by looking at figure 6.4, and at the detailed industry level, by looking at table 6.1. Personal service was a common cluster everywhere. Domestic service (a niche in all five places), laundry work (likewise in all five), and hotel employment (found in San Francisco, Miami, and Los Angeles) exemplify the types of low-status employment—often involving either tasks or personal relationships reminiscent of relationships between blacks and whites in a society under slavery—to which blacks were often confined, at least through the first half of the twentieth century.

Thus, the "job ceiling" that Drake and Cayton had observed in the 1940s and had described in *Black Metropolis* was still apparent in 1970, and nowhere more so than in Miami.[55] As the only southern metropolis among our five immigration regions, Miami contained the densest concentration in these traditional African American niches; elsewhere, opportunities had opened up in other sectors.[56] As emphasized by William Wilson and John Kasarda, manufacturing—from which African Americans had previously been excluded—opened its doors after World War II, with the result that industry became a linch-

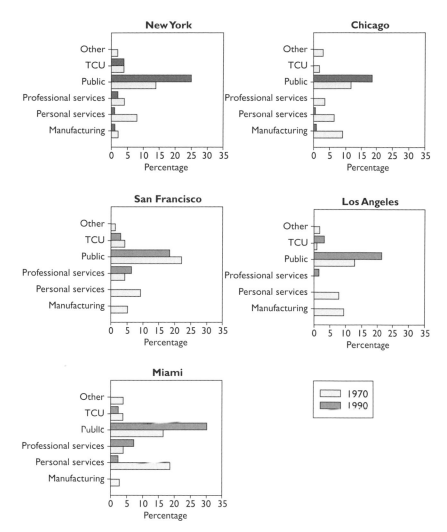

Figure 6.4.   Percentage of African American employment in niches, by major industrial sectors, 1970 and 1990

pin of African American employment in the urban economy.[57] Indeed, in all five places, the manufacturing sector included a number of industries that had evolved into African American niches by 1970. Only in Los Angeles and Chicago, however, did employment in manufacturing niches come close to providing 10 percent of all jobs held by African Americans, and in no case did manufacturing emerge as the principal sector of concentration.

TABLE 6.1.   MOST COMMON AFRICAN AMERICAN NICHES, 1970 AND 1990

	Year	New York	Chicago	San Francisco	Los Angeles	Miami
Public sector						
Welfare, service, and religious organizations	1970	✓	✓	✓		✓
	1990	✓	✓	✓	✓	✓
Street railways and busses	1970	✓	✓	✓	✓	✓
	1990	✓	✓	✓		✓
Postal service	1970	✓	✓	✓	✓	✓
	1990	✓	✓	✓	✓	✓
Other medical services	1970	✓	✓	✓	✓	✓
	1990	✓	✓	✓	✓	✓
Hospitals	1970	✓	✓	✓	✓	✓
	1990	✓	✓	✓	✓	✓
Local public administration	1970	✓	✓	✓	✓	✓
	1990					
Federal public administration	1970	✓	✓	✓	✓	✓
	1990	✓		✓		
Private sector						
Hospitals	1970	✓	✓	✓		✓
	1990					
Motor vehicles	1970	✓		✓	✓	✓
	1990	✓	✓	✓		✓
Private household services	1970	✓	✓	✓	✓	✓
	1990	✓	✓			✓
Street railways and busses	1970	✓	✓	✓		✓
	1990					
Telephones	1970	✓	✓	✓	✓	✓
	1990					
Hotels	1970		✓	✓	✓	✓
	1990					
Laundering	1970	✓	✓	✓	✓	✓
	1990					

Rather, African Americans were more likely to gravitate to government employment, which topped all other sectors as a locus of African American niches everywhere and played a particularly notable role in San Francisco. For the most part, as of 1970, blacks gravitated to the same set of functions everywhere—in particular, the postal service, public transit, and public hospitals.

At an absolute level, demographic differences among the five places influenced the degree to which an immigrant labor force was likely to find its way into those industries in which African Americans had established concentrations. Although employers are unlikely to hire workers according to their proportion in the population or the workforce, composition nonetheless usually yields some effect. In 1970, however, compositional factors alone would have had only a modest effect everywhere but Miami, where immigrants already constituted more than one-fifth of the workforce. In Los Angeles, by contrast, barely 1 in 10 workers was foreign-born in 1970.

For the most part, the African American niches of 1970 were concentrated in industries in which immigrants were underrepresented, as shown in figure 6.5. In the figure, African American employment niches are divided into three groups: (1) industries in which immigrants are highly overrepresented (index of representation [IR] greater than or equal to 1.5), (2) industries with slight immigrant overrepresentation (IR less than 1.5 but greater than 1), and (3) industries in which immigrants are underrepresented (IR less than or equal to 1). The figure summarizes the distribution of immigrants across African American niches in 1970 and 1990.

At a time when a third of African American New Yorkers were employed in industries that could be classified as African American niches, just over 60 percent of that group found itself in industries in which immigrant employment stood below parity. Thus the immigrant share of jobs in these particular black niches did not equal the immigrant share of jobs in the economy overall. In broad sweep, Chicago and San Francisco looked roughly like New York; Los Angeles and Miami provided alternative, polar types. Although Los Angeles then had a relatively modest immigrant population, it was heavily concentrated in industries in which African Americans had also clustered.

The pattern can be glimpsed in figure 6.6, which contrasts levels of African American and immigrant employment in all of the African American niches of 1970. The niches are further divided into those that remained as African American niches in 1990 (open circles) and those

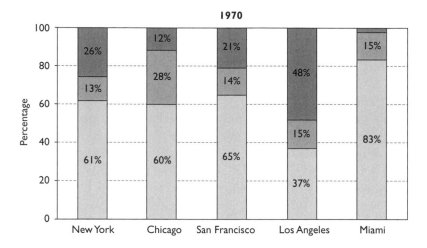

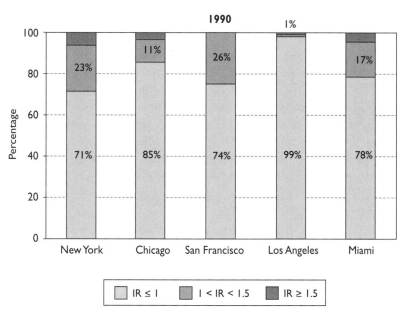

Figure 6.5. Percentage of African American employment in niches, by level of immigrant representation, 1970 and 1990

Note: IR, index of representation.

that no longer had high levels of African American representation by 1990 (filled circles). Two lines are added to enhance interpretation. A vertical dotted line shows the percentage of the region's workforce that is foreign-born. By contrast, the line at a 45-degree angle from the axes provides a measure of correlation between the sizes of the black and immigrant workforces at the industry level: points close to the 45-degree line indicate that an industry relies on black and immigrant workers to a comparable degree; points off the 45-degree line signal that one of the two groups is more heavily represented. For 1970 most observations lie to the left of the parity line, indicating that immigrants were generally underrepresented in African American niches in 1970, though in a few industries the two groups were equally represented.

Still, there are notable exceptions. In Los Angeles, apparel manufacturing had already absorbed a large immigrant workforce: indeed, no other industry among the top 10 African American niches in each of the five regions came close to tilting toward such a high level of immigrant dependency in 1970. Immigrants were also overrepresented in laundries, private households, hotels, and auto repair shops. By contrast, the industries in which black Miamians had concentrated did not attract a disproportionately large foreign-born workforce. The Miami case also illustrates the public-sector effect: the path to work on government payrolls proved far more difficult for Miami's foreign-born workers than for their native African American counterparts. As figure 6.6 shows, immigrants were employed below parity in each of the four black public-sector niches in Miami and at very low levels of representation in three of those four industries. In Miami the single largest African American niche—domestic service—remained far more impervious to immigrant penetration than in America's other leading immigrant destinations. The literature provides no clue as to why Miami was so different in this respect. I suspect that the silence is telling: perhaps the relatively selective group of Cubans, though still not quite recovered from the losses sustained in the flight from Cuba, already had better alternatives than to work in domestic service, surely more stigmatized than the factory or other service jobs that they readily took.

Thus, we observe substantial interurban differences in the degree of immigrant representation in the African American niches of 1970, but we also note certain similarities. In general, public-sector niches appear to have absorbed a relatively modest immigrant workforce: of the public-sector niches identified in figure 6.6, immigrant employment stood above parity in just one industry—hospitals in New York.

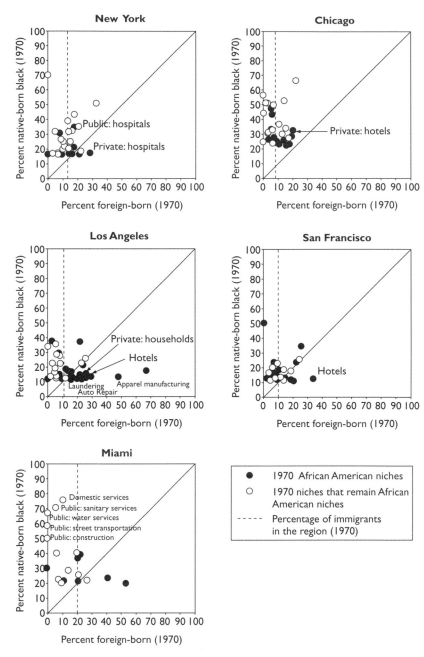

Figure 6.6.   African American niches: percent foreign-born by percent African American, 1970

Indeed, the hospital case underscores the specific barriers posed by government work itself, as immigrant representation was always higher among private-sector as opposed to public-sector hospitals. By contrast, immigrants had made substantial inroads into the niches most clearly linked to African Americans' historically subordinate role. Hotels, for example, were places of African American concentration in Chicago, Los Angeles, and San Francisco; in each of these three places, it was also an industry of immigrant overrepresentation. With the exception of Miami, private household work also involved a substantial immigrant contingent, as did laundry work.

The situation looked quite different 20 years later. The striking change was due in part to the convergence of African Americans onto public-sector employment. By 1990, as figure 6.7 highlights, the public sector had emerged as the overwhelming black niche in all five places. Part of the shift involved the personal services industries. This traditional employer of African American workers emptied out; its major components no longer qualified as African American niches in San Francisco and Los Angeles and retained only a residual African American workforce in New York, Chicago, and even Miami. The African American presence in manufacturing also severely eroded—and not just in Chicago, where the goods production sector as a whole was hard hit, but also in Los Angeles and San Francisco, where it thrived. Moreover, the outflow from these two sectors was part of a general retreat from private-sector niches overall. As can be seen from figure 6.6, which uses filled circles to identify the 21 industries in which blacks were overrepresented in 1970 but that no longer qualified as niches in 1990, every case involved private-sector employment.

Were African Americans pushed? Or did they go on their own? To answer these questions, further examination of the 1990 employment configuration is in order. The most significant trait distinguishing African American employment patterns in 1990 from those in 1970 involved lower exposure to immigrant employment, as shown in figure 6.5. Los Angeles presents the most striking turnaround: in 1970 the industries in which African Americans were most concentrated were also likely to rely, disproportionately, on immigrant ranks; by 1990 the industries with the strongest African American presence were, for all practical purposes, industries in which immigrants were underrepresented.

A comparison of figures 6.6 and 6.7 illuminates how African Americans' exposure to immigrants diminished during this period. First, African American concentrations in those industries in which immigrants

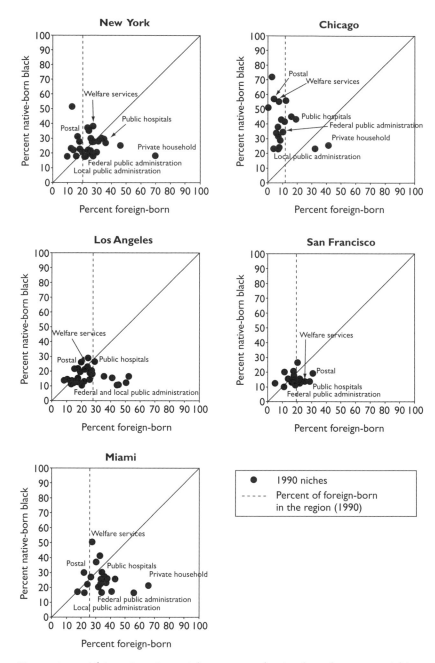

Figure 6.7.   African American niches: percent foreign-born by percent African American, 1990

were overrepresented—private household service, apparel manufacturing, laundering, hotels, and auto repair—simply disappeared. Second, concentration in the three public-sector niches established earlier—the postal service, welfare services, and hospitals—persisted, and at comparable levels of African American density. Third, many African Americans shifted into industries with relatively low immigrant penetration rates. Thus, by 1990, six new African American niches—federal and local public administration, public utilities, telephone, private mass transit, and private-sector welfare and religious services—appeared. Although the three latter industries involve private-sector employment, they share some of the defining traits of government employment—namely, a large bureaucracy that tends to engage in formal recruitment and whose visibility makes monitoring easy. Whether public or private, all 10 of the most important African American concentrations in Los Angeles were also industries in which immigrants had yet to gain a job share equivalent to their proportion of the region's jobholders as a whole. Indeed, immigrant employment in the key African American concentrations was often strikingly low—nowhere more so than in local public administration, in which fewer than 1 out of every 10 workers was foreign-born, as opposed to more than 3 out of every 10 workers for the region overall.

Roughly speaking, a similar change transpired in the four other places, though nowhere quite as drastically or dramatically as in Los Angeles. Chicago was closest to the LA mode. Overall, the African American niches of 1990 involved industries of considerably lower immigrant penetration than those two decades before. Unlike the situation in Los Angeles, immigrants in Chicago held jobs above the parity level in 2 of the 10 largest black concentrations—public-sector hospitals and bakeries. But, for the most part, as shown in figure 6.7, African American workers in Chicago were clustered in industries in which immigrant penetration levels fell well below parity. As in Los Angeles, black Chicagoans persisted in public-sector niches that had been established earlier and did so at very high levels of African American density—as in the case of the post office, where more than half of all employees were African Americans. They also established new niches that if not equally high in black representation were nonetheless industries in which immigrants had difficulty establishing themselves. Once again, the case of local public administration serves as an example of the economic environments that provided comparatively easy access to African American workers and yet remained largely closed to the growing foreign-born population.

Certainly, there are individual specificities to be noted in a detailed examination of the three remaining regions, but none involves major departures from the patterns characteristic of Los Angeles or Chicago. Naturally, compositional factors affected the absolute level of immigrant penetration in black niches. In the most immigrant dense of all regions, Miami, the industries of African American concentration also tended to rely heavily on foreign-born contingents—and far more so than somewhere like Chicago, where the immigrant workforce was, in relative terms, almost one-third as large. Even so, one is struck by the degree to which immigrants in Miami, with its large, relatively affluent, and politically influential Cuban population, remained substantially underrepresented in many of the key African American niches.

Moreover, the 1990 data underscore the high degree of isomorphism among the five regions, a major shift from the earlier period. In 1970 African American niches often varied from region to region; the concentrations reflected the particular types of opportunities available in each place—for example, in Chicago blast furnaces, which were never a possibility in New York or Miami. To be sure, the historical patterns to which I referred earlier—including confinement to low-status, menial fields such as private domestic service—generated considerable interurban uniformity.

Nonetheless, the convergence on government employment and a set of government-like functions—most notably mass transit and telephones—reveals a degree of similarity among the cities not seen before. By 1990, as shown in table 6.1, six public-sector industries—welfare services, mass transit, the postal service, other health service, hospitals, and federal public administration—had become black niches in all five regions, a trait characteristic of local public administration in all regions but San Francisco. More striking was the thinning out in the number of black niches, as the remaining clusters, which still absorbed a large proportion of total black employment, now concentrated in a very small number of industries. Examining the 10 largest African American niches in each of the 5 regions, it turns out that these 50 cases actually involved only 18 separate industries.

The similarities among the regions point toward a tentative answer to the questions about competition posed previously. Isomorphism underlines the ethnic nature of the black employment pattern: clustering in the industries identified in table 6.1 represents one of the distinguishing traits of this group. The isomorphic nature of the niches further suggests that the underlying force producing concentration was likely to have been endogenous. Although the five regions encompass America's leading immigrant destinations, they vary greatly in the relative size and composition of their immigrant populations, as noted elsewhere in this book. And, yet, the types of concentrations toward which blacks have gravitated differ little from place to place: roughly the same set of clusters show up in Miami—where immigrants constitute 41 percent of the workforce—as in Chicago—where the foreign-born workforce is just over 15 percent. Much the same can be said for the specializations from which African Americans exited. For example, why should laundries have disappeared as an African American concentration in all five regions unless there were some other set of factors—independent of immigration—that weakened African Americans' attachment to this industry?

Moreover, immigration counts as only one of the exogenous factors affecting blacks' employment opportunities. Others were clearly at work during the same period, as evidenced by the emergence of new niches. Local public administration is the best case in point: not a concentration in 1970, it emerged in 1990 as an African American employment niche in all regions except San Francisco. The period under review was one in which local governments everywhere faced severe pressures to improve recruitment of African American employees and enhance their promotional opportunities. Factors specific to the politics of local government undoubtedly played a role as well: in retrospect, the period of the late 1980s is likely to be seen as the heyday of African American influence in local politics, a decade in which the city halls of the nation's largest cities were all captured by African American mayors—David Dinkins, in New York; Harold Washington, in Chicago; Tom Bradley, in Los Angeles. As Raphael Sonenschein has shown in *Politics in Black and White,* a study of Los Angeles during the Bradley years, the advent of a black mayor substantially altered African American Angelenos' access to public employment. And as Waldinger showed in *Still the Promised City?* New York saw much the same outcome—notwithstanding the absence, until 1989, of an African American mayor, a turn of events that testifies to the strong political pressures bearing down on any big-city mayor, as well as to the dynamics of government as a specific type of labor market.[58]

The contention that African Americans were pulled into the concentrations established by 1990—as opposed to having been pushed from the clusters they had occupied in 1970—would rest on stronger grounds if we could also show that the shift during this period involved the replacement of bad jobs with better ones. It hardly seems difficult to characterize the contrast between the black niches of 1990 with the concentrations held 20 years earlier in just this way. Consider the comparison of the quintessentially "old" versus "new" black niches—domestic service versus public employment. On the one hand, the large body of literature on domestic service highlights not just the stigma and low pay associated with this particular line of work but also the great uncertainties in compensation and the arbitrariness in the definition of job responsibilities—attributes deeply resented by the workers who perform these functions.[59] On the other hand, the public sector offers higher wages, greater certainty of employment, and something likely to be still more valued by its African American employees: a particularly low likelihood of discrimination.[60]

To the extent that schooling signals something about the quality of jobs, it is relevant to note that workers in the African American niches of 1990 had considerably higher levels of education than those in the 1970 niches, a characteristic found in all five regions. Because my data derive from the Census of Population, I note that this indicator conflates the education of workers with the skill requirements of their jobs. Therefore, some portion of the educational upgrading of African American niches may simply reflect the entry of younger African American workers who are better educated than their older counterparts. However, it seems unlikely that work in local or federal public administration was actually no more skilled than the jobs involved in personal service work. Indeed, in 1970 a large gap in median schooling levels distinguished workers in the public-sector niches from persons employed in personal service, a differential that persisted through 1990. Although the contrast in median wages is not quite so stark, the 1990 pattern still represents a shift to industries with higher real wages, a change all the more impressive if we recall that real earnings overall during this same period essentially stagnated.

Conclusion

I began this chapter by asking whether immigrants' movement into the American economy has occurred "on the back of blacks." Nothing contained in the evidence presented here precludes the possibility of competition. Most important, immigrants began the period with sizable concentrations in the same industries in which African Americans tended to be clustered. If we accept a widely held view that migration is a network-driven process, then those industries of early immigrant concentration would have been the likely targets of subsequent migration. Our knowledge of the specific industries in question—apparel manufacturing, private household work, and hotels, to name just a few of the important cases—provides detailed documentation of how immigrant networks were implanted at an early stage and subsequently delivered a burgeoning immigrant workforce.

In general, the industries toward which African American workers had gravitated by 1970 did not rely—or, at least, had not yet relied—disproportionately on an immigrant workforce. Because African Americans held dense concentrations in a number of key industries in which immigrants had already established themselves at high levels of representation and that were subsequently the targets of the immigrant inflows that expanded in the two decades after 1970, one can infer the potential for displacement.

However, that conclusion is difficult to reconcile with the characteristics of the African American employment niches that had emerged by 1990. As I have noted, the same pattern essentially emerged in all places, regardless of the sharp differences in the size and characteristics of the immigrant populations among the five regions in question. Although these five regions also differ substantially in the structure of their economies, they showed little variation in the types of niches from which African Americans departed or the types of niches that they created. The new areas of employment concentration appear to be of better quality than clusters that African Americans occupied in the past. Further, the configuration of 1990 involved much less exposure to high immigrant employment, implying that African Americans proved increasingly successful in gaining access to jobs that immigrants found particularly hard to obtain.

Of course, a transformation of this sort may well have involved many instances of individual competition. It is quite likely, for example, that after 1970 African American sewing machine operators in Los Angeles found it increasingly difficult to either find or retain jobs, because the industry steadily tilted toward an immigrant workforce. But I doubt that immigrant convergence on such traditional African American concentrations as apparel manufacturing, or domestic service, or laundry work yielded large net effects. As we have seen, sizable opportunities opened up in sectors that had previously contained a much smaller African American presence, a change that most clearly reconfigured the position of African American niches in the one metropolis in which immigrant and African American employment concentrations most closely overlapped—Los Angeles. Relatively speaking, more African American workers were equipped to take advantage of those opportunities by 1990: owing to improved levels of education, the proportion of African American workers whose limited schooling confined them to jobs in apparel manufacturing or domestic work significantly declined during the period in question.

That African Americans found employment gains in the public sector highlights both the positive and negative factors associated with immigration. The decades following 1970 were years when America's leading immigrant destinations were losing their hold on their native-born populations. If not for immigration, the populations of these cities would have almost certainly shrunk, which in turn would have made for a greatly reduced demand for public services and the public funds allocated for such services. To the extent that immigrants swelled the demand for public employment, even as the employment structure of the public sector remained closed to foreign-born workers, the inflow of immigration may have generated distinctive benefits for native-born African Americans, whose dependency on public-sector jobs has grown over the years.

Thus, this chapter provides a sociological reinforcement of the empirical findings supplied by economists. Yet the story told here seems more in line with the approach adopted by sociologists. After all, the emergence and persistence of ethnic niches testify to the pervasive and enduring effects of social structures—whether of an informal nature, such as social networks, or of a more formal kind, such as the bureaucratic mechanisms involved in government work. Attention to differences in social structures and to the role these social structures play in allocating particular jobs to particular groups helps explain why immigrant inflows of the scope experienced by Los Angeles or Miami had little if any impact on the jobs available to native-born African American workers.

The shift toward public-sector niches may have both diminished the effects of immigrant competition and put African Americans in a position to absorb the positive effects associated with population gains produced by immigration. But we should not downplay a serious consequence of the types of niches that African Americans have consolidated since 1970. As I noted earlier, these industries employed workers with relatively high levels of education—from which I infer that high levels of schooling are either required for the job or are seen as normative, if not absolutely necessary, for task completion. While that characteristic prevents immigrants from making inroads into the sectors, it also tends to exclude African American workers with limited schooling from those industries with the greatest African American densities. For instance, skill or credential requirements in the public sector make it difficult, if not impossible, for the least skilled of African American workers to exploit the ethnic networks implanted in government employment. At the same time, these least-skilled workers must find employment in a market increasingly saturated with immigrants and in which the likelihood of working as a member of a small minority—and, therefore, being easily harassed and vulnerable—grows steadily. Moreover, the circumstances under which African Americans moved into the public sector no longer hold. For much of the time in question, government was a growth sector, enabling federal and local governments to incorporate African American workers without alienating the established white rank and file. Government is now clearly a declining enterprise.

What is more, immigrants—or if not immigrants then their descendants—increasingly want greater access to public-sector jobs. The same processes that opened up public jobs for African Americans in the late twentieth century are likely to work in an opposite direction in years to come. The visibility of public-sector employment made it a particularly convenient target for the application of affirmative action policies. Transparency made it difficult for government officials to defend functions that did a poor job of recruiting African Americans and likewise made it easier for advocacy groups to focus their efforts on those departments that were lagging in the effort. That same characteristic, however, now highlights the degree of African American overrepresentation when their population shares are at best stagnant if not declining and the new immigrant populations have generally yet to attain parity. What is more, the changing demographic situation is also steadily undermining black political influence in the leading immigrant cities, a process bound to accelerate as rates of naturalization and voting increase.

Under these circumstances, what future lies ahead for African Americans with limited schooling? It is clear that their situation will not be improved by simply reducing the flow of immigration. In the era of the North American Free Trade Agreement (NAFTA), any decline in the supply of low-skilled immigrants will simply push employers to move their businesses abroad. One obvious strategy is to concentrate resources on further improvements in the educational levels of African

Americans, so that more will be able to take advantage of the group employment niches in the public sector. But this approach is likely to yield only short-run effects, for all the reasons I have just stated. The only viable long-term alternative involves expanding private-sector employment opportunities. The policy challenge therefore entails a search for instruments that will increase the number of employers willing to hire African Americans with limited schooling. Some employers may respond to incentives; others will only react to the type of legal sanctions that we have had in the past, such as affirmative action. Whatever the mechanism, drawing less-skilled African American workers into the economic mainstream remains an imperative: the twenty-first century will continue to grapple with the central dilemma of the last: the problem of the color line.

Notes

1. Toni Morrison, "On the Backs of Blacks," in *Arguing Immigration: Are New Immigrants a Wealth of Diversity . . . or a Crushing Burden?* ed. Nicolaus Mills (New York: Touchstone, 1994), 97–100.

2. For a recent summary of studies on racial inequality, see M. Alexis, "Assessing 50 Years of African-American Economic Status, 1940–1990," *American Economic Review* 88, no. 2 (1998): 368–375. To be sure, researchers disagree on what is the state of racial inequality and the socioeconomic conditions of African Americans. For example, William A. Darity Jr. and Patrick L. Mason ("Evidence on Discrimination in Employment: Codes of Color, Codes of Gender," *Journal of Economic Perspectives* 12, no. 2 [1998]: 63–90) document the continuing significance of race in the labor market, whereas James J. Heckman ("Detecting Discrimination," *Journal of Economic Perspectives* 12, no. 2 [1998]: 101–116) contends that it is not race but the skills of African Americans that sustain the apparent racial gap in the labor market.

3. Charles A. Murray, *Losing Ground: American Social Policy, 1950–1980* (New York: Basic Books, 1984); Finis Welch, "The Employment of Black Men," *Journal of Labor Economics* 8, no. 1 (1990): S26–S74; John Bound and Richard B. Freeman, "What Went Wrong? The Erosion of Relative Earnings and Employment among Young Black Men in the 1980s," *Quarterly Journal of Economics* 107, no. 1 (1992): 201–232.

4. Lawrence M. Mead, *The New Politics of Poverty: The Nonworking Poor in America* (New York: Basic Books, 1992). Gerald D. Jaynes ("Race and Class in Postindustrial Employment," *American Economic Review* 88, no. 2 [1998]: 357–362) makes a more sophisticated, sociopsychological argument for high joblessness among African Americans. Harry Holzer, "Reservation Wages and Their Labor Market Effects for White and Black Youth," *Journal of Human Resources* 21 (1986): 157–177; Welch, "Employment of Black Men."

5. Harry Holzer, "Black Employment Problems: New Evidence, Old Questions," *Journal of Policy Analysis and Management* 13 (1994): 699–722; James H. Johnson Jr. and Melvin L. Oliver, "Structural Changes in the US Economy and Black Male Joblessness: A Reassessment," in *Urban Labor Markets and Job Opportunity,* ed. George E. Peterson and Wayne Vroman (Washington, D.C.: Urban Institute, 1992), 12; William J. Wilson, *The Truly Disadvantaged* (Chicago: University of Chicago Press, 1987); idem, *When Work Disappears: The World of New Urban Poor* (New York: Vintage Books, 1997).

6. Thanks to Mark Ellis for helping to clarify this point.

7. James P. Smith and Barry Edmonston, *The New Americans: Economic, Demographic, and Fiscal Effects of Immigration* (Washington, D.C.: National Academy Press, 1997).

8. Smith and Edmonston, *New Americans,* 6.

9. Daniel S. Hamermesh and Frank D. Bean, *Help or Hindrance? The Economic Implications of Immigration for African Americans* (New York: Russell Sage Foundation, 1998), 12.

10. For a detailed discussion about the orthodox labor economics, see Ronald G. Enrenberg and Robert S. Smith, *Modern Labor Economics: Theory and Public Policy* (Reading, Mass.: Addison-Wesley, 1997). See also John Isbister, *The Immigration Debate: Remaking America* (West Hartford, Conn.: Kumarian Press, 1996); Rachel Friedberg and Jennifer Hunt, "The Impact of Immigrants on Host Country Wages, Employment, and Growth," *Journal of Economic Perspectives* 9, no. 2 (1995): 23–44; and Smith and Edmonston, *New Americans,* for discussions of the different theoretical models and their implications.

11. Wins, that is, in the sense of getting a job. Overall, all workers lose as wages decline.

12. George J. Borjas, "The Economic Benefits from Immigration," *Journal of Economic Perspectives* 9, no. 2 (1995): 9, 19; Friedberg and Hunt, "Impact of Immigrants"; Smith and Edmonston, *New Americans,* 140.

13. George J. Borjas, "Do Blacks Gain or Lose from Immigration?" in *Help or Hindrance? The Economic Implications of Immigration for African Americans,* ed. Daniel S. Hamermesh and Frank D. Bean (New York: Russell Sage Foundation, 1998), 51–74.

14. For further discussion on this subject, see Isbister, *Immigration Debate*; George J. Borjas, "The Economics of Immigration," *Journal of Economic Literature* 32, no. 4 (1994): 1667–1717; Borjas, "Economic Benefits from Immigration," 9; and Friedberg, and Hunt, "Impact of Immigrants."

15. George J. Borjas, Richard B. Freeman, and Lawrence F. Katz, "On the Labor Market Effects of Immigration and Trade," in *Immigration and the Work Force: Economic Consequences for the United States and Source Areas,* ed. G. J. Borjas and R. B. Freeman (Chicago: University of Chicago Press, 1992); G. J. Borjas, R. B. Freeman, and L. F. Katz, "Searching for the Effect of Immigration on the Labor Market," *American Economic Review* 86 (1996): 246–251; G. J. Borjas, R. B. Freeman, and L. F. Katz, "How Much Do Immigration and Trade Affect Labor Market Outcomes?" *Brookings Papers on Economic Activity* no. 1 (1997): 1–90. I cannot overemphasize that their estimates are deduced from a theoretical model, and the estimated negative effects are

combined effects from immigration and trade. Many readers seem to be confused about the nature of these studies. Isbister *(Immigration Debate)* points out that "the study [Borjas, Freeman, and Katz, "Effect of Immigration"] did not directly measure the effect of immigration on the incomes of high school dropouts in the country. Rather, it made deductions from a model. The only variable it measured directly was the increase in unskilled labor caused by immigration. Beyond this it deduced, on the basis of an understanding of economic theory and general quantitative relationships in the economy, the effect that this increase in unskilled labor *must have had* on wage rates. The study had no way of looking directly at the relationship between immigration and wage rates, however. Consequently, although it is filled with tables and numbers, it should be thought of as belonging to . . . abstract model building, rather than . . . empirical estimation" (148).

16. In his article "Do Blacks Gain or Lose from Immigration?" George Borjas estimates that "immigration has probably reduced the income of the typical black native in the United States by perhaps more than one hundred dollars annually" (p. 69).

17. For a list of important studies, see Appendix B in Michael Fix and Jeffery F. Passel, *Immigration and Immigrants: Setting the Record Straight* (Washington, D.C.: Urban Institute, 1994) for an exhaustive list of the empirical studies and summaries of their findings.

18. David Card, "The Impact of the Mariel Boatlift on the Miami Labor Market," *Industrial and Labor Relations Review* 43 (1990): 245–257. Card did speculate that reduced in-migration of natives could also have contributed to the pattern he found.

19. Robert LaLonde and Robert Topel, "Immigrants in the American Labor Market: Quality, Assimilation, and Distributional Effects," *American Economic Review* 81 (1991): 297–302.

20. Joseph G. Altonji and David Card, "The Effects of Immigration on the Labor Market Outcomes of Less-skilled Natives," in *Immigration, Trade, and the Labor Market*, ed. J. Abowd and R. Freeman (Chicago: University of Chicago Press, 1991), 201–234.

21. Kristen F. Butcher and David Card, "Immigration and Wages: Evidence from the 1980s," *American Economic Review* 81, no. 2 (1991): 292–296.

22. Borjas, Freeman, and Katz, "Labor Market Effects"; idem, "Effect of Immigration"; Borjas, "Economics of Immigration."

23. David Card, "Immigration Inflows, Native Outflows, and the Local Labor Market Impacts of Higher Immigration" (Department of Economics, Princeton University, Princeton, N.J., 1996).

24. Ibid., 3.

25. Ibid., 20.

26. Ibid., 26, emphasis added. These findings contradict the findings of other studies (Randall K. Filer, "The Effect of Immigration Arrivals on Migratory Patterns of Native Workers," in *Immigration and the Work Force: Economic Consequences for the United States and Source Areas,* ed. G. J. Borjas and R. B. Freeman [Chicago: University of Chicago Press, 1992]; William Frey, "The Impact of Recent Immigration on Population Redistribution within the United States" [Re-

search report 96-376, Population Studies Center, University of Michigan, Ann Arbor, 1996]) that indicate that low-income, less-skilled domestic migrants are moving away from high-immigration areas. David Card acknowledges this contradiction and points out that "none of the previous studies has attempted to estimate skill-group-specific migration responses, holding constant city-wide aggregate factors" ("Immigration Inflows," 31). However, similar results have been reported by Richard Wright, Mark Ellis, and Michael Reibel ("The Linkage between Immigration and Internal Migration in Large Metropolitan Areas in the United States," *Economic Geography* 73, no. 2 [1997]: 232–252). Nonetheless, one can safely conclude that more research is needed to resolve this controversy.

27. Ibid., 38.

28. Ibid., 39.

29. Hamermesh and Bean, *Help or Hindrance?*

30. Kristen F. Butcher, "An Investigation of the Effect of Immigration on the Labor-Market Outcomes of African Americans," in *Help or Hindrance? The Economic Implications of Immigration for African Americans,* ed. Daniel S. Hamermesh and Frank D. Bean (New York: Russell Sage Foundation, 1998), 149–182; Cordelia Reimers, "Unskilled Immigrants and Changes in the Wage Distribution of Black, Mexican American, and White Non-Hispanic Male High-School Dropouts," ibid., 107–148.

David Card acknowledges this and points out that "none of the previous studies has attempted to estimate skill-group-specific migration responses, holding constant city-wide aggregate factors" ("Immigration Inflows," 31).

31. Reimers, "Unskilled Immigrants," 142.

32. Michael J. Piore, review of *The Handbook of Economic Sociology,* by Neil Smelser and Richard Swedberg, *Journal of Economic Literature* 34 (1996): 741–754; Charles Tilly and Chris Tilly, *Work under Capitalism* (Boulder, Colo.: Westview Press, 1998); Charles Tilly, *Durable Inequality* (Berkeley and Los Angeles: University of California Press, 1998).

33. Mark Granovetter, "Economic Action and Social Structure: The Problem of Embeddedness," *American Journal of Sociology* 91 (1985): 481–510.

34. Alejandro Portes, *The Economic Sociology of Immigration: Essays on Networks, Ethnicity, and Entrepreneurship* (New York: Russell Sage Foundation, 1995), 6.

35. Richard Swedberg, *Economics and Sociology: Redefining Their Boundaries* (Princeton, N.J.: Princeton University Press, 1990), 100.

36. Tilly and Tilly, *Work under Capitalism,* 73.

37. Ibid., 80.

38. Roger Waldinger, "Black/Immigrant Competition Re-assessed: New Evidence from Los Angeles," *Sociological Perspectives* 40 (1997): 370.

39. Ibid., 371.

40. Ibid., 372.

41. Portes, *Economic Sociology of Immigration,* 17.

42. Ibid., 12; A. Portes, "Social Capital: Its Origins and Applications in Modern Sociology," *Annual Review of Sociology* 24 (1998): 1–24.

43. Suzanne Model, "The Ethnic Niche and the Structure of Opportunity: Immigrants and Minorities in New York City," in *The Historical Origins of*

the Underclass, ed. Michael Katz (Princeton, N.J.: Princeton University Press, 1993), 166.

44. Joleen Kirschenman and Kathryn M. Neckerman, "'We'd Love to Hire Them, But . . .': The Meaning of Race for Employers," in *The Urban Underclass,* ed. C. Jencks and P. Peterson (Washington, D.C.: Brookings Institution, 1991), 203–234; Wilson, *When Work Disappears,* 140.

45. Waldinger, "Black/Immigrant Competition Re-assessed," 376.

46. Katherine Newman, *No Shame for My Game: The Working Poor in the Inner City* (New York: Alfred A. Knopf, 1999), chapter 8 and p. 309.

47. Lester C. Thurow, *Generating Inequality: Mechanisms of Distribution in the U.S. Economy* (New York: Basic Books, 1975); Rober W. Hodge, "Toward a Theory of Racial Differences in Employment," *Social Forces* 52 (1973): 16–32; Stanley Lieberson, *A Piece of the Pie: Blacks and White Immigrants since 1880* (Berkeley and Los Angeles: University of California Press, 1980); Barbara F. Reskin and Patricia A. Roos, *Job Queues, Gender Queues: Explaining Women's Inroads into Male Occupations* (Philadelphia: Temple University Press, 1990).

48. Gary S. Becker, *The Economics of Discrimination* (Chicago: University of Chicago Press, 1957).

49. George A. Akerlof, *An Economic Theorist's Book of Tales* (New York: Cambridge University Press, 1984), 14–15; and Kirschenman and Neckerman, "'We'd Love to Hire Them, But.'"

50. Card, "Immigration Inflows," 16.

51. LaLonde and Topel, "Immigrants in the American Labor Market."

52. I refer to economists exclusively, since social demographers who have done quantitative studies of the issues rarely specify the theoretical underpinning of their statistical models. Yet the statistical models that they use are identical to the ones that economists use. I do not wish to leave a wrong impression that this statement is about economics as a discipline. In fact, one of the most exciting areas of labor economics has been incorporation of sociological and psychological assumptions into the standard theories of the labor market. However, those efforts have yet to be incorporated into the study of immigration.

53. Waldinger, "Black/Immigrant Competition Re-assessed," 383.

54. Ibid., 368.

55. St. Clair Drake and Horace R. Cayton, *Black Metropolis: A Study of Negro Life in a Northern City* (New York: Harper & Row, 1962).

56. In an early publication, the geographer Harold M. Rose underlined the unusual centrality of domestic service and related jobs for the employment of Miami's black population. See Harold M. Rose, "Metropolitan Miami's Changing Negro Population, 1950–1960," *Economic Geography* 40 (1964): 221–238.

57. John Kasarda, "Cities as Places Where People Live and Work: Urban Change and Neighborhood Distress," in *Interwoven Destinies: Cities and the Nation,* ed. Henry Cisneros (New York: W. W. Norton, 1993), 82; idem, "Jobs, Mismatches, and Emerging Urban Mismatches," in *Urban Change and Poverty,* ed. M. G. H. Geary and L. Lynn (Washington, D.C.: National Academy Press,

1988), 148–198; William J. Wilson, *The Truly Disadvantaged: The Inner City, the Underclass, and Public Policy* (Chicago: University of Chicago Press, 1987).

58. Raphael Sonenschein, *Politics in Black and White* (Princeton, N.J.: Princeton University Press, 1993); Roger Waldinger, *Still the Promised City? African-Americans and New Immigrants in PostIndustrial New York* (Cambridge, Mass.: Harvard University Press, 1996), chapter 7.

59. See Judith Rollins, *Between Women: Domestics and Their Employers* (Philadelphia: Temple University Press, 1985). Though Rollins's sample was very small, all but one of the domestic workers she interviewed in the Boston area in the early 1980s were of southern, small-town, or foreign background, certainly factors relevant to the exodus of African Americans from personal services, as observed here.

60. See Waldinger, *Promised City*, pp. 114–118; and Peter Eisinger, "Local Civil Service Employment and Black Socio-Economic Mobility," *Social Science Quarterly* 67, no. 2 (1986): 165–180.

Chapter 7

THE IMMIGRANT NICHE
Pervasive, Persistent, Diverse

Roger Waldinger and Claudia Der-Martirosian

At the top of the immigration research agenda stands the question of how newcomers change after they have arrived. The conventional wisdom, both academic and popular, says that immigrants *should* change by entering the American mainstream. The concept of assimilation stands as a shorthand for this point of view.

In its canonical form the theory of assimilation begins with the assumption that immigrants arrive as "ethnics," an identity reinforced by their tendency to recreate their own social worlds. Cultural change occurs as Americanization transforms the tastes, everyday habits, and preferences of the second generation. But Americanization can proceed even as the ethnic social structure of interpersonal relations largely stands still: as long as immigrants and their descendants remain embedded in ethnic neighborhoods, networks, and niches, integration into the fabric of American society must wait; once ethnic boundaries are crossed, however, the increased probability of exposure to outsiders inevitably pulls ethnic communities apart. With the move from ethnic ghetto to suburb, interethnic friendships, networks, and eventually marriages all follow in due course. Thus, the advent of *structural assimilation*, to borrow the influential term coined by Milton Gordon, signals entry into the mainstream and the beginning of the end for any distinctiveness associated with the immigrant generation.[1]

All this is now entirely familiar to students of American ethnicity—but perhaps too much so, since the canonical view has little, if anything, to say about the driving force behind the changing probability of contact with outsiders, namely, movement out of the socioeconomic cellar. All one can do is to infer the likeliest answer: that economic progress takes the form of dispersion from the occupational or industrial clusters that immigrants initially establish. From the assimilationist standpoint, such concentration is a source of disadvantage explained by lack of skills and education: with acculturation and growing levels of schooling and American experience, immigrants and their children naturally move upward by filtering outward from their ethnic niche.

Today's scholars, however, tend to disagree with this model. Instead, they emphasize the connections that bind newcomers together and the resources generated by the contacts that crisscross immigrant communities. These ties constitute a source of "social capital," providing social structures that facilitate action, such as the search for jobs and the acquisition of skills and other resources needed to move up the economic ladder. Networks connecting veterans to newcomers allow for rapid transmission of information about job openings and opportunities for new business start-ups. Networks also provide useful information within workplaces, reducing the risks associated with initial hiring and similarly connecting coethnic entrepreneurs, who take membership in the community as an index of trust.[2] Once in place, the networks are self-reproducing, since each incumbent recruits friends or relatives from his or her own group, and entrepreneurs gravitate to the cluster of business opportunities that their associates in the community have already identified. Because relationships among coethnics are likely to be multifaceted rather than specialized, community effects go beyond their informational value and engender both codes of conduct and the mechanisms to sanction those who violate norms.[3] Concentration is beneficial, as the search for advancement takes a collective rather than an individual form, and network-dense communities provide the informational base and support mechanisms to create a pattern of parallel movement up the economic ladder.[4]

So goes the now conventional wisdom among many of today's immigration specialists. These views are most likely to resonate with sociologists and anthropologists, but they are hardly confined to these particular disciplinary tribes alone. The economist Glenn Loury, one of the first to invoke social capital as a factor facilitating movement up from the bottom, argues that "each individual is socially situated, and one's location within the network of social affiliations substantially affects one's access to various resources."[5] George Borjas, certainly a card-carrying neoclassical economist, has essentially endorsed the same point of view, showing that access to resources shared by the group as a whole can redound to the individual's benefit.[6] Similar perspectives can be found among political scientists and those in other disciplines.

Of course, not everyone has signed on to the program. There remain numerous defenders of the old-time religion who continue to argue that dispersion remains the best and the most common way for immigrants and their descendants to move up the economic ladder.[7] And even exponents of the new perspective are divided on almost as many points as they agree. They are uncertain about how best to characterize the clusters that immigrants have established: Are they ethnic economies, ethnic enclaves, ethnic niches, or perhaps even some other neologism that better captures the phenomenon? Just what name to use matters, because each concept denotes a somewhat different phenomenon, each varying in nature and extent. Whether one opts for the most restricted or most expansive appellation, questions of size and persistence loom large, since an exceptional phenomenon, not the everyday, more prosaic mean, may attract attention. Even if concentration is pervasive at any one time it may simply result from the large immigrant inflows of recent years and may thus be a phenomenon of passing importance.

This chapter is designed to provide a new look at the economic concentrations immigrants have established in America's largest urban regions. As we will show, clustering is indeed pervasive; it is found in every place and is typical of every major immigrant type, regardless of skill level or reason for migration. Admittedly, this portrait is somewhat dated, as our concern with examining patterns at a high level of disaggregation forces us to rely on the large sample base that as of yet only the 1990 Census of Population can provide. But if the picture is not fully contemporaneous, it offers a novel point of view, as we deploy a new technique for illuminating the multidimensional nature of the clusters immigrants have established.

As we shall show, understanding concentration provides important but limited information, since the clusters vary greatly across groups: some confine immigrants to the very worst segments of the labor market, others provide access to opportunities of a far more favorable nature, and still others offer intermediate options. Still, whatever the nature of the clusters, they are an enduring phenomenon. As we will show later in this chapter, once established, patterns of concentration exercise an enduring attraction for immigrants, even as they deepen roots in the United States. We will describe these patterns shortly, but let us first return to the debate over ethnic clustering that we have just begun to sketch out.

Ethnic Enclaves, Economies, or Niches: The Play of Debate

That immigrants tend to gravitate toward a narrow set of economic activities and then stay there is neither new nor news. The historical literature on American immigration is replete with observations on the predilections of immigrants for trades and occupations of various kinds. Scholars studying chain migration naturally noticed that newcomers moving from the same hometown not only became neighbors in the New World but often worked alongside one another. As today, clustering was always more pronounced among some groups than among others. Jewish immigrants from Poland were a particularly noticed and noticeable example, establishing not only *landsmannschaften*—hometown associations— but also a *landsmannschaft economy,* a striking concept coined by Moses Rischin that somehow never got much intellectual circulation.[8]

Immigration scholars have always been sensitive to the specializations with which newcomers so frequently begin. But ideological and academic preoccupation with assimilation focused attention elsewhere; the social science analysis of immigrant adaptation developed analytic tools and concepts to study such phenomena as intermarriage and residential change but not the ethnic structuring of the occupational order. Stanley Lieberson, in his influential 1980 book *A Piece of the Pie,* aptly captured the state of thinking: he used the term *special niches* to note that "most racial and ethnic groups tend to develop concentrations in certain jobs" that reflect cultural characteristics, special skills, or opportunities available at the time of arrival, but he did not probe deeper into the issue.[9]

The Ethnic Enclave

What led social scientists to think differently was renewed interest in, and appreciation of, that much-maligned social category, the petite bourgeoisie. Small business had always been an immigrant and ethnic specialty but it commanded little more than a passing academic nod until Ivan Light wrote his seminal *Ethnic Enterprise in America*. Light's central point, that ethnic solidarity propelled business growth among Japanese, Chinese, and West Indian immigrants, can now be seen as a formulation of embeddedness *avant la lettre;* but, although the book was widely read, its historical focus blunted its broader impact on the ways in which social scientists thought about contemporary immigrant progress.[10]

Instead, the catalytic intellectual development was the publication of Kenneth Wilson and Alejandro Portes's article on the Cuban immigrant enclave in Miami, more than 20 years ago.[11] Reporting on the initial wave of a longitudinal survey of newly arrived Cuban refugees and their labor market experiences in Miami from 1973 to 1976, Wilson and Portes found that a sizable proportion of the newcomers went to work for coethnics. They also discovered that those who worked for immigrant bosses were doing better than refugees employed in white-owned firms in the secondary labor market—which in turn prompted a piece of scholarly revisionism that became known as the "ethnic enclave hypothesis." What earlier observers had seen as a sweatshop, Wilson and Portes recast as an apprenticeship: low wages for a couple of terms of labor in the ethnic economy—dubbed the "enclave"—in return for which one learns the tools of the trade in order to set up on one's own and thus move ahead.

The scholarly news about Miami's Cuban ethnic economy and its impact provoked immense interest in terms of both policy and theory. After all, the central question in immigration research concerns the prospects for immigrants and their children. The research on Cubans suggested that at least some would move ahead successfully, and, more startlingly, they would do so on their own, turning disadvantage to good account. But if so, researchers then had to explain how Cubans and possibly other entrepreneurially active groups could use business as a stepping-stone. An earlier wave of research had shown that other visibly identifiable minorities were trapped in the "secondary labor market," unable to move into the "primary labor market," where employment was more stable, job arrangements allowed for upward mobility, and workers were rewarded for investments in skill and training.[12] Indeed, Portes and Bach's research showed that this pattern persisted among recent Mexican immigrants.[13] The puzzle was all the more compelling because the industries that comprised the Cuban ethnic economy also made up the secondary sector. The same structural factors that impeded skill acquisition, attachment (to a particular firm, industry, or labor market), and upward mobility in the secondary sector also characterized the ethnic enclave. Yet workers in the enclave appeared to enjoy some of the advantages associated with the primary sector.

As would be expected with any attention-grabbing piece, the ethnic enclave hypothesis quickly led to an ethnic enclave debate. It soon became apparent that the phenomenon to which Portes and his colleagues drew attention was not so easily identified in the other capitals of immigrant America. In the unusual immigrant metropolis of Miami—where most newcomers were middle-class refugees—Cubans appeared to provide ample employment to others of their own kind. Although, by definition, employment of coethnics served as a distinguishing feature of the enclave, scholars eventually noted that this characteristic was relatively uncommon: immigrant entrepreneurship could be found aplenty; instances in which immigrant owners *and* workers were overrepresented in the very same activity were a good deal more rare.[14]

The concept of the ethnic enclave also proved limiting. *Enclave* denotes segregation within a particular territorial configuration. And Portes's original elaboration further narrowed the parameters of the enclave, depicting it as both geographically distinct and encompassing a self-supporting economy that itself generated a variety of inputs and outputs. The notion of self-sufficiency was a nonstarter from the very beginning: if the largest cities are far from self-supporting, how could small ethnic enclaves do any better? Moreover, we know that immigrant economies are not spread throughout the larger economy but rather are highly specialized in a few industries or business lines in which ethnic firms can enjoy competitive advantages. Likewise, the emphasis on spatial concentration proved a red herring: though many immigrant neighborhoods serve as the fount of business activity, immigrant entrepreneurs spring up throughout the urban landscape—whether or not there are many coethnic customers to be found. Clearly, space may be a variable affecting the outcomes of immigrant entrepreneurship, but there seems little reason to treat it as a defining characteristic.[15]

The greatest problems had to do with the central finding itself: that immigrant workers laboring for a coethnic boss did better than those employed in *comparable jobs* but engaged by an Anglo employer. The immediate issue was how to explain this apparent anomaly; the initial literature did not help matters by offering a number of different accounts. Ethnic solidarity was one of the possibilities invoked: "Immigrant entrepreneurs," wrote Portes and Bach in *Latin Journey,* "rely upon the economic potential of ethnic solidarity."

> Ethnicity modifies the character of the class relationship—capital and labor—within the enclave. Ethnic ties suffuse an otherwise "bare" relationship with a sense of collective purpose in contrast to the outside. But the utilization of ethnic solidarity in lieu of enforced discipline in the workplace also entails reciprocal obligations. If employers can profit from the willing self-exploitation of fellow immigrants, they are also obliged to reserve for them those supervisory positions that open in their firms, to train them in trade skills, and to support their eventual move into self-employment. It is the fact that enclave firms are compelled to rely on ethnic solidarity, and that the latter "cuts both ways," which creates opportunities for mobility unavailable in the outside.[16]

This story was plausible, but *Latin Journey* provided no evidence that ethnic solidarity operated in the hypothesized way. For all their emphasis on the effects of ethnicity on relationships within the immigrant business, Portes and Bach had little to say about the immigrant firm itself: with the exception of an item on the ethnicity of a worker's employer, they collected no information about the internal organization of ethnic firms, their recruitment and training practices, or their connections to other firms. In effect, this formulation assumed solidarity, a presupposition that there was never any necessity to entertain. A more parsimonious view would simply have suggested that the development of ethnic networks would generate the infrastructure and resources for ethnic small businesses before a sense of group awareness or solidarity need develop. In the end, Portes himself moved on to a view of this sort, arguing that "bounded solidarity" and "enforceable trust"—*emergent* community characteristics related to the development of ethnic networks—provided the necessary ingredients to both mobilize resources and limit obligations, thereby making exchanges within the ethnic enclave reciprocal and not exploitative.[17]

Conceptual niceties aside, the nub of the problem involved replication. Jimy Sanders and Victor Nee fired the opening salvo: looking at the Chinese in San Francisco and Cubans in south Florida, they found that self-employment was good for the immigrant bosses but much less satisfactory for the immigrants most likely to work in their shops.[18] Min Zhou and John Logan then added nuance, showing that male Chinese immigrants in New York indeed benefited from working in industries of Chinese concentration but that their female counterparts had no such luck.[19] Greta Gilbertson and Douglas Gurak, who examined the experience of Colombians and Dominicans in New York, came up with results that essentially supported Sanders and Nee's critique.[20] Portes, needless to say, fired back, but with conclusions a good deal more modest than those he had originally advanced—namely, that workers in the enclave *do no worse* than those at work elsewhere.[21] Debate on the matter continues, but in the meantime the theoretical action has moved elsewhere.

The Ethnic Niche

As we noted earlier, the particular economic configuration identified as an enclave is a relatively rare element in the immigrant employment scene. Miami may have an enclave, as conventionally defined, of sizable dimensions; so, too, do the Chinatowns of San Francisco and New York, but then one quickly begins to run out of cases. Moreover, some of the immigrant groups with the highest self-employment levels seem to be particularly unlikely to exhibit the pattern associated with Miami's Cubans. Koreans, for example, are renowned for their entrepreneurial success, with self-employment rates well above the levels attained by Cubans. But Korean owners largely make do with a non-Korean workforce, in part because small business ownership has simply swept up so many Korean immigrants that there are too few coethnics for Korean bosses to hire.[22] And the Korean story is hardly unique, as we have shown in our study of Iranians in Los Angeles. Admittedly, members of this group are not typical, as they are refugees with the good fortune of arriving with ample capital and entrepreneurial experience to boot.[23] Even so the example is entirely relevant: Iranians have garnered tremendous business success and have done so without a co-ethnic labor force. Similar stories can be told for Israelis, Arabs, Russians, Greeks, Asian Indians, and various other immigrants who have made their mark in small business.[24] In effect, the old middleman minority pattern of ethnic entrepreneurs selling to an out-group clientele, exemplified in earlier immigration history by American Jews, remains alive, well, and a good deal more common than the ethnic enclave of immigrant bosses and their coethnic workers.

Moreover, the underlying sociological processes—involving the mobilization of information, capital, and support through ethnic social networks—characterize both the middleman minority phenomenon and the ethnic enclave. Although differences may exist between immigrant-owned firms that recruit outsiders and those that rely on insiders, these seem to be differences of degree rather than kind, with plenty of within-group variation along the coethnic employment axis and over time. Just as one would consider immigrant businesses that sell to a coethnic clientele and those that sell on the general market as variants of a common type, so, too, does it seem appropriate to think of the ethnic enclave and the middleman minority situation exemplified by Koreans and Iranians as special cases of the ethnic economy writ large—as convincingly argued by Ivan Light and Stavros Karageorgis.[25]

Self-employment is a particularly prominent—and, these days, much discussed—instance of immigrant economic specialization, but it is hardly the major feature. As an ethnic phenomenon, employment concentration shows up elsewhere—most notably, in the well-known propensity to find jobs in the public sector, a tradition pioneered by the Irish and taken up by others, especially African Americans. As we have shown elsewhere, the public-sector example has some distinctive elements, but the crucial ingredients involved in the establishment of an employment concentration seem much the same whether the locus is the private or government sector—or wage and salary work or entrepreneurship.[26]

Immigrants tend to cluster in activities in which others of their own kind are already established. Initial placements, just as Lieberson noted in *A Piece of the Pie,* may be affected by any range of factors—prior experience, cultural preferences, or historical accident. But once the initial settlers have established a beachhead, subsequent arrivals tend to follow behind, preferring an environment in which at least some faces are familiar and discovering that personal contacts prove the most efficient means of finding a job. More important, the predilections of immigrants match the preferences of employers, who try to reproduce the characteristics of the workers they already have. Managers appreciate network recruitment for its ability to attract applicants quickly and at little cost; they value it even more for its efficiency. Hiring through connections upgrades the quality of information, reducing the risks entailed in acquiring new personnel; since sponsors usually have a stake in their job, they can also be relied on to keep their referrals in line. The process works a little differently in entrepreneurship, where early success sends later arrivals an implicit signal about which types of companies to start and which to avoid. An expanding business sector, then, provides both a mechanism for the effective transmission of skill and a catalyst for the entrepreneurial drive: the opportunity to acquire managerial skills through a stint of employment in immigrant firms both compensates for low pay and motivates workers to learn a variety of jobs.[27]

Thus, the repeated action of immigrant social networks yields the ethnic niche: a set of economic activities in which immigrants are heavily concentrated, here defined in terms of representation rates at or above the 1.5 level. Although most scholars seem willing to concur with this highly generalized definition, just how to implement it has been a matter of some uncertainty. Almost all will agree that a niche denotes a "job" or, at best, a set of clearly related jobs, as specified by Suzanne Model in her pioneering article "The Ethnic Niche and the Structure of Opportunity." But Model then left considerable ambiguity as to what she meant by a job, writing that a job could denote "an occupation, an industry, even a set of related industries."[28]

One could argue that niches are best thought of in occupational terms, in which case the emphasis rests on the similarity of jobs, as they extend horizontally across a number of possibly quite unrelated industries. To the extent that niches are the product of networks developed in a particular institutional context, one would prefer to underscore relatedness among a set of somewhat different but usually interacting occupations. For this reason, we have previously argued for the industrial view: whatever the portal of entry, niches grow as immigrants move into the related jobs within an industry to which initial starting points provide access, information, and opportunities to pick up the relevant skills.[29]

A case can be made for either conceptualization of niches, though, as we shall see, they are pervasive however they are defined. But, in a sense, neither specification adequately captures the phenomenon of interest: the actual jobs around which immigrants develop their concentrations. From this perspective, industry does not quite qualify, since industries contain a diversity of jobs, some of which may prove susceptible to immigrant infiltration and others of which may be such as to make entry difficult or impossible. Is it meaningful to talk of the hospital industry as an immigrant niche, for example, when it is highly unlikely that the meaningful sociological properties of a niche—ethnic social networks—will connect orderlies with physicians (though they may link X-ray technicians with nurses and orderlies with nursing assistants)? As a transversal category, occupation cuts across the types of institutional conditions that either facilitate or hinder the entry of immigrants, with bureaucratic or governmental institutions far more resistant to the operation of immigrant networks, regardless of occupation. And what we call occupations are really official categories that aggregate a set of activities that often vary considerably depending on context. While the actual "job" varies too greatly from one workplace to another to be fully caught by any system of classification, pinpointing the intersection of occupation and industry links institutional context and level of employment, thus bringing us closer to the job.[30]

Controversy revolves not around definitional matters but around the types of groups likely to establish concentrations and the degree to which those clusters persist. Contemporary immigration, as we note throughout this book, is characterized by socioeconomic diversity: unlike in the past, when newcomers were concentrated at the bottom of the socioeconomic ladder, today's arrivals span the entire occupational spectrum, with a sizable portion moving into the middle or upper ranks. But the literature, otherwise so emphatic about the importance of ethnic clustering—whether thought of as ethnic enclave or ethnic niche—assumes that these highly educated immigrants are quickly assuming the occupational or industrial distribution of other workers with like skills. Portes, for example, has long argued that professional immigrants "are primarily hired according to ability rather than ethnicity," enjoying "mobility chances comparable to those of native workers" and "work conditions and remuneration not . . . different from those of domestic labor at similar levels."[31] Ironically, the reasoning follows from the arguments of Victor Nee and his collaborators, otherwise highly critical of Portes's point of view: firms "may be predominantly Anglo in character" but "have formal rules and procedures" and "legally . . . cannot discriminate by race or ethnicity and may be pressured to hire and promote minorities and women."[32] And, thus, there is considerable consensus as to how high-skilled immigrants make it in America: as Portes and Rumbaut put it in their influential synthesis, *Immigrant America,* professionals "tend to enter at the bottom of their respective occupational ladders and to progress from there according to individual merit," overcoming initial difficulties with "remarkable success."[33]

And yet the conventional wisdom has probably had more influence than it truly deserves. Clearly, immigrant professionals are not quite so convinced, as evidenced by the ongoing and increasingly prominent controversy over the glass ceiling. And the controversy itself sends an important signal about the phenomenon in question: one would hardly expect complaints about promotional obstacles if there were no sizable immigrant concentrations at the upper echelons of the occupational hierarchy. It is precisely the establishment of notable clusters, in engineering, computer specialties, and other like fields, that draws attention to potential problems experienced in moving ahead.[34] As we shall show, high-skilled immigrants are in fact likely to develop ethnic niches, though, as one would expect, those niches take a very distinctive form.

Ethnic Niches in the Immigrant Metropolis

Our interests lie in the extent, nature, and persistence of the niches that newcomers have established in America's largest immigrant regions. But as the literature has repeatedly shown, the category of "immigrant" hides almost as much as it reveals. As we have already noted, today's immigrants are socioeconomically diverse; they also vary according to the circumstances of their migration, some arriving as economic migrants and others as refugees. Portes and Rumbaut's now well-known schema—differentiating among entrepreneurial, professional, labor migrant, and refugee types—nicely captures these crucial lines of variation, and we have used this framework to select the groups in question.[35] Asian Indians, Filipinos, and, to some extent, the Chinese exemplify professional migration; Koreans serve as the exemplar of the entrepreneurial type; the Vietnamese and Cubans fit into the refugee category; and Mexicans and Dominicans belong to the genus of labor migrant. Needless to say, this linkage of particular national flows with specific migration types involves considerable simplification: even if some type of skew characterizes every flow, each one also exhibits at least some degree of heterogeneity. But for the purposes of this chapter, the skew is precisely what we seek to capture; at the very least, the type captures the modal category for the group.

Moreover, there seems to be only modest within-group variation in the key category; the Chinese are most likely to fall across types, as the newcomers to Los Angeles, for example, mainly fit into the categories of professionals and entrepreneurs, whereas their counterparts in New York and San Francisco are far more proletarian in origin.[36] Only West Indians seem to provide an awkward fit with the available categories: while clearly not refugees, and certainly not entrepreneurs, their migration histories and occupational positions are such that they straddle the divide between the professional and labor migrant types. Although including this group slightly muddies our comparisons, the benefits seem to outweigh the costs, if only because of the group's numerical importance and intrinsic interest.[37]

The relationship between immigration type and settlement pattern, as described in chapter 2, precludes the type of interurban consistency we would have preferred. In general, the networked nature of immigration makes for regional concentration. The more dependent on networks for information and support—a characteristic usually linked to lower levels of marketable skills—the more likely are the immigrants to converge on a limited number of places. Mexicans, for example, whose presence in

California has a long and distinguished pedigree, have only recently gravitated to New York in sizable numbers.[38] Likewise, West Indians and Dominicans have yet to penetrate far beyond the East Coast in great numbers, just as the Vietnamese have developed a noticeable concentration in southern California but nowhere else. Another part of the story involves a sort of regional specialization: geography, history, and accident ensure that the immigrant regions themselves receive certain flows and not others. Although Miami is a heralded immigrant region, it is also an anomalous one, as noted earlier in this book, because it hosts a very small Asian population. Thus, none of the groups we have selected span all five immigrant urban regions. Koreans, the Chinese, Filipinos, Asian Indians, and Mexicans are found in four regions, having yet to establish a large base in Miami; Cubans cluster in three (Miami, a veritable sun, surrounded by the distinctly lesser moons of New York and Los Angeles); and West Indians, Dominicans, and the Vietnamese have built up settlements in two (Miami and New York, in the former two cases, and Los Angeles and San Francisco, in the latter).

Notwithstanding the distinctions among immigrant types, as well as the differences among immigrant niches, clustering seems to be a pervasive phenomenon, as can be seen in table 7.1. As the conventional wisdom would suggest, the labor migrant groups have moved heavily into a limited number of occupations and industries. Thus, Mexican immigrants working in Los Angeles are particularly likely to be employed in niches, as we have shown elsewhere.[39] But Mexicans who head to San Francisco or Chicago or any of the other urban regions in question appear no different in this respect: in each place, ethnic niches account for a very sizable share of Mexican employment. The same generalization applies to the other group that clearly qualifies for the labor migrant designation—Dominicans. As one would expect, the highly entrepreneurial Koreans are also heavily niched wherever they are found.

But neither Mexicans nor Koreans are out of line with the other groups in question. Our selection of groups and cities, each divided into occupational and industrial niches, yields a matrix of 54 cells—in which ethnic niches account for more than 50 percent of a group's employment in more than half of the cases. To be sure, Mexicans are the only group with concentrations above the 50 percent mark in every place, whether measured from the occupational or the industrial standpoint. Still, the others follow closely behind. Consider, for example, Filipinos, the purest instance of the professional migrant type, as members of this group are particularly unlikely to work on their own, indeed far less

TABLE 7.1.　PERCENTAGE OF THE FOREIGN-BORN EMPLOYED IN NICHES

	Chicago		Los Angeles		Miami		New York		San Francisco	
	Occupational	Industrial	Occupational	Industrial	Occupational	Industrial	Occupational	Industrial	Occupational	Industrial
Dominicans	—	—	—	—	41	50	54	59	—	—
West Indians	58	68	—	—	31	31	43	40	—	—
Mexicans	60	64	55	55	—	—	68	74	62	64
Chinese	55	57	50	49	—	—	49	51	39	41
Filipinos	50	57	47	50	—	—	49	53	41	50
Koreans	57	57	47	45	—	—	59	54	53	53
Asian Indians	—	—	49	53	—	—	50	43	54	54
Cubans	—	—	—	—	15	19	35	33	—	—
Vietnamese	—	—	48	50	—	—	—	—	57	57

Source: 1990 Census of Population, Public Use Microdata Sample.

likely than the native-born population against whom immigrant populations are typically compared. Notwithstanding the usual insistence that
professional migrants filter into a broad cross section of occupations at
the level for which their education qualifies them, Filipinos look much
like their less-skilled counterparts in their tendency to cluster in niches.
At least half of Filipino employment falls into industrial niches in each
of the four regions where Filipinos are found in sizable numbers; only in
San Francisco do Filipinos display a notably lower tendency to cluster in
a narrow tier of industrial niches, though even here the level of niching
is far from trivial. Overall, we see little deviation from this pattern
among the remaining groups and considerable parallelism from place to
place; the high-skilled groups are quite similar to the low-skilled groups
in their propensity to gravitate to a clearly defined tier of jobs.

Only one group—Cubans in Miami—clearly departs from the general
pattern. This was an exception we did not expect to find, given the
widely accepted depiction of the Cuban ethnic enclave, whose importance no one has yet disputed. Although a full explanation for the dis-
crepancy between the conventional wisdom and our findings goes beyond the scope of this chapter, consideration of group and city sizes and
characteristics may provide the clue to the puzzle. While Miami may
have a notable immigrant concentration, as a metropolis it is far smaller
than the other urban regions in question. Cubans are Miami's very
largest immigrant group, which may make it more difficult for them than
for the far less numerous Dominicans or West Indians to secure a distinctive position within the region's economy. Cubans also have at least average qualifications. Thus, unlike LA's Mexicans, whose numbers lead to
dominance in many occupations and industries but whose limited schooling impedes movement out of the low-skilled sector, Cubans have many
options; the relatively large size of the Cuban population, within the
Miami context, also reduces the potential that a small set of industries or
occupations could absorb much of the group, yielding the dispersion implied by the low concentrations we have recorded. While the issue remains to be settled, we have enough information to exclude the possibility that definitional considerations—the focus on niches, most generally,
rather than the subspecies of ethnic enclaves or economies—account for
this tendency toward scatter. Whether inside or outside niches, or considered as a whole, Cuban self-employment rates are not trivial but are
far from overwhelming and indeed quite close to those for the Miami region as a whole. For the most part, this is a population making a living in
wage and salaried employment and whose propensity to gravitate be-

yond the ethnic niche remains a matter for others to explain. Further surprises regarding the Cuban niche in Miami and its evolution follow.

The Quality of the Ethnic Niche

Immigration is a network-driven process, with the connections among veterans and newcomers making niches common and salient components of the immigrant employment experience. From a strictly sociological standpoint, one might leave the matter here since the pervasive nature of the ethnic niche demonstrates the importance of social ties in structuring participation in a realm—namely, the market—in which everyday and much scholarly thinking assumes that the cash nexus principally applies. While the phenomenon of the niche implicitly demonstrates the role of social connections in shaping and delimiting employment opportunities, the next logical question involves the quality of the jobs to which immigrants' networks give them access.

Considerations

The question of employment—*not* immigrant—quality already looms large in this particular scholarly debate, as we have previously noted. Contrary to simplistic readings, the original ethnic enclave hypothesis did not claim that those Cubans who found employment acquired good jobs, as such. Rather, it contended that jobs in the enclave were better than comparable positions—that is, relatively lousy jobs in the secondary sector—to the extent that the enclave provided greater opportunities for skills acquisition and earnings improvement. The ethnic enclave hypothesis concerns the *relative* merits of an ethnic concentration within a particular segment of the labor market, without implications for the overall quality of jobs in the enclave.

Thus, whether right or wrong, the enclave hypothesis does not preclude the possibility that the significance of concentration principally derives from the characteristics of the particular clusters immigrants establish. Do immigrant niches pack newcomers into the economy's lousiest jobs? Or does the phenomenon extend to higher segments of the economy, in which immigrants develop clear concentrations involving jobs of notably higher quality?

The first possibility is hardly to be dismissed. As we suggest in chapter 3 of this book, immigrant networks may perform wonderfully in linking up newcomers with jobs yet also possess the considerable drawback of filtering immigrants into positions of entirely the wrong type. Concentration may essentially involve the development of dead-end mobility traps, in which immigrants pile up in occupations or industries from which there are no ready outlets.[40] Indeed, the dead-end mobility trap is the logical end point to which network theory itself points: while immigrants gain jobs through the "strength of strong ties," connections of this sort involve dense, overlapping networks that choke off the flow of new information, constraining dispersion and the search for new opportunities. Moving ahead seems to involve developing ties with nonredundant contacts.[41] Instead, immigrants typically depend on an overlapping set of shared connections that threatens to funnel them into a narrow tier of the economy where newcomers quickly saturate demand and compete with one another for any available slots.

Although plausible, there is little reason to assume that the dead-end mobility trap exhausts the list of possibilities. Clearly, high levels of niching among such well-educated immigrants as Asian Indians, Filipinos, and the Chinese suggest that clustering at the bottom is not the only option. As noted earlier, our knowledge of specific occupations and industries points to high levels of immigrant concentration in highly skilled, highly remunerated occupations in the professions and elsewhere. And newcomers of more middling backgrounds, such as West Indians, who have moved so heavily into health care, similarly seem to have connected with employment sectors offering wages and conditions that are unlikely to be worse than average. In other words, migration networks may have a similar structuring role among high- and low-skilled newcomers, but the former embed networks in more advantageous segments of the economy than do the latter.

Concepts and Indicators

Our concern principally involves characterizing the quality of the jobs contained within the industries and occupations in which immigrant niches are found. This effort differs significantly from our previous attempts to describe the characteristics of niches and, we believe, from the efforts of other researchers as well. Lacking information about the jobs themselves, we have described niches in terms of the characteristics of workers. This procedure serves reasonably well in identifying the gross features of niche jobs, distinguishing, for example, between those in manufacturing and those in professional occupations. But it also tends to confuse the occupants of a position with the position itself, as, for example, when one describes a niche as involving high-skilled jobs when in fact one only has information about the education of workers filling those positions and not the skill requirements of the jobs themselves.

For this chapter, we have drawn on job ratings derived from the *Dictionary of Occupational Titles (DOT)*, which contains information on the requirements, contents, and structures of more than 10,000 occupations, based, in part, on extensive on-site observation of jobs as they were actually performed.[42] Each of the occupations identified in the *DOT* is rated according to 3 worker functions (the complexity of work in relation to data, people, and things) and 41 worker traits, having to do with such aspects as training times; the aptitudes, temperaments, and interests best suited for satisfactory job performance; and the physical demands of the job. Because the worker function and worker trait indexes tend to be redundant, with considerable intercorrelation among the items, numerous researchers have sought to reduce them to a much smaller set of underlying dimensions, each one of which is intended to capture a different dimension of the job. For this chapter, we draw on the efforts of Xiaoling Shu and her collaborators, who used latent confirmatory factor analysis to identify seven latent constructs, of which we focus on four—substantive complexity, physical demand, social skills, and working conditions. Shu and her coauthors also assigned the *DOT* scores, which cover more than 10,000 occupations, to the much smaller, though still large, number of detailed occupational classifications contained in the 1980 Census of Population; in turn, we have reconciled the 1980 occupational categories with their counterparts in the 1990 Census of Population.[43] Because we have defined the ethnic niche as the intersection of industry and occupation, we have developed *DOT* scores for industries as well; in this procedure, we first calculated *DOT* scores, on each dimension, for all occupations, industry by industry, and then assigned each industry a single score, based on the mean for the industry-specific occupations.[44]

The dimensions that Shu and her collaborators identified can be thought of as falling into two categories, one having to do with cognitive skills, the second with aspects related to raw physical exertion and exposure. *Substantive complexity* and *social skills* serve as indicators of required cognitive skills. Jobs characterized by substantive complexity involve relatively high levels of "intelligence, verbal and numerical aptitudes, advanced educational development, long vocational preparation, involvement in abstract and creative processes, and high complexity of function in relation to data."[45] Although the concept of social skills overlaps somewhat with substantive complexity, this dimension is more closely linked to those aspects of jobs that involve coordination with others. By contrast, *physical demands* and *work conditions* tap into the environmental aspects and requirements of the job. Jobs with high physical demands are those that involve stooping, climbing, loading—brawn rather than the finely developed manual proficiencies involved in the traditional skilled crafts. *Work conditions* picks up not so much the tasks involved in the job as the environment in which the job takes place, with negative scores pointing to unfavorable conditions. The cognitive skill and physical exertion and exposure dimensions define the polar ends of the quality spectrum; the most desirable jobs are those that require high social and cognitive skills, have low physical demands, and provide favorable work conditions.

Our interest in the nonmonetary attributes of niche jobs diverges from the main focus of debate, which has thus far been entirely preoccupied with earnings and their determinants. Earnings provide a valuable but highly limited indicator of job quality. On the one hand, other aspects of job quality are likely to vary even more greatly than earnings, which means that level of earnings inadequately summarizes the traits worthy of interest; on the other hand, earnings covary with other aspects of job quality, such as the characteristics profiled in this chapter.[46] Indeed, correlations of this sort are precisely what one would expect, given the nature of a phenomenon in which groups tend to cluster in distinctive sets of positions. And, thus, jobs that appear to be "good" or "bad" using the indicators employed in this chapter would be likely to retain those designations if we added earnings to our list of measures.

Analysis

Since our interest lies not in all jobs but in the particular jobs contained in immigrant niches, we developed a procedure to assign an occupational and an industrial score to the niches occupied by each of the 54 combinations of immigrant groups and cities, as we described them earlier in this chapter. First, for each region, we identified all of the occupations and industries in which the relevant groups were represented at the 1.5 level or above; second, we calculated *DOT* scores for each of these occupations and industries; third, we weighted the scores by the proportion of the group employed in either the industries or the occupations; last, we took the mean of the industrial and occupational scores and multiplied by 100. With this procedure, we generated 54 scores for each dimension, which we then plotted on graphs in which industry defined the y-axis and occupation the x-axis.

We thus generated a series of maps of the location of immigrant niches, in which the intersection of the industrial and occupational scores pinpoint both their absolute and relative qualities, while highlighting the degree to which ethnicity is a common structuring factor, as opposed to the distinctive influence exerted by each urban region.[47] In an absolute sense, the better niches are those that fall above the zero point; the greater the distance above zero, the better the job. The opposite relationship obviously holds for the less desirable immigrant concentrations. Quality also varies along occupational and industrial dimensions: location in a common or different quadrant of a map tells us whether occupational or industrial niches both have higher or lower scores than the mean for all industries and occupations or whether they diverge. Within a quadrant, distance from the diagonal highlights disparities between occupational and industrial scores.

Whether the notion of niche is seen as good or bad, it implies specialization; as we have argued elsewhere, the process of niche creation is part of an ethnic division of labor in which groups gain privileged access to particular types of jobs and thereby reduce access by others.[48] To assess specialization, our unit is the ethnic group, whose component parts are defined by each of the relevant regions represented in the analysis. A group's position within the map, relative to the others, indicates differentiation, with a group occupying spaces that overlap with another unlikely to be distinct and, of course, vice versa. To check for differentiation, we calculated spatial means and radii for the ellipses surrounding them: nonoverlapping ellipses indicate distinctiveness. Within a group, the spread represents the ethnic, as opposed to the urban, effect. Tightly clustered groups are those in which a common ethnic factor exercises the principal influence on specialization; among dispersed groups, the niche is more affected by factors specific to the regions in which they concentrate. The relative size of the radii within each ellipse illuminates the comparative variation along industrial and occupational axes; the longer the vertical radius, the greater the difference in occupational scores; the longer the horizontal radius, the greater the difference in industrial scores.

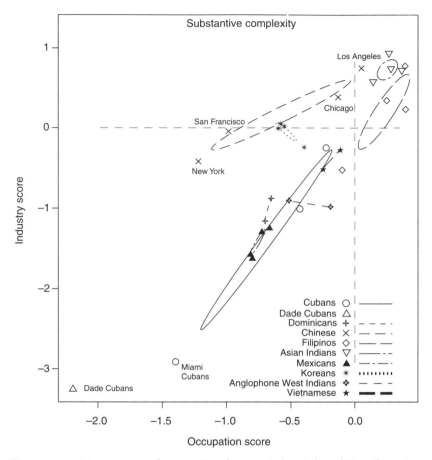

Figure 7.1.   Mean scores of occupational versus industrial qualities of immigrant niches: substantive complexity

Source: Employment in Niches: 1990 Census of Population, Public Use Microdata
Samples; *DOT* scores: tabulations by Xiaoling Shu et al. (note 44).

For simplicity's sake, the graphs do *not* identify specific regions,
though exception is made in two cases: the Chinese, in which the four
key regions are associated with migrations of different types, as we've
already discussed; and the Cubans, for whom we identify the point representing the Miami region. Given the special interest in the Cuban ethnic economy, and the literature concerned with its spatial arrangement,
we add an additional point to denote Cuban niches in the Dade county
portion of the Miami CMSA.

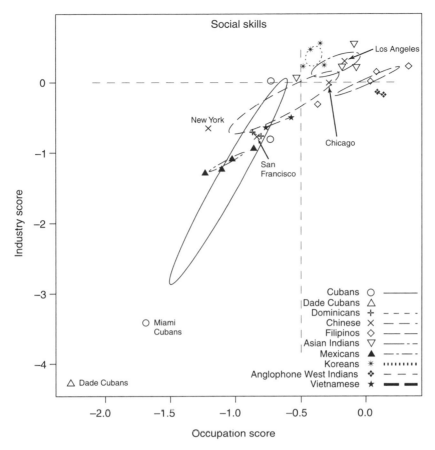

Figure 7.2.   Mean scores of occupational versus industrial qualities of immigrant niches: social skills

Source: Employment in Niches: 1990 Census of Population, Public Use Microdata Samples; *DOT* scores: tabulations by Xiaoling Shu et al. (note 44).

High- and Low-Skilled Niches: Asian Indians Compared to Mexicans

Although there is considerable variation across dimensions, at least one clear, consistent pattern emerges: the niches occupied by Asian Indians and Mexicans, the groups most clearly differing in the immigrant typology of Portes and Rumbaut, also define the polar ends of the quality spectrum in all of the places where they are found. If we focus on those dimensions related to cognitive skills—such as substantive complexity and social skills—Asian Indians consistently fall into the upper right-hand quadrant, denoting niches that are above the mean with respect to

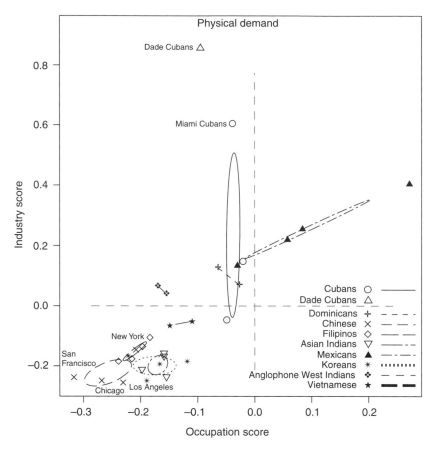

Figure 7.3.   Mean scores of occupational versus industrial qualities of immigrant niches: physical demands

Source: Employment in Niches: 1990 Census of Population, Public Use Microdata Samples; *DOT* scores: tabulations by Xiaoling Shu et al. (note 44).

both occupational and industrial scores, whereas Mexicans in all regions fall below the mean. The same contrast shows up upon inspection of the dimensions related to physical exposure and exertion: Mexican niches at once are physically demanding and involve unfavorable work conditions, whereas Asian Indian niches fall into the quadrants denoting light physical demands and better than average work conditions.

The two groups differ starkly not only from one another but also from other like groups. The dimensions related to cognitive skills, for example, highlight the specificity of a niche that one would expect of a group that clearly exemplifies the professional migrant type. Figures 7.1 and 7.2 show Asian Indians tightly clustered on both the substantive

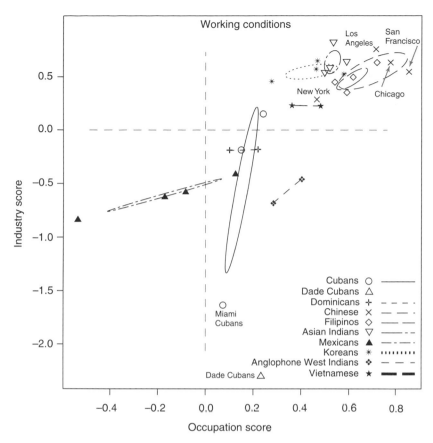

Figure 7.4.   Mean scores of occupational versus industrial qualities of immigrant niches: working conditions

Source: Employment in Niches: 1990 Census of Population, Public Use Microdata Samples; *DOT* scores: tabulations by Xiaoling Shu et al. (note 44).

complexity and social skill dimensions, indicating a strong ethnic effect and limited impact of place. On neither dimension do they occupy a completely isolated position, though the overlap in substantive complexity is slight and limited to one group, Filipinos. By contrast, Asian Indians fall out much less neatly on the dimensions related to physical demand (figure 7.3) and working conditions (figure 7.4), with the ellipse surrounding Asian Indian niches on the physical demands dimension entirely surrounded by the ellipse for Koreans, with whom there is also some overlap on the work conditions dimension.

The findings for Mexicans appear no less distinct. Mexican niches stand apart from Asian clusters regardless of group or region. Among

Asian groups, only the Vietnamese resemble Mexicans in falling into the lower quadrants of the two cognitive skill dimensions. Even so, the Vietnamese never overlap with Mexicans on these dimensions. And the physical demands and work conditions of the Vietnamese niches yield ratings that are more favorable than those of Mexicans.

This picture of Mexican and Asian Indian specialization derives from an effort to reduce the information about many occupations and industries to just a handful of points. This conciseness is its virtue, but also its vice, since we lose some of the concrete detail used in previous efforts to describe ethnic niches. A more disaggregated look at the data indicates that our abstracted representations of the quality of Mexican and Asian Indian niches are precisely what one would expect: medical doctors in Chicago and New York and engineers in San Francisco make up the most sizable Asian Indian occupational niches; by contrast, sewer, janitor, cook, and assembler top the list of Mexican occupational niches in Los Angeles, San Francisco, New York, and Chicago, respectively. Taking yet another snapshot, this time summarizing occupational, industrial, and educational characteristics of the specializations in which immigrants cluster, provides a view entirely consistent with the figures: regardless of place, Asian Indian niches involve professional or semiprofessional occupations, with little reliance on manufacturing, and Asian Indian incumbents of niche jobs possess impressively high levels of education. Mexican niches take an entirely opposite form, tilted toward manufacturing, involving scant employment of a managerial or professional type, and grouping immigrants with very modest levels of schooling.

Labor Migrants: Variation within an Immigrant Type

Mexican niches also highlight the distinctive manner by which groups of a similar type—in this case, labor migrants—nonetheless get inserted into the economy in very particular ways. The comparison to West Indians is especially illuminating in this respect. Although the latter are subject, like Mexicans, to considerable stigmatization, they arrive with somewhat higher skills; more important, they have found their principal entry point in the service sector, especially health care, securing jobs at the bottom half of that job hierarchy. Thus, while West Indian niches tend to be of lower than average quality on all dimensions, their clusters never overlap with the positions occupied by Mexicans. Moreover, they always occupy a more favorable position on the industry axis, reflecting the differences in industrial mix between the two groups and the great importance of health care–related employment among West Indians. The figure for social skills (figure 7.2), in which the distance between West Indian and Mexican locations is particularly great, highlights the impact of industry, as it reveals that the industries in which West Indians have concentrated involve much greater demands for dealing with people than do those in which Mexicans have concentrated.

By contrast, the niches established by the only other group distinctively categorized in the labor migrant group—Dominicans in New York—fall into the same general location as the Mexican concentrations. Even so, the figures illuminate both the urban and ethnic factors that make for ethnic specialization. Dominican niches most clearly overlap with Mexican niches on those dimensions related to cognitive skills. But they take up a different space on the figures that highlight the dimensions related to physical aspects, reflecting New York's distinctive economic structure, in which heavy industry—important to the Mexican employment scene in Los Angeles, San Francisco, and Chicago—plays a relatively minor role. Within New York, moreover, Mexican niches are more unfavorable on all counts than Dominican niches, an indicator of Mexicans' status as the most recently settled of New York's immigrant groups and their initial clustering in the bottommost positions available.

By the same token, ethnic effects show up most clearly in the general positioning of Mexican niches: they almost always cluster in the quadrant containing the least favorable scores on both occupational and industrial axes. Moreover, the regions are all tightly clustered on the two dimensions related to cognitive skills, telling us that the common experience of labor migration pushes Mexican immigrants into jobs of comparable skill levels wherever they settle. By contrast, region-specific factors yield a much larger impact on those dimensions related to physical environment at work, yet another indicator of the relevance of differences in regional economies.

Chinese, Filipinos, and Koreans: The Specializations of Professionals and Entrepreneurs

A quite different pattern characterizes the Chinese, and the figures highlight a pattern of within-group difference, a characteristic noted previously, though not emphasized. The Chinese exemplify the socioeconomic diversity of contemporary immigration; each major settlement includes niches made up of accountants and waiters, engineers and sewing machine operatives. However, the flows also tilt toward one end of the skill spectrum or another: a fundamentally middle-class migration has decamped in Los Angeles and Chicago, whereas a more proletarian flow has gravitated toward San Francisco and, especially, New York. In turn, these differences in class composition have yielded populations embedded in niches of quite different types. The niches fall out in similar ways on each of our dimensions: the data points are captured with narrow ellipses, in which Chicago and Los Angeles cluster together at a more favorable range on the spectrum and San Francisco and New York form a group at a less desirable end. Although location among the quadrants varies from dimension to dimension, the key factor differentiating the two clusters is cognitive skills. In substantive complexity and social skills, the Chinese niches in Chicago and LA rank above the average, whereas the New York and San Francisco concentrations fall into the bottom parts of the map. By contrast, niches in all four places occupy the same quadrant on those dimensions related to physical exposure and exertion—though the identical pattern of within-group clustering reemerges.

A more detailed comparison of Los Angeles and New York provides the substance on which these abstracted representations are based. If New York—with its ever-expanding Chinatown, dominated by restaurants and garment factories—highlights the continuity of the contemporary with the historical patterns, Los Angeles illuminates the new style of immigrant niching. In Los Angeles 45 percent of Chinese immigrants working in ethnic niches are employed in professional or managerial occupations; to be sure, cooking, waiting, and sewing remain ethnic niches as well, but these occupations employ just a fifth of niche workers. In New York, by contrast, the ethnic trades still reign supreme: just three occupations—waiter, sewing machine operative, and cook—account for almost half of all Chinese immigrants working in ethnic niches. Industry also separates Los Angeles from New York— where more than 60 percent of ethnic niche workers hold jobs in either restaurants or apparel manufacturing—but it additionally shows that the new pattern has not yet fully taken hold. Restaurants and apparel manufacturing top the list of Chinese industrial specializations in Los Angeles, a factor reflected in the very modest rankings in substantive complexity as they appear on the industry axis. Nonetheless, the relative weight of these traditional trades is not nearly as great as in New York, and they also allow for higher levels of self-employment, suggestive of a shift to a middleman minority situation compatible with the higher-class background of the local Chinese population. Furthermore, the census data show the development in LA of a new type of ethnic economy—with roots in high technology, business services, and other industries in which the linkage to China and Taiwan serves as a source of competitive advantage—that is barely visible in New York. For all these differences, the Chinese niches in New York and Los Angeles do share some underlying similarities: they rank better than average with respect to work conditions and physical demands. Although one might quarrel with the *DOT* rankings, apparel manufacturing and restaurants do not fall terribly far from the mean on the indicators related to physical conditions and exertion, which is why all the Chinese niches fall into the same quadrant on these two dimensions.[49]

Although some Chinese niches allow for high levels of self-employment, as in restaurants and a number of retail and wholesale lines, wage and salary employment characterizes most niche jobs, whether the positions are high or low skilled and regardless of place. Only among Koreans do we find a clearly different pattern, in which the movement into American cities has produced an economic profile involving a distinctively entrepreneurial flavor. Koreans show an impressive propensity toward self-employment, even in industries or occupations with relatively modest levels of Korean concentration. But entrepreneurship is most pronounced in those specializations that make up the Korean ethnic niche, of which small retail is the defining trait. Retail contains more than half the jobs in the Korean niches of New York and Los Angeles, almost half of niche employment in San Francisco, and just under a quarter in Chicago, where, for some peculiar reason, almost 30 percent of niche employment is found in laundries, a small business sector classified as services. While small retailing provides a fertile environment for immigrants seeking to start their own businesses, it also yields a depressed occupational structure—evidence of which can be seen among the occupations in which Koreans cluster. Regardless of place, Korean niches in the professions, though not of trivial dimension, are outweighed by the concentrations in retail and service industries; moreover, none of the professional clusters is comparable in relative or absolute size to the similar specializations established by Asian Indians or Filipinos or the Chinese. Rather, Koreans have gravitated to occupations compatible with the industries in which they concentrate—which is why "sales supervisor or proprietor" is the leading Korean occupational niche in each of the urban centers studied.

Thus, Koreans occupy a unique role as petty entrepreneurs; the figures show how this specialization in business differentiates Koreans' position in the ethnic division of labor from the other, principally Asian, groups that have entered the United States under quite similar circumstances and also bring relatively high skills. For Koreans, ethnicity exercises a particularly powerful structuring force on the two dimensions related to cognitive skills; the figure for substantive complexity, which yields a particularly tight cluster, underscores the ways in which the distinctive social structure of Korean migration overrides any difference in the economic structures of the various regions. Moreover, the situation of Koreans contrasts with that of Asian Indians, who are also quite tightly clustered but are grouped in a very different space. The latter are in the upper right-hand quadrant, close to the diagonal, indicating that jobs in the ethnic niche rank favorably with respect to both occupation and industry. By contrast, Koreans are grouped near the zero point for occupations but well below the mean for industry. This particular location neatly represents the occupational and industrial matrix in which Koreans find themselves. The industries of Korean concentration have a compressed job structure, weighted toward the bottom end; within these industries, Koreans occupy the more demanding jobs, but, even so, selling in small retail is typically a highly routinized task of limited substantive complexity. Similar considerations influence the positioning of Korean niches on the figure displaying social skills: in this case, their location in the upper right-hand quadrant reflects the nature of the demands of dealing with the people involved in retailing occupations and industries. By contrast, Korean niches appear more favorable on the dimensions related to physical exposure and exertion, where Koreans occupy a space that overlaps with that of Asian Indians and Filipinos.

Cubans: The Characteristics of an Unfavorable Niche

Taken as a totality, the niches occupied by Mexicans enjoy the dubious honor of being of the worst quality; the prize for the worst concentration occupied by any single group in any one place, however, goes to Cubans in Miami. As a visual inspection of figures 7.1 through 7.4 reveals, the niches occupied by Cubans in New York and Los Angeles do not display any enviable qualities, though Dominicans are positioned in a more or less similar space and Mexicans occupy a still less favorable space. Cubans in Miami, however, appear as an outlying group, clearly occupying the least desirable location in the figures that depict substantive complexity and social skill. Visual interpretation is a little more complicated when assessing those dimensions related to the physical environment of work, because the industrial mix is far less unfavorable than are the types of occupations in which Cubans in Miami have clustered. However, calculation of Euclidean difference from the zero point shows that the work and physical conditions encountered by Miami Cubans in their niche rank still lower than those of Mexicans in San Francisco, the least well positioned of this group.

The figures are entirely consistent with our knowledge of the detailed industries and occupations in which Cubans cluster. Examined from the optic adopted in this chapter, the Cuban niche has none of the virtues often ascribed to it, as the industries and occupations of Cuban concentration uniformly fall at the bottom of the hierarchy. For example, none of the high-end or even middle-level activities in which many Asian groups cluster—engineering, medicine, hospital, pharmacy, nursing—show up in the Cuban profile. Nor is there concentration in retail—a notable finding since we define industry here at a highly disaggregated level, which means that Cubans could have a concentration in retail apparel and not retail fish stores or in retail drugs and not retail grocery. But barely any concentration in a retail industry or analogous service industry appears: hardware stores, variety stores, barbershops, and dressmaking shops are the only niches of the type associated with flourishing ethnic economies, and together they account for less than 1 percent of total Cuban employment in Miami. Similarly, only one small sales occupation emerges as a Cuban cluster.

However, as the Cuban niche is the most modest of all, its import on the group's overall well-being is modest as well. Cubans working in ethnic concentrations appear to be engaged in lousy jobs, as registered on our indicators. Nonetheless, several qualifications apply. First, most Cubans are scattered over a wider and better range of the Miami economy—evidence that Cubans are getting ahead, not via ethnic enclaves or niches, but through assimilation as conventionally defined. Second, some of the largest niches might look better when examined from another standpoint. For example, the occupation of greatest Cuban concentration is truck driving, which rates poorly on working conditions, social skills, and substantive skills but rewards its occupants with a reasonable coin. But even were we to systematically assess the qualities of the Cuban concentration in light of monetary returns, that one-fifth of all Cubans working in their niches makes a living in the apparel industry—

well-known for its low wages—suggests that the picture would remain largely the same as the one we have already presented.

Niches: Pervasive *and* Persistent? Or Simply Transitional?

The ethnic niche stands out as a characteristic of almost every major immigrant group and is found in each of America's major immigrant destinations. With only one major exception—Cubans in Miami, about whom we will provide further details in a moment—immigrant groups congregate in specific occupations or industries, where they achieve high levels of concentration. Clustering occurs regardless of immigrant type, holding among labor migrants and professionals, among refugees and entrepreneurial groups.

The nature of the niches established by the groups we have surveyed suggests that the concept of an "ethnic division of labor" provides an apt description for the broader phenomenon in question. While clustering is an immigrant commonality, immigrants have gravitated to very different types of positions within the economy; consequently, the jobs contained in those niches also vary, and not just on one but on a series of orthogonal dimensions. To some extent, the variation among groups reflects the skill cleavages within the immigrant population. The more favorable locations in the figures tend to be occupied by educated Asian groups, while the less favorable positions tend to be filled by less well educated Hispanic groups, suggesting that schooling exercises considerable influence on the mechanisms that sort immigrants into one type of job over another. Nonetheless, the ethnic factor appears even more important. On the one hand, groups that are roughly similar in education—whether high or low skill—typically occupy distinctive locations. And, on the other hand, ethnicity seems to override the influence of region: though America's leading immigrant destinations are hardly alike, a tight ethnic clustering, rather than a regional spread, reappears from dimension to dimension and from group to group.

The ethnic niche is pervasive—an interesting fact, perhaps, but one of limited relevance if the clusters simply serve as way stations to something else. For scholars inclined to emphasize the assimilatory capacity of American society, niching is essentially a transient phenomenon linked to the early stages of settlement, a time when immigrants are still learning the ropes. As immigrants learn the new rules of the game, they come to appreciate the downside of embeddedness in ethnic networks. The ethnic workplace—whether immigrant owned or simply immigrant staffed— may be a good place to find a starting job, but it provides little room to move ahead. Obligations to the kith and kin who originally provided the job have the potential to turn an ethnic niche into an ethnic mobility trap. Staying within the community, therefore, means getting stuck. Better to venture into the open market, which, as Victor Nee and his associates have put it, "encourage[s] open social relationships [and] for this reason, function[s] as an integrative institution. . . . [F]irms seek the best qualified and least expensive workers, regardless of ethnicity."[50] And because filtering out of the niche generates superior rewards, or so the argument goes, out into the "mainstream economy"—whatever that is—immigrants go.

Such arguments resonate with the assimilationist cast of most sociological research. However, the time frame for assimilation extends across generations; given our interest in the foreign-born, this is a question with which we cannot engage. But we can examine change over a limited time span, first tracing shifts in the relative size of the immigrant niche and then zeroing in on the experience of specific immigrant cohorts. Given the multiplicity of places and groups, we focus only on occupational niches; we further limit this part of the analysis to the immigrant capitals of New York and Los Angeles, venturing beyond them only to pursue the unexpectedly unique situation of Cubans in Miami.

Change over Time

The "new immigration" is still too new to have much of a history; thus, under the best circumstances, we can examine change only over the 1970–1990 period. Moreover, many of the groups in question did not begin moving to the United States in numbers significant enough to produce meaningful regional clusters until the 1970s. The only new immigrant group with a long migration history, Mexicans, has also been so highly regionalized that it did not gain a sizable presence in New York until the 1980s.

The eight groups whose experience can be traced from 1970 to 1990 do indeed provide some support for the conventional view of ethnic niching, as can be seen from figure 7.5. The 1970 patterns show very high levels of concentration, just as one might expect of groups that are at once newly arrived and sufficiently few in number to be accommodated in just a handful of occupations or industries. The 1970–1980 period, however, shows a considerable transition from this concentration,

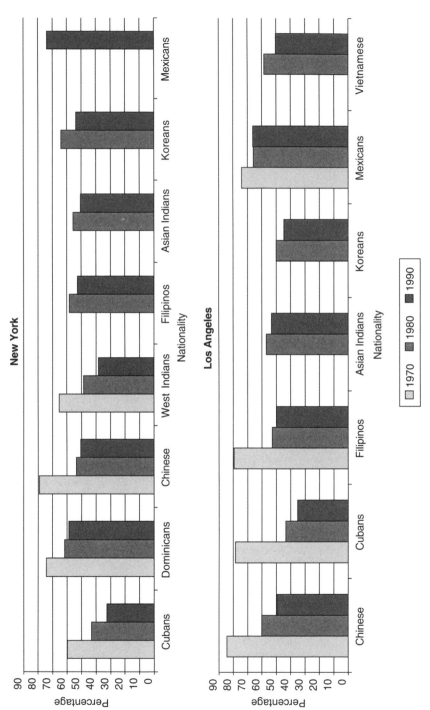

Figure 7.5. Percentage of immigrants in occupational niches, 1970–1990

Source: 1990 Census of Population, Public Use Microdata Samples.

with the one exception of Los Angeles Mexicans, who also constitute the very largest group.

Despite the declines of the 1970–1980 period, all groups maintained high concentrations in niches. Cubans in New York and Los Angeles registered the lowest levels of clustering, but even at this low ebb more than 40 percent of Cubans were employed in occupational niches in each place. In both places Cubans were also unique in yet another respect: their numbers had increased only slightly over the decade, reflecting the extraordinary magnetism of Miami for this group. Consequently, the relatively low concentrations of Cubans are probably most suggestive of the pressures toward continued clustering, even under those circumstances most conducive to dispersion. Overall, the new groups, many of them highly educated, such as Filipinos and Asian Indians, began with a high proportion of the group nested in a narrow tier of occupations.

In general, the 1980–1990 data yield a picture consistent with a tendency toward dispersion, but only to a very modest degree. Concentration fell off most drastically among Cubans in Los Angeles, with the proportion employed in niches down almost 25 percent over the 10-year period; however, this remains a highly unusual case, as concentrations generally remained unchanged during this period of increasing immigration. Of greater relevance is the experience of the Chinese and Vietnamese in Los Angeles and West Indians, Cubans, and Koreans in New York, where concentrations slipped by one-fifth to one-sixth. Other groups, such as Filipinos and Asian Indians of both regions and Dominicans and the Chinese in New York, saw much lower levels of dispersion toward occupations of lower ethnic density. In Los Angeles Mexicans actually increased their tendency to cluster in niches. Regardless of the rate of attenuation—reversed in the Mexican case—all groups retained concentrations close to or above the 50 percent level, as we have already noted.

Immigrant Cohorts

The immigrant niche is a phenomenon with staying power, at least in the short run. But its apparent persistence might be an artifact of a spurious correlation: if immigrant numbers are growing rapidly, as they are, and the newest immigrants converge on the industries of highest ethnic density, as they do, we may fail to observe the underlying tendency of long-term immigrants to head toward occupations in which their compatriots are less likely to work.

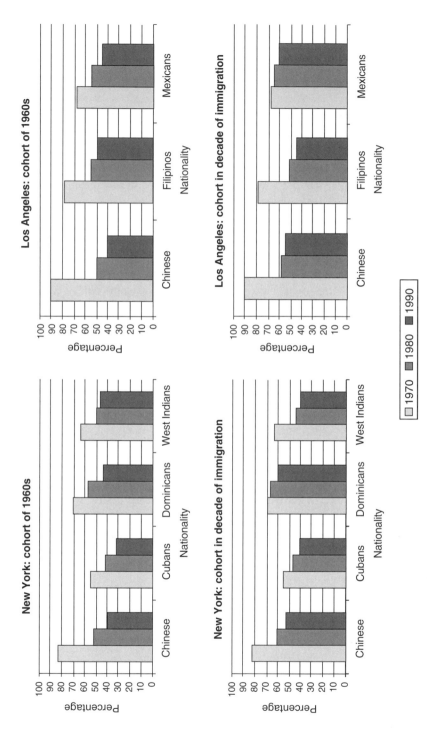

Figure 7.6. Percentage of immigrants in occupational niches, by cohort

Source: 1990 Census of Population, Public Use Microdata Samples.

Examining the behavior of veteran immigrants offers one way to assess this possibility. Figure 7.6 displays concentrations, as of 1970, for immigrants who moved to the United States between 1960 and 1969 and then shows how those patterns changed over the course of the next two decades. Once again, we observe a marked decline from the peaks registered in 1970, though in this case samples are still smaller, necessitating caution in our interpretation. While attenuation persisted from 1980 to 1990, it took place at a greatly reduced rate; only the case of Cubans, a group whose numbers actually declined during this period, appears to deviate from the broader pattern. In general, a large portion of the cohort of the 1960s—though not quite a majority—remained in occupations of high ethnic density at least 20 years after arrival in the United States.

But one could also look at the question from a different angle: if it is newness that leads immigrants to cluster, with the first wave most dependent on help from the limited number of veterans and still small enough to find accommodation in a handful of occupations, then later cohorts might be less likely to start out by clustering. This proposition does garner support, as suggested by the data graphed in the bottom two panels of figure 7.6. Insofar as small sample size does not distort the experience of the cohort of the 1960s, no other group of newcomers seems to have begun with comparable levels of clustering. But the situation of the arrivals of the 1980s looks barely different from the pattern established by their predecessors a decade earlier. In four of the seven groups, the cohort of the 1980s began with concentrations above the 50 percent mark. And in the case of the two labor migrant groups in question—Dominicans in New York and Mexicans in Los Angeles—the degree of clustering in niches barely changes from one cohort to another. To be sure, such data hardly settle the matter: more time is needed if we are to fully assess persistence, and it would be useful if we could compare persistence in the niche against some other benchmark. Nonetheless, concentration appears to be a trait that lasts over an extended period, shaping the experience of both new and old cohorts. If we recall that the concentrations are truly distinctive, separating the groups from one another, then the tendency to maintain employment in occupations of high ethnic density highlights a fundamental aspect of ethnic social structure.

The Great Exception

But not in the case of Cubans. Although the discovery of the Cuban ethnic enclave played a crucial role in directing scholarly attention to the phenomenon of ethnic economic concentration, Cubans appear to have followed a different script. As the immigration literature suggests, the various waves of exiles that arrived in Miami during the 1960s clustered together: by 1970, 40 percent worked in occupations and almost 50 percent worked in industries in which Cuban densities equaled or surpassed niche levels. But thereafter, as figure 7.7 shows, those who immigrated in the 1960s dispersed and did so more rapidly than their much less numerous counterparts in New York and Los Angeles, as well as Miami immigrants of similar vintage from all other groups. By 1990 niches, whether of the occupational or industrial variety, provided less than 15 percent of the jobs held by the working members of this cohort.

Later arrivals showed even less propensity to find jobs where their compatriots worked. Members of the cohort of the 1970s started out with employment at much lower levels of ethnic density than their predecessors and thereafter gravitated away from the niche. Although the degree varies, depending on whether one focuses on occupation or industry, the trend toward dispersion is unmistakable. As for those Cubans who moved to Miami during the 1980s, industries or occupations of high Cuban density accounted for only a small minority of total employment as of 1990.

In a sense, the basics read the same for Cubans as for other groups: veteran immigrants move to jobs of lower ethnic density over time; later arrivals never start out with the same levels of concentration as the pioneers. But Cubans clearly differ in the rate at which this change has taken place: in no other case do concentrations fall to comparable levels, nor do succeeding cohorts start with such a large proportion of the group working outside ethnic niches—however they are defined.

Critics might note that the literature does not so much concern the Cuban ethnic niche as the Cuban ethnic enclave, and we would not disagree. However, the ethnic enclave could not possibly be larger than the ethnic niche as we have defined it here. Bracketing questions as to the importance of spatial concentration, experts converge on one point—namely, that the ethnic enclave includes those economic activities in which group members are overrepresented as both bosses (i.e., the self-employed) and employees. While any such activity would also qualify

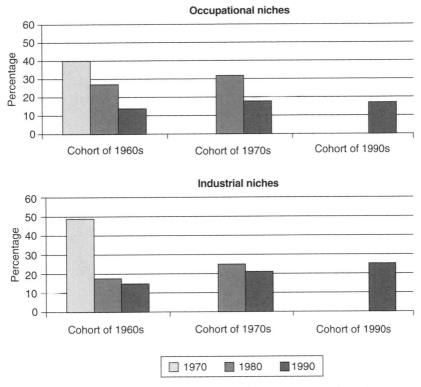

Figure 7.7.   Miami Cubans: percentage in niches, 1970–1990, by cohort
Source: 1990 Census of Population, Public Use Microdata Samples.

as an ethnic niche, our classification scheme also captures those activities in which group members are overrepresented as workers but not as bosses. Although we may miss those activities in which overrepresentation occurs only among the self-employed, we also know that Cuban self-employment rates only modestly exceed the average for the region. Hence, our portrait of the ethnic niche is more likely to inflate than obscure the size of the ethnic enclave, whatever that might be.

Accounting for the distinctiveness of the Cuban experience in Miami exceeds the scope of this chapter, but we suggest the following possibility: just as the literature tells us, Cuban refugees who settled in Miami in the immediate aftermath of the revolution crowded into a narrow set of occupations and industries, where they were likely to work alongside their compatriots. But this immigrant wave differed from other migrant streams in its prevalence of middle-class immigrants with relevant skills and prior experience who were able to trade on their assets to move beyond the niche. Other factors facilitated dispersion: Cubans' growing political weight, which influenced established organizations to open their doors, and the growing role of trade with Latin America, which motivated Anglo-owned or Anglo-dominated companies to hire Cubans not just as entry-level workers but for positions of greater responsibility. Unlike the other migrations in question, the Cuban experience is also unique for the numerical dominance of the very first wave. Later cohorts were smaller, which reduced the need for help from one's coethnics. With the first wave increasingly working outside the ethnic niche and in positions of some influence, the later arrivals found it easier to get started in jobs of lower ethnic density. And they had good reason to do so, as the ethnic niche was largely a concentration of lower-quality jobs, as we have repeatedly seen.

Conclusion

In a sense, this chapter tells the oldest of stories, confirming that today's immigrants are following the timeworn paths of immigrants past: linked by connections to and moving with the help and guidance provided by veterans, newcomers gravitate to the jobs where their compatriots have gotten started. Because migration is driven by networks, it also involves a process of social reproduction, in which the current crop of workers begets a new bunch that looks very much like the first.

But there is also something new under the sun: the ethnic niches of the early twenty-first century are not quite the same as the ethnic niches of yore. They are still to be found at the bottom rungs of the occupational ladder, where workers with no other resource but social support necessarily rely for help from others of their own kind. But the distinctively new breed of immigrants—newcomers who arrive with high levels of education—turn out to be no less likely to converge on niches than their less-skilled counterparts. The nature of migration tends to feed newcomers into clusters of similar type, regardless of skill level. Although the economies of America's major immigrant urban regions offer striking contrasts, immigrants of any one group secure niches of much the same type, regardless of place. As we have seen, niches tend to be clustered on almost every dimension, highlighting the importance of ethnic over urban effects.

However, the niches established by today's immigrants differ in kind. High-skilled immigrants tend to establish concentrations in jobs with above-average levels of cognitive skills, which also tend to be positions with favorable physical environments. By contrast, the less skilled work in jobs that involve much physical effort but demand little in the way of cognitive skills, all the while providing few physical amenities. Even though skill sorts immigrants into better or worse jobs, groups of roughly comparable skill level nonetheless build up niches of different types. And thus, contrary to the established approach, ethnicity is not simply an imported cultural characteristic but rather a principle of social organization that deeply shapes the role immigrants play in the dynamic economies of twenty-first-century America.

Notes

1. Milton Gordon, *Assimilation in American Life* (New York: Oxford University Press, 1964).

2. Thomas Bailey and Roger Waldinger, "Primary, Secondary, and Enclave Labor Markets: A Training Systems Approach," *American Sociological Review* 56 (1991): 432–445.

3. Alejandro Portes and Julia Sensenbrenner, "Embeddedness and Immigration: Notes on the Social Determination of Economic Action," *American Journal of Sociology* 98 (1993): 1320–1350.

4. For a fuller elaboration of this argument, see Roger Waldinger, *Still the Promised City? African-Americans and New Immigrants in PostIndustrial New York* (Cambridge, Mass.: Harvard University Press, 1996).

5. Glenn Loury, "Discrimination in the Post–Civil Rights Era: Beyond Market Interactions," *Journal of Economic Perspectives* 12, no. 2 (1998): 119.

6. George Borjas, "Long-Run Convergence of Ethnic Skill Differentials: The Children and Grandchildren of the Great Migration," *Industrial and Labor Relations Review* 47, no. 4 (1994): 553–573.

7. Richard Alba and Victor Nee, "Rethinking Assimilation Theory for a New Era of Immigration," *International Migration Review* 21, no. 4 (1997): 826–874.

8. Moses Rischin, *The Promised City* (Cambridge, Mass.: Harvard University Press, 1962).

9. Stanley Lieberson, *A Piece of the Pie* (Berkeley and Los Angeles: University of California Press, 1980), 379.

10. Ivan Light, *Ethnic Enterprise in America* (Berkeley and Los Angeles: University of California Press, 1972).

11. Kenneth Wilson and Alejandro Portes, "Immigrant Enclaves: An Analysis of the Labor Market Experiences of Cubans in Miami," *American Journal of Sociology* 88 (July 1980): 295–319.

12. See David Gordon, *Theories of Poverty and Unemployment: Orthodox, Radical, and Dual Labor Market Perspectives* (Lexington, Mass.: Heath, 1972); and Michael Piore, *Birds of Passage* (Cambridge: Cambridge University Press, 1979).

13. Alejandro Portes and Robert Bach, *Latin Journey* (Berkeley and Los Angeles: University of California Press, 1985).

14. John R. Logan, Richard Alba, and Timothy L. McNulty, "Ethnic Economies in Metropolitan Regions: Miami and Beyond," *Social Forces* 72, no. 3 (1994): 691–724.

15. For further elaboration along these lines, see Roger Waldinger, "The Ethnic Enclave Debate Revisited," *International Journal of Urban and Regional Research* 17, no. 3 (1993): 444–452. For a further discussion of the impact of spatial factors on ethnic economies, see Roger Waldinger, David McEvoy, and Howard Aldrich, "Spatial Dimensions of Opportunity Structures," in *Ethnic Entrepreneurs: Minority Business in Industrial Societies,* ed. Roger Waldinger, Howard Aldrich, Robin Ward, and associates (Newbury Park, Calif.: Sage, 1990); and David Kaplan, "The Spatial Structure of Urban Ethnic Economies," *Urban Geography* 19, no. 6 (1998): 489–501.

16. Portes and Bach, *Latin Journey,* 345.

17. Portes and Sensenbrenner, "Embeddedness and Immigration"; for a fuller elaboration of these concepts see Alejandro Portes and Alex Stepick, *City on the Edge* (Berkeley and Los Angeles: University of California Press, 1993); and Alejandro Portes and Min Zhou, "Gaining the Upper Hand: Old and New Perspectives in the Study of Ethnic Minorities," *Ethnic and Racial Studies* 15 (1992): 491–522.

18. Jimy Sanders and Victor Nee, "Limits of Ethnic Solidarity in the Ethnic Enclave Economy," *American Sociological Review* 52 (1987): 745–767.

19. Min Zhou and John Logan, "Returns on Human Capital in Ethnic Enclaves: New York City's Chinatown," *American Sociological Review* 54 (1989): 809–820; see also Min Zhou, *Chinatown: The Socioeconomic Potential of an Immigrant Enclave* (Philadelphia: Temple University Press, 1992).

20. Greta Gilbertson and Douglas Gurak, "Broadening the Ethnic Enclave Debate," *Sociological Forum* 8, no. 3 (1993): 205–220; Greta Gilbertson, "Women's Labor and Enclave Employment: The Case of Dominican and Colombian Women in New York City," *International Migration Review* 29, no. 3 (1995): 657–670.

21. Alejandro Portes and Leif Jensen, "The Enclave and the Entrants: Patterns of Ethnic Enterprise in Miami before and after Mariel," *American Sociological Review* 54, no. 6 (1989): 929–949.

22. On Koreans, Illsoo Kim's *The New Urban Immigrants* (Princeton, N.J.: Princeton University Press, 1981) remains the classic treatment; Pyong Gap Min's *Caught in the Middle: Korean Communities in New York and Los Angeles* (Berkeley and Los Angeles: University of California Press, 1996) adds depth, brings the story up to date, and highlights the growing dependence of Korean entrepreneurs on non-Korean labor.

23. Claudia Der-Martirosian, "Immigrant Self-Employment and Social Capital," *Ethnic and Racial Studies* (forthcoming); idem, "Economic Embeddedness and Social Capital of Immigrants: Iranians in Los Angeles" (Ph.D.

diss., University of California, Los Angeles, 1996); Ivan Light, Georges Sabagh, Mehdi Bozorgmehr, and Claudia Der-Martirosian, "Beyond the Ethnic Enclave Economy," *Social Problems* 41 (1994): 65–80.

24. See, for example, Steven Gold and Bruce Phillips, "Israelis in the United States," in *American Jewish Yearbook 1996* (Philadelphia: American Jewish Committee, 1996), 51–101.

25. Ivan Light and Stavros Karageorgis, "The Ethnic Economy," in *The Handbook of Economic Sociology,* ed. Neil Smelser and Richard Swedberg (Princeton, N.J.: Princeton University Press, New York: Russell Sage Foundation, 1994).

26. Waldinger, *Promised City,* chapter 7.

27. Ibid., chapters 1 and 9; see also Roger Waldinger, "The Making of an Immigrant Niche," *International Migration Review* 28, no. 1 (1994): 3–30.

28. Suzanne Model, "The Ethnic Niche and the Structure of Opportunity: Immigrants and Minorities in New York City," in *The Historical Origins of the Underclass,* ed. Michael Katz (Princeton, N.J.: Princeton University Press, 1993), 164.

29. See Waldinger, *Promised City,* chapters 3 and 4 and the footnote on p. 340.

30. "To say that two people belong to the 'same' occupation," write Chris and Charles Tilly in their book *Work under Capitalism* (Boulder, Colo.: Westview Press, 1998), "means that their employers have equivalent claims on them, not that they perform their work in the same manner or maintain the same relations with their fellow workers and people outside their firm" (26). In their view, by contrast, a "job" involves much greater specificity, entailing a set of rights and obligations between a given person and the organization within which he or she is employed (83). From this perspective, any effort at aggregation beyond the organizational level moves one away from the "job"; on the other hand, the Tillys also argue that jobs stand at the intersection of producer and categorical networks, and the networked nature of the jobs in question emerges clearly from the patterns we report in this chapter. For a similar effort to study niches as the intersection of jobs and occupations, see David Howell and Elizabeth Mueller, "The Effects of Immigrants on African-American Earnings: A Job-Level Analysis of the New York City Labor Market, 1979–89" (Working paper no. 210, Jerome Levy Economics Institute, Annandale-on-Hudson, N.Y., November 1997).

31. Alejandro Portes, "Modes of Immigrant Incorporation" in *Global Trends in Migration: Theory and Research on International Population Movements,* ed. Mary M. Kritz, Charles B. Keely, and Silvano M. Tomas (Staten Island, N.Y.: Center for Migration Studies, 1981), 282–283.

32. Victor Nee, Jimy Sanders, and Scott Sernau, "Job Transitions in an Immigrant Metropolis: Ethnic Boundaries and the Mixed Economy," *American Sociological Review* 59, no. 6 (1994): 852.

33. Alejandro Portes and Rubén G. Rumbaut, *Immigrant America: A Portrait,* 2d ed. (Berkeley and Los Angeles: University of California Press, 1996), 19.

34. See U.S. Federal Glass Ceiling Commission, *Good for Business: Making Full Use of the Nation's Human Capital* (Washington, D.C.: U.S. Federal Glass

Ceiling Commission, 1995); Joyce Tang, "The Career Attainment of Caucasian and Asian Engineers," *Sociological Quarterly* 34, no. 3 (1993): 467–496; idem, "Caucasians and Asians in Engineering: A Study in Occupational Mobility and Departure," *Research in the Sociology of Organizations* 11 (1994): 217–256.

35. Portes and Rumbaut, *Immigrant America,* chapter 1.

36. See Roger Waldinger and Yenfen Tseng, "Divergent Diasporas: The Chinese Communities of New York and Los Angeles Compared," *Revue Europeene des Migrations Internationales* 8, no. 3 (1992): 91–116; Yu Zhou, "How Do Places Matter? A Comparative Study of Chinese Ethnic Economies in Los Angeles and New York City," *Urban Geography* 19, no. 6 (1998): 531–553; and Min Zhou and Rebecca Kim, "A Tale of Two Metropolises: Immigrant Chinese Communities in New York and Los Angeles" (paper presented at the conference New York and Los Angeles in the New Millennium, University of California, Los Angeles, May 1999).

37. Philip Kasinitz, *Caribbean New Yorkers* (Ithaca, N.Y.: Cornell University Press, 1992); Waldinger, *Promised City,* pp. 118–122.

38. See, for example, Robert C. Smith, "Transnational Localities: Community, Technology, and the Politics of Membership within the Context of Mexico and U.S. migration," in *Transnationalism from Below,* ed. Michael Peter Smith and Luis Eduardo Guarnizo (New Brunswick, N.J.: Transaction Publishers, 1998), 196–238.

39. Roger Waldinger, "Ethnicity and Opportunity in the Plural City," in *Ethnic Los Angeles,* ed. Roger Waldinger and Mehdi Bozorgmehr (New York: Russell Sage Foundation, 1996), chapter 15; Vilma Ortiz, "The Mexican-Origin Population: Permanent Working-Class or Emerging Middle-Class?" ibid., chapter 9.

40. Norbert Wiley, "The Ethnic Mobility Trap and Stratification Theory," *Social Problems* 155 (1967): 147–159; for a contemporary example, see Ortiz, "Mexican-Origin Population."

41. Ronald S. Burt, *Structural Holes: The Social Structure of Competition* (Cambridge, Mass.: Harvard University Press, 1992).

42. U.S. Department of Labor, *Dictionary of Occupational Titles,* 4th ed. (Washington, D.C.: U.S. Government Printing Office, 1977).

43. The 1990 Census of Population provided data for more than 500 (three-digit) occupations.

44. X. L. Shu, P. L. Fan, X. L. Li, and M. M. Marini, "Characterizing Occupations with Data from the *Dictionary of Occupational Titles,*" *Social Science Research* 25, no. 2 (1996): 149–173. For a complete assessment of the utility of the *DOT* ratings, as well as an earlier effort to apply *DOT* scores to census occupations, see Ann Miller et al., *Work, Jobs, and Occupations: A Critical Review of the "Dictionary of Occupational Titles"* (Washington, D.C.: National Academy Press, 1980).

45. Shu et al., "Characterizing Occupations," 171.

46. Christopher Jencks, Lauri Perman, and Lee Rainwater, "What Is a Good Job? A New Measure of Labor-Market Success," *American Journal of Sociology* 93 (1988): 1322–1357; Neal Rosenthal, "More than Wages at Issue in Job Quality Debate," *Monthly Labor Review* 112, no. 12 (1988): 4–8.

47. Because our data consist of a set of point patterns, our analysis utilizes spatial statistics, which may be relatively unfamiliar to many readers. We first calculate the mean center of the spatial distribution for each group cluster on each dimension; since we are interested in the pattern of dispersion, which varies by direction, we calculate the ellipse of standard deviation. This measure is centered on the mean center, with its long axis in the direction of maximum dispersion and its short axis in the direction of minimum dispersion. Since the boundaries of the ellipse are defined by the standard deviations along the short and long axes, the points often lie outside the ellipse itself. For details, see David Ebdon, *Statistics in Geography,* 2d ed. (New York: Basil Blackwell, 1985), chapter 7. We are grateful to Bill Clark and Mark Ellis for suggesting these measures.

48. See Waldinger, *Promised City.*

49. On the distinctive characteristics of the Chinese ethnoburb in Los Angeles, see Yu Zhou, "Beyond Ethnic Enclaves: Location Strategies of Chinese Producer Service Firms in Los Angeles," *Economic Geography* 74, no. 3 (1998): 228–251.

50. Victor Nee, Jimy M. Sanders, and Scott Sernau, "Job Transitions in an Immigrant Metropolis," *American Sociological Review* 59, no. 6 (1994): 870.

Chapter 8

PROGRESS, DECLINE, STAGNATION?
The New Second Generation Comes of Age

Min Zhou

The question of immigrants' progress lies at the heart of the contemporary immigration debate. For more than 10 years now, the scholarly discussion has framed the question in its own arcane terms, trying to determine whether immigrants are of "declining quality," a phrase that implies that the skills of the most recent arrivals are lower than those of their predecessors. Although the controversy shows no clear resolution, it is certain that a large portion of today's immigrants come to the United States with levels of education sufficient to get started but too low to get ahead without great difficulty.

As with so many academic tempests, the issue of declining quality may be beside the point. Immigrants are, after all, a transitional generation, caught between here and there, and their own assessment of their American condition is heavily influenced by a dual frame of reference. Although their economic situation may leave much to be desired when compared to the U.S. average, in contrast with the circumstances they knew back home, they are far better off. Were they asked to rate their progress since leaving home, the great majority of the foreign-born generation would almost surely answer in highly positive terms.

Their children, especially the American-born, are likely to take a rather different view. For immigrants' offspring, the U.S. standard provides the relevant benchmark. In contrast with their parents, the second generation is unlikely to be mollified by reminders of how much worse things were in the "old world," wherever that might be. But the home country legacy, combined with difficulties engendered by the immigrant situation itself, may put the attainment of a conventional American dream in doubt. Getting ahead in America is likely to require skills far above the minimal competencies—in reading, math, and writing—with which most of the parental generation arrived. So some sizable portion of today's second generation, especially that of the least-skilled immigrants, may find itself stalled or even worse—falling below the ranks of the lower working class in which their parents have established themselves. Worries about "declining quality" pale beside either outcome.

Of course, the advent of the second generation comes with some delay. Although many immigrant children move with their parents, the great majority are born in the United States—which, to restate the obvious, means that their presence occurs sometime after their parents arrive. Still, that fact bears mentioning, since the "new immigration" is still of relatively recent vintage: close to half of the immigrants who currently reside in the United States came here after 1980. Consequently, the "new second generation" is an overwhelmingly youthful population, consisting mostly of children and adolescents, with a small but quantitatively significant portion maturing into adulthood. Their time may not be now, but it will come very shortly.

The scholarly literature will then be ready, as the libraries already contain a sizable and still growing body of literature on the new second generation. In a sense, today's researchers have rediscovered the "second generation problem," as it was called early in the twentieth century, though they have framed it with a new twist. Put broadly, that literature sounds two themes: one has to do with the direction of change, and the second with differences among groups. The difficulties of children of the least-skilled immigrants resonate with earlier concerns, but they now appear in a more ominous light. Yesterday there were plenty of jobs for workers with relatively low skills, and immigrants could take several generations to overcome their original disadvantages. Today, the economy has obliterated much of the low-skilled sector, putting generational advancement in doubt. As Herbert Gans speculated with his customary sharpness, we may be facing an unprecedented situation of "second-generation decline."[1]

On the other hand, many children of today's immigrants are making it—and doing so better and faster than immigrant children have ever done before. Some of the difference is clearly associated with the effects of class among the immigrants themselves, who are far more diverse in socioeconomic circumstances than were their predecessors. But if class backgrounds explain why children of foreign-born physicians, engineers, or computer specialists are highly represented in elite universities, they fall short in accounting for the divergent outcomes among groups that begin under modest circumstances. Consider the children of the Vietnamese fisherfolk living in New Orleans, about whom I have written with Carl Bankston: their parents started out on the very bottommost rungs, and yet a considerable portion of the children seem destined for success as defined in modest, middle-class terms. By contrast, the children of Cambodians or Laotians may be doing better than their own parents and than their American peers with similar socioeconomic backgrounds, but they do not fare as well as the Vietnamese I studied.[2] If most groups are getting ahead, but at markedly divergent rates, the central intellectual issue does not involve predicting second-generation decline but rather accounting for ethnic differences—a long-time academic pursuit.

Thus far, much of the research on the second generation has, appropriately and necessarily, focused on children. Appropriately, because the great majority of the new second generation consists of children. And necessarily, because the great workhorse of the American statistical system—the U.S. Census of Population—ceased asking questions about parents' place of birth in 1970, making it impossible to track the children of immigrants once they had moved out of their parents' homes.

But it is now possible to more fully capture the new second generation, owing to changes in the Current Population Survey (CPS), the characteristics of which are described in chapter 1 of this book. Because the CPS asks all respondents about their parents' nativity, the second generation no longer "disappears" from our statistical system—and thus, for the first time in almost three decades, we are able to study the entire second generation in great detail. That capacity makes all the difference, since the debate over second-generation prospects, although focused mainly on adolescence and school years, entirely hinges on what happens to the children of immigrants once they leave home. In this chapter I use this new data source to illuminate second-generation trajectories, showing the variations among second-generation immigrants in America's largest immigrant cities; using the information available on adults, I examine the fate of those pioneering children of the new immigration who are now themselves moving into the labor market.

Lessons from Past and Present Research

First, let us return to the scholarly debate. The body of academic literature identified with classical assimilation theories predicts a linear trajectory: the children and grandchildren of immigrants move beyond the
status of the first generation and progressively become less distinctive
from other Americans. This particular perspective shares a series of assumptions: outsider groups, however diverse and initially disadvantaged, all absorb a common culture and gain equal access to the opportunity structure; they do so in a more or less natural way, gradually
deserting old cultural and behavioral patterns in favor of new ones. The
whole process, once set in motion, moves inevitably and irreversibly toward the dissolution of the original group. Consequently, observable
ethnic differences are largely a function of length of time in the United
States and generational status. Although the time span for assimilation
is sometimes prolonged, distinctive ethnic characteristics eventually
fade and retain only symbolic importance.[3]

Classical assimilation theory arose as an abstraction from the experience of the earlier immigration from Europe, especially newcomers
who arrived during the gigantic wave of the 1880–1920 period and the
very large second generation that appeared as their legacy. The theoretical reflections largely developed while the process of adaptation was
under way. Now that it is over, one can safely conclude that the descendants of the 1880–1920 wave have overcome earlier disadvantages, achieving parity with, if not outdistancing, Americans of English
ancestry—or what Milton Gordon earlier called the "core cultural
group."[4] Unfortunately, assimilation theory cannot explain why this
outcome transpired—unless one subscribes to that variant of modernization theory that most earlier writers embraced but many contemporary social scientists have now challenged. Moreover, past success may
have been due to the specific circumstances yesterday's second generation encountered, including the long period of restricted immigration
between the 1920s and the 1950s, which almost certainly weakened attachment to the immigrant culture and patterns of group affiliation. If
the success of yesterday's second generation depended on restrictive immigration policy, the past is unlikely to prove a useful guide to the future, since we appear to be headed for more, not less, immigration.

To the extent that assimilation theory seeks to distill other essential elements of that earlier experience, the picture it presents stands at some
variant from the lessons of the modern historiography of immigration and

immigrant adaptation. As Steven Thernstrom showed more than 25 years ago, the Irish, Italians, and Jews moved ahead at very different rates, and in very different ways.[5] Joel Perlmann's more sophisticated analysis of the Irish, Jews, Italians, African Americans, and Yankees of Providence, Rhode Island, underscored wide differences in both educational and occupational attainment among the second generation, and these differences persisted after controlling for an extensive array of background variables.[6] Both Thernstrom and Perlmann used longitudinal data, which reinforced the reliability of their conclusions. Working with time-series data, George Borjas demonstrated that 1910 literacy levels in immigrants' countries of origin continued to be correlated with the economic position of their descendants in 1940 and again in 1970 and 1990.[7] To be sure Borjas, like Thernstrom and Perlmann before him, noted that later generations moved a considerable distance beyond their immigrant ancestors. But the notion of straight-line assimilation seems to clearly imply a *single* line—an idea that is very difficult to reconcile with the historical record of significant differences in the rates at which various groups moved upward.[8]

Ethnic Differences Today

From the standpoint of assimilation theory, time in the United States moves groups ahead and produces intergroup convergence. But time does not appear to work equally for all, as it matters little for upwardly mobile immigrants and their children. For example, Hirschman and Falcon, in their 1985 study of educational attainment among 25 ethnoreligious groups, found that neither generation nor length of U.S. residence significantly influenced educational outcomes. Moreover, children of highly educated immigrants consistently fared much better in school than did fourth- or fifth-generation descendants of poorly educated ancestors, regardless of ethnoreligious background. In this case, time, as measured by generational status, proved far less important than class status, itself highly correlated with national origin.[9] In a more recent study, Vernez and Abrahamse demonstrated that the lower educational attainment of Hispanic students, relative to Asian, black, and white students, was largely explained by their generally lower scores on all key socioeconomic characteristics, such as family income and parental education.[10] The effect of time in the United States is largely eclipsed by socioeconomic background, particularly in predicting the direction of structural assimilation for higher-status immigrant groups and the rate for lower-status immigrant groups.

Thus, much current research emphasizes the overriding importance of socioeconomic status; class position yields an independent effect on mobility outcomes, because its influence is so pervasive as to affect where people live and go to school, the types of contacts they can make, and the community resources to which they can gain access. Wealthier and skilled immigrants, more representative of contemporary immigration than past immigration, may experience temporary downward mobility; some also encounter the glass ceiling phenomenon. Nonetheless, today's educated newcomers seem to be remarkably successful in securing professional occupations and middle-class livelihoods, which in turn facilitate direct settlement in suburban middle-class communities. The prospects for poorer and unskilled immigrants are not nearly as bright: they have few options but to take up low-wage jobs and settle in declining urban areas, starting their American life either in poverty or on public assistance. Class factors also affect, but do not fully determine, the modes by which immigrants incorporate into American society. These modes of immigrant incorporation, as Portes and Rumbaut have shown in their synthetic work, *Immigrant America,* involve a complex of insider and outsider reactions that can sometimes reinforce initial class disadvantages—as among such labor migrant groups as Mexicans—but can also reduce their import—as among many of the entrepreneurial groups that came to the United States as refugees.[11]

Class factors occupy a particularly prominent place in the reinterpretation of second-generation prospects developed by Perlmann and Waldinger, who go so far as to argue that the problems facing children of today's working-class immigrants are essentially a variant of the difficulties of *all* working-class Americans, regardless of ethnic background.[12] But this perspective ends up reducing ethnicity to class, when it turns out that ethnicity often exercises its own effect, regardless of the economic factors that might otherwise distinguish or lump together diverse ethnic groups. Clearly, ethnicity plays a prominent role in structuring adolescent lives, both in and out of school. Many studies have shown that students of Asian origin outperform non-Hispanic white students, who, in turn, outperform black and Hispanic students by significant margins. However, Laurence Steinberg's book *Beyond the Classroom* demonstrated that these ethnic differences appeared among each of the nine different high schools that he studied and persisted after controlling for social class, family structure, and parents' place of birth. Steinberg also showed that significant ethnic differences exist in a set of beliefs and behaviors—a conviction in the payoff to schooling, attributional styles, and peer-group association—that are considered important determinants of school success. And Steinberg is far from the only scholar to arrive at conclusions of this sort.[13] Rubén Rumbaut, for example, who used language proficiency as a proxy for nativity or immigration status in a large-scale study in the San Diego School District during the 1986–1987 and 1989–1990 school years, found that first-generation Chinese, Korean, Japanese, Vietnamese, and Filipino students had the highest grade point averages of all students, including whites of often higher socioeconomic class backgrounds, in the district. More remarkable, even the Hmong, who came from a preliterate peasant background, and the more recently arrived Cambodians outperformed all native-born English-only American students attending the same school.[14]

Thus, a significant body of research points to distinctive effects associated with particular ethnic groups—positive in the Asian case, negative in the Mexican and other Hispanic cases—that are clearly observable after controlling for the class status of both the individual and the group, as well as the corresponding modes of incorporation. Ethnicity also interacts with broader structural factors in such a way as to reinforce the advantages or disadvantages associated with membership in a particular ethnic group. Portes and MacLeod, who worked with the National Educational Longitudinal Survey and employed hierarchical linear models, reported that the negative effect of disadvantaged group memberships among immigrant children was reinforced rather than reduced in suburban schools but that the positive effect of advantaged group memberships remained significant even in inner-city schools.[15] Using the same data set, but employing a two-stage least-squares method, Hao and Bonstead-Bruns found that immigrant status increased educational expectations for Chinese, Korean, and Filipino families more than for Mexican families. They also found that Chinese background consistently exerted positive effects on educational achievement, whereas Mexican background showed significantly negative effects, and that the ethnic effects persisted after controlling for important individual and contextual factors.[16]

Second-Generation Decline?

As I noted earlier, research on the "old" second generation of European-origin groups highlighted the importance and persistence of ethnic effects. While contemporary research shows continuity in this respect, scholarship on the new second generation sounds an important new note, indicating that ethnicity may do more than influence the rate at which groups progress. Instead, it can accelerate the upward progress of some groups while keeping others from advancing or even maintaining their status; second-generation decline is thus a scenario worth careful consideration.

But what accounts for the divergent effects of ethnicity? The advantages and disadvantages of ethnic group membership do not simply derive from the class status with which the first generation starts life in America; they are also a function of the different levels of social structures in which individuals and groups participate. At the macro level, the system of ethnic stratification functions to provide different ethnic groups with unequal access to economic resources and political power. At the micro level, the networks of social ties, which are often ethnically based and varying in structure from group to group, prescribe strategies and offer support in coping with structural disadvantages. Consequently, groups encountering similar levels of disadvantage nonetheless respond in different ways. Ogbu argues that they either accept and internalize socially imposed inferiority as part of their collective self-definition, thereby fostering an oppositional outlook on the dominant group and mainstream institutions, or else create a positive view of their heritage on the basis of cultural and ethnic distinctions, thereby establishing a sense of collective dignity.[17] The latter approach yields survival strategies that enable members to psychologically cope with structural barriers, keeping the host society at arm's length—precisely the pattern described in my book on the Vietnamese in New Orleans.[18] The former approach often produces a strategy of reacting to structural disadvantages by constructing resistance to assimilation.[19] In this case, symbolic expressions of ethnicity and ethnic empowerment may hinder rather than facilitate social mobility. This pattern is exemplified by the forced-choice dilemma confronting the Chicano and Puerto Rican youth studied by Margaret Gibson and Philippe Bourgois, both of whom found that Chicano and Puerto Rican students who did well in school were forcefully excluded by their coethnic peers as "turnovers" acting "white."[20]

Dissonant acculturation, to borrow the concept coined by Portes and Rumbaut in their second edition of *Immigrant America*, increases the likelihood of second-generation decline. Immigrants' tendency to settle in poor, inner-city neighborhoods brings their children into close contact with the adversarial culture of ghetto youth, as Portes and I wrote in our article on segmented assimilation.[21] But the adversarial culture would not be so enticing were it not for its elective affinity with the dispositions engendered by the immigrant situation itself. The first generation responds to discrimination and downward mobility with a dual framework of reference, regarding its current disadvantaged status as temporary. By contrast, immigrants' children, born American or raised to be American, expect to be judged by the same standards as other Americans, an orientation that yields little tolerance for the inferior treatment the foreign-born generation may have found objectionable but still bearable. The children want far more than their parents; however, they lack the resources—economic, educational, neighborhood, and institutional—that would allow them to gain the school-based skills needed to progress beyond the levels their parents have reached.[22]

Unlike in the past, today's job market allows for few alternatives, as both the demand and the pay for manual work are declining. Consequently, children of immigrants find themselves facing a situation of blocked mobility, and they respond by drawing on the lessons of the adversarial culture absorbed on the streets and in the schools. Unfortunately, this approach launches immigrant children into a vicious circle, since oppositional strategies work to their further disadvantage by putting them at risk of disruptive behavior, school failure, and labor force marginalization. This mismatch between rising aspirations and shrinking opportunities is likely to lead to second-generation decline, a process by which immigrant children are either pushed out or drop out of the bottom tier of urban economies. Granted, the same circumstances could provoke "second-generation revolt," as Perlmann and Waldinger speculate, but that possibility seems more relevant to an earlier era and far less likely in today's climate of limited collective action.[23]

Second-Generation Outcomes and the Metropolitan Context

Context affects how the second generation responds to the dilemmas it encounters. For those in the second generation, as for their parents, the context is likely to be urban, because of parents' tendency to converge on the five large urban regions profiled in this book. Life in the major immigrant regions necessarily entails heightened in-group contacts, a factor likely to slow the pace of assimilation. But as noted elsewhere in this book, America's leading immigrant cities differ significantly in their ethnic and national-origin compositions, so that, for any group, the probability of exposure to others of "one's own kind" varies a good deal from place to place. While urban economies generate jobs for immigrants, the shape of the metropolitan labor market aggravates the problems associated with the adaptation of second-generation immigrants. As shown in earlier chapters, the capitals of immigrant America have been unloading their manufacturing industries along with their related low-skilled sectors, a transition that has shifted urban economies to activities increasingly dependent on a highly educated labor force. For the children of poorly educated immigrants, this is bad news: to move beyond their parents, who have gotten by with a few years of high school or less, they will need to secure jobs that require much more schooling.

If the economies of the leading immigrant regions are all moving in this same direction, however, they are progressing at different rates. Deindustrialization may have swept New York, for example, but it has been less prominent in Chicago and Los Angeles. Likewise, San Francisco has transitioned to a high-tech economy that has no parallel in Miami. Thus, second-generation outcomes will likely hinge on who and where one is; this is the story to which I will now turn.

The New Second Generation Comes of Age: A Demographic Profile

The shift in national origins—from Europe to others parts of the world—is perhaps the single most distinctive aspect of the new immigration. But the transformation of the second generation is a more protracted development; though clearly in evidence, it is far from complete. The last second generation was dominated by cohorts born in the 1910s and 1920s, tailed by a much smaller, though not insignificant, group born in the 1930s. While these immigrant offspring are now aging, they remain a sizable presence, their numbers augmented by the descendants of the smaller waves of European immigration of the 1930s and the immediate postwar period. On the other hand, the new immigration is still of quite recent vintage, and rates of immigration have increased significantly since the late 1960s and early 1970s. Moreover, many of today's major groups are very recently arrived: for all practical purposes, Vietnamese and Central American immigration dates only from the late 1970s. Consequently, the composition of the second generation takes a distinct form; unlike the foreign-born, immigrant offspring retain a clear European plurality. But children of more recent newcomers have only begun to make their mark; many second-generation immigrants have Mexican-born parents, reflecting the long-standing nature of this flow, but a very diverse group of Asians as yet constitutes only a small share of today's second generation. Although the makeup of the second generation will change in due time, the nature of the demographic processes at work—including mortality rates among the aging descendants of European immigrants and fertility differentials among new immigrants—means that second-generation immigrants will continue to look quite different from first-generation immigrants for quite some time.

The demographic transitions at work nationwide parallel the shifts occurring in the leading immigrant cities. But the second generation has arrived as a notable force in the key immigrant urban regions, even while it is relatively inconspicuous elsewhere. As figure 8.1 shows, first-generation immigrants are more numerous than second-generation immigrants in every region but Chicago and in the United States as a whole. Here we see both the impact of the regionally concentrated nature of contemporary immigration and the continued demographic weight of the last second generation, which is far less likely than today's immigrant population to live in the key immigrant regions. Los Angeles and Miami, the regions of greatest immigrant density, also lead in the proportion of the population belonging to the second generation. Both are also new immigration regions, in the sense that they never exerted much attraction for earlier emigrants from Europe, Miami's lure as a retirement colony notwithstanding. For this reason, the immigrant presence is more marked in these regions than in either New York or San Francisco, with their continuing residue of immigrant offspring of the 1880–1920 wave. And although Los Angeles and Miami are quite similar in generational composition, Miami is distinct in one important respect. As the recipient of an even greater immigrant flow, in relative terms, than Los Angeles, Miami contains the smallest proportion of individuals of third or later generations. By contrast, Chicago looks mostly like the rest of America, with a large population of immigrant offspring, a remnant of its immigrant past, that outnumbers the foreign-born population.

As I noted previously, history and place make for marked interregional contrasts in ethnic composition between first- and second-generation populations. Chapter 1 designated Los Angeles and Miami as immigrant places dominated by Hispanics, a description that can also be detected from figure 8.2, which displays regional ethnic composition

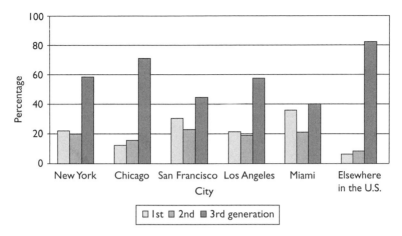

Figure 8.1. Distribution of immigrant generations in major immigrant regions
Source: Current Population Survey, 1994–1998.

by generation. Only Los Angeles contains a Hispanic-dominant second generation; a similar trend in Miami has been slowed by its large concentration of white second-generation retirees, making Miami's second-generation population a Hispanic plurality group. New York and Chicago, both earlier designated as immigrant cities with a Hispanic plurality, contain a second-generation population dominated by whites, yet another reflection of the impact of earlier immigration flows on these regions. San Francisco, the only region with an immigrant population dominated by Asians, boasts the greatest variety in the ethnic composition of its second generation and the most pronounced Asian tilt. The least regional variation appears in the third and later generations, of which whites constitute at least 60 percent in every region.

Though I am speaking of the second generation as a demographic category, I have already suggested that, sociologically, it splits into two: those immigrant offspring linked to the 1880–1920 wave and those who are children of the wave conventionally dated as of 1965 (although in some key cases, most notably Mexico, there is an earlier migration history of significant dimensions). The second generation's distinctive age profile signals this fissure, as shown in figure 8.3. Unlike the foreign-born, whose population tends to peak in the early adult years, the age distribution among the children of immigrants takes a distinctive U-shaped curve, with the largest second-generation contingents either under age 15 or over age 55 and relatively small cohorts resting in

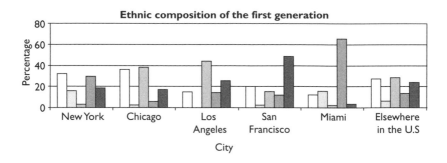

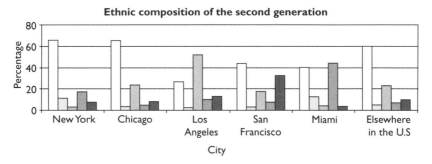

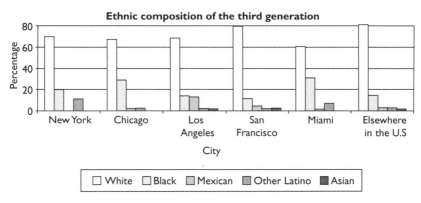

Figure 8.2.   Distribution of major ethnic groups by generational status in
major immigrant regions

Source: Current Population Survey, 1994–1998.

between. The U-shaped curve not only reveals a high level of variation
among the second generation but also indicates that the relative weight
of this population differs greatly according to age. Most important, the
second-generation presence is of relative importance among the
youngest and oldest groups. Among adults between the ages of 25 and

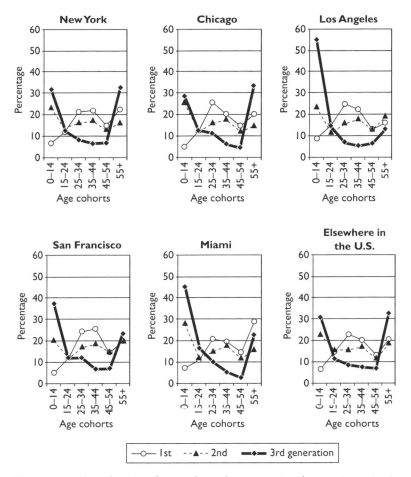

Figure 8.3.   Distribution of age cohorts by generational status in major immigrant regions

Source: Current Population Survey, 1994–1998.

54, however, immigrant offspring are still a relatively inconspicuous minority.

The U-shaped curve, though always observable, nonetheless assumes a different form in each of the immigration regions. The curve for Los Angeles is especially distinct, with a disproportionately large population of second-generation children and a disproportionately small population of second-generation elders, making for a very peculiar looking U-shaped curve. Miami again resembles Los Angeles, differing only in the relative weight of elderly immigrant offspring, most of whom are undoubtedly

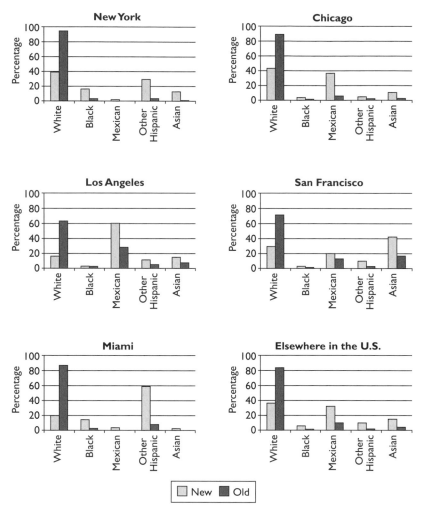

Figure 8.4.   Ethnic composition of the old and new second generations in major immigrant regions

Source: Current Population Survey, 1994–1998.

refugees from the colder climates of the Northeast and Midwest. Although the fissure point obviously varies from place to place, splitting the second-generation population into those born before and after 1960 highlights the ethnic contrast between the old and the new second generation, as figure 8.4 shows. Immigrant offspring born before 1960 are predominately white in all five regions, and almost exclusively so in New York, Los Angeles, and even Miami. By contrast, those born after 1960 are a far more varied lot, with whites topping out at 40 percent in New York and Chicago and not quite reaching the 20 percent mark in Los Angeles.

The age and ethnic structures of various immigrant regions are linked. Whereas the shift from the old to the new second generation can be seen in the youngest cohort in every place, nowhere has the majority of the new second generation yet come of age. But within age cohorts, the shift from old to new is considerably more advanced in some places than in others. In Chicago, only the youngest cohort has seen the white second-generation group change from a quantitative majority to a quantitative minority; in New York the same transition has already transpired among adolescents and the youngest of adults but not among any other cohorts. By contrast, the ethnic origins of second-generation adults ages 25 to 35 have already tipped from a white dominance in Los Angeles and San Francisco, with Miami lagging only slightly behind.

Thus, the future trend is beginning to take root, at least in three of the five leading immigrant destinations. Second-generation school success, on which so much research on immigrant children has focused, is undoubtedly crucial. But its importance rests, in part, on its linkage to labor market outcomes. The long-term significance of the educational problems experienced by immigrant children hinges on their consequences for subsequent employment options. It could well be, as put forth in the pessimistic scenarios of second-generation decline, that second-generation adolescents who performed poorly in school find themselves excluded from the job market—or, if not excluded, are opting out of it. Yet one can also imagine that today's immigrant offspring will move ahead at very different rates; the poorest performers may simply repeat the experience of previous working-class immigrants, finding a place in the labor market that, however modest, represents an improvement over that of their parents. Which option appears to be more common is a question that the CPS uniquely allows us to answer.

Generational and Ethnic Differences in Schooling and the Labor Market

Educational Adaptation

We begin with education, since schooling is a prerequisite for advancement in the twenty-first-century America in which the new second generation will mature. The first hurdle is the high school diploma, a credential

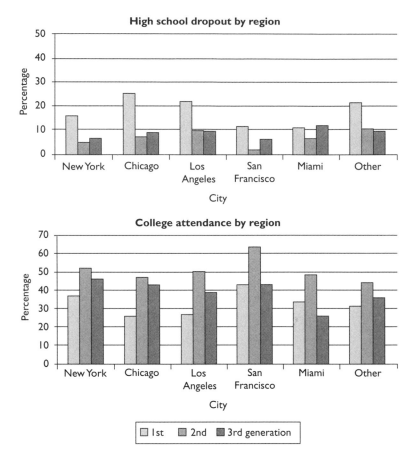

Figure 8.5. Educational outcomes by generational status: interregional and interethnic comparisons

Source: Current Population Survey, 1994–1998.

that most adult Americans have attained, at higher levels with each subsequent generation. But as shown elsewhere in this book, many immigrants arrive in the United States with just a few years of secondary schooling, and often less. Thus, completing high school is often a major leap for immigrant offspring in moving beyond the socioeconomic status of their parents. To examine this crucial advancement from one generation to the next, I first look at 16- to 19-year-olds.

I classify all 16- to 19-year-olds who neither attend high school nor possess a high school degree as high school dropouts. Immigrant (first-generation) youth are in big trouble on this count, as can be seen from

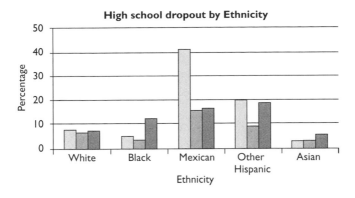

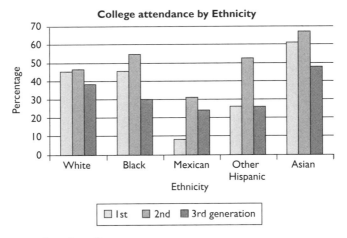

Figure 8.5. *(continued)*

the top panels in figure 8.5. "Dropout" may not be the most appropriate label for foreign-born children, as many of them may never have "dropped into" high school to begin with because they headed straight to the labor market as soon as they set foot on U.S. soil.[24] This minor qualification aside, failure to attend or complete high school is a distinguishing feature among foreign-born youth. But that generalization varies somewhat depending on one's perspective. Relative to their second- or third-generation counterparts, immigrant youth are a good deal more likely to be dropouts in every region except Miami, a southern metropolis that boasts the relatively largest black third generation and where black youth are particularly likely to have difficulties in school. Some clear regional disparities also emerge, with low rates of high school completion among foreign-born youth in Chicago, LA, and New York. Taking a somewhat different view, the foreign-born disadvantage, though still perceptible, varies across major ethnic categories. The gap between first and later generations is greatest among Mexicans, mainly because the first-generation dropout rate is so high.

These high first-generation dropout rates imply that this indicator will provide evidence of second-generation progress rather than decline. Not surprisingly, Mexicans show the greatest improvement in this category, although this change qualifies as improvement only in relation to the dismal first-generation pattern: second-generation Mexicans attend or complete high school at rates that compare unfavorably with those of third-generation blacks; third-generation Mexicans do still slightly worse. In contrast to outcomes for the first generation, those for the second generation vary more obviously across regions; second-generation adolescents are less likely to drop out than their third-generation counterparts in San Francisco, New York, and Miami and more likely to do so in Los Angeles and Chicago. Part of the regional variation is undoubtedly related to each region's distinctive ethnic mix, the impact of which is most visible in San Francisco; the only region with a second-generation population with an Asian plurality, it benefits from the extraordinarily low dropout rates among second-generation Asian youth.

Ideally, high school graduates will go on to college, with the relevant population consisting of persons ages 18 to 24. This indicator again highlights the foreign-born disadvantage, as the bottom panels of figure 8.5 show; however, one would hesitate to qualify the gap as inherently disastrous. If some young immigrant adolescents never drop in to high school, their slightly older counterparts, many of whom are drawn to the United States by the opportunity to work, are even less likely to attend school. In some regions, with San Francisco again leading the pack, the foreign-born are attending college at remarkably high rates; even at the lowest level, recorded in Chicago, foreign-born college attendance rates are not much worse than those of native-born blacks—which puts the matter in some perspective. Ethnic differences are again more dramatic than regional differences: more than 60 percent of all Asian-born youth attend college, whereas less than 10 percent of their Mexican-born counterparts attend college, regardless of place.

But college attendance rates for the second generation strike a blow against the hypothesis of second-generation decline: the second generation attends college at considerably higher rates than not only the first but also the third generation. Clearly, regional patterns are deeply confounded with a compositional bias: the very high college attendance rate for San Francisco is almost certainly related to the high college attendance rates among Asians, whereas the stark decline in second- and third-generation rates in Miami is likely a reflection of the problems encountered by blacks in this relatively poor southern metropolis. Nonetheless, the regional patterns are roughly consistent with the intergenerational differences within ethnic categories. Most important, all categories—with the exception of whites—show an increase in college attendance from the first to the second generation.

Economic Adaptation

Schooling is more strongly associated with socioeconomic attainment than ever before, since the steady educational upgrading of the economy puts at risk all those who fail to reach the societal norm for education. That immigrants with little education seem to find a place in today's economy may be an outcome related to the migratory condition itself, a function both of the social networks that propel movement to the United States and the dual frame of reference to which I have already referred. Since neither condition applies to immigrant offspring who are born and grow up in America, I move on to generational differences in employment, focusing on adults ages 25 to 64.

In a sense, the discussion about immigrant integration takes place in the shadow of the "underclass" debate, with much of the immigration anxiety—insofar as it has rational roots—linked to the possibility that newcomers and their descendants might also fail economically. Though underclass has always been a nebulous formulation, it clearly implies a thoroughly marginalized population involved in neither schooling nor gainful employment. As the top panels of figure 8.6 show, marginalization is most common among the foreign-born and blacks. As one might expect, marginalization is most likely among immigrant Mexicans, although the ethnic differentials on this count are much smaller than the gaps observed earlier for educational indicators. By contrast, the second generation is more clearly integrated into the labor market, with the distinctive patterns of San Francisco and Asians that I noted earlier showing up again.

Considering the extraordinarily low educational levels of many immigrants, it is hardly surprising to find them most at risk of marginalization;

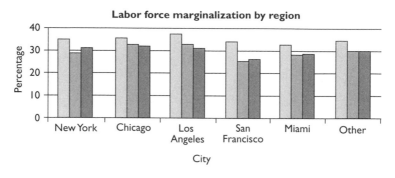

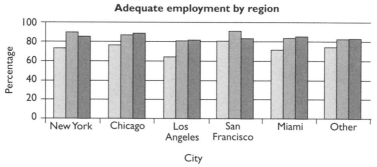

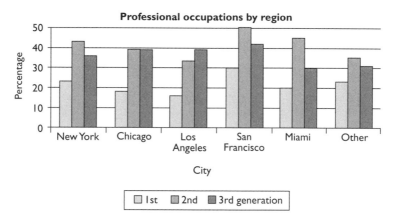

Figure 8.6. Economic outcomes by generational status: interregional and interethnic comparisons

Source: Current Population Survey, 1994–1998.

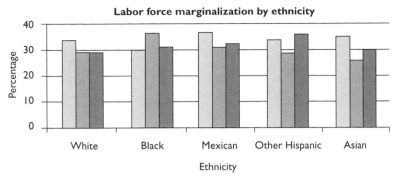

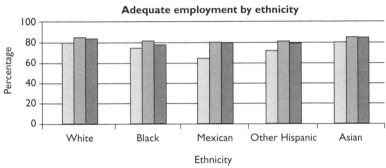

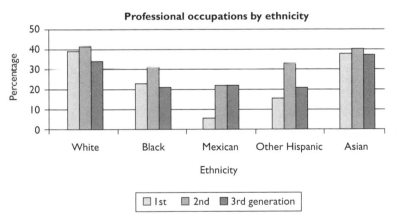

Figure 8.6. *(continued)*

the more relevant issue, addressed in part by an earlier chapter 3, concerns the income-generating capacity of the jobs urban residents find. In this chapter I turn again to the concept of employment adequacy, discussed at length in chapter 3. This indicator, as can be seen from the center panels of figure 8.6, highlights the persistent disadvantage of the foreign-born: immigrants are the least likely to have jobs of adequate quality in every place and in every category. Likewise, it reveals the progress of immigrant offspring relative to their predecessors, with particularly high rates of employment adequacy registered in New York, Chicago, and San Francisco. Second-generation Mexicans are more likely than Mexican immigrants to find adequate employment, and they do so at rates similar to those of native-born Hispanics other than Mexicans and third-generation blacks—a less than satisfactory rate from the perspective of structural assimilation.

I also examine a more selective indicator of labor market success, levels of professional and managerial employment (see bottom panels of figure 8.6). The now-familiar pattern—of first-generation disadvantage, second-generation improvement, and mild third-generation decline—reappears, though with some variation among regions and groups. San Francisco leads in the rate of second-generation upper-white-collar employment, followed by New York and Miami; the situations in Chicago and Los Angeles are somewhat less impressive. Clearly, a substantial portion of the second and third generations are moving well above the bottommost rungs. Nonetheless, access to these higher-level jobs varies greatly by group. Second-generation Mexican workers are much more likely than first-generation Mexicans to be employed in professional occupations, but they appear at a greater relative disadvantage on this count than on any of the employment indicators examined so far; the gap separating U.S.-born Mexicans from their white and Asian counterparts is significant.

Generational Status, Ethnicity, and Spatial Concentration: Net Effects

Instead of second-generation decline, the descriptive statistics I have just reviewed suggest that second-generation immigrants are moving ahead; they are doing better than the foreign-born population and often appear favorably situated relative to their counterparts with three or more generations in the United States. The passage from first to second generation yields a dramatic change, but the shift from second to third is much more modest. At the intergroup level, Mexicans do the worst, Asians do the best, and blacks and Hispanics other than Mexicans display a good deal of variation from place to place.

Although suggestive, the evidence is hardly definitive. On the one hand, ethnic differences may have an effect, as suggested by the literature, but class is also likely to be a significant factor. Similarly, it is not clear how to interpret the interregional differences. Do they reflect a genuine place effect? Or are they bound up with interregional differences in generational and ethnic composition? To answer these questions, I move on to a multivariate analysis, by which I seek to determine the net effects of generational status, ethnicity, and specific immigrant receiving contexts, controlling for observable demographic and socioeconomic differences.

Model Specification

My analysis focuses on the same outcomes reviewed earlier: high school attendance or completion for persons ages 16 to 19 (with dropout coded 0); college attendance for those ages 18 to 24; employment status (with labor force marginalization coded 0) for those ages 25 to 64; and, for out-of-school, employed persons ages 25 to 64, employment adequacy and professional or managerial employment. Each of these outcomes represents a dichotomy (e.g., attending or completing high school or not, attending college or not), making logistic regression the appropriate statistical technique. My substantive interest lies in the relative effects of generation, ethnicity, and region. I included two dummy variables to capture the effects of generational status, one for the foreign-born and one for U.S.-born descendants of the foreign-born, thus leaving U.S.-born of U.S.-born parents as the omitted category. Similarly, I employed four dummy variables to measure the effects associated with ethnic category: non-Hispanic black, Mexican, Hispanic other than Mexican, and Asian; non-Hispanic white was the omitted category. I used five dummy variables for each of the key immigrant regions, which made all other places the omitted category. Last, I entered a series of interactive terms to capture ethnic effects associated with specific places: being Mexican in Chicago or Los Angeles; being Hispanic other than Mexican in New York or Miami; and being Asian in San Francisco. Since I wanted to isolate net effects, I controlled for a series of background factors that could also contribute to the outcomes of interest. I controlled for four demo-

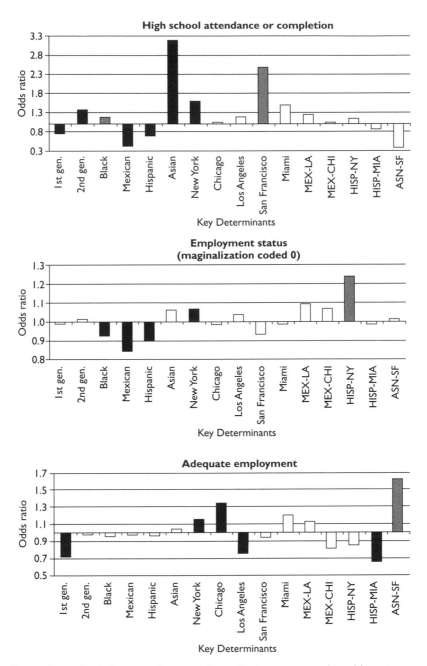

Figure 8.7. Logistic regression models predicting outcomes by odds ratios

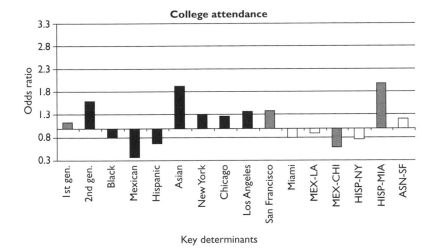

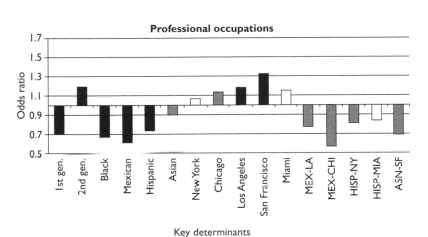

Figure 8.7. *(continued)*

Note: Significance levels: black = .01; gray = .05; white = n.s. 1st gen., first generation; 2nd gen., second generation; MEX-LA, Mexicans in Los Angeles; MEX-CHI, Mexicans in Chicago; HISP-NY, non-Mexican Hispanics in New York; HISP-MIA, non-Mexican Hispanics in Miami; ASN-SF, Asians in San Francisco.

Source: Current Population Survey, 1994–1998.

graphic factors: age (as measured in years), sex, marital status, and household size. I also added a set of controls for four socioeconomic factors: inner-city residence, poverty status, two-parent households, and home ownership. The models predicting labor market outcomes also included controls for education and the nonlinear effect of age.

My discussion focuses on the generational, ethnic, regional, and ethnic-place effects, controlling for all of these background factors; coefficients for all variables in the models can be found in the appendix to this chapter. I present all of the key results in graphic form, as displayed in figure 8.7. To ease interpretation, I have converted logit coefficients to odds ratios. Values greater than 1 indicate a positive relationship between any independent variable and the relevant outcome variable; values less than 1 denote a negative relationship. Black bars signal significant effects at the .01 level, gray bars indicate effects at the .05 level, and white bars denote levels short of statistical significance.

Educational Adaptation

The multivariate analysis lends weight to many, if not all, of the conclusions I draw from the examination of descriptive statistics. Neither the revisionist hypothesis of second-generation decline nor the conventional scenario of successive generational improvement holds true: the first generation does significantly worse than the third, which, in turn, does significantly worse than the second. Ethnicity also matters, although its weight varies by outcome and group. Mexicans and other Hispanics are both less likely to complete or attend high school and less likely to attend college than whites. By contrast, blacks are significantly more likely than whites to complete or attend high school but a good deal less likely to attend college. The odds of school completion or attendance at either level are significantly lower for Mexicans and other Hispanics and significantly higher for Asians than for whites.

Place does matter—but not in the anticipated way. For the most part, residence in the key immigration regions has a positive impact on educational outcomes (although this benefit is offset by a modest inner-city effect of opposite direction). Immigrants and their offspring have done well by locating in these major metros—perhaps because one characteristic of dominant metropolitan status is a highly developed educational infrastructure, a trait particularly applicable to the higher education sector. Not all groups are affected by place characteristics in quite the same way, however. For Hispanics other than Mexicans, a Miami location has a strong positive effect; however, this finding may reflect the pronounced Cuban tilt of Miami's non-Mexican Hispanic population, as opposed to the Dominican tilt in New York and the Central American tilt in Los Angeles and San Francisco.

Economic Adaptation

As I have already noted, the possibility that immigrants or their descendants might simply fall out of the economic race is a major worry motivating the immigration debate; from this standpoint, the center panel of figure 8.7 provides a basis for the anxiety. One the one hand, the generational effects on labor force marginalization do not rival their influence on the educational outcomes just reviewed: the first or second generation does no worse than the third, although I suspect that my controls for the demographic and socioeconomic correlates of immigrant status are crucial in diminishing the penalty specifically attached to foreign birth. On the other hand, I observe strong ethnic effects on labor force marginalization and education. All of my ethnic variables, except for the Asian category, are statistically significant, and they point to ethnic disadvantage. Black, Mexican, or other Hispanic ethnicity weakens attachment to the labor force (and to college). By contrast, only one place yields significant effects: residing in New York reduces the likelihood of labor force marginalization, a by-product, I suspect, of the region's robust economy. The New York location is particularly beneficial for non-Mexican Hispanics, relative to their coethnics outside the region.

Among those in the labor force, the foreign-born disadvantage in employment adequacy is pronounced. Foreign-born workers may show as much labor force attachment as the third or later generation, but once they are in the labor force, they are significantly less likely than longer-settled workers to obtain minimally adequate jobs, as depicted in the center panel of figure 8.7. By contrast, second-generation workers are no less likely than workers of third or later generations to hold jobs of adequate quality. While residence in New York, Chicago, or Miami facilitates employment adequacy, residence in Los Angeles proves detrimental, suggesting that the region's concentration of low-skilled foreign-born population intensifies competition among immigrants. But Miami's opportunities seem to elude its non-Mexican Hispanic residents, whereas residence in Los Angeles yields a positive, if not significant, effect on Mexicans.

In terms of access to the best, as opposed to minimally adequate, jobs the first-generation disadvantage persists, whereas the second generation turns out to enjoy an observable advantage, as shown in the bottom right-hand panel of figure 8.7. Just who experiences generational advantage varies by group, as blacks, Mexicans, other Hispanics, and even Asians are a good deal less likely than whites to hold managerial or professional occupations. This last analysis underscores the potential advantages associated with residence in the immigrant capitals: the big immigrant centers are relatively rich in managerial and professional opportunities. However, these opportunities have so far been elusive; the likelihood of holding a professional or managerial job is negatively associated with being Mexican in Los Angeles and Chicago, being non-Mexican Hispanic in New York, and being Asian in San Francisco.

Conclusion

The new sociology of immigration has naturally focused on the foreign-born population itself, since it was the renewal of mass immigration that distinguished the last three decades of the twentieth century from the midcentury years that preceded them. But immigrants' most lasting legacy is likely to be their children, some of whom are born abroad and grow up in the United States, though the great majority are Americans from birth. That legacy appears with some lag: after all, the phenomenon we label as the new immigration emerged in full blush over an extended period, and children take time to grow up. Because more than 44 percent of today's foreign-born population arrived after 1980, a percentage still higher among those of non-European origin (50 percent), most immigrant offspring have not yet reached adult years. But as I have shown in this chapter, the leading cadre of the new second generation is now entering the labor market, its presence particularly noticeable in the major immigrant centers of the United States.

The advent of the second generation is a momentous development, precisely because the aspirations of immigrant offspring are likely to be quite different from those of their parents. Meeting those quintessentially American expectations, however, will depend on the resources that second-generation immigrants can muster—most important, educational credentials and school-acquired skills but also the ethnic connections that lubricated their parents' entrance into the labor market. The concern that the grown-up children of today's immigrants will not make it—largely due to deficiencies on both counts—runs like a red thread through much of today's burgeoning scholarly corpus.

This chapter suggests that the most pessimistic renderings of second-generation scenarios lack warrant. As in the past, the children of immigrants appear to be progressing beyond the stations occupied by their parents, a generalization that holds for most groups and most key immigrant receiving areas and applies to the variety of indicators I have examined, including those related to education and labor market status. Moreover, the second generation does not appear to be paying a steep price for their parents' choice of destination; if anything, the evidence suggests otherwise, as the key immigrant centers are often associated with positive educational and labor market outcomes. Second-generation decline does not seem to be in the cards. On the other hand, rates of second-generation progress vary considerably. In general, Asians appear headed upward most rapidly, Mexicans most slowly, blacks and non-Mexican Hispanics at intermediate rates (though the angle of non-Mexican Hispanics seems more clearly pitched upward in Miami, where it picks up a sizable Cuban group). However, whether the children of low-skilled immigrants can catch up with the average socioeconomic levels of other Americans in the future remains to be seen.

Not all locations offer equal opportunities, on all measures, for all groups: Los Angeles does not seem to be serving Mexicans well with regard to educational and occupational opportunities, nor is New York a favorable location for non-Mexican Hispanics. But in comparison to the other regions, Los Angeles gives Mexicans a better chance of gaining minimally adequate employment, and Miami gives non-Mexican Hispanics a better shelter from labor force marginalization.

Some portion of the ethnic and ethnic-place disparities I have detected is probably related to class differentials that I have not been able to adequately assess with the data at hand. Although more fine-grained measures of household circumstances, for example, might reduce ethnic effects, I suspect that these ethnic effects are sufficiently large and consistent to persist, even under different specifications of the statistical model. The central question for today's research remains how to account for ethnic differences. Although this issue connects the scholarship on today's immigrants to the still-changing literature on their predecessors, it is also a subject on which many contemporary researchers evince more than a little discomfort. As I have argued in the past, groups that maintain both a distinctive identity and social structures that promote continued cohesion are more likely to succeed. I see nothing in the evidence presented in this chapter to suggest a different point of view. Grappling with this claim and the competing contentions about ethnic differences and their import remains at the top of the agenda for today's research on tomorrow's second generation.

TABLE 8.1. EDUCATIONAL OUTCOMES

Variable	Logistic regression coefficients predicting high school attendance and completion — High school dropout coded 0 — Population: all persons ages 16–19 — N = 22,610			Logistic regression coefficients predicting college attendance — College attendance coded 1 — Population: all persons ages 18–24 not currently enrolled in high school — N = 33,225		
	B	SE	Sig	B	SE	Sig
First generation	-0.2692	0.0878	0.0022	0.1248	0.0526	0.0177
Second generation	0.305	0.0890	0.0006	0.4577	0.0469	0.0000
Non-Hispanic black	0.1526	0.0788	0.0527	-0.1976	0.0443	0.0000
Mexican	-0.8433	0.0827	0.0000	-0.9494	0.0580	0.0000
Other Hispanic	-0.3522	0.1023	0.0006	-0.3675	0.0651	0.0000
Asian	1.1526	0.2314	0.0000	0.6513	0.0728	0.0000
New York	0.4595	0.1647	0.0053	0.2477	0.0650	0.0001
Chicago	0.0215	0.2106	0.9188	0.2203	0.0989	0.0260
Los Angeles	0.1669	0.1771	0.3461	0.303	0.0858	0.0004
San Francisco	0.9089	0.3586	0.0113	0.3134	0.1469	0.0328
Miami	0.3955	0.4015	0.3247	-0.2237	0.2057	0.2769
Mexicans*Los Angeles	0.2215	0.2345	0.3449	-0.099	0.1411	0.4827
Mexicans*Chicago	0.0151	0.3992	0.9698	-0.5396	0.2629	0.0401
Hispanics*New York	0.1365	0.2501	0.5852	-0.2654	0.1382	0.0549
Hispanics*Miami	-0.1488	0.5209	0.7751	0.6849	0.2759	0.0131
Asians*San Francisco	-0.9274	1.1306	0.4120	0.1871	0.3265	0.5666

Sex	−0.3169	0.0491	0.0000	−0.3652	0.0258	0.0000
Age	−0.399	0.0230	0.0000	−0.2007	0.0071	0.0000
Marital status	−1.9378	0.1136	0.0000	−1.7325	0.0500	0.0000
Central city	−0.1599	0.0567	0.0048	0.1218	0.0308	0.0001
Own home	0.6115	0.0559	0.0000	0.3843	0.0311	0.0000
Poverty status	−0.6164	0.0566	0.0000	−0.2712	0.0373	0.0000
Two parents in household	0.8229	0.0650	0.0000	0.7812	0.0382	0.0000
Number of persons in family	−0.0502	0.0153	0.0010	−0.1001	0.0102	0.0000
Constant	9.1841	0.4246	0.0000	3.781	0.1571	0.0000

TABLE 8.2. EMPLOYMENT OUTCOMES

Variable	Logistic regression coefficients predicting employment — Labor force marginalization coded 0 — Population: all persons ages 25–64 — N = 177,277			Logistic regression coefficients predicting employment adequacy — Employment adequacy coded 1 — Population: all persons ages 25–64 in labor force but not in school — N = 136,359			Logistic regression coefficients predicting employment in professional or managerial occupations — Professional or managerial occupations coded 1 — Population: all persons ages 25–64 in labor force but not in school — N = 136,359		
	B	SE	Sig	B	SE	Sig	B	SE	Sig
First generation	0.0025	0.0213	0.9068	−0.3221	0.0273	0.0000	−0.3399	0.0285	0.0000
Second generation	−0.009	0.0223	0.6870	−0.0134	0.0306	0.6621	0.1702	0.0271	0.0000
Non-Hispanic black	0.0733	0.0208	0.0004	−0.0408	0.0272	0.1337	−0.3905	0.0281	0.0000
Mexican	0.1663	0.0275	0.0000	−0.022	0.0332	0.5080	−0.4872	0.0377	0.0000
Other Hispanic	0.1071	0.0331	0.0012	−0.0281	0.0381	0.4611	−0.3029	0.0407	0.0000
Asian	−0.0574	0.0338	0.0896	0.0407	0.0452	0.3682	−0.1028	0.0423	0.0152
New York	−0.0617	0.0228	0.0068	0.1405	0.0412	0.0006	0.0644	0.0355	0.0700
Chicago	0.0113	0.0354	0.7495	0.2889	0.0678	0.0000	0.1268	0.0536	0.0179
Los Angeles	−0.0351	0.0302	0.2461	−0.2657	0.0483	0.0000	0.1652	0.0471	0.0005
San Francisco	0.0672	0.0497	0.1763	−0.0562	0.0825	0.4958	0.2772	0.0731	0.0002
Miami	0.0101	0.0635	0.8742	0.1847	0.1148	0.1075	0.1416	0.1028	0.1685
Mexicans*Los Angeles	−0.0886	0.0528	0.0930	0.1174	0.0822	0.1534	−0.2521	0.1041	0.0155
Mexicans*Chicago	−0.067	0.0936	0.4742	−0.2013	0.1616	0.2129	−0.5584	0.2329	0.0165
Hispanics*New York	−0.2138	0.0544	0.0001	−0.1577	0.0871	0.0703	−0.2032	0.1008	0.0438

Hispanics*Miami	0.0101	0.0951	0.9157	−0.4043	0.1556	0.0094	−0.1762	0.1621	0.2770
Asians*San Francisco	−0.0116	0.1187	0.9222	0.4871	0.2277	0.0324	−0.3656	0.1857	0.0490
CO	0.3205	0.0182	0.0000	0.5212	0.0204	0.0000	2.0861	0.0160	0.0000
HS	0.1993	0.0185	0.0000	−0.0665	0.0168	0.0001	−0.6213	0.0184	0.0000
Age2	−0.0005	0.0001	0.0000	0.0299	0.0248	0.2283	0.193	0.0236	0.0000
Sex	0.5762	0.0110	0.0000	−0.0339	0.0150	0.0236	−0.3011	0.0139	0.0000
Age	0.0465	0.0046	0.0000	−0.0054	0.0012	0.0000	−0.0012	0.0011	0.2633
Marital status	0.0338	0.0304	0.2662	0.716	0.0376	0.0000	0.5211	0.0447	0.0000
Central city	−0.0195	0.0137	0.1547	0.046	0.0186	0.0134	0.1005	0.0175	0.0000
Own home	0.1264	0.0135	0.0000	0.2419	0.0178	0.0000	0.2088	0.0179	0.0000
Poverty status	−0.8452	0.0191	0.0000	−2.1318	0.0252	0.0000	−0.8309	0.0398	0.0000
Two parents in household	−0.2972	0.0330	0.0000	−0.6375	0.0411	0.0000	−0.345	0.0476	0.0000
Number of persons in family	−0.0532	0.0044	0.0000	−0.0099	0.0060	0.0999	−0.0465	0.0061	0.0000
Constant	−0.4504	0.0941	0.0000	1.6903	0.0442	0.0000	−1.3097	0.0414	0.0000

Notes

1. Herbert Gans, "Second Generation Decline: Scenarios for the Economic and Ethnic Futures of Post-1965 American Immigrants," *Ethnic and Racial Studies* 15 (1992): 173–192.

2. Min Zhou and Carl L. Bankston III, *Growing Up American: How Vietnamese Children Adapt to Life in the United States* (New York: Russell Sage Foundation, 1998).

3. Richard D. Alba, *Italian Americans: Into the Twilight of Ethnicity* (Englewood Cliffs, NJ: Prentice-Hall, 1985); Herbert J. Gans, "Symbolic Ethnicity: The Future of Ethnic Groups and Cultures in America," *Ethnic and Racial Studies* 2 (1979); Milton M. Gordon, *Assimilation in American Life: The Role of Race, Religion, and National Origins* (New York: Oxford University Press, 1964); W. Lloyd Warner and Leo Srole, *The Social Systems of American Ethnic Groups* (New Haven, Conn.: Yale University Press, 1945).

4. Milton Gordon, *Assimilation in American Life* (New York: Oxford University Press, 1965), chapter 3.

5. Steven Thernstrom, *The Other Bostonians* (Cambridge, Mass.: Harvard University Press, 1973).

6. Joel Perlmann, *Ethnic Differences: Schooling and Social Structure among the Irish, Jews, and Blacks in an American City, 1880–1935* (New York: Cambridge University Press, 1988).

7. George Borjas, "Long-Run Convergence of Ethnic Skill Differentials: The Children and Grandchildren of the Great Migration," *Industrial and Labor Relations Review* 47, no. 4 (1994): 553–573.

8. Coming to the defense of straight-line theory, one could contend that it refers to the directionality of change within any given group and not to the comparison of pace across groups. However, the theory seems to have little, if anything, to say about rates of progress that vary by ethnicity.

9. Charles Hirschman and Luis Falcon, "The Educational Attainment of Religio-Ethnic Groups in the United States," *Research in Sociology of Education and Socialization* 5 (1985): 83–120.

10. Georges Vernez and Allan Abrahamse, *How Immigrants Fare in U.S. Education* (Santa Monica, Calif.: RAND Corporation, Institute for Education and Training, Center for Research on Immigrant Policy, 1996).

11. Alejandro Portes and Rubén G. Rumbaut, *Immigrant America: A Portrait*, 2d ed. (Berkeley and Los Angeles: University of California Press, 1996).

12. Joel Perlmann and Roger Waldinger, "Second Generation Decline? Immigrant Children Past and Present—A Reconsideration," *International Migration Review* 31 (1997): 893–922; Roger Waldinger and Joel Perlmann, "Second Generations: Past, Present, Future," *Journal of Ethnic and Migration Studies* 24, no. 1 (1998): 893–922. It is true, as Joel Perlmann reminded me in a personal communication (spring 1999), that "Perlmann and Waldinger do *not* argue that ethnicity does *not* matter for understanding assimilation patterns" (emphasis added); as he also correctly pointed out, both he and Waldinger have been attentive to ethnic effects in their previous work. Nonetheless, in my reading of their work on the second generation, they greatly

emphasize class—if not to the neglect of ethnic considerations, then at least as a factor of much greater importance.

13. Laurence Steinberg, *Beyond the Classroom: Why School Reform Has Failed and What Parents Need to Do* (New York: Simon & Schuster, 1996).

14. Rubén G. Rumbaut, "The New Californians: Comparative Research Findings on the Educational Progress of Immigrant Children," in *California's Immigrant Children: Theory, Research, and Implications for Educational Policy,* ed. Rubén G. Rumbaut and Wayne A. Cornelius (La Jolla, Calif.: Center for U.S.-Mexican Studies, University of California, San Diego, 1995), 17–69.

15. Alejandro Portes and Dag MacLeod, "The Educational Progress of Children of Immigrants: The Roles of Class, Ethnicity, and School Context," *Sociology of Education* 69, no. 4 (1996): 255–275.

16. Lingxin Hao and Melissa Bonstead-Bruns, "Parent-Child Differences in Educational Expectations and the Academic Achievement of Immigrant and Native Students," *Sociology of Education* 71 (1998): 175–198.

17. John U. Ogbu, *The Next Generation: An Ethnography of Education in an Urban Neighborhood* (New York: Academic Press, 1974).

18. Zhou and Bankston, *Growing Up American.*

19. Signithia Fordham, *Blacked Out: Dilemmas of Race, Identity, and Success at Capital High* (Chicago: University of Chicago Press, 1996); Herbert Kohl, *"I Won't Learn from You" and Other Thoughts on Creative Maladjustment* (New York: New Press, 1994).

20. Margaret Gibson, *Accommodation without Assimilation: Sikh Immigrants in an American High School* (Ithaca, N.Y.: Cornell University Press, 1988); Philippe Bourgois, *In Search of Respect: Selling Crack in El Barrio* (Cambridge and New York: Cambridge University Press, 1995).

21. Alejandro Portes and Min Zhou, "The New Second Generation: Segmented Assimilation and Its Variants among Post-1965 Immigrant Youth," *Annals of the American Academy of Political and Social Science* 530 (1993): 74–98.

22. Herbert Gans, "Second Generation Decline."

23. A point of clarification: I do not disagree with Perlmann and Waldinger's efforts to show continuity in the ways in which the children of immigrants experienced stigmatization, and responded resentfully, then and now. However, they explicitly made an additional argument: namely, that the resentment of the last second generation fueled the collective response that eventuated in the "New Deal regime," as they describe it. See Waldinger and Perlmann, "Second Generations."

24. Vernez and Abrahamse, *How Immigrants Fare in U.S. Education.*

Chapter 9

CONCLUSION
Immigration and the Remaking of Urban America

Roger Waldinger

This book has sought to tell the story of the new immigrant America and its urban capitals. That newcomers are urban bound is neither a surprise nor an accident. Although the immigrant geography of the United States at the turn of the twenty-first century barely resembles the pattern observed a century ago, the basic tendency to converge on a limited number of places remains much the same. Nor has the basic motivation for clustering changed. Networks, as we have emphasized throughout this book, lubricate the process of migration: the connections between veterans and newcomers attract the most recent arrivals to those places where the old-timers are well established. Rephrased in the jargon of the social sciences, immigrant settlement is path dependent, and the decisions of earlier immigrants exercise a profound effect on the options available to those whose departure from the old country comes later.

The tendency to cluster lies at the heart of the immigrant phenomenon itself. But geography and history influence the particular clusters toward which immigrants head. In a sense, the new geography of contemporary immigrant America reflects the resettlement of the American population itself. New York and Chicago still rank high in the hierarchy of urban places, but they no longer dominate as they once did. Instead, the nation's center of gravity has shifted away from the cities of the Northeast and Midwest, where immigrants of the turn of the twentieth century

massed. Not just the foreign-born but also millions of natives have decided that a better life is to be found in Florida and California. Still, the
accidents of history—the Cuban Revolution, the collapse of U.S.-sup-
ported regimes in Southeast Asia, the initiation of the Bracero program
and its subsequent abolition, civil wars in Central America—steered the
newcomers in the particular directions they have taken.

Thus, immigrants have an urban fate. Does it matter? The answer to
that question takes three parts.

The Urban Dimension.   The literature tells us that today's immigrants
are people who just happened to have settled in the nation's largest
urban regions. But this book puts things in a very different light: the
distinctive characteristics of the urban context in the key immigrant regions shape the very structure of opportunity that newcomers confront.
The capitals of immigrant America do not stand out just as concentrations of the foreign-born. They also happen to be places where the shift
toward the new, knowledge-based economy is most advanced. As we
have noted, not every urban region has moved in this direction at quite
the same pace; Miami lags behind the others, and San Francisco leads
the pack. But in each place, the structure of skills bears a very similar
stamp: compared to the rest of the United States, the leading immigration regions display a prominent tilt toward jobs for which advanced
training is required and away from jobs of an easy-entry sort and for
which the required skills can be picked up as one goes.

But if today's immigrant regions are dispensing with the activities for
which immigrants are usually deployed, then how to account for their
attraction to the foreign-born? Providing a full answer to that query exceeds the scope of this chapter; for our purposes, it is enough to say that
the native-born population has rearranged itself in ways that make
room for its newly found immigrant neighbors. Elsewhere in the United
States, the native-born population can be found on all rungs of the economic ladder. In the capitals of immigrant America, however, native-
born workers are an unusually well-educated lot, possessing the skills
that allow them to concentrate in the topmost jobs. The emergence of
this high-skilled contingent may partly result from the decision of less-
educated natives to respond to immigration by voting with their feet,
heading for places where competition for jobs is not quite so intense. In
the context of immigrants, however, accounting for the native-born

pattern seems less important than the pattern itself. Equipped with the proficiencies that employers in the growth sectors demand, native-born workers have largely vacated the low-skilled sector, providing entrée to the newest Americans, for whom work at the bottom beats the alternatives available back home.

Immigrants have plenty of opportunities to get started; unfortunately, they begin in a context particularly inimical to those among them with relatively low skills. The conventional wisdom about immigrant progress has shifted from optimism to pessimism, largely because the most recent cohorts of newcomers are experiencing ever greater trouble in narrowing the wage gap that separates them from comparable natives. As Mark Ellis showed in chapter 4, that conventional wisdom is largely right, but mainly for the wrong reasons. Newcomers living in the capitals of immigrant America lag further behind natives than their counterparts elsewhere in the nation, but not for the most commonly asserted reason—that their skills are inferior to those who have settled elsewhere. While the declining selectivity of urban-bound migration streams accounts for some of the disparity that expanded during the 1980s, that factor leaves much of the gap unexplained. The source of the problem of catching up, rather, lies in the new era of inequality in which we are living and the particularly severe form it takes in the regions to which immigrants have moved. While today's economy has reduced the earnings of the less skilled of all ethnic stripes, pay structures in the capitals of immigrant America have become more unequal than anywhere else. Moreover, the characteristics of native and immigrant workers have been changing in ways that unevenly equip natives and immigrants to benefit from the change in the structure of demand. Natives have been enhancing their skills just at a time when compensation for the better educated has improved. While immigrants' skills have also improved, they have advanced too slowly and have begun from too low a base—exposing them to the severely downward wage pressures at work in the low-skilled sector. Consequently, as Ellis explains, changes in the urban wage structure largely account for the declining relative wages of immigrant men and women, increasing the socioeconomic gap between them and their native-born counterparts.

Urban or Ethnic Effects?   Compared to the rest of the United States, then, the capitals of immigrant America appear to offer a troubled launching pad: here, the nature of the opportunity structure impedes the upward movement of less-skilled immigrants in ways unlikely to be replicated in other areas. But if we confine ourselves to the key immigrant regions on which this book is focused, the ethnic factor seems to be a more important influence than the specificities of any particular place.

Thus, the stories in the two chapters on ethnic niches (chapters 6 and 7) find little interurban variation. As Der-Martirosian and I found in our chapter on the immigrant niche (chapter 7), each group tends to occupy niches of a similar type regardless of where its members settle. Revisiting the figures in that chapter confirms this conclusion, as the spread among points represents an ethnic rather than an urban effect. Most groups are tightly clustered, which means a common ethnic factor exercises the principal influence on specialization. There is relatively little variation from one urban region to another, and the same pattern of concentration emerges along each of the indicators of job quality—whether, for example, social skills or physical conditions—examined. True, not all groups line up in the same neatly clustered way, but only one group stands out for its high level of interurban variation. Cubans in Miami follow a particularly unique pattern, to be discussed at greater length in the section that follows.

One might argue that this interpretation mistakes ethnic influences for those more powerful forces affecting the mode of immigrant incorporation. As Portes and Rumbaut convincingly argued in *Immigrant America*, a complex of factors relating to group characteristics and host society reactions channel immigrants into particular segments of the labor market and tend to keep them there.[1] But this perspective can easily be reconciled with the argument just developed. One could rephrase our conclusions by saying that different patterns of incorporation correspond to a basic variation in niche type: while labor migrants consistently occupy niches of low quality, entrepreneurial or professional immigrants gravitate toward more favorable niches. And one need not confine the analysis to polar types; for example, the contrast between Koreans, on the one hand, and Asian Indians and Filipinos, on the other, highlights the distinctive characteristics of these migration streams of higher-skilled immigrants. Korean niches not only compare unfavorably with Asian Indian and Filipino clusters in terms of quality but also illuminate the particular combination of traits—modest levels of substantive complexity and high levels of social skills—required by those employed in small business niches. However, a comparison of Filipinos and Asian Indians shows the degree to which ethnicity affects niche characteristics, even when the two groups greatly resemble one another in the mode of incorporation. And as an analytic construct, mode of incorporation does not seem sufficiently tight to capture the full range of variation that we find: Anglophone Caribbeans turn out to occupy a distinctive niche that cannot be easily placed in the heuristic scheme that Portes and Rumbaut propose.

Der-Martirosian and I examine a broad range of groups during a particular period; by contrast, Lim mainly focuses on one group but traces change over time. Lim's concern does not involve an immigrant group but rather African Americans and the evolving overlap between their niches and the clusters established by immigrants. Still, Lim's findings provide powerful evidence of the structuring role of ethnicity, though not in a mechanistic or deterministic way. While African American niches in our five immigrant regions were similar in 1970, urban influences then stood out in considerable relief. As of 1990, by contrast, urban differences had largely disappeared, replaced by a pattern of striking isomorphism in which African Americans occupied the very same niches, regardless of place.

Describing Lim's findings as evidence of ethnic effects does little more than provide a label; it falls a good deal short of explanation, leaving "ethnic" as a black box whose contents remain largely obscured. Reference to networks provides some illumination: the web of ties linking members of an ethnic population to one another shapes and constrains their ability to pursue opportunity, creating information fields and mobility channels that structure the fabric of ethnic life in ways that produce a tendency toward clustering. But it is not clear why networks would generate such similar results across a series of places. Nor is it quite certain why they would yield like effects at various reaches of the occupational spectrum, so that workers might be more dependent on social connections but professionals less so. Thus a supplementary explanation might invoke the concept of "parallel action": a process whereby persons sharing common traits respond similarly to a particular situation, seeking or selecting a niche in which their resources are best rewarded but doing so without a master plan or in the absence of any concerted behavior.[2] Since networks span most ethnic communities, these connections might subsequently shape clustering with even minimal exchanges of information and support. As Ivan Light and Edna Bonacich suggested in their work on Korean entrepreneurs, "ethnic facilitation" can involve no more than noticing the implicit signals sent when coethnics start to concentrate in fields of work or business lines that offer greater than average rewards.[3]

Compositional Factors.   The turn of the twenty-first century is a bad time to be a low-skilled worker in the United States; compounding this difficulty, the disadvantages associated with immigrant status and the very low educational levels of some immigrants puts immigrants in a skill class by themselves. While the key immigrant regions turn out to be particularly bad places for less-skilled immigrants to have settled, the variations in urban structure among these places do not seem to affect the opportunities available to the foreign-born. For example, in chapter 3, on low-skilled workers, I point out that the economic structure varies considerably among the three regions—Chicago, Los Angeles, and San Francisco—in which I examine Mexican employment experiences. Nonetheless, a basic pattern holds in all three places: education has little impact on job-holding probabilities among men, such that less-skilled Mexican immigrant men have much higher employment probabilities than their African American counterparts in all three places. But education sharply affects employment adequacy; less-skilled Mexican men pay a heavy price for their low skills, in much the same way, in all three places.

If the consequences of low-skilled status do not vary across the capitals of immigrant America, the distribution of low-skilled immigrants does; therefore, the *net effect* of this particular source of disadvantage is felt unevenly as well. In this respect, the key place of interest is likely to be Los Angeles. As announced from the start of this book, the center of immigration has shifted from the East Coast to the West Coast, with LA significantly outpacing New York as a destination for the foreign-born arrivals of the past 30 years. Los Angeles not only receives a disproportionately large immigrant flow but also attracts a disproportionately large group of low-skilled newcomers. If we are correct in arguing that low skills impede immigrant progress, then that obstacle will yield its most pronounced effect in LA.

But there is likely to be more. The literature on labor market competition, which Lim reviews in chapter 6, provides at best limited evidence that immigrants harm the wages or employment chances of natives. As to the matter of intraimmigrant displacement, however, there is little dispute: the higher the proportion of immigrants in the labor force, the greater the downward pressure on wages. Indeed, the tendency to cluster in niches only heightens the mismatch between supply and demand.

As we have noted throughout this book, network recruitment operates in such a way as to reproduce the characteristics of the existing labor force; it also creates a situation in which less-skilled immigrants find themselves crowded into the secondary labor market, from which exit proves awfully difficult. In Los Angeles, at least, employers have adapted to the increased availability of greenhorns by expanding low-skilled employment opportunities. But as newcomers headed for the same industries and occupations in which their kin and friends were already employed, they unwittingly depressed wages for all.

And the most lasting immigrant legacy takes the form of immigrant children. Across America, as Zhou notes in chapter 8, the new second generation is emerging at a very uneven pace. Overall, the second generation shows less of a tendency than immigrants to concentrate in the five urban regions on which we focus. But this pattern is largely an artifact of age. The category of second generation still includes many persons ages 65 and older who continue to reside in the older urban regions where the 1880–1920 immigrant population landed. But younger cohorts are disproportionately living where today's immigrants reside; if immigrant offspring run into problems as they attempt to get ahead, these bottlenecks will be narrowest in the immigrant concentrations on which this book has focused.

Once again, the crucible is likely to be Los Angeles. Numbers ensure that the future of the new second generation will unfold, to a disproportionate extent, on the West Coast. Zhou suggests that this new second generation is unlikely to constitute a new underclass, as the most dismal scenarios on second-generation immigrants have warned. We can expect that the children of immigrants will acquire a good deal more schooling and advance to a higher place in the occupational order than their parents did.

Even so, the prospects for these immigrant offspring are shaped by the resources of their parents, and their parents are disproportionately low skilled. At the household level, the difficulties children encounter are related to the level of resources parents may transmit; in Los Angeles, these resources are particularly likely to be low. But context is also likely to matter. To the extent that few in an immigrant community know how to navigate the worlds of school and office, and fewer still have done so, the models to whom children can turn are unlikely to be able to effectively motivate or facilitate achievement in school. That the largest group of ethnic outsiders also dominates the ranks of the region's working poor is a coincidence that will do nothing to improve the dominant group's view of the second generation, which is just now entering the employment scene.

Miami and the Cuban "Success Story" Revisited

As I signaled in chapter 1, and as authors have noted repeatedly thereafter, this book yields a picture of Miami and, in particular, of its Cuban residents unlikely to have been encountered elsewhere. But we did not expect to find this revisionist view ourselves; it emerged as we noted a series of anomalies, each one adding to the overall picture. Apart from a small section in chapter 1, we offered no extended discussion of the Miami situation or of the literature on Miami and its Cuban-origin population, though references can be found in various chapters. Thus, in this section, I step back and survey the intellectual context of this particular discussion and then distill the results of the various relevant observations made in preceding chapters.

Cubans represent a relatively small share of the total U.S. foreign-born and foreign-origin population, accounting for 3.6 percent of all immigrants and 2.2 percent of all immigrant offspring as of 1999. Nonetheless, Cubans are prominent in the immigration literature, probably to a disproportionate degree given their overall numerical importance. To some extent, historical events and timing played an important role in bringing Cubans to the forefront. As suggested earlier, the refugee influx of 1959 can be seen as the beginning of the new immigration, and the years since then have allowed ample opportunity to develop a body of scholarly literature. A series of interesting and controversial developments—including the Mariel crisis of 1980, the subsequent waves of *balseros*, and the saga of U.S.-Cuba relations, which has affected refugee policy in changing, unpredictable, and controversial ways—continue to attract public and scholarly attention. And Miami has proved to be a crucible of no unusual sort, its mix of Cubans, Anglos, African Americans, and Haitians providing ample opportunity for strife.

At the same time, the relevant scholarly literature has been unusually fertile, for reasons only partially explained by the intrinsic interest of the topic. The Cuban experience has been told by a particularly talented group of Cuban American researchers, for whom the effort at recounting and making sense of the story can be understood as an effort at self-understanding, among other things, of course. And whether fortuitous or not, the most prominent sociologist of contemporary immigration, Alejandro Portes, belongs to these ranks; Portes's highly influential writings have further drawn the attention of the broader scholarly community to the developments in Miami.

Although not always noted, the literature provides two accounts of the Cuban experience—one, linked to Portes and his associates, that provides the version that has filtered out broadly beyond the narrow group of specialists and a second, counternarrative that does not appear to have gained much notice in the larger immigration field. As reviewed briefly in chapter 7, Portes's view emphasizes the apparently successful incorporation of Cubans, with particular attention to Cuban business activities. While the explanatory account has evolved over the years, it has consistently highlighted those processes internal to the dynamics of settlement and community development. Thus, in their book on Miami, *City on the Edge,* Portes and his coauthor, Alex Stepick, accent the role of premigration ties and overlapping network affiliations in creating both the informational base and the level of trust needed to accumulate capital, build a client base, and secure skilled help. To be sure, the external factor is never missing. *City on the Edge* also underlines the importance of exclusion—by the local Anglo elite—and rejection of the exiles and their dream of counterrevolution—by Washington—as factors contributing to ethnic solidarity and community cohesion. *Immigrant America,* Portes's highly influential synthetic account, coauthored with Rubén Rumbaut, also develops a model of incorporation that accents the impact of the favorable "reception context" in addition to those community characteristics emphasized in *City on the Edge.* Nonetheless, *Immigrant America* does not disentangle the effects of the various forms of government support from the more general, positive ideological climate, and exclusion or rejection can serve only as a sufficient, not a necessary, condition of the community-level support mechanism on which the ethnic enclave is said to rest.[4]

The alternative view offers a very different interpretation of why Cubans have done so well, while also suggesting that the progress may be a good deal more uneven than the dominant account would allow. In the counternarrative, Cubans' relatively good fortune principally derived from the unusual level of government assistance they received and only secondarily from the community-level processes of the type Portes emphasizes. In briefest compass, the alternative account tells the following story: By the time of the first exodus from Cuba, Washington had already learned that refugees in flight from their communist homelands provided a new type of immigrant, one that could be showcased as part of the symbolic conflict with the Soviet Union. From the beginning, Cubans benefited from massive government aid, much of which initially served to resettle refugees away from Miami but some of which still managed to flow to penniless but experienced refugee en-trepreneurs. And while loans from the Small Business Administration, rather than the informal mechanisms of "enforceable trust" and "bounded solidarity," sparked the crucial wave of early start-ups, the large Central Intelligence Agency (CIA) payroll maintained in Miami provided substantial cash infusions to refugees in government service and those providing services by contract.[5]

In this account, then, macro political factors lie at the root of the Cuban ethnic enclave. But the counternarrative seems to suffer from an unresolved tension as it evinces skepticism about the "Cuban success story," all the while seeking to explain whatever success it can find in light of the political considerations noted. Thus, some writers note the importance of the Cuban working class and its expression in organized labor, while others point to patterns of persistent poverty and low wages.[6]

But the two sides have largely conducted this debate within the same parameters—that is, the contours of Miami, where the Cuban advantage, at least relative to other immigrant groups and African Americans, cannot escape notice and therefore requires explanation. True, Portes and Bach's important book *Latin Journey* traced the progress of a longitudinal sample of Cuban *and* Mexican immigrants, but the contrast took the form of parallel rather than comparative case studies. Cubans and Mexicans differ on too many different dimensions—class, the nature of the migration, the reception context—to determine the relative importance of community-level processes from a consideration of these two groups alone. And as noted previously, *Immigrant America* invokes a series of factors in its account of immigrant incorporation, but assessing the centrality of community characteristics requires a comparison with like groups that differ only on this one dimension—a requirement that naturally exceeds the scope of the effort at synthesis to which *Immigrant America* aspires.

Not surprisingly, then, changing the frame, as we have done in this book, also alters the story. Miami turns out to be an unusual immigrant region. Geography matters, and not simply because of the Caribbean connection, which itself has a more complicated consequence than much of the literature would allow. Miami, as we have emphasized, is part of the American South, where African Americans have consistently faced disadvantages, especially when compared to the other places that serve as America's key immigrant destinations. The political economy of the South, and not just Miami's peculiar history as a vacation spot, makes for a distinctive economic structure: Miami is a low-wage region, where the nature of the economy itself limits the potential for earnings growth. However glorious the progress of any particular group within this context, the place exercises its own constraints. Cursed with an off-center location, linked—albeit as a key node—to a peripheral region of the world economy, weak in manufacturing, and limited in the size of the professional and advanced services sector, Miami simply lacks the opportunities available in New York, Chicago, Los Angeles, and San Francisco. As a second-order urban area, Miami lacks the full range of economic specializations evident in its larger counterparts.

The Caribbean location, combined with the arrival of the well-educated, entrepreneurial component of the Cuban refugee stream, helped propel Miami to its role as commercial entrepôt for the entire region. But that same location meant that those likely to migrate there would turn out to be a relatively low-skilled group. As others have shown, Cubans fall roughly in the middle of the skill hierarchy for the nation's immigrant population; most of Miami's other key newcomer groups, however, lie in the bottom half of that distribution. Moreover, Asian immigrants, generally the most highly skilled among today's new foreign-born population, have yet to make an appearance of any note, making Miami the only immigrant region on which high-skilled immigrants have yet to converge. The association of skill and geographic origins at once reduces the ethnic diversity of Miami's foreign-born residents, while also pushing immigrant Miamians down in the earnings profile, at least as compared to the national average. And as Ellis's chapter showed, the 1980s made matters worse in this respect, as the wage inequality in Miami increased substantially, to the detriment of its foreign-born population.

As an immigrant center, then, Miami lacks allure. Within that context, it is still possible to conclude that the Cuban story is one of success, though success as tempered by the limits of the place in question. However, the chapters in this book speak in favor of a less rosy assessment. We note that the relevant information is not always gathered at the appropriate level of disaggregation. Clark, in chapter 5, shows that poverty levels among Miami's Hispanic immigrants, including long-settled immigrants, rank far above native-born white norms, but this finding does not capture the Cuban pattern alone. The same is true in chapter 4, by Ellis, who finds that in Miami Hispanic immigrants and natives earned significantly less than their white counterparts, with Hispanic immigrants of the 1980s more heavily penalized for recency than those who arrived in the 1970s. While the Hispanic pattern likely holds for Cubans, who constitute the great majority of the Hispanic group, these findings leave the question open.

But other chapters bring us closer to resolution. As Clark points out, poverty afflicts Cuban heads of households to a distressingly large degree; poverty is particularly common among Cuban households headed by women, whose numbers are far from trivial. As I find in chapter 3, on the working poor, Cuban men, but not Cuban women, display high levels of labor force attachment. Working Cuban men do reasonably well in securing jobs that meet the standard of employment adequacy, but only if one controls for education—which keeps overall Cuban levels well below those for native-born whites. To be sure, Cubans' situation looks better than that of Mexicans, but not so good as to be heralded an unvarnished "success."

Moreover, whatever success one finds does not seem attributable to the growth of an ethnic economy or enclave, however one might term it. As Der-Martirosian and I showed in chapter 7, ethnic niches account for a small portion of the Cuban employment base—a pattern particularly evident when compared to the configurations observed for almost every other group. Such as they are, the concentrations seem unlikely to provide the lever for accelerated upward mobility or diminished wage pressure. On the one hand, reliance on niches has been declining, with settlers dispersing to other activities and new arrivals less often converging on niches. And, on the other hand, Cuban clusters show up mainly in industries and occupations that rank poorly on a range of indicators measuring job quality. Admittedly, those indicators do not include income—though other studies have shown them to generally correlate quite closely with earnings.

Whether we are right or wrong about the particular niche Cubans occupy in Miami, its importance would necessarily diminish as Cubans' share of the region's population and labor force grew. Perhaps Cubans once converged on a cluster of jobs that generated significant advantages, at least relative to the alternatives at hand. But now that Cubans have such a dominant presence, the most important effects are those associated with the group's concentration in Miami and the economic characteristics of that region as a whole—as opposed to impacts that might derive from any cluster established within this particular regional economy. Although the ethnic economy offers many chances to get started, it provides limited opportunities to move up the socioeconomic ladder.

Unfortunately, we cannot provide a full account of the pattern of Cuban incorporation—a failing only excusable in that this was never our goal. But we can assay an alternative interpretation: In Miami, ironically, the incorporation of Cuban immigrants proceeded more or less as the conventional sociological accounts would have predicted, via assimilation. If we understand dispersion to denote assimilation, then our data on niches support the idea that Cubans are assimilating into mainstream Miami; that relatively few Cubans work in clusters implies dispersion to the occupations and industries where other Miamians work. Moreover, assimilation of this sort would not be surprising in light of the distinctive characteristics of both Cuban migration and the region on which Cubans converged: Cubans arrived with skills that were sooner or later likely to prove valuable, and the U.S. government sought to ease Cubans' entry into the Miami economy. In addition, in the particular Miami configuration, Cubans were unlikely to end up as a persistent bottom-level group. In Los Angeles, Mexicans have a long history as the preferred workforce for the least desirable jobs; and the magnitude of Mexican migration and the stigma Anglo Angelenos have long attached to Mexicans made it relatively easy for post-1965 Mexican immigrants to supplant African Americans at the end of the labor queue. But in Miami, Cubans always enjoyed the advantage associated with an ethnic order that put some other group—namely, African Americans—unambiguously at the bottom.[7] For this reason, the disrepute associated with refugees' initial jobs as busboys, waiters, or garment factory workers never stuck. Moreover, competition for better jobs was limited. Next in line were African Americans, who did manage to get government jobs, as Lim has noted, but were not difficult to bump out, or leap over, in the private sector.[8] And the expanded and diversified immigrant influx pushed Cubans up the ladder, as suggested by the very high foreign-born proportion in each of the black niches in the public sector—far higher in Miami than in any other immigrant region, a contrast that is particularly noticeable when the comparison is extended to LA. While I leave it to readers and other researchers to fully pursue the leads sketched out here, the findings of this book establish the peculiarities of this sun belt immigrant city. Miami appears to be a place of limited immigrant opportunity, one in which the patterns established by its newcomers are likely to diverge from the trajectories at work in the other capitals of immigrant America.

Conclusion: Urban America and the Immigrant Future

Immigration: The Long View

If we take the long view, immigration's persistence, *not* its restriction, distinguishes the American experience during the twentieth century. Granted, the forces of restriction did succeed in closing the open door that had allowed passage from old to new world more or less unhindered by the state. This old freedom never returned, even as the gateways to newcomers reopened after midcentury. But a close examination of the record underlines the difficulties encountered in closing the United States off to the world. The flow from Europe had no sooner abated than growers and industrialists in the Southwest stimulated migration from Mexico and their counterparts in the East and Midwest substituted African American migrants for the foreigners they could no longer recruit. The depression of the 1930s kept people in place—and encouraged U.S. authorities to expel Mexican immigrants, regardless of citizenship and other niceties. As soon as the economy revived with the advent of World War II, employers of alien labor remembered its charms—hence the Bracero program, to which modern Mexican migration owes its start. Before the war, America somehow could not muster the will and wherewithal to welcome refugees in search of safe haven; after the war, it faced new, ultimately irresistible, pressures to absorb persons stranded and displaced by Europe's devastation. Thus, refugee policy in the aftermath of World War II revealed greater benevolence, though the selection procedures involved a curious preference for former enemies rather than for those the enemies had persecuted.

Most important, the internationalism and anticommunism of the time made it hard to use immigration law as a cordon sanitaire; thus, the 1950s saw the doors reopen, first for Hungarian refugees and then for Cubans, who received an unusually warm welcome. In the mid-1960s, under the influence of the civil rights revolution, Congress sought to undo the wrongs it had perpetuated a decade before. On the one hand, it abolished the national origins quota, opening up the United States to areas of the world from which immigration had been hindered, most notably Asia. On the other hand, it ended the Bracero program, attempting to relieve a mainly Mexican American group of farmworkers from competition with lower-cost Mexican immigrant labor but ultimately driving the Mexican migration stream underground.

Various factors then amplified the immigrant presence. With the new immigrant influx came the buildup of ethnic networks that facilitated migration from the most recent sending countries; a legal framework that allocated quotas to persons with close kinship ties to U.S. citizens and permanent residents simply lent additional dynamism to the under-lying network-driven nature of the migration process. Immigrants also found friends in the labor market, among them immigrant employers, whose ranks expanded and diversified as the foreign-born presence in-creased at the high end of the labor market. The post–civil rights envi-ronment also emboldened immigrant advocates, including ethnic lead-ers and organizations and human rights, civil rights, and religious groups, all of which had a good deal more fight and influence than the immigrant organizations of the early twentieth century. For reasons of international politics, the United States facilitated several large-scale refugee flows, though the welcome mat was put out with only limited sensitivity to the need to protect the truly persecuted. Occasionally, as in the mid-1990s, anti-immigrant forces erupted; in 1996 laws were passed that significantly diminished the entitlements of legal residents while also increasing deterrence efforts in consular offices and at the borders and deportation efforts in the U.S. interior. But the spasm of re-striction soon passed, as Washington quickly revoked key aspects of the 1996 legislation. From this attack, immigrants learned that the best de-fense lay in the vote, an instrument whose invocation political leaders immediately appreciated, especially in the immigrant-dense states of New York, Florida, Texas, and California. Thus, in 1998 a Congress similar to the one that had sought to curb foreign inflows and penalize unwanted immigrants decided to facilitate the entry of an expanded group of professionals, who would officially arrive in the United States as temporary workers but would in many cases come to stay. The United States thus exited the twentieth century as an immigration coun-try of notable dimensions, with considerable pressure to keep the door open.

Of course, perspective is needed. One can speak of an immigrant tide, but as we pointed out in an earlier chapter, the foreign-born pro-portion of the U.S. population remains much smaller than it was a hun-dred years ago. Close to a million people are admitted to the United States as immigrants each year—far more than Congress envisioned when it passed the Hart-Celler Act in 1965—but millions more are waiting in line all over the world. The United States gains 300,000 un-documented persons each year, but the inflow is relatively modest when measured against the more than 5 million people who enter the United States legally each year for business, study, or pleasure—*not* immigration—and typically head home. Evaluated against the supply of potential immigrants, the immigrant inflow appears to be quite modest and under very good control.

Nonetheless, controversy over the immigration system continues. While questions of how many immigrants we should admit and according to which selection criteria—kinship, skills, or some combination of the two—certainly deserve attention, one should be wary of both the temptation to deliver novel answers and the relevance of this type of debate. In a sense, our options are largely shaped by the actions we have already taken and the changes in the world around us. The international flows of goods, services, and people are accelerating, and the United States is moving toward greater economic integration with its neighbors. Since the same changes in communication and technology that lubricate trade also facilitate migration, the ties between immigrant communities and their home societies are likely to consolidate, not wither. Moreover, America has spent recent decades establishing and consolidating networks that link veterans to new arrivals and potential migrants; in the immigrant-dense regions with which this book is concerned, the same networks deeply embed immigrants in particular sectors of the economy, which have now adapted to the inflow of a foreign-born labor force. Connections of these sorts are hard to uproot and are likely to exercise a deep inertial effect for years to come. The past also influences the politics of immigration. America's self-definition is that of a "country of immigration"; the most powerful interpretive frame thus situates immigration as a defining American trait, and the post–civil rights reinterpretation of the civic nation sanctions against restrictive measures of the type pursued earlier in the century. Immigrant Americans are also hardly powerless. They stand all the more influential when allied to native-born members of proximal host groups with an origin in a common place and an identity deriving from a similar experience—that is, the ethnic lobbies and advocacy organizations.

Immigration policy can change, but only incrementally, with shifts toward serious restriction encountering great, possibly insurmountable, opposition. But this policy debate proves of limited relevance at a time when roughly 10 percent of the country's population was born abroad and another 10 percent consists of the children of immigrants. While it is certainly true that many immigrants do return home—roughly 20 percent of 1980 to 1990 arrivals reemigrated—the great bulk of those living in the United States at any given time are here to stay.[9] The central question, then, does not so much concern the state and characteristics of tomorrow's newcomers—all the more so since those factors have largely been determined. Rather, the issue at hand concerns the prospects of today's immigrants and immigrant offspring. Will newcomers gain full membership in a society they have already joined? Or will they be excluded, whether implicitly or explicitly, from complete participation in the civic nation?

Broadly speaking, we can find two answers to questions of this sort, one accenting the positive and mutually reinforcing consequences of immigrants' search for opportunity, and the second emphasizing the obstacles newcomers will meet and the self-defeating responses that will result. The intellectual debate revolves around the competing narratives of assimilation or the underclass, the plausibility of each scenario enhanced by one's opposition to the other and the exclusion of alternative frameworks.

The Underclass Scenario

While there is nothing new in the imagery of immigrants as present or potential underclass, contemporary formulations take a distinctive twist. Capitalist societies have never had much fondness for the idleness of the poor, but until the advent of the social welfare state the poor had few alternatives but to work. It was immigrants *as* workers, therefore, on whom native-born observers projected their anxiety, viewing the laboring class as dangerous; the stigma attached to the hard and menial jobs the imported outsiders performed only added to the disrepute of the foreign-born. In the current context, work at the bottom continues to stigmatize those groups clustered in the lowest ranks, but those who do not work are the objects of greatest reprobation.

For the most part, immigrants have been shielded from the underclass brush. On the one hand, the foreign-born stand out for their high rates of employment, as we have seen. No reputational quality, including industriousness, is entirely good—thus hard-working immigrants can also be feared for being too much so and therefore stealing the jobs that Americans would otherwise want—but the traits associated with idleness, such as laziness, invite much greater scorn and dislike. On the other hand, there is a cultural place for the foreign-born in a self-proclaimed "nation of immigrants" that provides a degree of shelter not enjoyed by the one group around whom the underclass rhetoric has

crystallized: African Americans. To the extent that the underclass debate concerns the "ghetto underclass," it applies to a particular population infused by Euro-Americans with a negative affect, which the dominant groups have not (yet) extended to the foreign-born.

Once in place, however, the notion of the underclass provides a
frame for constructing an interpretation of the immigrant experience as
well. There are good reasons to be concerned about the possibility that
a small, but still significant, share of the immigrant population will be
unable to rise above poverty levels (as Clark mentions in chapter 5).
And though the debate over immigrants' utilization of welfare benefits
and other social services is partly motivated by narrow political concerns, it is at once legitimate and to be expected: regardless of the liabilities associated with foreign birth, the very low skills of certain immigrants increase the likelihood of welfare receipt—as shown by much
research. Still, poverty status does not inherently denote an underclass;
representing poor immigrants as an underclass involves a considerable
conceptual leap that has not yet been justified. And it is hard to imagine
that invocation of the underclass concept itself does not add to whatever stigma, and therefore liabilities, the poorest of immigrants have to
shoulder.

Assimilation in Question

Are we back to assimilation? If understood as progress pure and simple,
the answer might be yes. Clearly, that version of the assimilation story
receives ample support from the chapters in this book. While immigrants begin with considerable disadvantages, matters improve over
time, even among those who start out with skill deficits of the most profound sort. Wages rise, as do employment probabilities and the likelihood of holding an adequately paying job. And poverty rates are highest among the most recent arrivals, who have not yet had time to start
an ascent. Moreover, the factors pushing immigrants into poverty are
inversely related to those increasing labor force attachment: as immigrants secure positions of adequate quality, the degree of impoverish-
ment diminishes. Notwithstanding our emphasis on immigrants' widespread tendency to cluster in niches and remain there, only a minority
of immigrants persist in niches as settlement deepens. And the most
optimistic indicators are those gleaned from our examination of the
second generation, which appears to be escaping the dire fate forecast
for it.

But as noted in chapter 1, how one answers the assimilation question depends largely on how it is posed. If the standard is absolute progress, then this book has furnished positive evidence aplenty, but if the standard takes the form of relative progress, a different perspective is likely in order.

If we pose the question in relative terms, then the root deficiencies of the assimilation perspective loom a good deal larger. As the dictionary defines it, assimilation involves a process of growing similarity, in which immigrants and their descendants shed the differences that distinguish them from core members—whoever they might be—of the host society. But this definition suffers from a signal deficiency: the relevant differences do not simply include those immigrants bring with them but also those created by the very circumstances under which they come and the conditions under which they interact with the native-born. Consequently, as the literature emphasizes, context matters: individual fates are affected by self-understandings, as well as the understandings of others, of the social categories to which they are assigned. The views and expectations entertained by others of one's own kind and those who perceive and assign difference delimit one's options. Thus, the specificities of time and place circumscribe trajectories, without necessarily locking individuals in place.

For our purposes, context matters most for those who enter at the bottom, and still more in those regions where the immigrant concentration now defines what it means to occupy the lowest ranks. In this respect, it is important to remember precisely what the assimilation perspective forgets: from the standpoint of users of immigrant labor, the foreign-born are useful precisely because they are different; their dual frame of reference and their status as less entitled makes them ideal candidates to fill the jobs others do not want. From the perspective of employers, immigrants' suitability for the society's dirty work serves as one of immigrants' salient traits and, of course, their greatest virtue. Moreover, an economic habit of this sort is hard to curb. Absent immigrant cooks and hotel housekeepers, room and restaurant prices go up—not a desirable outcome in industries in which price competition is rife. One might want a larger number of better educated English-speaking workers, but improving the "quality" of workers assigned to low-status, unpalatable jobs would require a hike in wages and benefits that this new age of inequality seems not to allow. Thus, once started, dependence on immigrant labor becomes difficult to overcome.

Its persistence is of course fueled by networks, which are important both because of their efficiency and because of the resources that immigrants gain from their ethnic social connections as those ties build up. The process of migration creates the seeds out of which ethnic social structures develop. Most important, the contacts between veterans and newcomers make for an immigrant economic base that expands steadily, and with a dynamic of its own.

Thus, immigrants congregate at the bottom of the socioeconomic hierarchy. The functions immigrants fill then come to define them, adding further disrepute to whatever stigma is already associated with foreign origins. Immigrants' otherness is thus not solely a personal attribute but also a characteristic of the society they enter, which enhances rather than diminishes differences between the native- and foreign-born. In the conventional approach, such differences denote a lag, or even failure, in the rate of assimilation—but that perspective mistakes cause for effect. The most crucial differences, instead, are those created both through the process of migration and by members of the host group.

With these thoughts in mind, I return to the matter of second-generation fates. Zhou's chapter 8 points squarely in a different direction than that signaled by the specter of a second-generation underclass. In many respects, the story is a good deal more positive than the emerging literature would allow: when contrasted with comparable members of the first generation (though not to their parents, a comparison the data do not allow), the story appears to be one of second-generation progress, *not* decline. Mexicans, at once the largest second-generation group and the most numerous to have made their way into adulthood, provide the best case in point. Rather than slipping out of the world of work—to which the first generation is so strongly attached—the second generation actually remains more attached. Further disaggregations by gender would reinforce the point. As noted in chapter 3, employment rates for Mexican immigrants reveal a striking gender gap. For second-generation Mexican women, however, other evidence points to considerable convergence toward the Euro-American, native-born norm, as the U.S.-born daughters of Mexican parents show much higher rates of economic activity than the preceding generation.

And it is not simply a matter of just having a job—however much that counts. At some base level, later generations of Mexican Angelenos show clear signs of occupational improvement, relative to their immigrant counterparts, as Zhou shows. Moreover, the change is doing much to narrow the employment gap separating them from native whites. By the second generation, the uniformly proletarian nature of the immigrant population gives way to an occupational profile in white-collar employment more clearly in line with the economy of the times. To be sure, most of the gain involves a shift into the less-skilled, less-well-remunerated nonmanual sales, administrative, and clerical jobs. Even so, Zhou shows a large increase in the level of professional employment. Thus, if the issue at stake is whether the children of Mexican-born immigrants are stuck at the very bottom, the best answer appears to be no.

But that may be the wrong question to pose, since second-generation progress is entirely consistent with persistent disadvantage relative to dominant groups. As Zhou notes, many second-generation groups are likely to catch up to, if not surpass, Euro-Americans: the future of Asian Americans seems particularly bright. But prospects for the children of Mexican, Central American, and Caribbean immigrants of various origins do not glitter. For these groups, the most likely second-generation scenario would be movement into the ranks of the working and lower middle class, as in the past. That status may be impressive from the standpoint of the sending communities back home, but it is likely to seem much less grand if the group still falls short of the rewards enjoyed by the average American.

In addition, the regional factors we have highlighted throughout this book will probably weigh heavily in the process. Although second-generation immigrants are likely to drift away from the key immigrant regions, many will stay where they have grown up; to the extent that immigrants continue to occupy the bottommost rung, that presence will yield a persistent shadow, affecting the prism through which the children of immigrants will be seen. In the key immigrant regions, moreover, class and ethnicity are aligned in distinctive ways. As Ellis emphasizes in chapter 4, inequality is particularly noticeable in these capitals of immigrant America. More to the point, the remaining Euro-American residents are increasingly absent from the lower and even middle ranks. Class and ethnicity therefore tend to overlap in ways that cumulate advantages for Euro-Americans (and possibly Asian Americans) but reinforce disadvantages for second-generation groups of other origins. And if Euro-Americans set the standard to which others aspire, their distinctively high position in the regional class structure is likely to at once stand out and provoke resentment in those with much lesser prospects.

The future for America's immigrant regions, then, may take a very different road than that mapped by the governing narratives. Some immigrants and their offspring will undoubtedly slumber in a lower class, from which there is little, if any, opportunity to exit; others will rapidly move up the totem pole, putting the assimilation of yesterday's immigrants to shame. But the main drift is likely to be different, taking the form of a conflict among the new and old ethclasses that emerge from the intersection of class and ethnicity. That the new ethclasses will have advanced from the bottom is precisely why they will be ready to mount a challenge, as they have both the resources needed for mobilization and the awareness of just how much they lack. And the emerging ethclass conflict will be facilitated by the presence of an ethnic elite, stemming from immigrant or, more likely, second-generation ranks and fully equipped with the symbolic tools needed to mobilize their coethnics and make gains on their behalf. After the experience of the last century, one would be foolish to look to some new social group as the force destined to move history forward. But rather than projecting our anxieties or wishes on to immigrants, as either underclass or assimilation scenarios do, we would do better to acknowledge the potential for deep social conflict resulting from the immigrant quest for progress and the obstacles that such a search entails. Poor immigrant parents may have been relatively powerless, but not their children. We can count on them for concerted efforts to gain dignity and also to assert, through efforts both practical and large, a different vision of their place in the world. Such are the prospects for urban America and the newcomers who will transform it. Let us await exciting times.

Notes

1. Alejandro Portes and Rubén Rumbaut, *Immigrant America: A Portrait*, 2d ed. (Berkeley and Los Angeles: University of California Press, 1996).

2. I echo the argument of Jeremy Boissevain, Jochen Blaschke, Hanneke Grotenberg, Isaac Joseph, Ivan Light, Marlene Sway, Roger Waldinger, and Pnina Werbner, in "Ethnic Entrepreneurs and Ethnic Strategies," in *Ethnic Entrepreneurs: Immigrant Business in Industrial Societies*, ed. Roger Waldinger, Howard Aldrich, Robin Ward, and associates (Newbury Park, Calif.: Sage, 1990), 133.

3. Ivan Light and Edna Bonacich, *Koreans in Los Angeles, 1965–1982* (Berkeley and Los Angeles: University of California Press, 1988), 184–185.

4. The key works are Alejandro Portes and Robert Bach, *Latin Journey* (Berkeley and Los Angeles: University of California Press, 1985); Alejandro

Portes and Alex Stepick III, *City on the Edge* (Berkeley and Los Angeles: University of California Press, 1993); and Portes and Rumbaut, *Immigrant America*.

5. This paragraph synthesizes the arguments presented by a variety of scholars, most notably Silvia Pedraza-Bailey, *Political and Economic Migrants in America: Cubans and Mexicans* (Austin: University of Texas Press, 1985); Ramon Grosfoguel, "Global Logics in the Caribbean City System: The Case of Miami," in *World Cities in a World-System,* ed. Paul Knox and Peter Taylor (Cambridge: Cambridge University Press, 1995), 156–170; idem, "World Cities in the Caribbean: The Rise of Miami and San Juan," *Review* 17, no. 3 (1994): 351–381; and Raul Moncarz-Percal, "The Gold Cage: Cubans in Miami," *International Migration* 16 (1978): 109–114. For a view seeking to transcend the limitations of both competing accounts but generally agreeing with the more political interpretation, see Carlos Forment, "Political Practice and the Rise of an Ethnic Enclave," *Theory and Society* 18, no. 1 (1989): 47–81.

6. Guillermo Grenier, "The Cuban-American Labor Movement in Dade County: An Emergent Immigrant Working Class," in *Miami Now! Immigration, Ethnicity, and Social Change,* ed. Guillermo Grenier and Alex Stepick III (Gainesville: University Press of Florida, 1992), 133–159; Marifeli Perez-Stable and Miren Uriarte, "Cubans and the Changing Economy of Miami," in *Latinos in a Changing U.S. Economy,* ed. Rebecca Morales and Frank Bonilla (Newbury Park, Calif.: Sage, 1993), 133–159. For a discussion of the politics and vicissitudes of the "Cuban success story," see Sheila Croucher, *Imagining Miami: Ethnic Politics in a Postmodern World* (Charlottesville: University of Virginia Press, 1997), chapter 4.

7. Harold M. Rose, "Metropolitan Miami's Changing Negro Population, 1950–1960," *Economic Geography* 40 (1964): 221–238; idem, "Blacks and Cubans in Metropolitan Miami's Changing Economy," *Urban Geography* 10, no. 5 (1989): 464–486.

8. For an example of Cubans bypassing blacks in the labor market, see Alex Stepick and Guillermo Grenier, with Hafidh A. Hafidh, Sue Chaffee, and Debbie Draznin, "The View from the Back of the House," in *Newcomers in the Workplace: Immigrants and the Restructuring of the U.S. Economy,* ed. Louise Lamphere, Alex Stepick, and Guillermo Grenier (Philadelphia: Temple University Press, 1994), 181–198.

9. Bashir Ahmed and J. Gregory Robinson, "Estimates of Emigration of the Foreign-Born Population: 1980–1990" (working paper no. 9, Population Division, U.S. Bureau of the Census, Washington, D.C., December 1994), available at http://www.census.gov/population/www/documentation/twps0009/twps0009.html.

NOTES ON CONTRIBUTORS

Roger Waldinger is Professor and Chair, Department of Sociology, at the University of California, Los Angeles. He is the author of four previous books: *Still the Promised City? New Immigrants and African-Americans in Post-Industrial New York* (Harvard University Press, 1996), *Ethnic Los Angeles* (edited with Mehdi Bozorgmehr; Russell Sage Foundation, 1996), *Ethnic Entrepreneurs: Immigrant Business in Industrial Society* (with Howard Aldrich, Robin Ward, and associates; Sage, 1990), and *Through the Eye of the Needle: Immigrants and Enterprise in New York's Garment Trades* (New York University Press, 1986). His newest book, *How the Other Half Works: Ethnicity and the Social Organization of Labor* (with Michael Lichter), will be published by the University of California Press in 2002.

William A. V. Clark is Professor, Department of Geography, at the University of California, Los Angeles. His research interests include migration and residential mobility and the nature of demographic change in large cities, especially changing patterns of residential segregation. His recent work has focused on mobility and tenure choice and large-scale immigration into California. *Households and Housing: Choice and Outcomes in the Housing Market* (Center for Urban Policy Research, 1996) compares housing choice in the United States and the Netherlands. *The California Cauldron: Immigration and the Fortunes of Local Communities* (Guilford Press, 1999) examines the way in which large-scale immigration is changing California's communities.

Claudia Der-Martirosian received her Ph.D. in sociology from the University of California, Los Angeles. She has coauthored several journal articles and book chapters on immigration and has written a forthcoming article on Iranian immigrants and self-employment. Currently she works as a statistician for the UCLA School of Dentistry. Her research efforts have resulted in several coauthored publications in the field of public health dentistry.

Mark Ellis is Associate Professor, Department of Geography, and Research Affiliate, Center for Studies in Demography and Ecology, at the University of Washington, Seattle. He is interested in the racial and ethnic changes wrought by immigration in America's largest cities, especially the labor market effects of the arrival of new groups. His work has appeared in a number of journals including *Economic Geography, International Journal of Urban and Regional Research, Annals of the Association of American Geographers,* and *International Migration Review.* He is writing a book titled *Race, Region, and Nation: The Territorial Politics of Immigration* with Richard Wright.

Jennifer Lee is Assistant Professor, Department of Sociology, at the University of California, Irvine. Her research interests include race and ethnic relations, immigration, and the new second generation. She has completed a book, tentatively titled *From Civil Relations to Exploding Cauldrons: Blacks, Jews, and Koreans in Urban America,* forthcoming from Harvard University Press. Her current research project, "Multiracial Identities: The Fading and Persistence of America's Color Lines," examines the way in which interracial couples identify their children and multiracial adults self-identify.

Nelson Lim is a research associate at RAND Corporation and the research director of Los Angeles Family and Neighborhood Survey (www.lasurvey .rand.org). His research focuses on the causes and consequences of durable social inequality on the basis of ascribed characteristics such as race, gender, and nativity.

Min Zhou is Professor, Departments of Sociology and Asian American Studies, at the University of California, Los Angeles. Her main research interests include immigration, race and ethnicity, Asian American studies, and community and urban sociology. She has done extensive work on immigrant adaptation, the new second generation, Asian American communities, ethnic entrepreneurship, and community-based organizations. She is the author of *Chinatown: The Socioeconomic Potential of an Urban Enclave* (Temple University Press, 1992), coauthor of *Growing Up American: How Vietnamese Children Adapt to Life in the United States* (with Carl Bankston; Russell Sage Foundation, 1998), and coeditor of *Contemporary Asian America: A Multidisciplinary Reader* (with James Gatewood; New York University Press, 2000).

INDEX

affirmative action: in higher education, 20

African Americans: in Chicago, 71, 95, 101, 205–7, 206f, 207f, 208t, 210f, 211, 212f, 213, 214f, 215–18; education, 81, 288f, 289f, 295, 296f, 296f, 297f, 298; employment, 24, 80–83, 186–222, 304t, 305t; ethnic niche, 205–8, 206f, 207f, 208t, 209, 210f, 211, 212f, 213, 214f, 215–18, 312; high school attendance, 289f, 295, 296f, 302t, 303t; immigrant competition hypothesis, 190–222; in Los Angeles, 101, 205–7, 206f, 207f, 208t, 209, 210f, 211, 212f, 213, 214f, 215–18; men's employment and skills, 84, 93–94f, 95, 96f, 97, 98–100f, 101; in Miami, 53, 56, 205–7, 206f, 207f, 208t, 209, 210f, 211, 212f, 213, 214f, 215–18; movement to large urban centers, 8–9; "moving up," 80–82; in New York, 87, 101, 205–7, 206f, 207f, 208t, 209, 210f, 211, 212f, 213, 214f, 215–18; population statistics, 44–45; poverty, 160, 164; in San Francisco, 205–7, 206f, 207f, 208t, 209, 210f, 211, 212f, 213, 214f, 215–18; second generation, 284f, 286f, 288f, 289f, 293f, 295, 296f, 297f, 302–5t; skill level, 86, 88, 107; skills-mismatch hypothesis, 84; third generation, 293f, 295; unemployment, 187, 188f, 189; as "urban underclass," 9, 11, 23, 160, 164; vs. less skilled immigrants, 84, 93–94f, 95, 96f, 97, 98–100f, 101; wages, 123–29, 124f, 127f; West Indian immigration and, 34, 86–87, 88, 106; women's employment and skills, 101–4, 108

African immigrants: population statistics, 38f

amnesty, 36

Asian immigrants: in Chicago, 69–70; education, 20, 34, 288f, 289f, 295, 296f, 297f; employment, 293f, 295, 296f, 297f; geographic dispersion, 49; high school attendance, 289f, 295, 296f, 302–3t; in Los Angeles, 57; in Miami, 54–55; in New York, 61–62; population statistics, 38f; in San Francisco, 45, 65–67, 296f, 297f, 302–3t; second generation, 284f, 286f, 288f, 289f, 293f, 295, 296f, 297f, 301, 302–5t; third generation, 293f, 295; wages, 123–29, 124f, 127f; in Washington, D.C., 47. *See also under individual countries*

Asian immigration, 33–34, 38f, 44f

Asian Indian immigrants, 34; in Chicago, 70, 241t; education, 20; ethnic niches,

Compositor:	Impressions Book and Journal Services, Inc.
Text:	Sabon
Display:	Syntax
Printer and Binder:	Edwards Brothers, Inc.